America Inc.?

A volume in the series

Cornell Studies in Political Economy
edited by Peter J. Katzenstein

A list of titles in this series is available at www.cornellpress.cornell.edu.

America Inc.?

Innovation and Enterprise in the National Security State

Linda Weiss

Cornell University Press
Ithaca and London

First published 2014 by Cornell University Press
First printing, Cornell Paperbacks, 2014

Printed in the United States of America

Library of Congress Cataloging-in-Publication Data

Weiss, Linda (Linda M.), author.
    America inc.? : innovation and enterprise in the national security state / Linda Weiss.
      pages cm — (Cornell studies in political economy)
    Includes bibliographical references and index.
    ISBN 978-0-8014-5268-0 (cloth : alk. paper)
    ISBN 978-0-8014-7930-4 (pbk. : alk. paper)
    1. Military-industrial complex—United States. 2. National security—United States—21st century. I. Title. II. Series: Cornell studies in political economy
    HC110.D4W48   2014
    338.0973—dc23   2013038090

Cornell University Press strives to use environmentally responsible suppliers and materials to the fullest extent possible in the publishing of its books. Such materials include vegetable-based, low-VOC inks and acid-free papers that are recycled, totally chlorine-free, or partly composed of nonwood fibers. For further information, visit our website at www.cornellpress.cornell.edu.

Cloth printing   10 9 8 7 6 5 4 3 2 1
Paperback printing   10 9 8 7 6 5 4 3 2 1

Contents

Preface

How does a non-American academic come to write a book about the contribution of the U.S. national security state to America's industrial economy? The simple response is that the interplay of state and economy sits at the center of all my work. A more considered response—to the extent that one can answer these "origin" questions with any precision—would be that my interest dates from my days as a graduate student at the London School of Economics during the 1980s. There, the interdisciplinary Patterns of History seminar brought together a range of high-powered scholars who, inter alia, explored the impact of international pressures, most notably war, on domestic policies and institutions. Later, a series of workshops convened between 1989 and 1991 by international relations scholar Fred Halliday and historical sociologist Michael Mann enjoined participants to jettison their individual disciplinary conventions by creatively integrating the national and the international in their analyses.

In a halting and modest way, this is where I began. In *Creating Capitalism* (1988), which focused mainly on the postwar Italian political economy, I examined the influence of war and the legacy of occupation on national policies for industrial structure and the resulting diversity of political economies. In *States and Economic Development* (1995), with my colleague John Hobson, I set out to understand what kind of domestic structures and international challenges lay behind the rise and relative decline of industrial powers at different historical periods. It was this project that really tweaked my interest in the question of war, defense preparedness, and its impact on the industrial economy.

In later work I examined the interplay of state and economy from a European and East Asian perspective. But the issue of the role played by the state in the American political economy continued to intrigue me.

Comparing the United States with Britain in my 1995 study, for example, it seemed to me that for all the talk of declinism, America was more likely to revive its industrial economy because of the cooperative relationship between its industry and the defense sector. But this was more of an aside than a substantiated proposition. And even though that idea still seems to me to retain a kernel of truth, two decades on, my understanding of the U.S. experience has changed quite dramatically.

Indeed, I began this book with the notion that the United States was not essentially all that different from other countries when it came to supporting its own economy and its own industries. Like other scholars, I hypothesized that the U.S. government pursued a covert form of industrial policy—one that remained largely out of sight because delivered through its defense sector. Several years on, I no longer entertain that hypothesis. The United States is not like any other country. But neither is it distinctive for the usual reasons alleged, with emphasis on "freer" markets and the like.

Toward the end of this project, I began to have mixed feelings about the nature of my study. Although the national security state in this book is not the snooping state—as the term is more widely understood since 9/11— it became hard to ignore reports of the virtually unlimited surveillance of American and foreign citizens in the name of antiterrorism, a burgeoning intelligence apparatus that has grown like Topsy, and the CIA's drone attacks on unarmed civilians abroad that appear to be radicalizing a new generation. Nevertheless, here I was writing about the technological supremacy created by the national security state, and turning a blind eye to its darker side. This was a calculated choice to begin with. It is one I have sought to maintain— for two reasons. First, the appetite for critical views of all things military and security-oriented is already well served by a large literature. Second, the more I delved into the subject, the more its treatment seemed laced with policy (and political) agendas that can so often color one's conclusions. Who needs reminding that passions do indeed run deep in this arena?

On reflection, I believe that I have made the right choice in sticking to my original purpose, staying on message, and avoiding normative commentary. This will not be to everyone's taste. For those who want to read about what is wrong with American foreign and defense policy, there is an abundance of commentary, much of it thought-provoking, some of it constructively engaging rather than merely negative. But for those who want to understand how it is that America, since World War II, has come to host a panoply of revolutionary innovations and high-tech industries—and whether its free market/ antistatist narrative continues to serve it well—this book takes a step in that direction.

Abbreviations

ARCH	Argonne National Laboratory–University of Chicago joint GVF
ARPA-E	Advanced Research Projects Agency–Energy
ASCI	Advanced Simulation Computing Initiative
CBO	Congressional Budget Office
CCAT	Center for Commercialization of Advanced Technology
CECOM	U.S. Army Communications Electronics Command
CIA	Central Intelligence Agency
COTS	Commercial off-the-shelf
CRADA	Cooperative Research and Development Agreement
CRS	Congressional Research Service
CTTO	Commercial Technology Transition Office (Navy)
DARPA	Defense Advanced Research Projects Agency
DDR&E	Deputy Director of Research & Engineering (DoD)
DHS	Department of Homeland Security
DoC	Department of Commerce
DoD	Department of Defense
DoE	Department of Energy
DRAM	Dynamic random-access memory
DSB	Defense Science Board
FFRDC	Federally Funded Research and Development Center
GAO	Government Accountability Office
GVFs	Government-sponsored venture capital funds
HSI	Homeland Security Institute
HTS	High-temperature superconductivity
HTUF	Hybrid Truck Users Forum
ICT	Information, communications, and technology

IR&D	Independent Research and Development program
IRIS	Internet Routing in Space
ISN	Institute for Soldier Nanotechnologies
JCTD	Joint Capabilities Technology Demonstration
MIC	military-industrial complex
NCI	National Cancer Institute
NGA	National Geospatial-Intelligence Agency
NIA	National Institute of Aerospace
NIAID	National Institute of Allergy and Infectious Diseases
NIH	National Institutes of Health
NIST	National Institute of Standards and Technology
NITRD	Networking information technology R&D
NNI	National Nanotechnology Initiative
NRAC	Naval Research Advisory Committee
NRC	National Research Council
NRI	Nanoelectronics Research Initiative
NSF	National Science Foundation
NSS	National security state
OFT	Office of Force Transformation (DoD)
OMB	Office of Management and Budget
ONR	Office of Naval Research
OSD	Office of the Secretary of Defense
OSTP	Office of Science and Technology Policy
OTA	Office of Technology Assessment
R&D	Research and development
S&T	Science and technology
SBIC	Small business investment company
SBIR	Small business innovation research
SDIO	Strategic Defense Initiative Organization
SEI	Software Engineering Institute
TRP	Technology Reinvestment Program
UAV	unmanned aerial vehicle
UCAR	University Corporation for Atmospheric Research
VC	Venture capital
VCs@Sea	Venture Capitalists at Sea
VHSIC	Very high speed integrated circuit
VLSIC	Very large scale integrated circuit
VOC	Varieties of capitalism

America Inc.?

1

The National Security State and Technology Leadership

The PC industry is leading our nation's economy into the 21st century . . . There isn't an industry in America that is more creative, more alive and more competitive. And the amazing thing is all this happened without any government involvement.

Bill Gates, 1998

There is no getting around the governmental role in innovation. Even cowboy innovators usually have government technology supporters in their rearview mirror . . . The reality is that government support necessarily must pervade the market for radical technology advances.

William B. Bonvillian, 2009

But what, apart from the roads, the sewers, the medicine, the Forum, the theater, education, public order, irrigation, the freshwater system and public baths . . . what have the Romans done for us? (And the wine, don't forget the wine . . .).

Monty Python's Life of Brian, 1979

Bill Gates's "state-less" depiction of America's high-tech economy perfectly captures the prevailing understanding of U.S. techno-industrial preeminence. Both at home and abroad, the United States is widely portrayed as the quintessential free-market economy. In this reputedly freewheeling entrepreneurial setting, robust antistatism combines with weak state capacity to ensure that the U.S. government contributes little more to America's global technology leadership than a business-friendly environment.

This book tells a different story, one that links high technology with national security and (antistatist) political norms.[1] It proposes that there is more to American capitalism and the American state than meets the free-market eye. In getting to this "something more," we start from the sub-stantive observation that the U.S. has an unmatched capacity for transforma-tive innovation.[2] For half a century and more, the United States has been the uncontested high-technology hegemon, leading the world in virtually all the major technologies that drive the modern economy and underpin its prosperity. Think of innovations such as communications satellites, micro-electronics, computers, software, biotechnology, the internet—the list goes on. More striking still is that every one of these breakthrough innovations emanated from the United States precisely in the period since World War II, giving rise to entirely new industries.

My main argument focuses on the role of what I call the national secu-rity state or NSS (though I use the term in an unusual sense; more on this shortly). Since World War II, the NSS has dominated in high-risk, break-through technologies and emerging industries; this pursuit has established, and continues to secure, the foundations for a high-technology commercial sector. Nevertheless, the NSS pursues technology leadership in order to sus-tain U.S. military-political primacy, not to achieve commercial advantage. To do so it has to rely on the private sector to advance its technology goals. After all, the days when the military could source all it needed from its arsenals are long gone. But as leading-edge capabilities came to reside less and less within the pool of large defense contractors (core of what is traditionally described as the military-industrial complex), and more and more within high-tech firms reluctant to work on security-related projects, the NSS was compelled to retool its incentive system. As I explain in more detail below, increasingly since the 1980s the NSS has had to reach outside the traditional pool of large contractors to attract the most innovative companies, by building commer-cial goals into its programs. By placing greater emphasis on commercializa-tion opportunities, some of these incentives seek to sweeten collaboration with the Department of Defense (DoD) and other security-related agencies, and thus to increase NSS influence over the direction of technology. In this manner, commercialization becomes the sine qua non of technological-cum-military primacy. Far from being mutually exclusive, security and com-merce have become closely entwined in NSS policy and practice.

At one level then, this is a story about how the geopolitics of threat per-ception has generated a vast state machinery geared to perpetual innovation in the quest for technological superiority. At another level, it is a story about the domestic challenges and political obstacles that have reshaped the NSS and its relationship with the private sector, not only by integrating the goals of security with those of commerce but also by merging public and private resources in distinctive ways.

Although focused on innovation, this is not a study of the nature or process of innovation. I am interested in the sources of U.S. technological dominance because this issue opens a window onto larger concerns at the center of contemporary political science debates. Two in particular moti-vate the research for this book. One turns analytical attention inward and invites analysis of the U.S. model of capitalism—in particular, the question of the American state's transformative capacity in the techno-industrial realm. Here, the standard view is of a weak, limited, even dysfunctional state (aka governing apparatus) in which numerous veto points work against—and undermine—coherent problem solving and policymaking. To this conception must be added a strong dose of antistatism which—institutionally, politically, and ideologically—has regularly thwarted efforts to normalize the state's active role in promoting commercial activities.

A second debate turns attention outward and concerns U.S. primacy (or, if one prefers, preeminence) in the world of international relations. It asks: Whither U.S. power in the context of a rising China and financially weakened public and private sectors? Here, so-called American declinists have regularly painted a grim picture of the American future. Most often implicated in this declinist perspective is the role of the defense sector as an unmitigated burden on the U.S. economy. In speaking to both concerns, I bring to bear a fresh perspective that revises both the "weak state" view of U.S. economic dynamism and the "defense-burdened" view of U.S. economic decline.[3]

The U.S. Puzzle

The fact that all the major advanced industries of the past sixty years have been pioneered in the United States raises an obvious question: Where does this capacity for transformative innovation come from? Why the United States? In a quasi-foundational narrative, this uncommon (exceptional?) capacity is attributed to a culture of risk-taking and entrepreneurship in which creative individuals, working on their own initiative, push out new ideas and new widgets based on their own ingenuity and derring-do. The adulation accorded the late Steve Jobs for all the wonderful Apple gadgetry is merely the latest example of this influential story. Of course this view of the role of entrepreneurs is well founded, both in American economic history and in today's economy. But it is also extremely one-sided—and therefore false, since it leaves out what is equally important.

Looking with two eyes rather than one, we see another side to the innovativeness of such celebrated U.S. creations as Apple and Google namely, a medley of technologies that have emerged from costly and sustained state sponsorship. From the GPS to the cell phone, from the mouse to the Siri voice-activated personal assistant application on the new iPhone, or to Google Earth, Google Translate, and indeed Google's search engine—all have one thing in common. They, like the internet and the IT revolution that preceded it, emerged from patient federal investment in high-risk innovation, focused in the main on national security objectives. It is of course often recognized that the American state has played a catalytic role in nurturing technological innovation and founding new industry sectors. Nevertheless, explaining this uncommon capacity for transformative innovation requires less conventional thinking than either of the binary categories "state" or "market" allows. It also requires a less conventional focus than simply on R&D spending or defense spending or even the military.

The Argument

So what accounts for America's transformative capacity? Where do its break-through innovations come from? My answer traces the relationship between high technology, national security, and political culture. It advances three interlinked propositions regarding the role of the NSS as technology enter-prise and commercialization engine; its geopolitical drivers; and the institu-tional consequences of an antistatist constraint.

The national security state as technology enterprise. First, America's capacity for transformative innovation derives not merely from the entrepreneurship of its private sector, or simply from the state as such, but from the national security state—a particular cluster of federal agencies that collaborate closely with private actors in pursuit of security-related objectives. The NSS is a wholly new postwar creation that is geared to the permanent mobilization of the nation's science and technology resources for military primacy, and here I document and explain why it has had to become increasingly involved in commercial undertakings. Although centered on defense preparedness, the NSS is a good deal broader than the military, yet narrower than the state as a whole. In addition to its defense core in the Department of Defense, the NSS comprises several other components created at the height of the Cold War to pursue, deliver, or underwrite innovation in the service of securing tech-nological supremacy. Although some are designated as "civilian" in their ori-gins, evolution, and current mix of activities, these NSS components remain deeply enmeshed in national security or dual-use functions (as we shall see in chapter 2).[4] Acting as commander in chief, the president sits at the peak of this complex, supported by the Oval Office and, in particular, the Office of Science and Technology Policy. In sum, I discuss NSS activities not in the more popular sense of a surveillance state, but as a national "technology enterprise" in which the military is the central, but far from exclusive, actor.

In telling this story, I demonstrate and account for a major shift in NSS innovation programs and policies that involved the national security agen-cies in cultivating and undertaking commercialization ventures. At first (c. 1945 up to the 1970s), this process of fostering commercially relevant (general-purpose or dual-use) technologies took both direct and indirect forms. Then (especially from the 1980s onward) it also took a more proac-tive form, via patenting and licensing reforms and cooperative agreements to transfer technology from the federal labs to the private sector, via the launch-ing of new procurement and joint innovation initiatives, and via the creation of new venture capital (VC) schemes. By placing greater emphasis on commercialization opportunities, some of these incentives sought to sweeten collaboration with the DoD and other security-related agencies, and thus to increase NSS influence over the direction of technology. A significant problem for the NSS has been that since the late 1970s, it has become progressively more challenging to enlist innovative companies in the private sector to work on security-related projects. While traditional defense suppliers grew increasingly large and specialized in systems integration, by the 1970s the more innovative producer companies—above all, critical suppliers of integrated circuits—had begun to pull away from the federal market. Attracting nondefense firms to do defense work was at one time easy because the government market (in semiconductors and computers, for instance) was so much larger than the private market, and healthy profits could be made. But by the mid-1970s commercial markets had come into their own, leading firms to reorient production to suit the more standardized demand. One consequence of lacking the earlier pull power of massive demand is that NSS agencies have had to create new incentives to foster private-sector collaboration. One of the major incentives intended to reattract the private sector is the inclusion of commercial goals in NSS technology policies. Commercial viability therefore has to stand alongside security and technological supremacy in NSS policy. For instance, if a firm works with an agency to create a technology, service, or prototype for use by the U.S. Army, it will also be encouraged from the outset of the project to create a similar product for the commercial market. In this way, and many more, the NSS has progressively been drawn into promoting commercial innovation for security reasons. One implication, demonstrated in some detail, is that the NSS has achieved a much broader reach than commonly implied by the notion of a military-industrial complex.

Geopolitical drivers. What are the drivers of the NSS technology enterprise? Geopolitics and related threat perceptions have been the original catalyst for NSS formation and its evolution as an innovation engine. This state- (and technology-) building dynamic has occurred in three broad phases: the Cold War, the rise of Japan as techno-security challenge, and the post-9/11 era of asymmetric threats. The NSS emerged and expanded in fits and starts after World War II in response to a perceived international threat, emanating from the Soviet Union, that proved both enduring and persistent. It is instructive to note that in this phase the NSS bears at least some comparison with the erstwhile "developmental states" of Northeast Asia. They too emerged in response to an intensely perceived security threat, from neighboring China and North Korea, but instead sought national security more broadly via economic improvement, or industrial catch-up.[5] Living on the fault lines of the Cold War in the presence of a credible and unyielding security threat exerted an unusual pressure on the East Asian states to pursue security by building economic strength. More distinctively in the case of Japan, Peter Katzenstein has developed the argument that, against the backdrop of terrible defeat, domestic power struggles succeeded in reorienting Japan's conception of security in favor of economic rather than military strength. Thus the Japanese state practices a form of "technological national security" in order to ensure against its resource dependence and reduce its exposure to international supply disruptions (Katzenstein 1996, 2005; also Samuels 1994).

Fundamental motivations drawn from different historical experiences thus serve to underline a unique feature of the NSS. In contrast to Japan (and the East Asian developmental states more generally), America's national security state has been geared to the pursuit of technological superiority not for reasons of national independence, economic competitiveness, or resource dependency, but in order to maintain American primacy. For the United States, the experience of World War II drove home the point that science and technology (S&T) was a game changer—the key to winning the war—and that future preparedness would depend on achieving and sustaining technological superiority. Geopolitics is thus the driver, not economics. I emphasize this point because many analysts have viewed the Pentagon as the source of an industrial policy that is pursued beneath the radar[6]—a claim that this book disputes since it mistakes the nature of the primary driver.[7] From its inception, the NSS was tasked with ensuring the technology leadership of the United States for the purpose of national defense. Even as the Soviet menace retreated, security proved paramount as the U.S. confronted a newly resurgent Japan that threatened to dethrone it as the regnant technology power.

Appreciating the strength and intensity of the U.S. security focus means never underestimating the significance of this point: as long as U.S. military strategy continues to rely on a significant technology lead over its adversaries (real or potential), threats to that lead can never be simply (or even primarily) a commercial matter—even when the NSS "goes commercial."

It is in the post-9/11 era of multiple asymmetric threats that a shadow has crept over the NSS technology enterprise. In the first place, it has come to lack the strong geopolitical stimulus of a well-defined adversary, thus softening its laser-like focus on advancing the technology frontier. Add to this the problems of budgetary issues, rancorous politics, and an extreme offshoring movement that disconnects innovation from production, and you have a recipe for a deeply uncertain future—quite apart from any consideration of China's likely impact. This raises the question of whether the NSS qua innovation engine will continue to sustain U.S. military superiority and high-tech leadership, an issue I examine in Chapter 6 and respond to in Chapter 9.

To be sure, there is a commercial twist to this geostrategic story because of the way the NSS in general, and the military in particular, depend to a large extent on the private sector to supply their technology needs. Both stories—strategic and commercial—are intimately connected to the quest for global primacy, to the U.S. role of world superpower in a security environment that calls for permanent preparedness for war, and in an age when military preeminence requires perpetual innovation. It is as if the foundational NSS credo were: "To be safe, we must be cutting edge."

Antistatism. My third proposition is that American antistatism in the political arena helps to channel government involvement (the commercial activism of the national security agencies) toward a preference for hybrid organizational forms that merge public and private resources in distinctive and often intricate ways. Although hybridization has a lengthy history in the American setting, what I identify as "innovation hybrids" have come into their own since the 1980s, in the very period when "small government" rhetoric reached a crescendo. Through its hybrid creations, the NSS conducts commercial pursuits and business-style ventures and establishes a presence in the marketplace (chapter 7). In this manner, antistatism does not preclude a substantial public presence in private-sector activities; rather, it transforms the way that presence is organized and experienced.

I therefore draw attention to the primary influence of international imperatives (both geopolitical and geo-economic), and the mediating effects of domestic politics. My analysis of domestic politics focuses chiefly on how antistatist antipathy toward federal support for civilian technology programs often shapes the way NSS actors meet strategic imperatives for technology development. As recently highlighted with the ups and downs and ultimate termination of the Advanced Technology Program, the American political system remains highly resistant to institutionalized funding for outright commercial ventures, yet highly supportive of most things to do with defense and national security.[8] In order to understand how the NSS functions as a strategic engine of innovation, and entrepreneurship, and as a networking node for government-industry projects and why its extensive links with the commercial sector are rarely visible, let alone examined, I therefore introduce the concept of hybridization and explore it as a form of institutional compensation for (the absence of state leadership arising from) a national antistatist value set.

Re-viewing the NSS–Private Sector Relationship

In developing these arguments, my larger purpose is to establish the transformative contribution of the NSS (not just the military) to U.S. enterprise and innovation.[9] To this end, I discuss historical and contemporary cases that demonstrate three broad features of the NSS–private sector relationship that are often either not well understood or completely overlooked. By combining historical analysis with contemporary cases I demonstrate aspects of continuity as well as a significant shift in the NSS-industry relationship (chapters 3–6). These show that NSS activities have long been more complex than R&D as such; that its reach is now much more extensive than confined to the enclave of a military-industry complex; and that its interfacing with business and the commercial marketplace is more integrated than suggested by the more common categories of military spin-off and spin-on.

Beyond R&D. What does the NSS do that marks it out from the norm—from garden-variety R&D funding? One hardly needs reminding that almost all advanced states are involved in promoting innovation. The key distinction is not state involvement versus noninvolvement; it is rather the nature and character of that involvement—the extent to which a state is more or less present and proactive in the innovation process, and not least in the commercialization stage, thereby helping to bring innovations to the point of production for the market. Here we can envisage a spectrum that runs from the more passive end of techno-industrial governance, via simple expenditure on research, to the more active end where states are involved in one, some, or all of the following: procuring new technology; providing assured demand for the resulting innovations; devising the technology problem sets for industry to work with; generating public inventions/intellectual property for private firms to exploit; taking equity positions in innovative firms; devising with industry new technology standards to outflank foreign competitors, and so forth. Thus, leaning toward the more passive end of state involvement we would find Britain; moving further toward the middle and beyond we would observe a number of states in the developed world (France, South Korea) and emerging markets (Brazil, China) that use one or more of these tools to reduce risk for firms in the innovation process.

Of special interest, however, is the more active (or proactive) end of the spectrum—for it is here that we find the United States. Its innovation activism may indeed surprise in view of that country's characterization as the archetypal liberal market economy. Nevertheless, the United States is quite possibly the preeminent power in using all these active forms of industrial governance—but often in forms that are decidedly not conventional.[10] So how does the NSS deliver innovation and technology leadership? In chapters 3–6, some ten different ways are identified in which this occurs. The main highlights (with examples of relevant NSS components) are outlined below. In short, the NSS is a broad political formation that fulfils many of the most important functions associated with maintaining technological superiority—going well beyond traditional notions of R&D.

BOX 1.1. WHAT DOES THE NSS DO?

- Contracts with the private sector to make and buy things that do not yet exist—that is, technology procurement (DoD, NASA, DoE, CIA)
- Provides assured demand for the innovations through acquisition contracts (from semiconductors to renewable energy devices; e.g. DoD, NASA, DoE)

- Devises the problem sets for technology developers in the private sector to work with, often yielding major breakthroughs that establish new industry sectors (ONR, DARPA, DoE, NIH)
- Finances development of inventions in national laboratories, universities, and the private sector (NSF, DoD, DoE, NIH, NASA, CIA)
- Catalyzes the formation of new companies (all NSS components)
- Licenses inventions created in the national labs to U.S. industry; granting firms patents rights to publicly financed inventions (NIH; DoD; DoE);
- Establishes the foundational infrastructure for the modern VC industry to boost innovation;
- Runs VC firms that take equity positions in selected startups and innovative companies (CIA, U.S. Army, DoE, DoD)
- Creates new institutional forms that bring NSS-funded inventions to market (numerous examples, ranging from VC funds to commercialization entities)
- Plugs gaps in innovation networks by providing a public space for matching up actors at different points in the innovation chain—researchers, program managers, venture capitalists, manufacturers, and buyers.

Beyond the military-industrial complex. Second, in its economic-industrial reach, the NSS is much more extensive than we have come to understand via the enclave concept of a military-industrial complex. Thanks to President Eisenhower's farewell speech of 1961, with its Cassandra-like warnings against the perils of the military-industrial complex (a striking contrast with his former advocacy of closer military-industrial cooperation) this concept has become a standard reference point in American public debate.[11] The term has since been widely used in different ways, often pejoratively, to refer to the large defense conglomerates that, with the blessings of their military peers in the various armed services, lobby members of Congress to preserve or promote favored weapons projects. A broad understanding has emerged that companies that work on defense projects are a specialized group of firms walled off from the rest of the industrial base. Ann Markusen's (1991, 404, 400) reference to the military-industrial complex as a "separate but not equal segment of U.S. industry," "dominated by large firms," and "inflexible" because "unable to shift easily to commercial production" is representative of the enclave idea. This notion of a wall of separation between military and commercial technology is placed under the spotlight in chapter 5, where I examine the sources and consequences of the NSS's commercialization shift: in fact, the NSS operates within a commercial environment in a way that casts a new light on its involvement and influence in the private sector.

Spin-around: integration of security and commerce. In addition to being more complex and extensive, the NSS relationship with business and the commercial marketplace is also more integrated than we have come to understand via the standard categories of spin-off and (more recently) spin-on. The latter is the term for technology originating in the private sector for commercial use and acquired by the public sector, whereas "spin-off" is the term widely deployed to mean technology originating in the defense sector that has (serendipitously) led to commercial applications. Both terms portray the relationship between defense and commercial technologies as a one-way street along which the innovation traffic flows either from the defense sector to commerce (pre-1970s spin-off) *or* from private enterprise to the military (post–Cold War spin-on). Thus the pre-1970s relationship has been broadly conceived as one of serendipity (unintended military spin-offs), while the more recent relationship is often viewed as military dependency on commercial leadership. The assumption here is that the model of technological development has shifted from (military) spin-offs for commerce to (commercial) spin-ons for the military. At the Cold War's end, John Zysman and his Berkeley colleagues were among the first to articulate the argument that America's military and economic security would henceforth depend on the ability to adopt a spin-on policy, in the manner of Japan (Borrus and Zysman 1992; also Samuels 1994).

Yet, whether we examine how the mission agencies have long interfaced with the private sector to achieve their goals, or why they have increasingly supported commercialization and entrepreneurial undertakings (such as VC firms), these unidirectional terms seem unfruitful. Whereas "spin-off" underplays what was often pursued by NSS actors with a national security purpose—sustaining an industrial base that, through being commercially viable, could supply both military and commercial markets—"spin-on" overstates the exclusively private origins of much commercial innovation. Modifying these assumptions, I deploy the term "spin-around" to better capture the process whereby an innovation that originates in the national security setting becomes adapted for the commercial market, and is then spun around to users in the NSS. Although the term itself is my own, the process is sufficiently well understood by NSS users. This is attested by the extent to which the idea of a national security payoff has frequently provided a rationale for dual-use projects. Thus, to take just one example of spin-around, the recent enthusiasm for NSS agencies sponsoring VC funds that take equity in private firms (chapter 3) is directly informed by calculations of a technology payoff for national security. In such cases, the NSS insistence on a commercial market for the technology (as a criterion of investment) is designed to leverage the scale and cost advantages of the commercial market and thereby achieve affordable and sustainable delivery to the NSS community. While there is plenty of evidence of the spin-around process during the Cold War (see especially chapter 4), contemporary examples are even more abundant (chapters 5 and 6). Indeed, as we see in the evolution of government-funded venture capital (chapter 3), procurement (chapter 4), and commercialization (chapters 5 and 7), the integrated character of commerce and security becomes ever more self-conscious as practice—and as deliberate policy—from the 1980s onward.

There is of course no shortage of studies that acknowledge the federal role in innovation. To see how my argument both connects with and diverges from these existing accounts, I now turn to them.

Existing Accounts: Discounting, Sidelining, Civilianizing the State

In spite of the range and scope of federal involvement in the innovation process, the NSS remains an underexamined arena. Most studies have limited their focus to the defense sector proper, to the pre-1970s era, and chiefly to R&D. In some cases, such accounts have also been driven by a policy agenda that seeks either to curb the military influence over science and technology, or to advocate a civilian techno-innovation policy. As a result, whether intended or not, a consensus has formed around the view that the state-cum-defense sector's innovation role can be attributed for the most part to serendipity,[12] confined to the bygone era before the 1970s,[13] or in some major way walled off from the commercial economy since military requirements are so specialized that they have little commercial applicability. This consensus effectively, if not always intentionally, ends up discounting any kind of defense-specific commercial contribution.[14] But what happens when one controls for different sectors, different NSS components (beyond DoD), and the postwar years as a whole (after the 1970s)? What happens is that, as I show in chapters 3 to 6, these discounting claims become difficult to sustain.

Regardless of intent, the effect has been analytically to neutralize, and thereby minimize, the state's contribution to the transformative innovation enterprise. In particular, our models of comparative capitalism have served us poorly in this domain, completing ignoring the technological influence of the NSS. At best, the assumption is made that the state's role is limited to defense, and its significance is further sidelined on the assumption that the defense sector is disconnected from the mainstream economy. The standard notion of a military-industrial complex has surely contributed to this misleading analytical move, and its restrictive scope is eliminated in chapters 3 to 7.

Discounting the State. A substantial body of scholarship on S&T policy has debated precisely the question of the state's commercial impact. Technology policy analysts have undertaken some of the finest work on the contribution of the federal government to commercial innovation. Their accounts cover a wide variety of sectors, mostly limited to the early postwar decades, and focusing chiefly on the role of the defense sector in producing commercial spin-offs through R&D spending (and to a lesser extent procurement). Exemplary studies include David Mowery and Nathan Rosenberg's (1982) research on the impact of defense R&D on the U.S. commercial aircraft industry; Kenneth Flamm's (1988) study of the computer industry; John Alic's and his collaborators' (1992) analysis of the relationship between defense and commercial technology; and Vernon Ruttan's (2006a) overview of the role of defense-related procurement in generating the major general-purpose technologies of the postwar period. All point in various ways to the key role of the U.S. defense sector in providing commercial industry with a technological edge—primarily during the 1950s and 1960s. Surprisingly, political scientists have rarely strayed into this area. Glenn Fong's 2001 article on the defense origins of the microelectronics industry is one notable exception.[15] In very general terms as well, some political scientists do recognize that at least one component of the NSS, the Department of Defense, has been a "driving force behind the research and development programmes of the private sector" (Vogel 1987, 104). But detailed analyses are few.

Sidelining the State. If, inadvertently or otherwise, a good deal of the S&T policy literature has ended up discounting the American state as a transformative actor in the innovation process, the comparative capitalism literature completely sidelines its influence. In a two-step process, the state's role is confined to the defense sector, then that sector is analytically excluded on the assumption that it operates as a self-reproducing enclave, separated from the mainstream economy, with no further relevance to the U.S. innovation story. Where the United States is concerned, this state-excluding approach is a marked feature of the comparative capitalism literature as a whole. It is especially striking in the "varieties of capitalism" (VOC) framework associated with the work of Peter Hall and David Soskice (2001). VOC theorists link U.S. success in transformative innovation to the predominance of the free market. They characterize the U.S. as a liberal market economy in which the firm is free from nonmarket interventions; they propose that such economies, which have freer markets for capital, labor, and products, are more inclined to take risks that produce radical innovations than coordinated market economies like Germany or Japan, where incremental innovation is said to be more typical.[16] The VOC argument thus presents the complementary macro-account to the cultural micronarrative of entrepreneurial risk-taking.

The overall result is that the U.S. experience of breakthrough innovation and technological leadership is framed as a "state-less" process.[17] This makes sense, of course, only if you fence off a large part of the system, which is to say, only if you ignore the NSS and its interaction with the commercial economy. That is precisely what the VOC approach has done. With a view to sustaining the idea of a nationally coherent model, the VOC framework (applied to the United States) reinforces the idea of a defense-security sector that is completely detached and insulated from the commercial sector—and hence irrelevant to the workings of the broader economy.[18] One of this book's central propositions, however, is that there is no such divide between the military and commercial sectors; instead, there is a multilayered network of public-private arrangements in which security and commercial objectives, projects, and resources intersect and entwine.

Civilizing the State. Fred Block's edited volume offers an important recent exception to the "serendipity–bygone era" consensus (Block and Keller 2010). It covers a range of federal innovation activities in both the defense and the nondefense sectors. While some contributions to that volume seek to develop a rationale for U.S. government intervention to foster innovation, the emphasis of the study is on "normalizing" the American state by highlighting the role and capacity of civilian agencies as a form of hidden developmental state that undertake industrial policy functions. Normalization in this context simply means government's adoption of a deliberate and direct role in sponsoring and guiding commercial innovation. At a recent conference, Block explained the complementarity between our two studies using the vivid imagery of an ugly caterpillar being transformed into a beautiful butterfly.[19] In this metaphor, the NSS (the military, as Block would see it) is the caterpillar and the hoped-for (longed-for!) butterfly is a civilian-focused industry or technology policy that flies free of its origins.

While I sympathize with that project, my aims, approach, and arguments are different. I seek to illuminate what has hitherto been obscured as well as downplayed in the scholarly literature. In my argument, in the absence of the NSS and the permanent defense preparedness around which it has formed, there would be little to distinguish U.S. innovation from that found in most other advanced democracies. Whether one should applaud or regret such an outcome is not germane to my argument. Certainly, it is conceivable that once established, a transformative innovation capacity could be unmoored from its originating NSS institutions and its geopolitical drivers. But we must also factor in particularities of the domestic institutional setting, which make that outcome most unlikely—namely, the domestic strength of antistatism. As long as its antagonistic stance toward normalization endures, the emergent butterfly would seem permanently encased in its NSS cocoon.

Fear and Loathing of the Military? Could there be another reason that existing accounts have generally ignored or discounted this transformative state story? Could it be because it involves an actor—centrally the military—that is directly connected with the means of destruction? For many, the idea of linking something so inherently destructive (perpetual mobilization for war) with something potentially growth-enhancing (innovation, technological transformation) makes for a very unpleasant juxtaposition—and is thus an unthinkable proposition. It need hardly be said that such an inquiry does not sit comfortably with the modern intellectual temperament.[20] Defensive or otherwise, war and the activities of war preparedness are not simply unpleasant reminders of the failure of the Enlightenment project to rule the passions with reason. They are also an affront to the spirit of progressive liberalism, a waste of money, talent, and effort that could be more fruitfully directed at civilian pursuits. This theme of militarism's harmful impacts on domestic development runs through a substantial critical literature that forthrightly denounces the military role in science and technology, not least its impact on the public purse. Critical commentary focuses on aggregate defense spending as well as the defense R&D budget and is particularly sensitive to defense buildups (see chapter 8). Much of this literature thus comes in waves—specifically during the Vietnam war and the defense buildup under the Reagan administration, then inspired by anticipation of the peace dividend after the collapse of the Soviet Union, and most recently in response to the budgetary pressures associated with the "war on terrorism" and exacerbated by the financial meltdown.[21]

Just as I do not intend to sing the praises of militarism (in this case, "liberal militarism"),[22] so I do not seek to deny its negative aspects. Consonant with the view of historians of war and military technology,[23] I see modern militarism as a two-edged sword, both destructive and transformative. Much worthwhile effort has gone into examining its destructive[24] and resource-wasting side.[25] My interest lies in probing the more neglected transformative story that the United States uniquely encapsulates in our own epoch, however discomforting its telling may be.[26] It seems obvious to me that an effort to bring to light that which has hitherto remained obscure or largely overlooked is not thereby to endorse it. My intention is not to advocate war or militarism or even a national security state, but to understand and explain its transformative effects, for better or worse.[27] So much, then, for the different ways in which the catalytic role of the NSS in U.S. innovation has been effectively sidelined and obscured.

The Approach of This Book

It is no secret that federal agencies pursue their missions through myriad forms of partnering with nonstate actors in the university, corporate, and nonprofit sectors. What needs emphasis is that this whole NSS enterprise—the permanent mobilization of S&T for perpetual innovation—depends on a vast intertwining of the public and private, the military and civilian, the security and commercial sectors. In this respect, it is not a top-down or state-centric story. The NSS cannot achieve its goals on its own account; to maintain technological supremacy, it needs to harness the power and cooperation of the private sector. This requires effort: cooperation cannot be taken for granted (even during the national emergency of World War II), and is often problematic (as some argue is the case today).[28] Thus, in order to attract private actors to carry through their innovation projects and policies, various components of the NSS have to create, and periodically update, a whole system of incentives and organizational arrangements—ranging from the funding and design of technology development to intellectual property and procurement reforms. Over time, this motivating process draws the NSS further and further into promoting commercial technology from which both sectors can draw benefit. But throughout this process of give and take, the NSS continues to set the goals, make the rules (for example, by setting performance standards), and define the problem sets for industry and university researchers to tackle. The outcome is what I characterize as a system of governed interdependence—neither "statist" nor "free-market" in its approach to inducing transformative innovation.

For specific analytical purposes, the governed interdependence perspective offers an alternative to the conventional binary categories that privilege either a statist or a society-centered framework—neither of which adequately captures the relationship that underpins U.S. transformative capacity.[29] In my account, although the security imperative and the NSS to which it gives rise provide the driving force behind transformative technology development, governed interdependence is the obverse of statism (or top-down direction of the economy); it conceptualizes the collaborative and negotiated character of public-private sector relations as NSS components seek to achieve their goals (an example being the increasing emphasis that defense programs place on developing products and services that serve both military and commercial markets). I emphasize that the governed interdependence concept applies to situations in which a government body works with or through private actors and entities to achieve its own objectives, but at the same time maintains control over the goals to be pursued and the rules of participation. This does not mean that outcomes will always yield the results desired or that there will not be spectacular failures. Where technology development is concerned, however, the sharing of decision-making space (for example, devising problem sets while giving private actors a say in program design, not just implementation), has been found to produce more jointly productive results than if a program or policy is determined chiefly by state actors: compare the very high speed integrated circuit program and the Advanced Simulation Computing Initiative, discussed in chapters 4 and 5). To emphasize: governed interdependence is not a statement about the state as such, but rather about how some state actors in some settings for some purposes seek to interact with nonstate actors to achieve their goals—whether those goals happen to be national security (as in this case) or techno-independence or catch-up. In short, governed interdependence is neither universal nor generalized as a feature of states.

As this last point implies, the governed interdependence approach thus opens a window onto vexing questions about state-ness and state capacity in the United States. As subsequent chapters show, the NSS pursues its missions by involving nonstate actors in a myriad of public-private arrangements and partnerships. From the perspective adopted here, these publicly sponsored networks—which came into their own as a result of mobilization for

World War II—have an "elective affinity" with the U.S. system, which both demands a sizeable state to maintain its global preeminence, yet at the same time exudes a strong antistatism. Sometimes appearing to "privatize," at others to "hybridize" state activities (a distinction examined in chapter 7), these public-private partnerings also tend to enhance NSS effectiveness in its quest for technological superiority. This in turn raises the question of how this analysis intersects with a newly emergent understanding of the American state, and with the comparative institutions approach to American capitalism.

New Thinking on the American State

The governed interdependence approach challenges the "weak state" tradition in American political science. It seeks to contribute to the new understanding of American state power that has emerged from studies of American political development.

A central theme of this relatively youthful subfield of political science is the idea—made famous by Charles Tilly and creatively applied by other historical and macrosociologists—that "war makes the state."[30] Applied to the modern era, this means that national responses to international problems like war and trade have transformed political institutions.[31] Far from excluding the influence of domestic politics, this approach inverts the causal flow in a kind of "Tilly plus Marx" argument to the effect that war makes the state—but not exactly as it chooses. This is because existing domestic institutions (in the U.S., case for example, in the form of antistatist mechanisms) mediate between international imperatives and the domestic expansion of state power.[32]

This book builds on that double-stranded idea by incorporating and connecting two elements. The first is a largely overlooked political economy dimension ("war makes the state—and the high-tech economy"), which leads to a focus on the (geo-)politics of innovation.[33] The second is a state power dimension ("war makes the state—but not necessarily as it chooses"), which leads to a focus on the filtering role of domestic structures. The proposition here is that domestic political value sets, preferences, and institutions mediate the state's involvement in techno-innovation—not by diminishing or limiting state capacity but by extending its infrastructural power and creating a hybrid political economy.

It follows that in my account, antistatism is less a state-limiting constraint than a state-transforming force. Since this conception differs from the one advanced by Aaron Friedberg's influential study, it is important to be clear about where our accounts differ. In an illuminating analysis of the role of antistatist forces in curbing state expansion during the early Cold War period, Friedberg asks why America had not, as Eisenhower feared it might, imitated the USSR and become a "garrison state." His metric was "statism," in Weberian terms, defined as an increase in "the size and strength of the executive branch of the federal government" (Friedberg 2000, 10). Having examined budgets, force levels, weapons systems, research programs, institutions, and policies, he concludes that in spite of developing a commanding national security structure, America resisted statism throughout the Cold War. Antistatist forces deeply embedded in American ideas, institutions, and policies opposed the accumulation of power by the executive branch. Powerful statist tendencies, Friedberg claims, had been arrested at every turn. Antistatism thus constrained the expansion and centralization of state power and thereby proved a source of domestic economic and technological strength. A profit-seeking arms industry was more innovative and efficient than the one devised by the Soviets, and no more warmongering than an arsenal staffed with government bureaucrats would have been (Friedberg 2000, 345). As this brief summary indicates, Friedberg focuses on the "magnitude" of state expansion and concludes that its growth was kept in check by antistatism.

While I broadly agree with Friedberg's assessment of the significance of antistatist forces, I am less convinced by the conclusions he draws regarding their impact on the American state. My doubt stems from his use of a particular conception of state power more suited to despotic regimes (and implied by the term "garrison state"). As we know, certain states have historically wielded considerable despotic power, power over society, much as the Soviet Union came to do. However, the power of modern industrial states is chiefly infrastructural, not despotic. They possess the capacity to reach into society, to extract and redistribute resources on the basis of consent and negotiation (a capacity that preindustrial states lacked).[34] Friedberg sees antistatism defeating a despotic tendency toward centralized "control over" society.[35] But what of the American state's infrastructural power? Might it be that instead of simply curtailing this capacity, antistatist impulses have channeled it along particular paths—effectively reshaping the nature of state power expansion, rather than simply restricting it? This is a key contention of the present study.

Friedberg's argument turns on the idea of limited state involvement in shaping the U.S. high-tech economy and attributes American state minimalism to the influence of a robust antistatism. But the way he poses his principal question—garrison state or limited state?—forces thinking into a state-versus-market framework and thereby misses what is arguably most distinctive about the NSS, namely, its close entwinement with nonstate actors and the private sector and its spawning of innovation-driven hybrids. As I argue in chapter 7, rather than representing a shift toward classical statism, America's NSS drove the development of hybrid public-private institutional forms, enhancing the state's commercial influence at the same time as providing for national defense. Rather than merely providing a check-and-balance mechanism that kept the state from becoming all-powerful, antistatism (whether played out in Congressional politics or the White House, in public opinion or the business sector) exerts a hybridizing effect on the implementation of NSS transformative goals. Hybridization, I propose, is a preferred U.S. response to public policy problems that on one hand require the state's presence, but that on the other, precisely because of antistatism, are more effectively addressed outside conventional public entities. Creating something that looks more private than public is thus often a way of avoiding political blockage.

In short, whereas Friedberg is concerned with what antistatism helped to prevent, this book's perspective emphasizes what antistatism helped to create. It proposes that publicly sponsored networks, hybrids, and other forms of partnering arrangements are one way of resolving the tensions inherent in maintaining global preeminence in an antistatist political environment. On one hand, maintaining primacy entails technological superiority, thus demanding a significant degree of state activism in the technology development system. But on the other hand, antistatism demands a relatively small, passive state. As the political historian, Margaret O'Mara puts it in her study of Silicon Valley, "The Cold War required a strong state, but American political traditions demanded a weak one" (2005, 10).[36] In seeking a solution, she adds, universities and technology-intensive industries were empowered as partners with the federal government. As I would put it, governed interdependence rather than statism became the order of the day. And as one of its many manifestations, hybridization came to provide one state-enabling way of sidestepping the antistatist constraint.

In my analysis, governed interdependence opens a conceptual window onto an American state that transcends the "statelessness" account and thereby complements the emergent understanding of American state power. Here, a school of thought that includes political scientists, historians, and sociologists has begun to argue that the United States is far from a weak state and that this idea is "no longer reasonable or even interesting" (Novak 2008, 771). King and Lieberman (2008) note that in this emerging view, the state-building process as well as the state's capacity and strength are increasingly understood as the product of links formed with social networks, rather than as necessarily independent or autonomous from society. Although some are inclined to see these features as paradoxical and as a quintessentially American pattern, state-society partnering to achieve public goals appears to be an increasingly widespread tendency (though not commonly found in American-style, hybridized forms). Indeed, it has been argued in a broader comparative framework that certain forms of state-society partnering, understood here as governed interdependence, are important sources of the state's transformative capacity in the advanced technology-intensive economy. Neither simply bottom-up nor solely top-down, this form of governance has much in common with state-economy patterns found in certain sectors and settings where exposure to international competition has intensified.[37]

In a similar vein, my analysis intersects with O'Mara's argument that the peculiar public and private blend of "power structures and policy networks" that she observes in the making of Silicon Valley "enabled leaders to quietly and significantly increase the power and influence of the federal government while simultaneously condemning the idea of "big government" as dangerously communistic" (O'Mara 2005, 10). Thus we converge in our view of state capacity, even while our studies move in different empirical and theoretical directions. Whereas O'Mara focuses on a particular region, sector, actor, and early period, with a view to understanding the origin of industrial districts, my account covers a broader canvas (in terms of space, time, actors, and sectors) with a view not only to illuminating the power of the American state as a transformative economic actor, but also to probing its implications for understanding and reconceptualizing the U.S. model of capitalism.

By implication, the governed interdependence approach, by injecting a state capacity dimension, also challenges the conceptualization of the American model in the comparative capitalism/comparative institutions literature. Here, the seminal work of Hall and Soskice promulgated the core idea that models of capitalism cohere around a complementary set of institutions that reinforce one another, each contributing their own positive effects on economic performance. Complementarity for Hall and Soskice means that changes in one institutional arena (say, labor markets) are unlikely to be possible without accompanying changes in other arenas (capital and product markets). From this perspective, for instance, the U.S. model of free labor markets and high labor mobility serves to reinforce the system of "shareholder value" with its emphasis on maximizing short-term profits, on spot markets for goods and materials, and on stock-market finance.

Critics of this mutual reinforcement view of institutions have not been in short supply. But if the measure of a study's value is the extent of productive debate that it generates, then Hall and Soskice can be credited with pushing the boundaries of institutional analysis. For the central insight to emerge from this debate is that institutional complementarity consists of two basic types, not just one: complementarity may either reinforce a tendency or compensate for that tendency.[38] This allows for the possibility that models of capitalism are not necessarily institutionally coherent; that they may comprise institutions that oppose each other; and that some institutions may balance or compensate for the effects of others—though this offsetting effect occurs neither intentionally nor necessarily (Crouch 2005b, 2010). This insight can be fruitfully applied to the American national security state in order better to understand how aspects of its activities may offset potential imbalances created by liberal market institutions. In practical terms, this directs our attention to two market-compensating possibilities: first, the extent to which the NSS plugs gaps left by so-called free-market institutions (such as by providing patient capital, high-risk investment, and breakthrough inventions—areas in which the private sector is often weaker than free-market logic anticipates); and second, the extent to which NSS technology activism compensates for antistatist institutions that militate against a commercially driven technology policy.

Finally, I do not claim that U.S. activism in commercial technology is without precedent. Rather, my claim is that state activism in this arena has evolved from distinctive foundations in national security exigencies that gave rise to an institutional complex, a national security state, that was new to the postwar era. Its dispersion of programs and funding activity within a security-centric focus gives the NSS a level of strategic coherence centered on the development of a diverse array of breakthrough technologies, while its hybridized public-private character has imparted a transformative capacity.

While I do not reject the primacy of the national security motivation in my analysis of the NSS role, I do reject the implied dichotomy: either security or development, guns or butter. This book seeks to reconnect these elements. In focusing on how the NSS does both (in future, under a tightened budget), I argue that the American state is no less active than many other states in governing the market; it is however far less conventional in its activism, and thereby also less visible.

2

Rise of the National Security State
as Technology Enterprise

We are not, however, a warlike people. Our historic goal is peace . . .
We maintain strong military forces in support of this supreme purpose, for we believe that in today's world only properly organized
strength may altogether avert war.

Dwight D. Eisenhower, 1953

There is one thing we do know, we cannot settle for anything short
of technological leadership in R&D related to national security.

Melvin Laird, 1970

The genesis of the national security state (in the usual sense rather than
as I define it) has been richly detailed in several historical studies.[1] Rather
than retell that story here, I highlight just one aspect of pivotal importance
to the argument of this book: namely, the rise and evolution of the NSS
as an innovation enterprise that concentrates national responsibility for
science and technology. How that role emerged and took shape and how it
embraced a variety of actors in the private sector is a fascinating story in
itself. Nothing like it had ever been created before. Regarding the evolution of the NSS, I emphasize four important points. First, the national security state emerged not fully formed, but in fits and starts in the aftermath of
World War II in response to a persistent and intensely felt geopolitical threat.
Second, its creation had a major impact on American political development
insofar as it led to significant expansion (and concentration) of the state's
transformative capacity within the executive branch of government. Third,
the national security state has been protean in its responsiveness to threats
arising from both the international security environment and weaknesses in
its domestic sources of supply, wherever these were perceived to challenge

America's technological leadership. And fourth, rather than relying on heavy-handed, top-down controls or simply counting on the private sector to foster innovation from the bottom up, the national security state has fostered relations of governed interdependence throughout the American economy. These public-private relationships would often take the form of contractual synergistic partnerships between the NSS, industry, and academic institutions. However, they also generated more lasting institutional fusions which created distinctive hybrid arrangements for the pursuit of public goals. Through these partnerings and hybrid arrangements, the NSS came to revolutionize the nation's technological capabilities and stimulate commercial innovation for the purpose of national defense.

As mentioned, several excellent accounts of the early postwar period have described the emergence of institutions that have come to be identified with national security functions, and I draw amply on many of them. However, the purpose of this chapter is both narrower and broader than that of the extant literature. Its key objective is to clarify the nature, scope and sources of the NSS qua technology leadership/innovation enterprise. My account is accordingly narrower in focus, being concerned chiefly with those components of the NSS that play a significant role in technology development. It is however broader in scope, since (unlike the NSS literature I draw on in this chapter, which typically stops somewhere in the early 1950s, or at the latest the 1960s), the chapter traces key stages in the evolution of the NSS over the postwar period as a whole—again, always with a specific focus on those aspects of its evolution most relevant to technological leadership.

Since my aims differ from those of the historian, my account does not give priority to questions of periodization. While not ignoring the time factor, I frame my discussion of the rise and evolution of the NSS in terms of five broad phases. These correspond roughly rather than neatly to the designated periods: emergence (1945–57), growth (1958–68), crisis (1969–79), reform and reorientation in two phases (1980–89 and 1990–99), and re-visioning (2000–2012). In each phase, I seek to highlight those aspects of the international security environment, the domestic political context, and the technology leadership challenges that have influenced the formation and evolution of the NSS innovation enterprise. However, as a way of marking the important shift that I am emphasizing in this book, I also consider these phases as two distinctive but interconnected eras. These are the so-called "procurement era" (up to and including the 1970s) and the "commercialization era" (the 1980s to the present). The implication is not that procurement was abandoned after the 1970s, but rather that there was a heightened emphasis on bringing innovations to market in a way that meets both mission-centered and commercial goals. This is the core of my story.

Emergence (1945–1957)

It is no secret that World War II was a watershed event for both American political development and U.S. technology leadership. Prior to that national emergency, America could be characterized neither as national security state nor as technology leader.[2] In the early postwar decades, however, the United States could lay claim to being both. Neither development, however, was inevitable. The surprise attack on American territory in 1941 helped strengthen the postwar case for permanent military preparedness that gave birth to a vast national security infrastructure, but it was by no means a fait accompli at war's end. As public policy historian David Hart explains, "the establishment of the military as a patron worth having and national security as a label worth fighting for did not occur automatically or immediately after the victory in World War II." Rather, the immediate postwar years were marked by "frustration and bitterly won incremental gains for proponents of the national security state."[3] Intense struggles ensued between different parts of the bureaucracy, between the executive and Congress, and between powerful political actors over different organizational designs that conflicted with established power prerogatives and offended that cluster of American values aptly captured by Friedberg (2000) under the label of antistatism. It would take the Korean War to most effectively "break this bottleneck." And it would take a different kind of catalyst—the shock of Sputnik—to propel the NSS into a sustained race for technological supremacy, and in a way that transcended partisan rivalries.

The emergence of the NSS was kick-started and carried forward by a series of geopolitical events that spanned the marked deterioration of U.S.-Soviet relations after 1945 and the outbreak of the Korean War in 1950. But the eventual shape of the new structure was a product of domestic conflict and compromise, as the Truman administration sought to reconcile American antistatist values with the new ideology of national security and the expansion of executive power that this implied.[4]

The birth of the NSS is conventionally traced to the 1947 National Security Act, which provided a foundation for the expansion and centralization of the federal government's defense and intelligence operations under the direct authority of the president as commander in chief (Hogan 1998, 24). Under its mandate, the Truman administration unified the Army, Navy, and newly created Air Force within the National Military Establishment—a body replaced in 1949 by the newly created Department of Defense—placing all under the authority of a civilian secretary of defense. It also created the Central Intelligence Agency and the National Security Council, and provided a statutory identity to the Joint Chiefs of Staff. Finally, Truman established a number of S&T boards that proved ineffective and were later recast in a more centralized form under Eisenhower.[5] Separately, in the final weeks of his presidency, Truman united all signals intelligence within the National Security Agency, an agency within the DoD. In so doing, he created the last of the four institutions—NSA along with the NSC, DoD, and CIA—that evolved into the main hard-power pillars of U.S. national security. All of Washington's separate national security networks converged in the Oval Office. This was the node through which the incumbent president could use his authority to coordinate the activities of the many and varied agencies that came to constitute the NSS. Through special advisory councils, strategic programs, and—not least—the Bureau of the Budget, the president was positioned to coordinate technology policy, as shaped by its separate NSS components (Nelson 2007, 266). It would take a little over a decade for the key agencies of the national security state to acquire their longer-lasting institutional identities. Battles over missions, budgets, and influence would subsequently transform many of the new entities; nevertheless, the foundations were now in place.

Having established a set of powerful institutions for concentrating the management of science and technology, President Truman set about containing their budgets (Hogan 1998, 72–73). Geopolitical developments, however, soon trumped balanced budgets. Following several successive events—the Soviet blockade of Berlin in June 1948, the "loss" of 500 million inhabitants of China to the communist camp in 1949, and the Soviets' successful detonation of a nuclear weapon that same year—Truman and many of his closest advisers cast communism as a direct military threat, not just a dangerous subversive force. The Soviets' explosion of an atom bomb had such a profound impact that it generated vast new programs for a continental air and missile defense system as well as a strategic nuclear deterrent.[6]

In response to the newly perceived direct external threat of destruction to the American homeland, a landmark document, *National Security Council Paper 68* (NSC-68) outlined justifications for a rapid and massive U.S. military buildup. It cited Soviet consolidation of power in eastern Europe as evidence of its expansionist intentions, and called for the West to contain the Soviet Union as justification for the United States to pursue a major buildup of its conventional military and nuclear forces. Reticent about its cost projections, Truman held off approving the plan until after the outbreak of the Korean War, finally removing the cap that he had imposed on defense spending.

Technological Leadership beyond Defense: NIH, AEC/DoE, NSF

Looking beyond the DoD to the other arms of the NSS, we soon see how the process of establishing a national security state geared to securing technological supremacy could not stop with the DoD and the intelligence agencies. At different stages, it also drew into its orbit the Atomic Energy Commission, which in 1973 became the Department of Energy, as well as the National Institutes of Health, the National Science Foundation, and a little later, NASA.

National Institutes of Health. Like Energy, Health is a quintessentially dual-use agency, with one foot in the civilian sector and the other firmly planted in the NSS. The federal research labs known as the National Institutes of Health, the Public Health Service's research wing, are a case in point. NIH's connection with the NSS technology enterprise can be seen in at least three ways. First, the NIH inherited the responsibilities and contracts of the wartime Office of Scientific Research and Development Committee on Medical Research and continued to work closely with the NSS.[7] Indeed, the NIH budget was not permitted to grow until it inherited wartime projects (Swain 1962, 1235).

Wartime biomedical research was intended to ensure the health of U.S. service personnel and to defend against biological and chemical warfare, an effort that NIH activity continues to support. The Public Health Service, in partnership with the Army and the Department of Agriculture, then began research in the field of biological warfare in 1941 under the auspices of the Chemical Warfare Service.[8] Shortly thereafter, a Biological Warfare Committee composed of civilian scientists was established to advise the armed services; the military began funding research relevant to biological warfare in dozens of universities and industrial plants.[9] The principal effect of the BWC was to draw attention to the potential dangers of biological weapons to human beings, crops, and livestock. It called for an extensive program of biodefense emphasizing the development of vaccines and protection of the national water supply. Commenting on this early history, Bernstein notes that Secretary of War Henry L. Stimson hoped to legitimize the research at the Chemical Warfare Service by naming civilians as monitors and that senior Army officials preferred the establishment of a civilian agency with ties to the armed services. Stimson's reasoning behind this "civilianizing" policy is instructive: "Entrusting the matter to a civilian agency . . . would help in preventing the public from being exercised over any ideas that the War Department might be contemplating the use of this weapon offensively" (Bernstein 1987, 117). The rationale behind the NIH's launch of a "War on Cancer" (discussed below) was arguably similar.

The second point to note in establishing the national security relevance of the NIH is the fact that biomedical research did not lose its military significance simply because the nation had entered an era of "armed peace." The Chemical-Biological Coordination Center that succeeded the BWC continued to provide a forum to promote close cooperation between the Army, Navy, NIH, and the American Cancer Society, each providing the center with financial support. This mechanism allowed the armed services to exploit innovations and research driven by the NIH.[10]

Third, the NIH remains an integral part of the NSS because the body of knowledge required to cure naturally occurring human disease is in many cases the same as the knowledge required to counteract the threat of biological and chemical warfare, or to understand the cellular effects of exposure to other environmental hazards such as radiation (Kadlec and Zelicoff 2000, 14). Cancer research has thus become another mechanism through which the NIH serves national security.[11] Not coincidentally (it would appear), the National Cancer Institute shares the same address as the U.S. Army Health Services Command at Fort Detrick, exploiting facilities originally used for research and development related to biological warfare. This cohabitation was the result of the Nixon administration's 1969 decision to convert the nation's biological warfare program to a commercial biotechnology industry (discussed below). It signifies the close and continuing relationship between the DoD and the NIH, whose synergy has made lasting contributions to the postwar development of the U.S. biotechnology and pharmaceutical industries.[12]

Atomic Energy Commission/Department of Energy. Another core component of the NSS, the Department of Energy traces its origins to the former Atomic Energy Commission, whose roots lay in the Manhattan Project. In taking over the Manhattan laboratory system in 1947, the AEC acquired virtually unlimited control over all nuclear energy R&D. One of its early tasks was to assess the nascent atomic weapons program of the Soviet Union. "Since then," according to the Office of the Director of National Intelligence, "its security and intelligence functions have come to reside within DoE."[13] As the agency responsible during the Cold War for nuclear weapons development and testing and, subsequently, stockpile stewardship, a major part of the DoE's budget has been dedicated to national defense objectives. A smaller share of its budget would later also support the development of new energy-saving and renewable energy technologies, with more direct relevance to the civilian economy, but this aspect too is now enmeshed within the "new" focus on energy security (chapter 6). Today the DoE's primary missions include stewardship of the nuclear stockpile and ensuring America's "energy security" in collaboration with the DoD.[14] Like the armed services, it has relied on a system of contracting out R&D as an adjunct to the important work conducted in its extensive network of National Laboratories.

These laboratories, otherwise known as Federally Funded Research and Development Centers, form another important component of the NSS innovation enterprise. With thirty-nine labs overall, the DoE has the largest network, including the famous Los Alamos, Lawrence Livermore, and Sandia nuclear labs originally constituted for the purpose of creating nuclear weapons. Initially established under the Atomic Energy Commission to perform R&D for the mission agencies, their activities range from basic research all the way to patenting and licensing of inventions. As the Manhattan Project was wound down, the labs were given new missions, some of which included R&D applied to the use of fissionable and radioactive materials for biomedical, health, and military purposes. As a result, these in-house laboratories developed strong connections with private contractors, paving the way for entire new industries, ranging from radioisotopes in nuclear medicine to biotech and bioengineering.[15] Constructed as organizational hybrids for conducting research and developing technologies, in addition to sponsoring entrepreneurship and commercializing innovations (since the 1980s), these government-owned, privately operated labs have come to play a much broader role in the NSS innovation story than is conventionally conveyed by the term "R&D" (chapter 7). Similar public-private fusions were engineered by the DoD in its bid to outstrip the Soviet Union. Thus, in 1951, the prestigious U.S. Office of Naval Research sponsored the creation of MIT's Lincoln Laboratory. Its brief, a direct response to the Russians' atom bomb explosion was to develop an air defense system known as SAGE (Semi-Automatic Ground Environment). Following a pattern similar to the energy agency's research labs, the MIT lab was a hybridized arrangement that melded public and private resources in order to serve a national mission.

National Science Foundation. When created in 1950, the National Science Foundation had a tiny budget and limited responsibilities (for "basic, undirected" research that no other public agency had an interest in sponsoring). Vannevar Bush's proposal for a body that would centralize control of scientific research had languished in Congress during the first half-decade after World War II, largely because President Truman opposed its bid for control by unelected civilians. When the NSF was finally established in 1950, the AEC and other federal bureaus had already assumed control of much of the scientific research that Bush had hoped the NSF might support. Nonetheless, NSF had the broader mission "to promote the progress of science; to advance the national health, prosperity, and welfare; and to secure the national defense." As its meager budget grew, reaching $40 million in 1958, the NSF became an integral component of the NSS, often taking to completion projects begun or sponsored by a sister agency, such as managing twelve materials research labs transferred from the Defense Advanced Research Projects Agency in response to antiwar protests against defense research on campus. Indeed, NSF's budget would expand in step with various geopolitically significant events that spanned the launch of Sputnik (discussed below) and the Carter-Reagan defense buildup that followed the end of détente.

In the "battle for hearts and minds" during the Cold War, the NSF would also play an important soft-power role in the national security apparatus by fostering international scientific and technological cooperation. (NASA would later add its own soft-power thrust by enhancing national prestige through the Apollo Program that brought humanity to the moon.)[16] Science and technology were instruments of foreign policy, a way to show both allies and nonaligned nations that a particular form of government produced a superior, more desirable overall society.

The NSF, however, never came to centralize control of the nation's scientific research as Vannevar Bush had championed. By the time it was formed, the Navy (shortly followed by the Air Force and Army) had already established their own S&T programs, including extramural funding support. While Defense was funding a good deal more allegedly basic research in universities than the NSF, historians concur that it was much more applied than generic or fundamental in nature (Edgerton 2004, 43). With the exception of the life sciences where the NIH held sway, the AEC/DoE and the armed services dominated the postwar patronage of science and technology development. Together with the NSF and (later) NASA, these emerged as the key actors in the NSS innovation enterprise.

Partnering for Perpetual Innovation

The Eisenhower administration that came to power in 1953 oversaw the start of a long climb in federal support for technology development. Yet its strongest contribution to the NSS technology enterprise was institutional, not financial.[17] More than any other peacetime president, Eisenhower bolstered the NSS's ability to steer technological change throughout the American economy by creating robust public institutions and empowering them to enter into flexible and well-resourced alliances with the private sector. Although Eisenhower reversed many of the more "statist" industrial policies implemented by the Truman administration, relying instead on a "decentralized industrial policy of procurement" (Friedberg 2000, 22), he did not preside over a withdrawal of the national security state from the postwar American economy. Instead, he changed its forms of engagement. The resulting forms of public-private entwinement built upon both the system of contracting out inherited from World War II and the hybridization strategies rooted in American history (chapter 7).

In contrast to Truman's approach, favored by many New Deal liberals, Eisenhower envisaged a set of increasingly close and cooperative state-society relations focused on technology development. The "close integration of military and civilian resources," he argued, would engender better understanding of defense needs and civilian capabilities, benefit the armed forces, and enhance the nation's security. Eisenhower envisaged a model of technology development premised on the public-private integration that had led the United States to victory. Translated to peacetime, he declared in a 1946 memo for the civilian and military leadership of the War Department and military commands, this "pattern of integration will not merely familiarize the Army with the progress made in science and industry, but draw into our planning for national security all the civilian resources which can contribute to the defense of the country."[18]

In this model, state-based agents would ideally undertake three tasks: first, form partnerships and alliances with private actors throughout the national economy; second, negotiate private-sector support for state-directed projects; and third, leverage both public and private resources in pursuit of national technological objectives. "It is our job," Eisenhower argued, "to take the initiative in promoting the development of new resources, if our national security indicates the need. It is our duty to support broad research programs in educational institutions, in industry, and in whatever field might be of importance to the Army" (Melman 1970). Public and private actors would work together under the goal-setting auspices of the national security state in order to develop the cutting-edge technologies necessary for national defense. It was the NSS's job, in other words, to guarantee U.S. technological leadership. In short, this was the vision at the heart of the NSS innovation enterprise: permanent preparedness in pursuit of perpetual innovation.

The end of the Korean War provided Eisenhower with an opportunity to rationalize the structure of the emergent NSS. Having abolished the "unwieldy boards,"[19] Eisenhower affirmed the role of the armed services in science and technology policy, creating within the DoD centralized offices for research, development, engineering, and acquisition, each headed by a designated assistant secretary. For their part, each of the services established an Assistant Secretary for Research and Development and began to expand its own system of myriad institutionalized partnerships, programs, and projects.[20] In an incisive phrase, Eisenhower aptly defined this new structure as the "decentralization of operations, under flexible and effective direction and control from the center." (Eisenhower 1953).

Together with the more permanent (hybridized) forms of institutionalized partnering, the contracting-out model became the centerpiece of the national security state's S&T policy. In addition to the armed services, the AEC and NIH also increased their use of extramural contracts and hybrid arrangements to serve their missions.[21] In 1955 the second Hoover Commission declared that every effort should be made to conduct defense-led R&D in "the civilian economy," and this recommendation was promptly echoed in declarations of executive branch policy (Danhof 1968, 107).

From Contracting Revolution to Radical Innovation

Mobilization for World War II revolutionized technology procurement through new contracting arrangements that shifted the risk of innovation to the public sector. This was a turning point in the nation's science and technology development because it paved the way for a more radical and sustained form of innovation. In the process, the role of firms and universities was transformed as well.

Prior to World War II, the armed services relied on technological change driven mainly by private demand and the public-sector initiatives of European powers, especially Great Britain and Germany.[22] This situation changed dramatically under the National Defense Expenditure Act (1940) driven through by Roosevelt before America entered the war. Together with the War Powers Act (1941), this made a sweeping break with procurement tradition. Henceforth, the armed services could undertake developmental projects in partnership with the private sector through contractual arrangements that transferred the cost and risk from private actors to the federal government. The act gave the armed services authority to negotiate contracts using either a fixed-fee or a cost-plus-fixed-fee arrangement. Contracting reforms were most important because they allowed the armed services to steer developmental projects throughout the private sector while protecting private-sector partners from risk. In effect, by no longer relying on private-commercial demand to set the pace of innovation, the services came to occupy a leading position on the technological frontier.

Not only did the war transform the federal government's role within high-technology sectors of the national economy, it also transformed the role of American firms within the global economy. As Mowery and Rosenberg (1998, 6) have observed, American firms tended to excel at using and adapting technologies created elsewhere, but the U.S. economy rarely spawned radically new technological fields or industrial sectors. Prior to World War II, they argue, American firms "had few equals" in their ability to deploy and (sometimes) improve foreign technologies but until World War II, the U.S. position in science and technology was not one of leadership. The notable exception was the agricultural sector, historically a stronghold of federal government support.

The American university was another institution remade by the Cold War and the rise of the NSS, and that in turn generated an industrial ecosystem. Both MIT and Stanford figured prominently in Pentagon patronage that established permanent labs designed to achieve strategic goals. At MIT, the Air Force's Lincoln Lab (1950) in partnership with IBM created the SAGE air defense system (chapter 4). At a cost of $8 billion over ten years, it was the largest S&T enterprise mounted since the Manhattan Project.[23] On the west coast, Stanford University became a key institution in the growth of a radio and microelectronics industry that evolved into Silicon Valley. From modest beginnings, Stanford grew rapidly, by 1950 drawing almost one-quarter of its entire research budget from electronics research for the DoD, very little of it "undirected" (Geiger 1992, 33–34).

These changes, together with the growing weight of large military contractors, were not viewed in a wholly positive light. It was President Eisenhower himself who, in his 1961 farewell address, would first raise the alarm about the military-industrial complex as a political force. Yet it was not until the Vietnam War that the term came into its own in public discourse, whence it has emerged as both "lobby" and "trope" (Roland 2007, 344). More generally, the term has become firmly associated with idea of a wall of separation: a mission agency that interacts with a specialized, discrete group of companies, and that has little contact with the commercial economy.

The fledgling national security state thus emerged incrementally and somewhat messily, the product of geopolitical imperatives filtered by domestic politics and antistatist impulses. By the early 1950s the principal components of today's national security state were largely in place, actively harnessing the nation's scientific and technical resources for the purpose of military preparedness. Ironically, as Hart (1998, 176) observes, domestic political conflict over the nature of that enterprise helped translate geopolitical challenges into a technology policy that was heavily oriented toward the military and defense-related agencies. Nevertheless, the NSS role in national technology policy had yet to be fully established, a process that crystallized in response to Sputnik.

Growth: The Sputnik Effect (1958–1968)

> It's really an impressive story of how we turned a negative into a positive. We won the space race. We built miniaturized objects that became cell phones and GPS systems. We built the Internet. And at the end of the day, there is no Soviet Union.
>
> *CBS News,* February 11, 2009

In October 1957, at the height of the Cold War, the USSR launched Sputnik, a small, earth-orbiting satellite hardly bigger than a beach ball. This world first achievement was met by America with a mix of fear and awe. Its impact was momentous—broad, deep, and lasting. As Eisenhower's chief science adviser, James Killian, recalled:

> As it beeped into the sky, *Sputnik 1* created a crisis of confidence that swept the country like a windblown forest fire. Overnight there developed a widespread fear that the country lay at the mercy of the Russian military machine and that our own government and its military arm had abruptly lost the power to defend the mainland itself. . . . Confidence in American science, technology, and education suddenly evaporated. (Killian 1977, 7)

Not least, the Sputnik effect planted new shoots in the NSS and instituted a system of perpetual innovation for military preparedness. NSC-68 had emphasized the relationship between technological superiority and national defense; suddenly, however, it seemed that it was the USSR that had been actively building that relationship while the United States had been caught sleeping. The nation was still reeling from Sputnik 1 when one month later the Russians sent their second satellite into space. The contrast with America's own failed December effort (fast-tracked by the Navy), had a devastating impact on morale and led to a period of "genuine consternation, followed by a veritable orgy of national self-examination and self-criticism."[24]

As a result, Sputnik triggered the so-called space age and a new era of institution (and nation) building. School science curricula were strengthened; science education was prioritized; R&D funding was increased. In addition, to boost the innovation effort, the federal government founded two new research and technology-oriented agencies (the Defense Advanced Research Projects Agency and NASA), created another hybrid institution to seed a modern venture capital industry (the Small Business Investment Corporation), expanded the NIH, and centralized DoD science and technology policy by creating the position of Deputy Director of Research and Engineering. As historian Walter McDougall writes, "Sputnik triggered an abrupt discontinuity," transforming governments into "self-conscious promoters, not just of technological change but of perpetual technological revolution" (1982, 1011).

As for institutional development relevant to formation of the NSS technology enterprise, the Sputnik moment had four important effects. First, it made it politically easier to appropriate funds for defense- and national security–led research and development (Congressional Research Service 1986a, 41). In the name of defense, Congress provided NSS agencies with large infusions of funds to assist in the national innovation effort. Adjusted for inflation, the NSF budget increased from just under $173 million in 1957 to more than $1.2 billion in 1967, while NIH funding climbed from $950 million to $3.8 billion. Overall federal obligations for the five NSS agencies conducting R&D in this period more than tripled, climbing from just over $20 billion to more than $72 billion.[25] Whereas before Sputnik the nation spent roughly 1.5 percent of GDP on R&D, with government and the private sector contributing equal shares, a decade later that investment exceeded 3 percent of GDP, some 70 percent of which was provided by the federal government.

Second, Sputnik paved the way for centralizing the organization of technology development, giving Eisenhower the opportunity to drive through the Defense Reorganization Act of 1958, which enhanced the authority of the secretary of defense and the Joint Chiefs of Staff by giving them the power to impose a unified program on all the armed services. Most importantly, it was this act that established the position of Director of Defense Research and Engineering, who assumed the role of chief technologist for the DoD responsible for research and engineering. As Friedberg has observed, whenever the secretary of defense was prepared to use his powers under the act, "he now had available to him, for the first time, an instrument with which to exert substantial control over the pace and direction of the nation's entire military research effort" (Friedberg 2000, 319).

Third, Sputnik provided an imperative for preparedness against future "technological surprise," leading to the creation of two new agencies, the Advanced Research Projects Agency (later the Defense Advanced Research Projects Agency) and NASA. DARPA was founded in 1958 as a defense research agency independent of the three services, with a mandate to create and prevent technological surprise. The agency's broad charter gives it authority to develop both military and dual-use technologies in collaboration with commercial industry. As the central arm of the DoD's research program, DARPA became responsible for long-range, high-risk R&D of interest to the military as a whole, including the building of prototypes for new military systems. It is often credited with helping to put the DoD at the forefront of high technology. However, as Alex Roland points out with reference to U.S. computer development, "DARPA was just one of several federal agencies and several research-support paradigms that made a difference. Different agencies played more or less critical roles at various stages."[26] Although small by DoD standards (receiving less than 4 percent of the military's Research, Development, Test, and Evaluation budget), the agency's broad remit and agile form would spark numerous breakthroughs stimulating military and commercial innovation, ranging from stealth aircraft to the internet.

Whereas DARPA was intended to lead investigation and development of revolutionary technologies from within the Defense Department, NASA was established as an independent agency tasked with increasing national opportunities for scientific and technological advancement in space-related fields. Although designated as a civilian agency, NASA formed a key component of the defense establishment, as former science adviser to three administrations Harvey Brooks remarked in 1970 to a Congressional committee (cited in Geiger 1992, 26). As chief U.S. protagonist in the space race, NASA's technological prowess was a vital component of the national prestige on which America's soft power depended. In particular, the new agency spawned the Apollo Program that mobilized American science and technology in ways reminiscent of the World War II Manhattan Project. In a direct hard-power manner too, NASA served specific military purposes, working closely with the armed services, the CIA, and the DoD (Berkowitz 1970, 9; Geiger 1992). As a result of its broad Congressional mandate, NASA like DARPA engaged in dual-use technology development (with many major breakthroughs ranging from composite materials to communications satellites), and in 1962 created the Technology Utilization Program, which promoted commercial spin-offs through dedicated field offices and Industrial Applications Centers.

Mirroring the armed services, DARPA and NASA relied predominantly on the judicious use of contracts to conduct their work, further expanding the federal government's technology procurement networks and strengthening the role of the American research university in the national security system.[27] Federal funding for university research rose by 200 percent during the half-decade 1959–64, compared with a 91 percent increase in the preceding five years (Geiger 1997, 356–57).

In a separate innovation-boosting effort to win the Cold War, this time targeting the civilian economy, Congress passed the Small Business Investment Act of 1958. Designed to stimulate innovation through investment in young and emerging firms, this act authorized the funding of Small Business Investment Companies, creating a hybridized venture capital system that fused private ownership with public resources. This unique partnership between the public and the private sector provided vital equity and long-term loan support for high-technology startups and laid the foundation for the modern venture capital industry (chapter 3).

Notwithstanding incremental adjustments, the institutional complex in place at the end of the Eisenhower administration lives on. Whereas most of the arrangements implemented by the Truman administration were all "just for the interim" (Kevles 1975, 43), Eisenhower established a permanent and preeminent role for the national security state in the nation's science and technology policy, organizing it and equipping it for war on the technological frontier. The response of his administration to the Sputnik crisis completed the lineaments of the NSS as we know it, and its infrastructural reach grew in scale and scope right through the 1960s. It was the debacle of Vietnam that halted this trajectory.

Crisis: Legitimation and Innovation Deficits (1969–1979)

When Richard Nixon took over the presidency in 1969, he inherited a legacy of crises at home and overseas. Domestically, the nation's universities—drawn into the NSS's orbit during and immediately after World War II—became battlegrounds as radical students demanded the expulsion of the military and a small but vocal group of academic researchers called for sources of funding other than the DoD (Smith 1990, 73–74). Internationally, the strategic logic of the Vietnam War was being called into question; there was a growing awareness that the United States had to try to defuse a Cold War that was spinning out of control and which—as some in the administration feared—the nation was set to lose. While these issues formed the backdrop to defense conversion and a period of détente with the Soviet Union, the new decade also brought fresh concerns about an innovation deficit, heightened to an increasing extent by the seemingly relentless rise of Japan as a rival technological power. The implications for U.S. technological leadership and defense strategy would pave the way toward a new emphasis on military and commercial integration.

The decade that runs roughly from the late 1960s to the late 1970s thus begins with a legitimation crisis and closes with an emerging innovation crisis. Each challenge generated a distinctive response that tilted the NSS toward a more direct role in fostering commercial innovation, beginning with biotechnology.

The Legitimation Crisis and Its Impacts

The legitimation deficit (the anti-Vietnam effect) made itself felt in three main ways: first it sparked a biological weapons conversion effort that catalyzed the formation of a commercial biotechnology industry; second, it redefined the DoD-DARPA relationship with the university sector; and finally, it ramped up the NSS relevance of the NSF and the NIH, rerouting DoD's nondefense funding through these agencies.

Nixon's November 1969 decision to ban development of offensive biological weapons was responsive to the intense antiwar sentiment that gripped the country. It was also motivated by the realization that in an offensive bioweapons race, a secretive authoritarian system like the USSR would always have a large advantage. That calculation was reflected in the concurrent decision to ratify the Biological and Toxin Weapons Convention, finalized in 1972. Determined also to lead the emerging revolution in microbiology, the federal government deployed the conversion process to kick-start a commercial dual-use biotechnology industry, transferring to the private sector a good deal of the technology that had been locked up in government labs. Keeping control of U.S. technology once conversion to peaceful use had been achieved was also important. It was the desire to protect U.S. inventions once transferred to the private sector, argues Shelley Hurt, that set federal authorities on a path to major intellectual property reform, starting with a strengthening of the Patent Act in 1971 and culminating in the Bayh-Dole and Stevenson Wydler acts of 1980.[28]

In the conversion process, a major beneficiary was the Department of Health, Education, and Welfare. In 1972 its National Institutes of Health acquired a new biological research arm—the Frederick Cancer Research and Development Center (hereafter the National Cancer Institute). The NCI was the organization designated to fight a new battle, the so-called "War on Cancer," launched by Nixon during his reelection campaign.[29] The NCI would become highly relevant to the NSS, given that cancer research involves a knowledge base similar to that required for biodefense. In 1970, the journal *Nature* reported that the new NIH-run facility would "use Fort Detrick for the containment and large scale production of suspected viral tumor agents," while another NIH-run facility, the National Institute of Allergy and Infectious Diseases would undertake "research on hazardous viruses" among other viral diseases.[30] Both NIAID and NCI are the most highly funded institutes of the NIH, working in areas that also feed into the biomedical work of their next-door neighbor, the Army's Medical Research Institute of Infectious Diseases.

Symbolic of its entwinement with the NSS, the National Cancer Institute took possession of the Army's former biological warfare facilities. An official history of Fort Detrick remarks how "unusual" it was that a civilian agency establishing itself on a military reservation "be given full title to the land," including seventy buildings (Covert 1993, 110). But the NIH-NCI relationship to the NSS went beyond the occupation of military premises to embrace also its human resources. Following demilitarization of the biological labs, several hundred displaced Fort Detrick scientists and technicians were moved into the positions that were opened up by the new cancer institute. The move allowed the retention of critical scientific expertise that could deliver knowledge relevant to this quintessentially dual-use field of biotechnology. Indeed, the complementarity of Defense and NIH interests in this arena—perhaps stronger today than ever—played no small part in building a biotechnology industry, funding projects of fledgling companies aimed at both mission-oriented and commercial applications.[31] Today, in two-hatted mode, the U.S. Army Medical Research and Materiel Command runs an extramural research program that targets various forms of cancer (breast, prostate, and ovarian). One may only wonder how Congress came to nominate the Army to wage "war on breast cancer."[32] Thus, the conversion process provided the

United States with the makings of a biotechnology industry that played to the dual needs of defense and commerce. The important point, however, is that in doing so, conversion forged another link connecting the NIH to the NSS.

The legitimation crisis also helped to redefine the relationship of the military to the university sector, producing two outcomes relevant to the NSS technology enterprise. The first was an expanded role for the NSF and the NIH, which stepped into the breach created by the military's semiretreat from the funding of university research. As the Vietnam War escalated, unrest at university campuses inflamed debates over the propriety of DoD-DARPA sponsorship of university research, a good deal of which had included non-defense activities. As antiwar sentiment increased across American campuses, Congress responded with the Mansfield Amendment to the Military Procurement Act of 1970, which required mission agencies to divest themselves of broader, non–mission-oriented research. Ironically, to comply, the military services were forced to cancel numerous university research projects that did not have a "direct and apparent relationship" to the defense mission, while continuing to fund defense-specific projects (Congressional Research Service 1986a, 51–52). Though the requirement was softened a year later and eventually removed from legislation, for almost a decade, DoD-DARPA funding of university research emphasized military relevance. In the meantime, however, the extramural programs of the NSF and the NIH expanded to fill the vacuum created by the departure of the DoD from nonmilitary funding. Thus in 1971, NSF assumed responsibility for Defense's materials research laboratories in order to pursue industrial applications. The university-based program had been set up in response to post-Sputnik concerns, but faced extinction when Congress banned the use of Pentagon-sourced money from funding non–mission-related research. At one stroke, responsibility for the DARPA program was transferred to NSF.

The second outcome can best be described as a hybridizing response. Because of the fierce student reaction to the perceived militarization of research universities, some institutions were induced to hive off research units that owed their existence to military sponsorship. Innovation-focused ventures such as the famed Stanford Research Institute (established as SRI International in 1970) and Draper Laboratory (divested from MIT in 1973), among several others, were formally separated from their university bases and reconstituted as independent not-for-profits that effectively—in the spirit of public-purpose institutions—continued to draw the bulk of their income and research agendas from the NSS.

The Innovation Deficit and the Offset Strategy

As détente came to an end in 1977, the new Carter administration confronted a darkening geopolitical and economic landscape. Strategically, the military establishment saw itself struggling to stay ahead of the USSR in defense technology. Economically, there appeared to be no escape from the malaise that had gripped the United States since the mid-1970s, attributed by many not to the Vietnam War or the oil crisis but to the rise of Japan and a loss of innovation capacity. In due course, as Japan began to outstrip the United States in many of its own high-technology markets, the economic challenge would increasingly take on geopolitical significance. The Japan factor thus came to add a distinctive geopolitical threat of its own to these strategic and economic concerns. Overlaying and intersecting with these concerns was the perception of a mounting "innovation deficit"—a diminished ability of the NSS to access the advanced capabilities of the private sector as innovative firms turned their backs on the government market. It is worth pausing to consider both the geostrategic challenge and the innovation deficit as they emerged in the late 1970s because it was their intersection that provided the impetus in the subsequent decade to expand and consolidate the commercial reorientation of NSS technology policy.

The DoD's Offset Strategy. The Cold War was not simply an arms race but a science and technology race, as both the United States and the Soviet Union concentrated their resources to gain a technological edge over and impose technological surprise on each other. By the late 1970s, technology development initiatives begun under Eisenhower had achieved outstanding progress, an upshot of which was that U.S. intelligence agencies now had a relatively clear picture of Soviet military capabilities and technological accomplishments. By 1977, U.S. intelligence suggested that the Soviet Union had achieved parity with the United States in terms of nuclear weapons and their delivery systems. Since the USSR also had quantitatively superior conventional forces, it now possessed a potentially large strategic advantage. As a result, senior officials feared that deterrence was being threatened and looked for a strategy "to restore the conventional military balance" (Perry 2003, 2). This fear coincided with a collapse in détente, accelerated by the Soviet invasion of Afghanistan in 1978. Secretary of Defense Harold Brown thus determined that the United States needed once again to target its resources toward the development of technologically superior weapons systems able to offset the USSR's quantitative edge. He named this the Offset Strategy, and gave Deputy Director of Research and Engineering William Perry the responsibility and resources to develop the relevant technology as quickly as possible. Looking back, Perry recalled what this meant for technology development: "I decided . . . to base the Offset Strategy on information technology, a field in which the United States, even in those days, had a commanding lead. Very early in my tenure, I went to an organization called DARPA . . . for detailed briefings on the advanced sensors and smart weapons that were to be the basis of the Offset Strategy." (Perry 2003: 3).

Innovation deficit. The Offset Strategy has a particular analytical relevance because it coincided with an innovation deficit. In the same period as the strategy was devised, the Defense Science Board was pointing to a worsening state of industrial responsiveness to support current acquisition needs.[33] This concern became the subject of testimony before the House Armed Services Committee and led to formation of a special Defense Industrial Base Panel. In its report, *The Ailing Industrial Base,* the panel's key finding was that there had been "a serious decline in the nation's defense industrial capability. . . . An alarming erosion of crucial industrial elements, coupled with a mushrooming dependence on foreign sources for critical materials," the panel concluded, "is endangering our defense posture at its very foundation" (U.S. House 1980, 6).

Even allowing for some hyperbole, there was genuine cause for concern. The case of integrated circuits generated most disquiet. These devices had been typically sourced from smaller specialized firms such as Fairchild Semiconductor and Texas Instruments. Although government contracts had been critical to their crucial startup stage, these younger but fast-growing firms began to turn their backs on defense and space work, in favor of higher returns in expanding commercial markets where integrated circuits were being incorporated into all manner of electronic goods such as calculators and digital watches. As commercial demand for mass-produced chips soared, dwarfing the government market, the defense-space agencies found it ever more difficult to interest semiconductor firms in designing and manufacturing integrated circuits for their use.[34] As the Congressional Budget Office commented in a later report, stringent technical and other requirements (such as radiation hardening), had made defense-related semiconductors too expensive for the commercial market, "discouraging semiconductor firms from producing the integrated circuits needed by military planners" (Congressional Budget Office 1987, 61). As a result, the armed services began to experience shortages of customized chips. Addressing this problem was made more urgent by the renewed tensions with the Soviet Union and the decision to rely more heavily on an information technology–intensive strategy on the battlefield. Making the problem even more pressing was Japan's challenge to U.S. technology leadership, most vitally in microelectronics, the very basis of the Pentagon's Offset Strategy.[35]

The significance of this point should not be lost: many of the advanced design and manufacturing capabilities for achieving the goal of the Offset Strategy were located in the commercial arena, not among the large defense contractors conventionally identified with the military industrial complex.[36] This meant that the DoD had to explore new ways of procuring advanced technology that could also meet commercial interests if it were to access the so-called "nontraditional" suppliers (as the cases examined in chapters 4 and 5 demonstrate).

As America entered the new decade, its political and national security leaders thus confronted the two-pronged challenge of a rising power in high technology and an "ailing industrial base," one they saw as compromising the nation's technology leadership and endangering its military primacy. How they responded to this challenge marked the deepening and broadening of NSS engagement with commercial undertakings. For the most part, however, it left unresolved the erosion of high-tech manufacturing whose flight abroad would intensify from the mid-1980s onward.

Reform and Reorientation: Beginnings (1980–1989)

In discussing the next phase in the evolution of the NSS, it must be said at the outset that any effort to capture in a word key aspects of a period is bound to be contentious. But we must remember that the purpose is always to highlight and encapsulate only those changes most relevant to the evolution of the NSS as a technology enterprise. Attempting that task over a time span of three decades (running from the early 1980s to the present) presents its own difficulties of treatment. At one level, the task seems relatively straightforward because the unifying theme of the period as a whole is a major shift toward commercially significant involvement of the NSS. At another level, however, complexity sets in because that evolution coincides with a flagging U.S. economy and the rise of a national competitiveness narrative. It is therefore easy to overlook the national security enterprise that lay behind certain economic initiatives. I have therefore, found it useful analytically to divide this overall trajectory of the NSS into three phases: the beginnings followed by the consolidation of reform and reorientation, and then the re-visioning of the NSS's role in techo-innovation.

From the late 1970s, the enormous leverage that the federal government once exercised in terms of market pull began to weaken. Two structural changes that underpinned that process could not be reversed: the diminution in relative size of the government procurement market (dwarfed by commercial markets by the 1970s) and the falling federal share of total R&D spending (overtaken by private R&D outlays by the late 1980s). The case of integrated circuits dramatically illustrates the first trend whereby defense-related sales fell from 70 percent of the domestic market in the mid-1960s to 10 percent by the 1980s. Less dramatic, but nonetheless reflective of its diminishing pull, is the federal government's diminishing weight in R&D spending. Having funded almost twice as much R&D as private industry in 1960, it was funding slightly less than industry's share of the national total by 1980. (More detailed data are presented in chapter 5's analysis of how the changes impact the NSS technology enterprise.)

The key point is that, with its leverage reduced, the NSS had to create new incentives if it was to reattract innovative companies to work on its projects. Building commercial viability into technology procurement projects from the outset was one such incentive, and gradually over the next two decades it became a major means of procuring transformative innovation from nontraditional suppliers. More generally, it was over the course of this period that programmatic and institutional reforms tilted the NSS increasingly toward the commercial sector as a way of recapturing the technology high ground.

In briefly discussing these reforms, I seek to set them in their broader international and domestic context. As this period was marked by a darkening economic mood, it is important to distinguish strategic initiatives that also had commercial benefits from initiatives that had purely commercial payoffs. A secondary objective is therefore to indicate how overlapping economic and strategic concerns over the loss of industrial competitiveness and an ailing industrial base that threatened technological superiority created an impetus for government action that would feed directly into NSS initiatives to ensure U.S. primacy.

Two reforms to the patent system kicked off the 1980s decade. The first, the Bayh-Dole Act of 1980, gave smaller firms and universities the right to retain ownership of government-funded innovations. Patent rights emerged as an important issue for innovative firms in DoD-sponsored surveys conducted during the 1970s. Giving firms ownership rights over their inventions, even if stimulated by mission problem sets and investment, would be an inducement to the smaller, but increasingly crucial IT firms to work on mission projects. Shelley Hurt (2010) has argued that reforms to the patent and licensing system were also crucial to protecting actual federal inventions once Nixon had taken the decision to convert the biowarfare labs and kick-start a biotech industry.

The second reform, the Stevenson-Wydler Technology Innovation Act (like the Bayh-Dole Act, signed into law by the outgoing President Carter), focused on inducements for the National Laboratories to commercialize their innovations.[37] It was first in a series of laws making it a National Laboratory mission to transfer technology to the private sector. Throughout the Cold War massive public investment by the DoE (not to mention the Pentagon, NASA, and the intelligence agencies) did much more than build weapons with prime contractors. It also created "a technical archipelago of immense value, whose crown jewels are the three national weapons laboratories," Los Alamos, Sandia, and Lawrence Livermore.[38] Weapons labs are not the kind we associate with white-coated scientists and test tubes. They are populated by interdisciplinary teams of scientists and engineers that use theoretical and applied nuclear physics to "solve design and manufacturing problems as concrete as those at any consumer products company." Their vast practical experience and inventiveness made them a prime target for the licensing revolution stimulated by the incentives that sprang from subsequent enhancements of the Stevenson-Wydler reform. From this period onward, the national labs would be transformed from their chief status as R&D hybrids to embrace also entrepreneurial activities.

Thus, although strengthened throughout the 1980s, beginning with the new Reagan administration, these reforms owed their existence to earlier administrations that spanned both political persuasions. Indeed, wherever the NSS technology enterprise was paramount, or wherever it was married to commercialization initiatives that could take hybridized forms, bipartisan support could be counted on (see especially chapter 7).

Following the Soviet invasion of Afghanistan in 1979 and the full resumption of Cold War tensions, Ronald Reagan took office on a platform hosting two contradictory impulses. The new decade opened with a Republican administration seeking to square the circle with a promise to roll back government and a pledge to confront the Soviets by ramping up defense spending on advanced technology. Hardly had the Vietnam folly had time to recede from public attention when the new administration was being charged with remilitarizing technology. Its plans for a massively expensive project to create a shield against Soviet missiles were met with alarm and resounding opposition both at home and abroad, not least within the scientific community. The Strategic Defense Initiative, the so-called Star Wars project, while never brought to fruition, nevertheless created a new independent agency, within the Pentagon. Modeled after DARPA, the Strategic Defense Initiative Organization (SDIO) was given a broad remit to expand its development efforts in a wide range of areas, including sensors, lasers, space propulsion, ultra–high speed computing, advanced space materials, and the like.

But as one high-tech sector after another began losing market share to Japan, and as Silicon Valley entered a prolonged crisis, the administration would also have to deal with a newly emergent geopolitical threat deemed likely to dislodge U.S. technology leadership in the absence of measures taken. As if to reflect the worsening U.S. economic outlook, Japan's seemingly relentless rise thus translated national security into an issue of national competitiveness.[39] Thus, for example, as the SDIO emerged, a small specialized unit called the Office of Technology Applications was formed with the mission to find commercial applications for its defense technologies.

Throughout this period, the "Japan factor" loomed large in the concerns of both NSS officials and Congress, generating studies, reports, and remedial action. Following the Defense Science Board's 1980 *Ailing Industrial Base* report, defense officials, apprehensive about the geostrategic implications of U.S. industry losses to Japan, pushed for an interagency study of Japan's growing market share in memory chips—critical to its technological advantage. The Congressional Office of Technology Assessment was then called on to produce a *Report on International Competitiveness in Electronics* (1983). But by 1986, as the DRAM (dynamic random-access memory) crisis took its toll on Silicon Valley,[40] the worsening state of America's microelectronics industry could no longer be ignored. In the following year, a report on *Defense Semiconductor Dependency* warned that the nation's capability to deploy technologically superior weapons, which depended on superior electronics, could soon be "dangerously diminished" because of the loss of U.S. manufacturing capability (Defense Science Board 1987, 187). Ceding the high ground in producing and scaling up critical general-purpose technologies (not just in semiconductors, but also in computing, software, advanced materials, and the like), was seen as tantamount to relinquishing U.S. primacy. The key threat here of course was Japan, whose commercial industries (and access to the United States market) had made it a technology powerhouse. NSS agents and academic analysts observed, too, that Japan had strengthened the link between technology and manufacturing—"the application of innovation," as the Defense Science Board put it. By contrast, the United States seemed bent on severing that connection, closing industries and sending manufacturing offshore. Indeed, U.S. authorities in business and government put a confident construction on the exit of manufacturing industry—in the deluded belief that the decline of manufacturing and the offshoring of production signaled the emergence of a more advanced "postindustrial" economy. In their prescient analysis, Berkeley scholars Stephen Cohen and John Zysman (1987) warned of the devastating policy consequences such wrongheaded thinking would unleash. Thus, by the time the Soviet Union departed from the scene, it was not just U.S. technology leadership that was under fire, but its very ability to maintain capabilities in critical fields that depended on a thriving manufacturing base (Borrus and Zysman 1992).

Thus, in its implications for U.S. technological leadership and defense strategy, Japan's relentless incursions would have both shorter- and longer-term implications. In the shorter term, the NSS innovation deficit would pave the way toward a new emphasis on military and commercial integration, in full swing by the fall of the Berlin Wall (chapter 5). In the longer term, however, the emerging "production deficit"—the leakage of manufacturing industry offshore—would become a flood that could not be staunched. What this might mean for the NSS innovation engine today is an issue I will put on hold until chapter 9.

As subsequent chapters demonstrate, an array of programmatic and institutional reforms thus began to tilt the NSS toward commercially viable innovation as a way of recapturing and retaining technology leadership. These reform initiatives (box 2.1) included new technology procurement programs to attract commercially oriented firms; a strengthening of the patent system to encourage commercialization of government-funded or -created innovations; the formation of software and semiconductor hybrids to advance the state of the art such as the Software Engineering Institute and SRC Software; the establishment of industry consortia such as Sematech that integrate NSS and commercial objectives; and the reorganization of national labs to seed entrepreneurial endeavors and transform lab technology into market-ready products via cooperative R&D agreements with private firms.

**BOX 2.1. REORIENTING THE NSS TO DUAL-USE
AND COMMERCIALLY VIABLE INNOVATION**

- **Patent/intellectual property reforms:** Bayh-Dole Act (1980), Stevenson-Wydler Technology Innovation Act (1980) plus amendments (1984, 1987, 1989).
- **Programmatic and procurement reforms:** 1978–82 new technology procurement programs from VHSIC and VLSIC to SBIR; 1986 acquisition reforms: DoD Reorganization Act (Goldwater-Nichols) intended to reduce interservice rivalry and reform DoD's management of R&D and acquisition. In response to recommendations of the 1986 Packard Commission on Defense Management, the reforms subsume management of technology procurement under acquisition.
- **Organizational reforms:** Hybridization of national labs and creation of new "innovation hybrids" (not just "partnerships" but a merging of public and private innovation efforts, discussed in chapter 7); for example:
  - **1982:** Semiconductor Research Corporation formed by U.S. semiconductor device firms and co-funded by NSS components to undertake silicon-based R&D in U.S. universities. Semiconductor industry specialist Thomas Howell notes that "four U.S. government organizations participate in and contribute to its funding"—DARPA, NSF, the US Army Research Office, and NIST—and that "a number of its key leaders have backgrounds in Department of Defense microelectronics R&D programs." At the time, SRC was led by the former head of DOD's VHSIC program (Howell 2003, 197).
  - **1984:** DOD establishes the Software Engineering Institute, a privately operated hybrid, to develop and diffuse best practice in software architecture.
  - **1980, 1984, 1986:** DoE labs gradually revamped as entrepreneurial-commercialization engines; new internal entrepreneurial schemes, new incentives/mechanisms to commercialize innovations (e.g., the High Temperature Superconductivity Pilot Centers at Argonne, Oak Ridge, and Los Alamos, started in 1988, which spawned new ventures in lab-industry collaboration to develop and commercialize technology via Cooperative Research and Development Agreements.

Overall, the 1980s produced a decade of efforts by NSS planners and Congressional committees aimed at exploiting innovations sponsored or created by the federal government. Many of the reforms and S&T initiatives of the period sought to reverse the lagging status of U.S. industry and innovation and thereby address the challenge to the nation's technology leadership and its Offset Strategy.

Thus, President Reagan, though widely (and perhaps justly) considered the founding father of neoliberalism, was no slouch when it came to providing the NSS with resources that would also help to galvanize commercial regeneration. In the realm of science and technology at least, the Reagan administration's actions belied its small government, antistatist rhetoric, in keeping with the fact that it is in the S&T domain that both parties, in competing for the national security mantle, have generally reached across the partisan divide. Thus, in addition to the SDIO's broad mission to include promoting the commercialization of its innovations (which it claimed to have done with some success), in 1987 the administration announced its intent to double the NSF budget over the next five years and to establish national S&T centers within universities throughout the country, which the NSF would use also to drive commercialization of technology. As the Cold War wound down, however, and high-tech industry gradually recovered, the NSS technology enterprise would have to negotiate a rockier political path to sustain the transformative ambition.

Reform and Reorientation: Consolidation (1990–1999)

Whereas the Reagan era is often remembered for the militarization of technology, the following decade is typically perceived as reversing that trend. The drive to civilianize technology policy began to gather steam during the presidency of George H. W. Bush, with a Democrat-controlled Congress. Although philosophically opposed to government involvement in commercial undertakings, the Bush administration was nevertheless persuaded to support dual-use ventures such as the Sematech semiconductor research consortium and a fledgling nondefense initiative, the Advanced Technology Program. However, it was not until the Clinton administration's tenure that civilizing technology policy came into its own—though not in the sense normally understood, as we shall see.

The prospect of a peace dividend arising from the collapse of the Soviet Union and an end to Cold War hostilities dramatically altered the strategic environment of the 1990s and, with a Democrat installed in the White House, gave force to the campaign for a defense conversion that could strengthen commercial enterprise. However, programs perceived to prioritize commercial benefits soon renewed Congressional tension over technology funding. The George H. W. Bush administration had earlier dismissed DARPA Director Craig Fields for promoting an array of NSS-shaped ventures deemed to be more concerned with improving U.S. commercial competitiveness than enhancing military preparedness. Similarly, promising federal initiatives such as the Advanced Technology Program and the Technology Reinvestment Program, after failing to gain the support of a Republican-dominated Congress elected in 1994, were soon weakened and eventually terminated.

The DARPA-managed TRP was a federally funded dual-use program intended to strengthen links between defense and commercial firms by creating civilian applications of defense technologies. It directed some $800 million to several dozen dual-use technology projects in cost-shared arrangements with commercial firms, before its termination by the Republican Congress in 1996 as part of its general repudiation of nonmilitary and dual-use technology initiatives with apparently more obvious commercial than military benefits. In an effort to stave off that action, then Under Secretary of Defense for Acquisition and Technology Paul Kaminski felt it necessary to try to convince Congress that TRP was not "industry policy," underlining this point with a personal reassurance: "I have no interest . . . in these dual use programs or investing in these programs unless the net round trip to the DOD results in lower costs for our applications. Greater performance and lower cost is the objective" (Kaminski 1995a: 14). As a Congressional history of science policy had seen fit to comment a decade earlier, "The longstanding . . . debate about the principle of government support for industry, rather than its efficacy" is one with "few if any parallels" outside the United States (Congressional Research Service 1986b, 207). Ten years on, that debate—and the antistatist norms that animated it—still retained its currency.

Civilianizing Technology—Not Always What It Seems

In tracing the further evolution of the NSS as an S&T enterprise, we have begun to shift our gaze from what it looks like to what it does. By the 1960s, the NSS had already experienced its major growth phase, hence in organizational terms its key components were all well in place. But states are actors as well as organizational configurations, so the question of how the NSS has evolved as a technology actor is especially relevant. The story of acquisition (which entails production) is quite different from that of technology procurement (which entails innovation). In the realm of acquisition, constrained defense budgets and the rising costs of weapon systems made the expense of equipment a major issue that—with assistance from an aggressive new defense secretary in the Pentagon, William Perry—helped drive major reforms to defense acquisition. The upshot of the Perry reforms introduced in 1994 was a buying process designed to give more scope to commercially available items. In the realm of technology development, however, it was not so much cost as access to, and influence over, the commercial sector that became a major issue for NSS planners. The problem had deeper roots, but was exacerbated by the post–Cold War consolidation of defense-intensive firms (reduced from fifty to five by the end of the 1990s), which were focused less on enhancing innovation than on maximizing shareholder value— pouring the bulk of profits into share buybacks and dividends, leaving little for R&D. As a result, NSS actors became increasingly concerned to ensure the commercial viability of their investments as they engaged and encouraged nontraditional suppliers of innovation. This, indeed, is the story—detailed in subsequent chapters—that unfolds from the 1980s onward.

Thus, civilianizing (aka commercializing) technology should be understood not just in the conventional sense of a nonmilitary approach to technology policy. Increasingly in this era, we see the rise of two different civilianizing forms. One is a banal version, which can be summarized as the "buy more ready-to-use" commercial items approach, otherwise known as the commercial-off-the-shelf (COTS) approach. This was especially the case for software. Increasing dependence on information-intensive equipment meant that software was rapidly becoming the dominant item of expenditure in weapons systems. In an era of cost cutting and military downsizing, vigorous campaigning by firms like Microsoft in order to get Defense and other NSS agencies to use readymade software began to bear fruit.[41]

But there is a second, much more developmentally significant version of commercializing technology—the one of most relevance to this study and to the post–Cold War era. Rather than making defense technologies commercially relevant (one of the original aims of TRP), or financing firms to develop innovations for the commercial market (the purpose of the Advanced Technology Program), or buying in readymade commercial items (the COTS program), the thrust of this second approach is to make greater use of the commercial sector (or nontraditional suppliers) to innovate for the NSS.

Note that the second approach entails two alternative ways of fostering technological innovation: The first enjoins NSS planners to incorporate commercial objectives within their technology procurement programs, a process already begun, if somewhat haltingly, in the late 1970s under the VHSIC and SBIR programs in order to entice innovative firms to work on government projects (chapters 3 and 4). The most striking case in the 1990s was the DoE's ten-year, $5 billion program for advanced simulation computing (the Advanced Simulation Computing Initiative), a major dual-use project stimulated by the need to find a new mode of (computer-based) nuclear weapons testing following the 1988 Comprehensive Test Ban Treaty. Under the ASCI program, the nuclear labs combined with key computing companies to produce revolutionary technologies intended to meet the needs of stockpile stewardship by simulating weapons testing, and to revive a moribund supercomputing industry by producing commercially significant innovations (chapter 5). The second way the NSS would seek to foster innovation was to leverage the commercial scale and capabilities of private firms by investing directly in their emerging technologies in order to shape their future direction. This hybridizing route was pioneered by the CIA in 1999 when it created its own privately run venture capital fund, In-Q-Tel, for that purpose, a precedent that other NSS agencies soon emulated (chapter 3).

Thus, over the course of the 1980s and 1990s, the NSS experienced a period of policy reform and reorientation that focused on the creation of new technologies with broad application—and new vehicles with which to

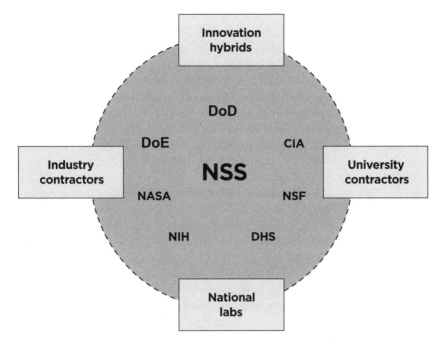

Figure 2.1 The national security state as technology enterprise.

access them. As questions of regaining access to (and influence over) advanced capabilities existing outside the traditional defense industry became paramount, the mission agencies thus made commercial relevance a test of their investment and innovation strategies. By the end of this period, the NSS technology enterprise embraced a vast array of innovation hybrids, national labs, industry, and university contractors (figure 2.1).

Re-visioning (2000–2012)

It is well known that the period following the 9/11 attacks has been one of strong expansion for the national security state. Whether understood in the conventional sense of surveillance or in the specific sense of technological innovation relevant to this study, the NSS is today considerably larger than its early–Cold War version. The question remains as to whether this growth has strengthened U.S. technological leadership or made it more vulnerable, an issue I return to shortly.

As threats to national security have multiplied to include everything from pandemics, terrorism, and weapons proliferation to energy supply, environmental crises, and cyber attacks, so new bureaucracies have been built, S&T agencies formed, and innovation hybrids created. Thus in 2003, a new Department of Homeland Security was set up to anticipate, prevent, and respond to domestic emergencies, notably terrorism. The DHS quickly established its own DARPA-style R&D agency, HSARPA (2003), with the stated mission to promote revolutionary changes in technologies for homeland security. The intelligence community soon followed in 2007 with the Intelligence Advanced Research Projects Activity (whose budget and activities remain classified), while the Department of Energy gained new funding for its own ARPA-E as energy supply was added to the portfolio of international threats. Even the Army got into the swing of targeting key technologies by creating innovation hybrids that included a venture capital fund (OnPoint Technologies) and a nanotechnology development institute at MIT (the Institute for Soldier Technologies), focused on revolutionizing combat gear for the warfighter. Thus, although security-oriented spending on S&T had already resumed by the late 1990s, the "war on terror" provided new motivation and momentum for NSS-led technology development—in fields including robotics (embodied in drones), biotechnology/biodefense, nanotechnology, cybersecurity, and renewable energy (chapter 6).

We know, of course, that bigger is not necessarily better. Critics point to political and social costs that stem from the NSS's enormous recent expansion. One such cost has to do with long-standing fears of a surveillance state. As *Washington Post* investigators Dana Priest and William Arkin reported in their "Top Secret America" series in 2010, the growth of organizations composing a "surveillance state" since 9/11 is vast, and much of this apparatus is turned inward, upon American citizens. Many commentators on both sides of politics agree that deploying the NSS apparatus to monitor and spy on one's own citizens (not to mention one's allies) does not sit comfortably with the vision of a healthy functioning democracy, thus raising a new kind of criticism that it weakens the very political order it is supposed to protect. In making this point, Fareed Zakaria pulls no punches as to the consequences of expanding the national security state to conduct "war on terror at home":

> Since September 11, 2001, the U.S. government has created or reconfigured at least 263 organizations to tackle some aspect of the war on terror. . . . The rise of this national security state has entailed a vast expansion in the government's powers that now touch every aspect of American life, even when seemingly unrelated to terrorism. Some 30,000 people, for example, are now employed exclusively to listen in on phone conversations and other communications within the United States. . . . We don't look like people who have won a war. We look like scared, fearful, losers.[42]

But there is perhaps another, less well-recognized cost of the NSS's recent expansion that relates more centrally to our focus on the S&T enterprise.

Big injections of funds for homeland security, biodefense, antiterrorism, and warfighting have dramatically increased the NSS budget for technology development and acquisition after the events of 9/11. The NIH, DoD, and NSF formed a biodefense complex to coordinate a $5 billion program, Project Bioshield, for the development, purchase, and stockpiling of vaccines; the new Homeland Security Agency commanded a $6.6 billion budget (constant dollars) in the first five years of its existence; while Defense's budgets for technology development, and procurement soared. Measured in sheer dollar figures (adjusted for inflation), the NSS technology enterprise has grown spectacularly (figure 2.2).

But this was no Sputnik effect. On the contrary, as the NSS has gained budget and bureaucracy, close observers have begun to raise the question: just how well focused are its S&T/innovation initiatives? What is the vision, where is the strategy? In its 2008 report, the Defense Science Board lamented the lack of a coherent forward-looking vision for a twenty-first century net-centric fighting force. A year later, the DoD think tank, MITRE, and its advisory body, the JASONs, warned of the steady loss of skilled people, including program managers, from DoD's core S&T units. They joined

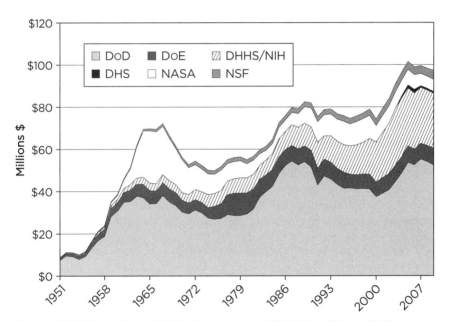

Figure 2.2 NSS spending on R&D by federal agency, 1951–2009 (millions of 2005 constant dollars). Calculations based on data from National Science Foundation, *Federal Funds for Research and Development, Detailed Historical Tables*, (various vols.), 1951–2009. NIH data for 1952–57 are not standardized with later years (hence slightly inflated): U.S. Department of Health & Human Services, NIH Almanac, Appropriations (Section 1), www.nih.gov/about/almanac/appropriations/index.htm. NIH data for 1958–66 supplied by Michael Yamaner (NSF) from printed publications of the Department of Health, Education, and Welfare.

others concerned that Congressional pressures for R&D to be focused on immediate "warfighting needs" was neglecting the longer-term demands of technology leadership (chapter 8). Even the Government Accountability Office joined the chorus of critics. A plethora of short-term Defense initiatives for rapidly satisfying urgent operational needs in the field, it observed, is of limited value in sustaining technological superiority.[43] Such comments raise the prospect that the NSS innovation engine is flagging. Importantly, this concern has emerged not because of a new era of restrained spending: indeed, critics of defense spending now include among their ranks such consummate insiders as Jacques Gansler and Robert Gates, both former defense secretaries who insist that the DoD can and must "do more [and better] with less."[44] Rather, the concern that technology leadership may be flagging reflects the perceived loss of a strategic unifying vision for the long haul, which has allowed Congressional politics and short-termism to hold sway.

The question of where the NSS may be headed is one that must await exposition and argument. Suffice to propose that the NSS technology enterprise—and its commercial influences—is neither as moribund as some fear (chapter 6), nor as problem-free as some would hope (chapter 9). Indeed, rather than stymying innovation, the need to do "more with less" may well be its salvation.

Let the distinctiveness of the American experience also be recognized. Although most modern industrialized countries have instituted "permanent preparedness" by building armed forces and arsenals for defense, with the singular American exception, none in that process have created an institutional complex resembling a national security state. This is the difference that sets the United States apart, for here, permanent preparedness is not just about "the military" or "defense," or even "intelligence." It is about the strategic goal of technology leadership that drives the quest for perpetual innovation. In the U.S. setting, the goal of military preparedness was immediately added to the ambition of scientific and technological superiority. This powerful American cocktail created an encompassing political-economic system in which the national security state became intricately bound to the development of the private sector and its capacity for innovation. It is to that part of the story that we now turn.

Investing in New Ventures

The United States is the most entrepreneurial country in the world,
due [among other things] to ready availability of venture capital.
Krishna Kumar, 2009

If we have heard pronouncements by Silicon Valley patriarchs, we
may begin with the view that government has nothing to contribute
to new ventures. Isn't this the realm of heroic entrepreneurs and investors, far removed from pointy-headed government bureaucrats?
Joshua Lerner, 1996

Under pressure of geopolitical competition, the NSS moved to become
an engine of innovation. Far from confining its activities to the funding
of "research," it took an active role in seeding new commercial ventures.
Consider for a moment what American icons like Intel, Apple Computer,
Sun Microsystems, Fedex, and America Online have in common: all received
government venture capital funding in their critical early startup phases.[1] As
we shall see, for the emergence and growth of many such entrepreneurial
initiatives, federally sponsored venture capital has long offered a significant
source of early-stage financing.

This chapter examines the NSS involvement in venture capital financing,
an activity commonly regarded as a quintessentially private entrepreneurial
function and an invention of the U.S. market. It traces the development of
government-backed venture capital funds (GVFs) since their emergence during the height of Cold War tensions up to their most recent incarnations, in the
wake of the twin threats to national security associated with 9/11 and the energy crisis. It revisits the role of Sputnik, launched in 1957, in helping to spear-
head the creation of a network of GVFs by galvanizing the federal government

to fill a gap in the investment infrastructure for high-risk innovation. It then focuses on the evolving role of NSS agencies in sponsoring and running more recent venture initiatives, from the Small Business Innovation Research program to the venture capital funds of the CIA, the DoD, and the DoE.

Throughout the postwar period, mounting concerns about diminished innovation capacities, at first in the commercial then in the military sector, have at various times stimulated new federal initiatives in venture capital (VC). As the timeline in figure 3.1 indicates, although this story of government-backed venture capital formally begins at the height of Cold War tensions, it is prefaced by the experience of military mobilization, is later stimulated by Japan's relentless technology incursions, and continues up to and beyond the 9/11 attacks, with the launching of new programs dedicated to funding innovations that serve both commercial markets and security missions.

Three main patterns are discernible in federal involvement with the venture capital industry: first, the importance of international geopolitical influences in stimulating the majority of programmatic responses; second, the risk-absorption role of GVFs focused on seed funding and early-stage activities; and third, the strategic emphasis on technologies with dual (commercial and military) applications. A fourth pattern is also evident in the creation of hybrid public-private partnering arrangements designed to attract private collaboration and thereby enhance NSS access and influence in technology development. This hybridization pattern has much broader relevance, beyond venture capital initiatives, and is dealt with separately. The overall result has been to expand the commercial reach of the NSS while at the same time

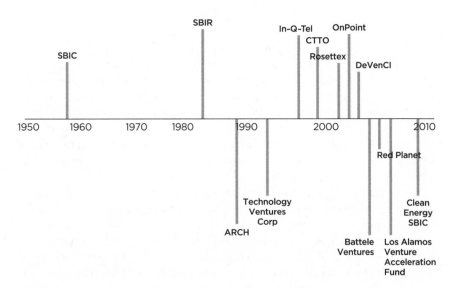

Figure 3.1 Timeline of government-sponsored VC Funds, 1950–2010.

giving the commercial sector a stake in implementing policy goals—the relationship that I earlier conceptualized as one of governed interdependence.

Geopolitical Roots of the U.S. Venture Capital Industry

Venture capital is widely recognized as a quintessentially American institution.[2] Writing in 1994 as a specialist in the field, Paul Gompers observed that "Venture capital in the U.S. is significantly larger and more active than in any other country" (1994, 22). Popular notions of why venture capital is relatively more vigorous, successful, and widely diffused in the United States than elsewhere typically emphasize America's risk-taking, entrepreneurial culture.[3] More scholarly arguments have emphasized alternately the influence of the national legal environment, the financial system, and the nation's science and technology base. The technology hypothesis is considered the more convincing for being more consistent with the general dominance of science-and-technology-intensive firms in VC funding (notably biomedical and ICT firms). As a recent study observes, "scientific and technological advance are the fuel for creating firms capable of generating the returns necessary to support a VC industry" (Kenney et al. 2008, 319).

My analysis adds to that perspective. Dominance in science and technology forms the cornerstone of NSS efforts to sustain global preeminence. Investing in high-technology enterprise by creating or sponsoring VC firms contributes in no small way to that effort. Analysis of the evolving role of the NSS in seeding, boosting, and, more recently, running venture capital initiatives reveals the critical role of government-backed venture funding for the majority of high-risk startups and early-stage technology enterprise—the very entrepreneurial activities in which the United States reportedly leads.[4] As we shall see, one such federal program alone recently accounted for 60 percent of all high-risk venture capital provision in the U.S. economy. It is also consonant with the broader argument of this book that although formed chiefly in response to national security imperatives, GVF investments give priority to dual-use innovations that transition easily into both military and commercial markets. Across the broad range of programs examined here, the dominant pattern is one of federal initiatives for boosting public-private collaboration in order to catalyze innovation and thereby advance the security goals of the NSS.

The Formative Role of World War II

The standard story of America's modern VC industry starts in 1946 with the Boston-based firm, American Research and Development. ARD was significant in a foundational sense for several reasons. First, it pioneered the modern (institutional) form of private equity investment by raising capital from sources independent of wealthy individuals, and by seeking to offer management expertise (not simply finance) to promising high-tech firms. Second, ARD cemented its paradigmatic status in the VC community when its 1957 investment in Digital Equipment Corporation, the minicomputer maker, returned more than five hundred times the original investment when the company's initial public offering took place in 1968 (Old 1981, 23).

Although ARD was clearly not a government-funded venture capital firm, the circumstances surrounding its creation are of some significance for my argument in which the NSS plays a formative role. Among those circumstances, mobilization for war had a prominent place. For this was a new kind of war: it crystallized within the military and scientific community a fresh understanding of the role of science and technological innovation. Importantly, ARD was established to take advantage of unexploited military innovations. Indeed, the very "goal of the company was to finance commercial applications of technologies that were developed during World War II" (Gompers 1994, 3). Equally important, ARD was led by someone who acquired firsthand venturing experience as a result of the war mobilization effort. That person was General Georges Doriot, the acknowledged "father of venture capital" and "the heart and soul of ARD" (Gompers 1994, 3).

In this respect, ARD's beginnings owe much to the NSS in its embryonic form. Copious notes in Doriot's personal papers written during and after the war reveal the extent to which experience gained in the mobilization effort was instrumental in ARD's creation.[5] In Doriot's case, seven different leadership roles in the Quartermaster Corps (which included managing procurement and heading R&D in the Military Planning Division) served to transform the Harvard business professor into "a world-class builder of innovative new enterprises" (Ante 2008, 80). As an explanation of the mission of Doriot's Division, the following could almost double as a description of DARPA's role today: "The purpose of his division was to identify the unmet needs of soldiers and oversee the development of new products to fill those needs. In order to pull off this engineering miracle, Doriot perfected the art of finding the right people for the right technical challenge, and then inspiring them to invent the future" (Ante 2008, 80).

The embryonic NSS was also a testing ground for another of ARD's founders, Karl Compton, MIT president, physicist, and one of Doriot's closest colleagues. Throughout the war, Compton provided scientific leadership and advice at the highest levels of government, serving also on the committee charged by President Roosevelt with jump-starting a new synthetic rubber industry in response to the shortage of natural rubber. Like Doriot, Compton remained informally "in service" for many years after the war, succeeding Vannevar Bush in 1948 as chairman of the Joint Research and Development Board until ill health took hold (Stratton 1992, 50–51).

As a result of these experiences, both men came away from the mobilization effort armed with the conviction that a potentially large stock of scientific innovations lay waiting to be exploited by budding entrepreneurs. As

Doriot's correspondence reveals, "ARD was conceived with a view to helping start up firms exploit those innovations" (Ante 2008, 87).[6]

But it was the ability to exploit the postwar innovations sponsored by the NSS that produced ARD's first and most famous startup success, Digital Equipment Corporation. Indeed the Digital-ARD case nicely illustrates the rich connections and synergies that typically exist between NSS personnel and programs, university researchers, and technology companies (often startups). Consider for example that Digital Equipment's founder, Kenneth Olsen was a former Navy veteran and engineer in the DoD's Lincoln Laboratory at MIT, who was recruited by the Office of Naval Research (ONR) and the air force to work on the Whirlwind project, all before leaving the laboratory to start up Digital Equipment Corporation. Olsen calls Whirlwind the first minicomputer and maintains that his company was based entirely on DoD-sponsored Whirlwind technology (Old 1981, 23). The NSS had a formative rather than direct role in these early VC beginnings, spurring the innovations that made ARD possible in the first place and, following Digital's success, made its emulation desirable.

Sputnik and the Technology Race: Launching SBIC, Federal Fund of Funds

The Small Business Investment Corporation initiative dates from the late 1950s, prompted by a serious concern that the Soviet Union's technological achievements might soon outpace those of America. Federal authorities, shocked at Russia's success in launching two satellites in 1957, decided to take an active role in financing the growth of innovative firms by participating in the development of venture capital (Gompers 1994). Expressing the mood of the time, Georgia Senator Richard Russell summarized American reaction to the event: "*Sputnik* confronts America with a new and terrifying military danger and a disastrous blow to our prestige" (U.S. House, Committee on Science and Technology 2008, 23).

Concerned to accelerate the development of advanced technologies, the U.S. government commissioned the Federal Reserve to conduct a study of financial obstacles to the development of what it called "entrepreneurial businesses." The Reserve's findings that small businesses could not get the credit required to keep pace with technological advancement paved the way for the SBIC initiative, with the passage of the Small Business Investment Act of 1958, one year after Sputnik.[7] As we saw earlier, the same impetus also gave rise to increased spending on scientific research and education, as well as to the creation of DARPA and NASA.

The SBIC program was set up within the Small Business Administration (SBA) in the context of this extreme political concern with the Soviet Union's technological progress. This was a national security response—not in the conventional hard-power sense of defense preparedness, but in the second way in which that term come to be understood—as the soft-power battle for hearts and minds. U.S. primacy in science and technology, concretized in innovation, was essential to America's international prestige and thus to establishing the superiority of the U.S. model of politics and economy.

SBIC venture capital firms are independently owned and run, for-profit investment companies that merge public and private resources. Under the Small Business Investment Act of 1958, the SBA is authorized to charter and fund new VC firms that intend to stimulate investment in the nation's small businesses with the provision of early-stage funding.

Since inception, these investment companies have derived from the federal government half to three-quarters of total funds raised and invested in the form of government-guaranteed low-interest loans and participating debentures or equity investment.[8] Over the life of the scheme, the SBIC hybrid has provided some $60 billion of long-term debt and equity capital to more than 107,000 U.S. companies, with more than $25 billion invested in firms less than three years old.[9]

But funding is not the end of the government's involvement: it also sets investment eligibility guidelines (excluding certain kinds of investment, for example, in real estate and financial services), mandates repayment terms, and then hands over operational autonomy to the SBIC company. Recipients of SBIC funding must have a minimum establishment capital of $5 million, be independently owned and operated, and meet certain threshold criteria to qualify as "small" investment funds. The SBA-licensed SBICs typically receive two-thirds to three-quarters of their capital from the federal government in the form of loans at below-market rates (or interest-free loans for five years in certain cases)—and more recently, via equity participation. This means that SBICs have been able to borrow up to four dollars for every dollar of private money they raise. In this way, a private investment of $1 million could generate an investment of up to $5 million, with the remainder coming from the federal program. (The ratio has oscillated over time, varying from 2:1 to 4:1). In return for its investment, the SBIC receives interest or dividend payments from equity. Although SBICs make up a diverse group in terms of financial form and investment focus, the programmatic emphasis on "filling the gap" by sponsoring early-stage, high-risk ventures has become more pronounced over time as certain types of investment (such as in financial services and unimproved real estate) were ruled out (Brewer & Genay 2005).

In spite of flaws requiring subsequent modifications, the program quickly filled a vacuum in the investment landscape as a fund of funds. From its inception, the number of SBICs increased rapidly and by the mid-1960s, "700 SBICs controlled the majority of risk capital invested in the United States" (Gompers 1994, 10). To put their role in perspective, from the 1950s through the 1960s, venture capital was still at the stage of a "cottage industry" and SBICs provided an estimated two-thirds to three-quarters of all venture capital funding allocated to American business during this period.[10] One may note that the venture capital industry in Silicon Valley—the largest VC concentration in the United States—emerged during the 1960s and 1970s when SBICs provided the major source of VC funding. In its first decade, the program "backed well over one billion dollars of lending to SBICs" and the SBICs in turn "collected more than two billion dollars of private capital and surplus," making an investment pool of more than three billion inflation-adjusted dollars (Fohlin 2005, 11).

As the financial consequences of the 1970s oil embargo severely tested firms young and old, by 1978 only 250 SBICs remained active. Even so, in 1983 SBICs still accounted for more than 75 per cent of U.S. venture capital investments (Gompers 1994, 8). This was soon to change dramatically as Congress, in a bid to rescue investment, altered the "prudent man" rule in the 1979 Employee Retirement Income Security Act to allow pension funds to invest in venture capital. Independent VC funds would soon thereafter make up the bulk of the industry.

It is worth pausing to consider the broader significance of the SBIC program. Existing studies indicate that the 1958 fund of funds was instrumental to the growth of America's VC industry in at least two ways that went beyond the financing of entrepreneurial firms. First, the SBICs created an infrastructure that served to grow the industry. As investment banking scholar Josh Lerner writes, the SBIC program seeded the infrastructure of much of the modern VC industry. The clustering of law firms, data providers, and other intermediaries, even many of the early venture funds themselves, emerged to service the SBIC funds, only gradually shifting their focus to independent venture firms (Lerner 2009, 10).

Second, these hybrid funds seeded a cadre of venture capitalists who learned their craft running government-backed funds in the formative years. Many went on to set up their own independent firms. A series of oral history interviews with Silicon Valley patriarchs of venture capital add some flesh to the dry facts. One such veteran, William Draper (who now runs Sutter Hill Ventures) puts it candidly:[11] "It [the SBIC program] was a bonanza for me, in that I never would've gotten into venture capital . . . it made the difference." In 1962, the Silicon Valley veteran started an SBIC, the Draper and Johnson Investment Company, with $150,000 of family money and a $300,000 government loan. "We were the twelfth one to start. . . . We made, I don't know, maybe ten or fifteen investments . . . a few years later, we paid back the government and we started a new limited partnership called Sutter Hill."

SBICs like those of Draper have been credited with fueling startup companies throughout the U.S. economy, backing numerous ventures that were exploiting breakthroughs in such fields as electronics, data-processing, and medical technologies. Intel, for example, received a $300,000 investment in 1969 from Wells Fargo Investment Company, an SBIC, when Intel had only 218 employees and less than $566,000 in revenues. In 1971, Intel went on to produce the first single-chip microprocessor, paving the way for the personal computer. As well as older American IT icons, new SBIC-backed companies have emerged from the venture program. Discussing amendments to the SBIC program in 2001, Congress reported that a year earlier when *Fortune Small Business* compiled its list of the one hundred fastest-growing small companies, six of the top twelve on the list received SBIC financing during their critical growth years (U.S. Senate 2002, 22717).

Although the relative weight of SBIC-backed funds in the VC system has fluctuated over time, at the end of FY 2003 they still provided more than $9 billion of venture financing to small firms. Combined with the federal contribution of $12 billion, they provided a hefty $21 billion pool for high-risk seed equity investments—by most measures a significant source of funding for American startups. Seven years on, in the wake of the worst financial crisis of the postwar period, SBIC continued to offer a stable source of venture funding. Most recently, the SBA announced that it had issued a record $1.59 billion in capital through its SBIC debenture program in fiscal 2010, "the highest level in the program's 50-year history."[12] Although the federal SBIC program forms a much smaller part of the venture capital industry today, it has provided generous support to U.S. startups since its inception. Even in 2010, SBIC financings (totalling $2.05 billion and benefitting more than 1,300 entrepreneurial companies), were significant. At the end of the decade, the federal fund of funds was still managing more than $8 billion in outstanding leverage and commitments, invested in some 300 private equity partnerships with more than $17 billion in capital under management.[13]

The government funded VC program has not been declining as private sector funds build up. To the contrary, SBICs have invested in more high-risk startups than the average VC fund. Between 1994 and 2002, for example, at least 64 per cent of seed/early-stage financing (totaling $14.4 billion) was performed by the hybrid SBICs (Small Business Administration 2003, 15). Though difficult to quantify, the impact of the program on the growth of the industry would seem hard to deny: as one SBIC recently announced on its webpage, "Through this program, the federal government is the largest single investor in U.S. private equity funds."[14]

It is instructive to compare this story of state involvement (well told for the earlier period by Gompers) with the standard narrative according to which the VC industry emerged as a spontaneous, bottom-up product of independent risk-taking entrepreneurship. In the less stylized more historically complex account, however, the private VC industry was slow to develop and depended on the helping hand of the government-backed SBIC to supply unmet demand.

Nor does the SBIC story end here. In keeping with the NSS's new security imperative to develop alternatives to carbon-based energy, the Energy Independence and Security Act of 2007 authorizes funding of SBICs dedicated to funding Renewable Energy ventures. Administered by the SBA, the new Energy Saving Debentures and Renewable Fuel Capital Investment

Program licenses a new type of SBIC called Renewable Fuel Capital Investment Company "to promote research, development and production of goods and services that generate or support the production of renewable energy." The new type of SBIC which can invest equity in early-stage companies has special new funding for renewable energy initiatives that reduce the use and consumption of non-renewable energy sources and promote the use and consumption of wind, solar, geothermal, hydrogen, ethanol and other biomass fuels.[15]

As a hybridization of public/private resources that formed part of a broader response to Cold War imperatives, the SBIC was conceived as an integral component of the NSS's technology and innovation policy. It was also the first U.S. example of a government-sponsored venture capital fund. It was not to be the last. But in the more recent cases, the NSS is no longer seeding venture capital firms; it is directly seeding the technology firms themselves.

Creation of "the World's Largest Seed Fund": SBIR

Tasked with funding high-risk, early-stage technology development, the Small Business Innovation Research program has emerged as the largest source of seed and early-stage funding for high-technology firms in the United States. It currently invests around $2.5 billion annually in U.S. firms, for which it has been aptly described as "the world's largest seed fund' (Connell 2006), its broader role notwithstanding (chapter 5). Venture capitalists are "an appropriate referent group," though not for direct comparison (National Research Council 2009a, 5). A key difference—one that is to the advantage of the technology firm and of the wider investment community—is that no equity is required from the technology firm in exchange for the federal investment provided. This makes SBIR a preferred venue for traditional venture funding—the NSS investment serving also as a "certification" mechanism that signals the technology's commercial potential to the VC community.

The design and implementation of SBIR are examined in chapter 5 where new (commercialization) approaches to procuring technology are the focus. Here the issues are how the SBIR program came to be embedded in the NSS thanks to its funding structure and the international and domestic influences that helped to catalyze the program; the program's contribution to the national venture capital effort; and its broader significance for the NSS technology enterprise.

Although not evident from its generic title, SBIR is firmly embedded within the NSS. Two aspects of the program establish its NSS pedigree: first, the geopolitical circumstances in which the idea for the program took shape, and second, the funding mechanism that sustains it.

International influences and security implications. At the end of a difficult decade marked by defeat in Vietnam, two oil shocks, and aggressive Soviet moves in Africa and Afghanistan, the feeling of strategic insecurity once again took hold within the NSS community. Big cutbacks in defense spending in the first half of the 1970s added to the concern that the United States was being outstripped by the Soviet Union. In particular, the conflict between the DoD's strategic posture emphasizing technological superiority against the Soviet strategy of numerical advantage on one hand, and the challenge of accessing innovative technologies on the other, made action all the more urgent.

On top of these strategic concerns, the United States appeared to be facing a renewed test of its technology leadership as new trading competitors, in particular Japan, gained significant ground in high-technology markets. The president's Office of Management and Budget, which presided over a ten-agency panel on the state of U.S. innovation, declared in a 1977 report that "there is increasing concern that the capability of the United States to continue its historic successes in technology is in a serious decline. While astonishing achievements have occurred since World War II, there is now considerable evidence that product innovation has either leveled off or declined in many industries" (Office of Management and Budget 1977, 1). The Senate Subcommittee on Science, Technology, and Space went further, linking what it perceived as a serious lag in innovation to a disturbing trend reported by a number of witnesses, notably "an astonishing drop in the creation of small high technology companies" and a dramatic decline of venture companies entering the market each year with new issue underwritings (Congressional Research Service 1978, 12).

A related cause for concern brought to the attention of the same committee was the fact that established firms were shifting away from investment in major product and manufacturing innovations "to relatively minor product and process improvements promising short-term returns."[16] At the same time, an important enquiry of the Senate Select Committee on Small Business into the "Underutilization of Small Business in the Nation's Efforts to Encourage Industrial Innovation" confirmed the earlier conclusions of two major Federal agencies that "the ability of the United States to innovate for commercial and defense purposes was in "serious decline."[17] A fall-off in innovation, coupled with a "dearth of venture capital," was not such a big deal in itself. What made it a big deal was that "it [was also a threat to] U.S. technological leadership," the same report declared. Drawing attention to the security consequences, the 1979 Report reiterated the message of the Office of Management and Budget report that the lack of venture capital and the declining "capability to invent" compromised the nation's ability to produce "new products essential for defense."

Leaving to one side the tendency to hyperbole in some of this literature, nevertheless the impact was clear. The conclusion of these extensive hearings, briefings, pilot studies, and reports was that of a need for high-risk research and investment in order to generate scientific and market breakthroughs. A related concern was how to find better ways to convert the results of federally funded R&D into commercial benefits for the nation—specifically by inducing university researchers and private companies to ramp up the commercialization effort. That effort would be stimulated by patent reforms under the 1980 Bayh-Dole Act. Among the other initiatives and reforms that sought to meet this newly perceived leadership threat was the 1982 funding arrangement that targeted innovation with early-stage investment. As the designer and program manager of the original SBIR program argued on the occasion of SBIR's reauthorization, this was an area where private investors often feared to tread (Tibbetts [1979] 1999, 129–30).

Although mandated by Congress in 1982, the program was first piloted by agencies of the NSS: the NSF in 1977, followed by the DoD in 1981. In Defense's own words, the "scope and intent" of the program already had a "solid foundation in the DoD": "The Department . . . committed itself, with the inception of the Defense Small Business Advanced Technology (DESAT) Program in 1981, to encourage and marshal the ingenuity and technological capability of the nation's small businesses to address problems of importance to DoD."[18]

In the view of a DoD insider, Jacques Gansler, the most important trend behind the pilot SBIR (DESAT) program was the U.S. strategic focus on technological superiority as required by the Offset Strategy, coupled with the recognition that cutting-edge technologies were most likely to be found outside the large contracting firms, in younger companies.[19] Importantly for the DoD, SBIR was also about reuniting R&D with acquisition, two processes that had been drifting apart, creating barriers for DoD access to the greater innovative capabilities that existed outside the large contracting firms. These access constraints, compounded by a precipitous drop in the post-Vietnam procurement budget of roughly $77 billion between 1976 and 1980), redirected DoD attention to untapped sources of technological innovation.

Thus the SBIR, although administered by the SBA, emerged with firm roots in the NSS as it sought to sustain leadership in a new strategic and economic environment. One further feature adds to this NSS-centric picture of the program—the funding mechanism itself.

Funding structure: who uses SBIR? All federal agencies with external R&D budgets greater than $100 million must set aside a fixed percentage of their annual R&D budget for awarding to firms under the SBIR program (currently 2.5 percent). It is this funding arrangement that ensures that SBIR is principally an investment fund for NSS agencies. Of the eleven participating agencies, only a handful are substantial investors (figure 3.2).

At a glance, we see the overwhelming predominance of the NSS agencies in the SBIR program, providing around 97 percent of the funds. The DoD's vast R&D budget ensures that it remains the single biggest source (48 percent of total funding), followed by the NIH/Department of Health and Human Services (26 percent), then NASA, DoE, and NSF. Other (non-NSS) agencies provide less than 5 percent. This distribution has remained relatively unchanged since the program's inception. Since it is the defense- and

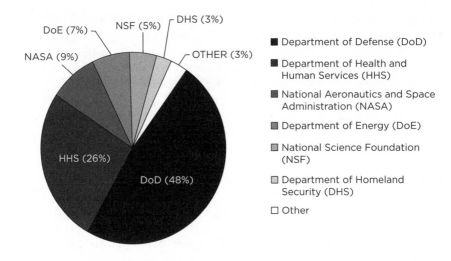

Figure 3.2 SBIR award funding by federal agency (1983–2006 average). Calculations based on data from SBA, SBIR *Annual Report* (various years).

security-related agencies that have the largest R&D budgets and are thus the largest users of the program, this weighting anchors SBIR firmly within the NSS.

Contribution to Venture Capital. How significant is SBIR as a source of investment capital for technology development? Compared with the private venture capital market, which averaged $20–$29 billion per year for the 1995–2008 period,[20] SBIR's current annual funding of $2.5 billion may seem like small change. But disaggregate those figures and a different story emerges. The key difference between the two sectors is technology targeting. In contrast to SBIR, the bulk of private investment finances buyouts, marketing activities, and late-stage expansion; only "a fraction" of venture capital funding "directly supports the development of new technology" (Branscomb and Auerswald 2002, 67).

By contrast, SBIR focuses 100 percent of its resources on the front end of innovation (from proof of concept to production of a prototype) where uncertainty and risk are highest. Over the 1995–2008 period, for example, the private VC industry invested just 5.3 percent of total funding in seed and startup activities, compared with more than 76 percent of capital allocated to "expansion" and "later stage" activities.[21] If we consider that the private-sector data for "early stage" financing includes activities such as "initial expansion, commercial manufacturing, and marketing," what emerges is a relatively reduced-risk (risk-averse?) profile. Venture capital firms invest most of their money in product development and expanding the sales of existing products. Almost a decade on from the NIST study cited above, the trend was even more pronounced (Atkinson 2010,10).

Indeed, of the U.S. total of $4.2 billion invested in high-risk technology in 2009, SBIR provided no less than 60 percent.[22] According to the SBIR-Inknowvation website, since the first investments were made in 1983, the SBIR program has funded more than 130,000 early-stage projects and provided more than $34 billion to technology development in young firms.[23] Seen in this light, SBIR would appear to provide the most significant source of capital for high-risk technology development. For a program that has attracted so little scrutiny from the scholarly community, SBIR's importance as a source of investment capital is all the more surprising [Gompers and Lerner 2004, 309).

As a three-phase program that goes all the way to commercialization and procurement, SBIR is designed to leverage further investment from private VCs. Federal agencies start the process by funding the cutting-edge research to explore the technical feasibility of an idea, leading all the way to production of a prototype. If results look promising, interested VC firms will then step in to invest in the company, usually a startup (Tibbetts 2006, 4).

This suggests that for the more risk-averse venture capital investor, the SBIR-funded firm has the advantage of providing a form of "certification"; it establishes technical feasibility and thus lowers the risk to a level more acceptable to the private VC industry. Further enhancements to the program to speed commercialization now enable an agency like DoD to provide 4:1 matching funds for private financing raised by SBIR firms.

For the innovative firm, SBIR confers three advantages. First, the company gains investment without contracting debt or conceding equity interest. A successful SBIR participant can receive as much as $1 million in direct investment (in the form of a contract) to support its product development and commercialization work for private-sector and military markets. Second, special patent and data rights provisions enable the firm to develop and retain ownership of intellectual property. Third, this establishes the firm in a stronger position should traditional VC funding be sought. Contrast each of these three features with the usual onerous requirements of private VC and it becomes clear why SBIR maintains its important role for high-risk technology development. In the words of one successful SBIR firm: "Our strategy is to maximize the extent [to which] we can get public funding before going to private investment. . . . The more that we can prove our technology before going to venture capitalists [the better position we'll be in, with respect to] how much of the company we'll be giving up for the funding."[24]

SBIR's broader significance for the NSS technology enterprise derives from its design as a technology program for which applications can potentially find both NSS and commercial outlets (see chapter 5). Its effectiveness in catalyzing innovations that serve both markets is reflected in various ways: in the high marks regularly awarded to the program by the Government

Accountability Office;[25] in the annual SBIR commercialization brochures produced by the DoD; in the breakthroughs achieved by some of America's most dynamic companies while receiving early SBIR support—a line-up that includes, for example, Amgen, Chiron, Compaq, Dell, Intel, Symantec, Titan, Qualcomm, Nanosys, and Genentech; and in the strong Congressional support for the program's periodic reauthorization. Scholarly assessments have concluded that DoD's SBIR Program is stimulating not only R&D but also efforts to commercialize that would not otherwise have taken place.[26] To reiterate: the SBIR is firmly embedded in the NSS technology enterprise. This is the engine that moves it forward.

Post-Cold War Trends: New Funds for a New Security Environment

The new millennium witnessed a boom in NSS venture capital initiatives. By the end of 2010 the CIA, DoD, the Army, the Navy, the National Geospatial-Intelligence Agency (NGIA), NASA, and Homeland Security had all started down the path of creating, piloting, or exploring different models of VC funds to help plug their technology gaps. As former USAF Colonel Bernard Chachula explained:

> . . . as we in the defense sector continue to adjust from the demobilization of the Cold War, we are experiencing a new type of mobilization in the wake of the attacks of 9/11. This . . . relies less on massive numbers of personnel and heavy equipment but, instead, looks to capitalize on innovation and the leveraging of technology to take the battle to an elusive enemy. And so it is that numerous agencies have looked to venture capital activities to fast-forward the integration of new technologies to support their mission. (Chachula 2004)

Although many of the new VC initiatives took shape in the wake of the 9/11 attacks, these events did not so much redefine the security environment as help to dramatize more diffuse challenges already in play in the previous decade following the Soviet collapse. In this altered environment, security and intelligence priorities shifted from well-defined targets determined by the Soviet presence toward more diffuse threats associated with nonstate actors and the spread of nuclear, chemical, and biological weapons.

For the defense and intelligence agencies, the problem was how to access and influence nascent technologies for dealing with these less conventional threats—and to do so in both an affordable and timely manner. A similar set of assumptions to those that helped shape the SBIR program lay behind the NSS turn to venture capital. Since most innovation occurs in young high-tech firms, developing links with entrepreneurial companies was clearly essential—if somewhat unconventional given the emphasis in the popular view on the minimization of state involvement in the commercial arena. Standard defense contracting arrangements would not suffice. Lengthy budgeting cycles, ponderous procurement regulations, and complicated intellectual property rights had long repelled the most innovative firms from doing business with DoD, particularly in the critical sector of information technology.[27] A new mechanism was needed to attract and motivate the private sector to collaborate. In response to these challenges, the CIA took the first step with the formation of In-Q-Tel, which soon generated a round of venture funding initiatives within the NSS.[28]

In all such cases the fundamental priority has been to fulfill national security missions. However, as we shall see in later chapters, the means for meeting these objectives has increasingly drawn the NSS well outside the security space, into more directly commercial endeavors. Sustaining technological superiority now thoroughly entwines commercial and military activities. NSS investment strategy must therefore seek out firms whose innovations have potential for both nondefense commercial and military applications, both private and public markets. The rationale for this doubled-sided approach is neatly summarized in the 2002 edition of DoD's annual *Report to Congress on the Activities of the DoD Office of Technology Transition*: "The ultimate goal is to achieve technically superior, affordable Defense Systems technology while ensuring that technology developed for national security purposes is integrated into the private sector to enhance the national technology and industrial base" (Department of Defense 2001, 1).

In establishing venture funds, agencies within the NSS have thus assumed that the appropriate technologies for venture investment will typically be those that meet a security requirement while having strong commercial potential (batteries, biofuels, and networking being three such cases). For the relevant agency, this dual-use focus is pivotal to engaging the innovative private sector in technology development and has the added benefit of enhancing capacity to leverage additional resources from private venture capital. Further side benefits underlined by RAND analysts include the promise of a return on investment that can support future R&D, and capacity to contribute to the formation of new industries vital to the defense industrial base.[29] This effectively is the appeal of dual-use technology strategies, including those of venture investment.

Acting like venture capitalists—but with a technology- rather than profit-oriented focus—the aim of the NSS venture capital funds is to gain early access to emerging technologies in the commercial sector in order to influence their development, to rely on the competitive advantages of market demand in the private sector to drive down production costs, and finally to transition the innovations to military systems. This spin-on process is often more accurately described as "spin-around," in the sense that there is frequently an early-stage NSS contribution to the innovation (via problem setting, startup funding, and licensing), followed by ongoing synergistic developments that come from repeated public-private collaboration. The development of the so-called "military-entertainment complex"—based on video-gaming, virtual reality, and simulation technologies—is a case in point (see, e.g., Lenoir and Lowood 2005).

The CIA's In-Q-Tel

The CIA took the lead in the new experiments with venture funding, creating In-Q-Tel in 1999 as a way of dealing with shrinking budgets, new security threats, and changing technology requirements. In particular, the agency needed access to the most advanced information technology to conduct its mission. The problem was that numerous advances in the IT field were occurring among the very technology firms that traditionally did not do business with the defense sector. The proposal to start a venture fund was first mooted in 1997 and came to fruition two years later with the creation of Peleus, later renamed In-Q-Tel. As Donald Tighe, former vice president of the fund, remarked in a 2006 press interview, "To their great credit, it didn't take a sputnik or a 9/11 for [the CIA] to realize that the pace of innovation was suddenly ahead of their ability [to keep up]."[30]

As an independent, nonprofit hybrid—government-funded but privately operated—In-Q-Tel uses venture capital not simply as a passive purchaser and user of technology but as a problem-setting co-developer. It conceives venture capital as a tool to attract private-sector collaboration and thereby access nascent technologies in order to influence and accelerate their commercialization for delivery to the intelligence community. This strategic intent is not unique to the CIA's fund, as we shall see. Defense too views venture capital as a way of influencing technology development in the commercial arena, by becoming "a partner at the table, figuring out and having some input into where that technology development goes."[31]

In-Q-Tel achieves this goal mostly by making equity investments in startups or young firms with promising technology, often coupled with product development funding.[32] By taking stakes in those companies, In-Q-Tel acquires a position on the board of directors, which enables it to track new products under development and to play an influential part in shaping emerging technology. As In-Q-Tel's vice president, Catherine Cotell, explained in her 2006 statement to Congress: "As an investor, In-Q-Tel can influence the product development roadmap to ensure that the commercial products will indeed meet the Intelligence Community's needs while adding value for the commercial customers as well."[33]

In addition to providing developmental input as an equity investor, In-Q-Tel (like DARPA) creates spin-off companies. This strategy involves engaging "at a very early stage, before the technology has been spun out of the laboratory." In such cases, "In-Q-Tel will strategize to move the technology from the laboratory into a spinout, by assembling a management team and providing seed funding." Summing up the fund's approach, Cotell put it this way: "By utilizing equity investments, sometimes coupled with work programs and market guidance, In-Q-Tel fosters the development of strong companies which produce commercially viable technologies . . ."

Whether In-Q-Tel's investment involves a spinout or an equity partner, the technologies and companies selected must be principally directed at the commercial market. In-Q-Tel will invest only if the technology—in addition to solving critical mission challenges—can potentially sustain large markets in the private sector and thereby capture the economies of scale unavailable with government contracts alone. The insistence on a commercial market for a technology is thus designed to leverage the advantages of large-scale demand and thereby ensure cost-effective, sustainable delivery to the intelligence community. As Cotell emphasized in her Congressional statement, "Rather than seeking point solutions or one-off custom products designed explicitly for the Intelligence Community, In-Q-Tel invests in companies that build successful technology solutions intended for the high growth commercial market and introduces these solutions to the Intelligence Community." An early article recounting the founding logic behind In-Q-Tel makes clear the commercial, developmentally oriented role that the CIA leadership envisioned for the new fund: "The leadership . . . understood that, in order to extend its reach and access a broad network of IT innovators, the Agency had to step outside of itself and appear not just as a buyer of IT but also as a seller. The CIA had to offer Silicon Valley something of value, a business model . . . that provides those who joined hands with In-Q-Tel the opportunity to commercialize their innovations" (Yannuzzi 2000, 26).

The CIA's venture fund follows the tradition of the NSS's problem-setting role, which, together with its technology procuring and commercialization activities, has played no small part in spawning new industries in the postwar period. The fund intends that "In-Q-Tel's partner companies" will gain, in addition to investment capital, "another valuable asset," namely, "access to a set of very difficult CIA problems that could become market drivers" (Yannuzzi 2000, 26). In this role, In-Q-Tel is guided by a special interface center, QIC, whose task is to define the problem sets that provide a focus for In-Q-Tel's activities by translating the needs of the CIA (Chachula 2004, 8).[34]

To gain a more rounded picture of how the GVF fits into the broader technology enterprise, however, we need to include another fact of some significance, namely that the majority of the companies in which In-Q-Tel has invested (approximately 140 by 2011) turn out to be spin-offs from NSS-sponsored research conducted at universities and laboratories (largely supported by DoE, ONR, DARPA, and NSF through such programs as SBIR) (Cotell 2006, 5). This effectively completes the national security state's R&D → GVF → private-sector commercialization → product acquisition circle.

As evidence of the broad commercial reach of In-Q-Tel, consider that as of August 2006, it had cultivated a vast network that included 200 venture capital firms, 100 labs and research organizations, as well as public and private technology transfer offices and program managers at government funding agencies; it had reviewed more than 5,500 business plans, invested some $150 million in more than 90 companies, and delivered more than 130 innovative solutions to the intelligence community.[35] Its investment in software, information infrastructure, and materials sciences has resulted in products ranging from military-themed video games, miniature cameras, and mobile power products to advanced mapping and tracking devices and shape-shifting medical implants—many of them also commercially significant.

As further evidence of its capacity to mobilize private-sector collaboration, consider In-Q-Tel's ability to attract co-investment from private VC funds. According to Cotell's 2006 Congressional testimony, for every dollar In-Q-Tel invests, it leverages an average of eight dollars of private investment to commercialize technologies. As one Silicon Valley CEO commented, "When we mention to other Silicon Valley investment firms that In-Q-Tel is one of our investors, that earns us brownie points."[36]

Another measure of the "In-Q-Tel effect" in the commercial arena is the extent to which its portfolio companies are acquired by established businesses. Google's 2004 acquisition of Keyhole Inc. is the most widely reported but by no means the only example of the "In-Q-Tel effect."[37] Keyhole, the company that developed the software now known as Google Earth, was one of In-Q-Tel's portfolio companies in 2003. More recently, In-Q-Tel partnered with Google to back another startup, Recorded Future, a company that monitors the web in real time and uses the information gleaned from tens of thousands of websites, blogs, and social media accounts to identify relationships and to predict future actions and events. The Google-NSS partnership is an interesting if controversial example of governed interdependence: it involves a private company that not only co-invests in a company together with America's spy agency (both having seats on Recorded Future's board), but that also enlists the help of the National Security Agency to secure its networks, and in turn sells equipment to that secret signals-intelligence organization.[38]

Success has also made In-Q-Tel the darling of the national security community, resulting in expansion of its operations to support other intelligence agencies and inspiring wider emulation within the NSS. Several of these more recent initiatives are outlined in table 3.1, which captures the main types of government-sponsored venture capital funds since 1958.

Venture Initiatives of other NSS Agencies

As shown in table 3.1, some GVFs, like In-Q-Tel, are organized as quasi-independent companies that take direct equity positions in the firms in which

TABLE 3.1
Government-sponsored VC funds, 1958–2010

Sponsor	Name	Started	Funding source	Form
SBA[a]	SBICs	1958	Federal-leverage 2:1–4:1 (public:private)	Financial risk Underwriting
NSS[b]	SBIR	1982	Levies on agencies' R&D budgets	Direct investment
DoE-Argonne	ARCH	1986	DoE/Chicago U	Direct investment
DoE-Sandia	Technology Ventures Corp[c]	1993	DoE/Lockheed Martin	Tech transfer; VC scouting start-ups
CIA	In-Q-Tel	1999	Largely CIA	Direct investment
DOD-NGA-CECOM	Rosettex	2001	NTA contract "fees"	Direct investment
DoD-Army	OnPoint	2002	Army: levy on R&D budget	Direct investment
DoD-OFT	DeVenCI	2002	Works with VCs	Information/ collaboration
DoE–Oak Ridge	Battelle Ventures LP	2003	Private/DoE[d]	Direct investment + Tech transfer
DoD-Navy	VCs@Sea NRAC VC Panel	2004	Works with VCs	Information/ collaboration
NASA	Red Planet Capital[e]	2004	NASA & private firms	Direct investment
DoE–Los Alamos	Los Alamos National Security LLC Venture Acceleration Fund	2006	Private/DoE	Direct investment + Tech transfer
SBA[a]	Energy SBICs	2007	Federal-leverage	Financial risk underwriting

Source: Adapted (with additions and updates) from Homeland Security Institute 2005, 84).

[a] Administrative agency only.

[b] NSS agencies account for about 97% of program funding.

[c] Founded by Lockheed Martin, co-funded with DoE; a nonprofit designed to move technologies out of Sandia and other national labs to the private sector; uses its funds to help start-up companies commercialize lab technologies and to find the right investors (Harold S. Morgan, Senior Manager, Industrial Partnerships, Sandia, personal communication, March 2011).

[d] DoE contributes intellectual property, giving Battelle unique access to the federally funded technologies of six DoE national laboratories, which provide the catalyst for its investment activities.

[e] NASA's fund was stillborn, a victim of cuts by the George W. Bush administration.

they invest (for example, the Defense Department's OnPoint Technologies and Rosettex, and DoE's laboratory funds). OnPoint Technologies, the U.S. Army's fund, focuses on mobile power and energy innovations for the soldier and targets the investment area of portable power, such as nanosolar power, fuel cell devices, and battery storage devices. Its primary mission is "to facilitate finding and creating dual-use products—products addressing the needs of commercial markets that will also meet the needs of the individual soldier . . ."[39] As an investment-procurement vehicle, the Army fund triangulates between the innovator enterprise (which may be either a startup or an established technology company) and its potential customers, which are often prime contractors already contracted to the Army's program managers to supply a product (Wessner 2007, 65). Indeed, part of the OnPoint management team's salary package is based on whether the innovation is adopted ("transitioned") by the Army.[40]

From the NSS to the private sector. Note that whereas the Defense and CIA venture funds are tasked with transitioning technology from the private to the public sector (a route that may originate in the public lab, producing a public-to-private-to-public sequence that emphasizes "spin-around"), the DoE funds are mostly focused on transferring technology from the public to the private sector. The typical route is via the creation of spin-off companies that commercialize innovations from the energy agency's labs. Thus, for example, Los Alamos National Laboratory's Venture Acceleration Fund looks for lab technologies with high potential for new company formation and product development; the DoE-supported Lockheed Martin Fund helps spin out companies from Sandia National Laboratory; and DoE's Technology Commercialization Fund finances the most promising projects from eight of its national labs. The rationale behind the new mission of the nuclear weapons labs is that it not only creates an income stream for the labs through licensing their intellectual property, but also, by getting innovations into the market, exploits competitive processes to lower costs and mature products for later acquisition.

Coordinating deals between investors and users. A second group of government-sponsored venture initiatives is structured as information outreach and networking nodes that connect the relevant NSS agency with the venture capital community and early technology opportunities. The DoD's DeVenCI (Defense Venture Catalyst Initiative) and ONR's Naval Research Advisory Committee VC Panel are organized in this manner (table 3.1). In these cases, the "fund" makes no investment; instead it seeks to generate deals between the VC investor and the acquisition community—by identifying a procurement market to catalyze private VC investment in a company whose technology may look promising, but too risky for the venture capitalist in the absence of a defined market.[41]

A Roundup of GVF Activities

Across the spectrum of GVF initiatives, the NSS leans more toward the active developmental than the "passive user" end of the technology spectrum. This orientation of the GVFs is evident in at least three typical activities: financing startups; influencing product development for the commercial market; and finding markets to prompt private venture capital firms to invest in nascent companies.

Enterprise catalyst. GVFs often create startups, the latter frequently originating in NSS labs and mission-sponsored research and technology development. In addition, SBIR-backed companies (almost wholly funded by NSS agencies) are a significant source of technologies for the VC initiatives. The CIA fund is not alone in this regard; the Army's OnPoint Technologies and the NGIA's Rosettex, though structured differently from In-Q-Tel, also seek out young companies with emerging technologies in their investment approach.

By way of contrast, DoE-sponsored funds are largely structured around the technology spin-off or the company "spin-out" principle: they commercialize technologies that originate in the federal laboratories by partnering with private firms to which they transfer their innovations, either by assisting lab scientists to create spin-out companies or by licensing their technology to established firms via Cooperative Research and Development Agreements.[42] The DoE funds are thus entirely dependent on NSS-created innovations that can then be licensed or spun out to create a new company. As an illustration of the principle, consider one of the first hybrid funds, ARCH Development Corporation, established in 1986 to commercialize patented inventions from Argonne National Laboratory in collaboration with the University of Chicago.[43] As the manager of Argonne (whose origins lie in the Manhattan Project) the university could take title to the lab's intellectual property. ARCH's founding CEO, Steven Lazarus, suitably embodied the experience of both military and academic worlds, having been a naval officer who later became the associate dean of Chicago's Graduate School of Business. The new body was given a mandate to licence technologies and to form new business ventures with the provision of early stage finance (Holl 1997, 481).

As for the domestic conditions under which ARCH was created, these were the years of intense political concern to put to broader use the inventions and know-how that were concentrated in the national labs and in many cases lying dormant. Domestically, this Congressional interest converged with the broader Reagan emphasis on cutting back on government outlays and expanding market opportunities. Thus, squeezed of funding (from the decline in nuclear power demand) and feeling vulnerable, the Argonne lab remade itself as a more commercially oriented entity, to become "a corporate laboratory for the nation."[44]

Since inception, this productive partnership has launched dozens of new companies—not to mention highly successful spin-off VC funds now run as private for-profits. The group's for-profit venture fund, launched in 1989, became the first VC fund to be established between a major U.S. laboratory and a university. The ARCH Venture Fund began with $9 million in capital, fully pledged by a group of investors. It became so successful that it produced two independent for-profit funds, one of which now manages over $1.5 billion of investment.[45] ARCH is pertinent because although it required a great deal of effort from other actors, without the NSS system and the Argonne hybrid to which it gave rise, this massive venture capital undertaking would very likely not exist.

In a process that encapsulates in miniature the way the NSS ecosystem comes together, one of ARCH's portfolio companies is Sapphire Energy, an SBIR-backed venture (generously supported by the NIH and NSF) that has developed a green fuel for the Navy made from pools of algae. Since successfully powering a Boeing 737 with this fuel, the company has begun constructing a biorefinery to scale up production of algal "green crude," encouraged by loan guarantees from the Department of Agriculture) and the promise of handsome contracts from the U.S. Navy (chapter 6). figure 3.3 depicts this "enterprise catalyst" aspect of the government-sponsored venture funds.

Fostering products for commerce and security. In addition to funding startups, the GVFs influence product development for the commercial market by making commercialization for nonmilitary markets a requirement of investment. As we saw in the case of In-Q-Tel, the potential of a company to produce commercially viable products for the wider market is now a key criterion

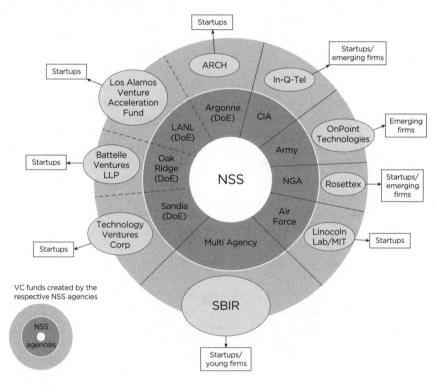

Figure 3.3 The government-sponsored venture fund ecosystem.

of support: "We don't want them building in anything that's just intended for the government," declared the then In-Q-Tel president, Mike Griffin, in 2003. "That tends to leave an orphan product and that doesn't contribute to a company's success."[46] Although smaller than the CIA fund, OnPoint, which focuses on new power and energy sources for foot soldiers, takes a similar approach, stating that its primary mission is to "discover, invest in, and support companies at the intersection of Army and commercial marketing needs."[47] We can include in this second type of developmental activity the for-profit Rosettex Venture Fund funded by the NGIA and established under contract with SRI International to serve the National Technology Alliance.[48] Rosettex focuses on seed and early-stage capital investment to develop "next-generation information systems for military and private sector use." At the time of its inception in 2002, it anticipated that the technologies developed for CECOM, the Army's Communications Electronics Command, would eventually move a new generation of information technologies into industrial and consumer use while serving the military purposes for which they were originally intended.[49] Rosettex and OnPoint, together with In-Q-Tel, seek the widest possible use for the technologies they fund. Insisting on applications with a potentially large market in the private sector overcomes the reluctance of private actors (VCs and technology firms) to collaborate with the defense and security agencies; at the same time, the NSS acquires sustainable suppliers that can remain viable without the promise of substantial government demand. The VC model also gives the NSS a means to influence future development of the funded companies without requiring an intrusive hand.

Market scouting. A third, developmental thrust of the NSS venture capital initiatives is the emphasis given to identifying markets for nascent innovations, sometimes brokering deals that will clinch the development of a technology with the high probability of a final market. While all the GVFs perform this market-scouting role, it is the sole purpose for which the Department of Defense's DeVenCI and the Navy's VC Panel were established. As mentioned, these GVF initiatives forego direct equity investment; instead, they seek to match technologies with markets, using the high probability of firms securing federal acquisition contracts (reducing investment risk) in order to catalyze private VC investment in companies with relevant technology.

In sum, the government-sponsored venture funds blend equity investments and product development funding; they target young companies to create dual-use, commercially profitable products that meet the needs of the agencies; they finance companies spun out of the labs and research institutions; and they broker deals with other VC firms to bring the technologies to market. In all cases, they seek out markets for the final product. In the words of an In-Q-Tel insider: "We're absolutely not passive. Once we've invested money into a company, we have a strong interest in seeing that company succeed."[50]

It should not need stating that the investments carried out by NSS-linked GVFs are not always successful. That would be an unlikely outcome for any investor in nascent technology, whether public or private. Indeed the absence of failure would indicate that insufficient risk was being taken, without which few innovations would be likely. In any case, many GVFs work in tandem with the private sector, hedging risk by leveraging their funds to create a larger investment pool. The hybridized nature of this investment system is the focus of chapter 7, but what matters here is the institutionalization of this funding approach for high-technology ventures—thereby reducing risk for firms and private investors alike—that makes the NSS a critical actor in this arena.

In the story of America's VC industry, the national security state occupies a special place. As well as seeding a modern VC industry, NSS agencies—with an eye to the geopolitical implications of diminishing access to transformative technology—have created a network of venture capital funds involving different mixes of ownership and operational arrangements with the private sector. These funding arrangements, ranging from the more passive to the more active end of government involvement in the innovation process, contribute significantly to the earlier stages of product development where outcomes are uncertain and the risk substantial. Although it is conventional to associate America's vibrant entrepreneurship with an equally dynamic private VC industry, the reality is that federal programs, not private VC, provide the majority of the high-risk startup and early-stage capital for U.S. innovation.[51] Moreover, the NSS employs VC not only to help develop, commercialize, and acquire the latest technology *from* the private sector, but also to effect its transfer in the other direction, spinning out technology from the federal laboratory *to* the private sector, via product development partnerships.

GVFs act not just as passive recipients of technology; they often play an active role in its development. Indeed, whereas the language of spin-off and its association with serendipity may have partially reflected earlier NSS experience, nowadays it is the language of spin-around that more accurately reflects the synergistic aims and efforts of the government-sponsored venture funds.

In the broadest sense, then, GVFs are important instruments of the NSS technology enterprise. These funds make investments in private companies with "dual-use" technologies, leverage positions in other (private) venture capital firms, aid technology propagation and commercialization, and take responsibility for transitioning promising technologies into the market. As a key mechanism of investment in high-technology ventures, government-sponsored venture funds effectively extend the influence of the NSS throughout the commercial economy.

Beyond Serendipity

Procuring Transformative Technology

New technologies are seldom created by luck; they are instead the
result of private and public sector investments of time, money, and
effort.

Ronald Reagan, 1983

Ever since World War II, technology procurement has been a key instrument of U.S. high-technology leadership. With its modern roots in military
contracting during the war, technology procurement soon evolved into a
means to drive American firms to undreamed-of technological feats. Its catalytic role in the emergence of high-tech industries in postwar America has
been well recognized in policymaking circles and its contribution to breakthrough innovations has been well documented by analysts of technology
policy. But for much of the postwar period the prevailing view has been that
commercial applications that grew as spin-offs from defense and security-
related technology were mostly serendipitous, limited, and increasingly
scarce from the 1970s onward. This view was one that suited American policymakers, argued John Alic and his collaborators in a major study of the issue
published in 1992.[1] By clinging to this belief, governments could continue to
justify nonintervention and the virtues of the free-market paradigm.

In this chapter I draw on a wealth of existing research to challenge and
revise this standard story as it applies to the period up to the late 1970s. After
this period, as the standard story tells it, the role of technology procurement
declined to the point where it ceased to have much commercial influence,
serendipitous or otherwise. Thus, in the next chapter I present several case
studies that show the continuing commercial significance of NSS technology procurement right up to the present. In this way, I hope not only to
show how, but also to explain why NSS actors have increasingly sought to

encourage commercial applications of NSS innovation—at first early in the Cold War era, then increasingly from the 1980s onward.

The period before the 1980s was one of NSS-wide sponsorship of general-purpose innovations, via the mechanism of technology procurement. It was also one of the beginnings of a new emphasis on commercially relevant technology development designed to attract the most innovative firms that operated outside the traditional defense-industry circle (the subject of extended treatment in chapter 5). In this way technology procurement was not just a means of acquiring from the private sector innovations that had military-security relevance; it was also a formative tool in catalyzing commercial innovation and new enterprise.

Since I am to some extent following a path carved out by Alic et al.'s pioneering study, *Beyond Spinoff*, which two decades ago also tackled the myth of the serendipitous spin-off, it is important to emphasize where we differ. Reflecting the policy ambitions for a post–Cold War era, Alic and his distinguished collaborators undertook to show why the pervasive view of spin-off as a serendipitous process was fundamentally misleading. The thrust of their case was to argue that the serendipity assumption was mistaken not because spin-offs do not occur, but because it assumes that the process is automatic, free of effort and cost. What makes the spin-off story a half-truth, they argue, is the fact that spin-offs from defense technology are limited and costly precisely because unplanned. The fact that companies must modify and adapt defense technologies for commercial use thus makes spin-off ineffective as a public policy approach to commercial innovation. The study, well timed for the new Clinton administration, made a convincing case for promoting dual-use technologies (and more generally, dual-use firms and a dual-use relationship between commercial and military sectors) as part of a broader call for a commercially oriented technology policy. This is because the authors saw the commercial sector (both in the United States and abroad) coming to be much more important in the development of new weapons systems than traditional defense firms. To a significant extent, Alic et al.'s dual-use advocacy has come to pass (chapters 5 and 6).

So how does my account differ? On the issue of cost and effectiveness as a policy for commercial technology, I have no disagreement, even if measurement of these outcomes has proved elusive. But the main thrust of Alic et al.'s analysis is to dismiss serendipity by focusing on the efforts needed from the private sector to bring innovations to fruition. I am approaching the same issue, but from a different angle: serendipity misleads because it ignores the extent to which public-sector actions and motivations drove broad support for the major general-purpose technologies. My account therefore differs from Alic et al.'s as follows: the serendipity argument underplays what was often pursued by NSS actors on purpose, and with a view to what I call spin-around: broad support for an industrial base that can supply both public and private markets for reasons of national security. I seek to explain not just how but why NSS actors have pursued purposive or intended spin-offs.

NSS purposiveness arose out of its efforts to meet geopolitical concerns—strategic rivalry with the USSR and then increasingly technological rivalry with Japan—while responding to the domestic challenge of attracting unwilling actors in the private sector to work with the government. While the need to leverage commercial resources for cost reduction played into these considerations, it was not the primary motivating force. In the discussion that follows I explain the role of technology procurement in driving innovation before turning to address the serendipity myth head on.

Technology Procurement versus R&D: The Activist Element of Government Purchasing

For many analysts and policymakers, the federal contribution to innovation begins and ends with the funding of research, or R&D. But as a number of analysts now concur, "R&D investment alone is not sufficient" to bring about innovation or to bring innovations into use.[2] A vital component in that process is the role of assured demand by a government agency that wishes to use the innovation—a critical factor often overlooked in accounts that stress the more passive "research" side of R&D.

Here, one must distinguish between two basic categories of public contracting. In the one case, authorities buy already existing products and services—such as paper or PCs or readymade software—off the shelf, as it were. In the other, authorities acquire a technology, a product, a service, or a system that either does not yet exist or that requires further development and testing prior to deployment (examples range from lightweight batteries and unmanned vehicles to medical devices, lasers, and geospatial information services). In these latter cases, R&D, technical change, or cutting-edge innovation is required for eventual incorporation into a marketable outcome. Here, "technology procurement" is the appropriate term.[3] It involves programs whose major objective is the creation of products and services for the federal government (acting either as final end user, or as catalyst for broader general use), sometimes with a view to their playing a commercial role as well. Whereas the objectives of "basic R&D" programs are confined to the advancement of knowledge, there is then an "activist" dimension to technology procurement that the generic labels "R&D" and "research" obscure in discussions of public funding.

Beyond funding, technology procurement provides the pull of assured demand: it creates a ready market for the resulting innovation. In this sense, government acts as a catalyst of innovation both by investing in and buying goods, services, and systems not yet in existence, and by adapting existing technologies to new purposes and end users (Edquist 2005). As a demand-based instrument, it pulls new technologies and products into the marketplace through competitive and negotiated federal contracts, backed by a ready buyer. For all its importance in understanding the U.S. innovation story, however, the term "technology procurement" is virtually absent from the U.S. literature.[4] While the role of federal R&D funding has been amply examined, the more comprehensive focus on technology procurement has received much less attention.[5]

Absorbing Private-Sector Risk, Seeding Revolutionary Innovations

The massive requirements of World War II triggered a major shift in the means by which the federal government went about procuring advanced technology. Prior to the war, the armed services were compelled to rely almost completely on a process of competitive bidding that discouraged innovation by placing the burden of risk on the private sector. The 1940 National Defense Expenditure Act changed all that, granting the authority to buy technology through negotiated contracts.[6] The "cost-plus" contract proved to be a particularly important innovation tool because it allowed the armed services to fund product development prior to acquiring the resulting product, and thus to absorb the considerable risks inherent in the process of creating a novel technological device (Danhof 1968, 32).[7] The risk-shifting role of the new contracting arrangements thus paved the way for a new partnership between public and private sectors, which was critical to establishing the NSS technology enterprise.

The NSS did more than absorb the risk of advanced technology development; its massive appetite for new types of defense and defense-related equipment launched revolutionary general-purpose technologies that gave rise to a host of leading commercial sectors. Well-documented examples of sectors jump-started by Cold War technology procurement projects include microelectronics and information technology (computers, software, semiconductors, more recently the internet), and aerospace (aircraft, communications satellites, GPS).[8] The NSS not only funded much of the physical science and engineering that led to advances in semiconductors, computers, communications and aircraft; it also purchased a large fraction of the products themselves, especially the most advanced products. In a succinct historical overview of six general-purpose technologies, Ruttan (2006a) examines the role of military-space demand as a key source of commercial development. Military-space demand for general-purpose technologies, he argues, produced America's leading high-technology commercial sectors, in particular, aerospace, computers, and semiconductors.

Up until the late 1960s, NSS agencies were the "lead users" (sometimes the only users) of the most advanced technological products (notably aircraft, semiconductors, computer hardware, and even software). Moreover, they were able and willing to pay premium prices for products that met their demanding performance requirements. As well as providing a constant and plentiful source of demand, the defense and defense-related sectors (mainly

DoD, NASA, AEC/DoE, and NSA) demanded products and services whose technological level was far more advanced than that initially required in civilian markets. This was the critical catalytic role that NSS agencies played through technology procurement. They went way beyond conventional notions of R&D in helping to place American industry on constant alert that it was expected to keep itself at the technological cutting edge.

In sector after sector we see this formative role of technology procurement. In microelectronics (and subsequently in semiconductors), for example, under industrial preparedness contracts in the 1950s, the NSS played the seminal role of first customer and "training coach" for the domestic industry.[9] The following are examples of U.S. defense-led and defense-supported innovations in widespread civilian use by the 1980s [2000s].[10]

- Applications of wartime radar to air traffic control and microwave communications links
- Atomic energy
- Radioisotopes for industrial and medical applications
- Antibacterial drugs
- Cryogenic blood preservation
- Resuscitators and heart pumps
- Genetic medicine
- Jet aircraft
- Computers, solid state electronics, and integrated circuits
- Computer mouse
- Workstations
- Communications and weather satellites.
- Robots and computer-controlled machine tools
- Lasers (multiple applications)
- Chemical pesticides
- Fire- and weather-resistant clothing
- Industrial air filtering
- Power steering
- Large-scale earth-moving machinery
- Solar-electric cells
- Storm windows
- Microwave ovens
- Wide array of advanced materials and composites
- [The internet]
- [Global Positioning System]

Indeed, "the federal government was the *only* customer" for American-made integrated circuits until 1964 (Department of Commerce, Office of Technology Policy 1996, 19, emphasis added). Massive demand for the new products at premium prices, especially from NASA and DoD for the Apollo and Minuteman programs—together with ample assistance in constructing pilot production lines—drove early investments in integrated circuit manufacturing capability. But it was the partnership with their demanding customers that pushed the fledgling U.S. semiconductor firms to rapidly improve production capabilities and equipment, and reduce manufacturing costs (National Research Council 1999, 33). As high demand from the military and space sectors continued, prices for integrated circuits dropped rapidly from about $50 per device in 1962 to $2.33 by 1968 (Wilson et al. 1980, 147). Demand thus produced the classical learning curve effect that made the components affordable and so more widely available. But this was not a simple learning-by-doing process. It was a collaborative effort in which semiconductor producers worked in conjunction with space-defense engineers and program managers to improve quality and yield.

Even the computer software industry took root in NSS requirements, chiefly those of the defense sector. According to Kenneth Flamm, of the forty-five major advances in computer software that originated in the United States between 1950 and 1980, no fewer than eighteen were developed with federal government sponsorship, all but one receiving Pentagon technology procurement funding (Flamm 1988, table A-4).

Crucible of Entrepreneurial Initiative and Learning

In this respect, federal demand did more than seed revolutionary innovations; it also acted as a crucible of entrepreneurial initiative by supporting the formation and growth of new firms in their early learning phase that leveraged the experience gained in defense production for new commercial opportunities. As a 1984 study of the semiconductor industry observed, early production was often so faulty and the learning curve so steep that around 90 percent of the devices produced for the space-defense programs failed to meet federal specifications. Indeed, in order to get the number of devices it needed from the twelve firms contracted, the DoD had to pay for up to twelve times the number it actually wanted. In this generously endowed and fully compensated teaching-learning environment, integrated circuit producers gradually turned out more and more usable devices, ramping up their production capacity, which in turn stimulated the search for new markets (Borrus, Millstein, and Zysman 1984, 534). But this was far from a quick or easy process. As Kenneth Flamm comments, military support remained central in this crucial period because following its invention in 1959, "close to a decade passed before the integrated circuit was cheap enough to become widely used in commercial electronics" (Flamm 1988, 18).[11] Thus the NSS was responsible for setting the emergent semiconductor industry and its jewel in the crown, Intel, on the firmest foundations. Similar observations apply to other key sectors (aeronautics and computing, for example) as we shall see.

As well as supplying companies with a ready market, problem sets, technical know-how, learning experience, and investment, work on space-defense applications gave firms the necessary confidence in the technologies involved to take the first commercial steps. A comprehensive 1986 report prepared for Congress on DoD support for science and technology underlined this aspect of technology procurement: "Military applications provided the confidence in [the technologies'] feasibility and cost which has permitted the private sector to plan with confidence for commercial exploitation" (Congressional Research Service 1986b, 427–30).

The effectiveness of defense-related technology procurement as a driver of transformative (and commercially relevant) innovation has been carefully studied (e.g., Ruttan 2006a). Three factors have been highlighted that help to explain technology procurement's effectiveness as an engine of innovation. One is that technology procurement is user-focused and therefore demand-driven. NSS agencies were often, in the end, the users of the technology that they sponsored (or at least brokers for other NSS actors) and generally had an important strategic vision of what they were looking for. Pushing the known boundaries and taking risks, rather than making a profit, was the underlying logic. Risk-taking of course has its costs in terms of failed programs, so that transformative "effectiveness" is not the same as "efficiency." Another factor is that the NSS agencies clearly understood (and still do) that wide deployment and high-volume demand is a critical driver of cost reduction over and above the emphasis placed on developing the technology itself; hence also the importance of encouraging commercial applications that would be honed in the competitive space. A third factor is that the NSS could draw on a vast decentralized system of specialized subcontractors, which encouraged technology diffusion and the emergence of sophisticated suppliers. This last factor of course belies the notion of an enclave-style military-industrial complex built around a group of big defense firms (chapter 5). This synergistic relationship between assured NSS demand for breakthrough innovations on one hand and private-sector applications on the other would become a recurring feature of the national science and technology enterprise.

In sum, the role of space-defense procurement in generating new general-purpose technologies, advanced industry sectors, and (to a lesser extent) technology startups is well documented in the official histories—most notably for the early decades. Nonetheless, this role has often been downplayed—and at times discounted. Two assumptions have played their part in this discounting effect. The first is that because the mission of the agencies in question was that of national security, not economic competitiveness, commercial spin-offs from defense-driven innovation were therefore simply fortuitous—neither sought nor encouraged.[12] The second (the main focus of chapter 5) contends that whatever the commercial impact of defense- and security-focused innovation in the early postwar years, its relevance is now long past because of growing barriers between defense and commercial industry (a so-called "wall of separation").

Closer attention to all three factors indicates that the NSS was both directly and indirectly aiding commercial applications even in this earlier period. Indeed, the intention of the military, and of the wider NSS, has always been to procure not just ready-to-use products but technology that is in advance of the best available. The process that this entails can only be described as intentional, strategic, and over time increasingly commercially sophisticated, informed as it is by a deep understanding of what is needed to grow a new market and thus support an industrial base. To characterize NSS commercial impacts as serendipitous or of declining relevance is to misconstrue much of the thinking and effort that underpins the pursuit of American technological superiority.

Spin-Off and Spin-Around—Serendipitous and Purposeful

It has been claimed that when the national security motive is paramount, commercial considerations must be absent. Following this reasoning, the commercial applications of mission-sponsored technologies that gave rise to a host of advanced industry sectors were little more than unintended by-products of national security projects.[13] True, commercial innovation was hardly ever the primary motivation. But neither was it always uninvited, nor the result of blind chance. In practice, commercial and security goals were often unavoidably connected. In the case of several general-purpose technologies, federal support straddled national security and civilian applications because the space-defense and defense-related agencies perceived the necessity of a commercial industry for maintaining technology leadership. Sometimes, NSS agencies learned this lesson the hard way. For instance, when the DoD pursued microwave monolithic integrated circuit (MIMIC) technology as a strictly military development, the high cost stymied widespread use of the devices. DoD eventually changed course by encouraging MIMIC contractors to pursue commercial applications.[14] A report to Congress on federal technology partnerships summed up the "payoff to defense" as "the world's best radar at a lower cost by leveraging [mission R&D for] commercial production" (Department of Commerce, Office of Technology Policy 1996, 32). This is an instance of what I call spin-around effect.

Indeed, there is a broad perception throughout the NSS that commercialization is integral to the national security mission. One of the DoE's nuclear defense laboratories explains why, on the eve of launching a spin-off company to market one of its inventions: "National security decision makers are conservative. They want to see the technology widely used in applications like cars or television before they consider it for weapons. Getting the technology out of the labs and into commercial applications will give us the confidence needed to deploy it in critical defense applications."[15]

This understanding of the spin-around effect, predominant at first in programs for computing and aircraft while sometimes stifled in the military arena, became more pronounced over time as the DoD in particular found it increasingly a challenge to elicit advanced information technology from the nontraditional suppliers in the private sector whose innovative capabilities were outpacing those of the prime contractor defense firms.

We turn now to examine specific ways in which the serendipity assumption misleads, by focusing on the variety of NSS actors (not just DoD) that helped to bring commercial applications into existence by their direct and indirect efforts; the diversity of sectors in which such efforts bore fruit; and the evolution of the DoD's own approach to technology procurement which increasingly emphasized commercial viability.

Agency diversity. It is true that as a matter of policy, as distinct from practice, up to the late 1970s the Pentagon did not offer much directed support for commercial innovation. However, other NSS agencies with broader technology mandates, including the Defense Department's own DARPA, from the start pursued broadly based programs that served both defense-related needs and commercial uses. Computers, semiconductors, software, aerospace, biomedicine, and biotechnology are among the better-documented cases of sectors that emerged from such programs fostered by NASA, the DoE, and NIH as well as by DARPA and the Pentagon.[16]

There is, of course some element of truth to the serendipity claim: until the 1970s, there was little direct encouragement of commercial applications from the DoD itself. However, there is ample evidence that DoD provided broader support to nonmilitary technology. A 1972 report by the Government Accountability Office makes this clear, stating that "Budgetary restrictions and the unpopularity of military involvement in nondefense activities have imposed strong pressures on DoD to confine its activities strictly to the defense mission" (1972, 10). Such pressures reflected widespread opposition to the Vietnam War and the perceived militarization of university research, leading to the Mansfield Amendment that required defense funding of university R&D to be tied strictly to military projects. By the end of the decade, however, fears of losing the technology edge were nudging policy toward greater military-commercial integration. Thus, for reasons already indicated and revisited below, the DoD also began to factor commercial considerations directly into its technology development and procurement programs.

A related point is that within the DoD itself, commercial spin-offs from technology procurement were not always unanticipated or publicly unassisted— even when given largely indirect support. Consider the Independent Research and Development (IR&D) program. These Defense-funded projects, initiated by contractors but not performed under contract, can be seen as a form of "stimulated innovation"—the practice whereby the NSS came to offer its contractors financial and technical support for pursuing "independent" technology development. The DoD, NASA, and several other agencies allow contractors to recover a portion of their independent R&D expenditures as overhead payments on their cost-based procurement contracts.[17] In the case of the DoD, under a 1971 amendment, the program enabled commercial applications of military-sponsored innovations, provided that the work involved had potential military relevance. Equivalent to about 7 percent of DoD's RDT&E (Research Development Test and Evaluation) budget, but not counted as part of that budget, IR&D is "an adjunct to DOD's mainstream research and development activity," estimated to cost the department more than $6.9 billion annually by 1985, adjusted for inflation and just under $10.7 billion if we include other NSS components (Congressional Research Service 1986a, 343). Indicative of its continuing significance, by 2009, IR&D spending amounted to $7.7 billion for all NSS components, of which DoD accounted for $5.3 billion.[18] The important point is that DoD agents not only expected the private sector to commercialize defense technologies when operating within the IR&D policy framework; they also provided the means for defense contractors to leverage federal resources in order to commercialize military innovations. Indeed, an early review of IR&D by the Government Accountability Office (1974) found that DoD was (unwittingly?) absorbing a large share of the costs of developing an engine for commercial aircraft.

If anything, Defense is more proactive today than in the 1970s in its efforts to use the IR&D program to encourage two-way spillovers between military and commercial innovation—aka the spin-around effect. Indeed, the department's stated policy is to use its financial support of contractor IR&D, inter alia, to "encourage the commercialization of dual-use technologies to ensure the . . . availability of those technologies for application to future military systems and for the economic benefit of the United States."[19] In late 2011, Defense official Frank Kendall reported to the Senate Armed Services Subcommittee that the department's IR&D program had reimbursed some twelve hundred firms for their efforts and thereby provided a stimulus for innovation at all levels of the supplier base (Kendall 2011).

Part of the rationale for this kind of support that blurs the boundaries between mission-based and commercially oriented technology is the spin-around effect: NSS actors want to see their technologies commercialized in order that they might have access to a stable and affordable supply of tried and tested products on the market. As DARPA explained in a 1985 commissioned study of its activities: "Such spin-off has direct military value when the armed services later buy commercial products that embody that technology" (Havelock and Bushnell 1985, ix). Though not labeled as spin-around, the effect appears to be well understood by NSS insiders. As the landmark report *Funding a Revolution* stated in its discussion of DARPA's role, the agency "put significant effort into getting the results of its research programs commercialized so that DoD could benefit from the development and expansion of a commercial industry for information technology" (National Research Council 1999, 102).

Sector diversity. Closer attention to individual industry sectors suggests another way in which the serendipity argument mis-specifies what is often a purposeful endeavor. In computing, information technology, and aerospace, for example, defense and space programs sought to encourage broad deployment of these inherently general-purpose (or dual-use) technologies.

In the case of computing and aerospace, the connection between sustaining U.S. technological superiority and supporting commercial diffusion of general-purpose technology was clearly understood by NSS actors from the outset. In the fall of 1945, Pentagon managers, perceiving the military's need for an extensive infrastructure in order to benefit from digital processing, undertook to diffuse knowledge of computing methods and devices as widely as possible.[20] Subsequently program managers within ONR, the Air Force, and later DARPA and NASA encouraged broad deployment across both military and civilian sectors. In the case of computers, spin-offs from the critically important SAGE and Whirlwind projects—in the form of firms, innovations, and industry sectors—rather than being unintended, were actively encouraged, significant impacts of which have been well documented (box 4.1).[21]

BOX 4.1. COMMERCIAL IMPACTS OF NSS'S SAGE AND WHIRLWIND PROGRAMS

- DoD funded Whirlwind as a general-purpose computer program to provide the basis for the Semi-Automatic Ground Environment (SAGE) air defense system for tracking and intercepting enemy bombers. Developed in the 1950s in response to Russia's explosion of an atomic bomb. First reliable, real-time digital machine designed to drive a Navy flight simulator (Whirlwind), intended as a platform technology. Whirlwind ran in a support role for SAGE until 1959.
- Whirlwind provided in turn the basis for the SAGE Air Traffic Integration (SATIN) system, a dual-use technology funded by the Federal Aviation Authority and the first automated air traffic control system.

Innovations Generated by Whirlwind
- *Hardware*: ferrite/magnetic-core memory (dominant form of memory until 1973); digital communications (phone-line transmission and modems); computer graphics (early graphical user interface); time-sharing.
- *Software*: pioneered use of real-time software; concepts that evolved into assemblers, compilers, interpreters; software diagnosis programs; time-shared operating systems; structured program modules; table-driven software; data description techniques.

Licensed and Spin-Off Computer Companies and Core Memory Suppliers
- IBM; Univac; RCA; General Electric; Burroughs; NCR; Lockheed; Digital Equipment; Ampex; Fabri-Tek; Electronic Memories & Magnetics; Data Products; General Ceramics; Ferroxcube.

Computer Stars: The Case of IBM
- IBM, as a company outside the defense sector, was self-admittedly a major beneficiary of (mostly planned) spin-offs arising from long and close collaboration with NSS agencies (working with MIT's Lincoln Lab on SAGE; and later with Lawrence Livermore on the ASCI project). IBM gained know-how by working on SAGE with MIT; built fifty-six computers for SAGE, earning over $500 million, contributing to its emergence as the world's largest computer manufacturer (Edwards 1996, 101–2; Freeman 1995, 33). At the project's peak, up to eight thousand IBM employees worked on it.

Software Spin-Offs: The Case of RAND's SDC
- The RAND Corporation spun off the Systems Development Corporation (SDC), a "developmental hybrid," to handle the software for SAGE. By 1963, SDC had trained more than ten thousand employees in the field of computer systems, serving both military and commercial clients. Of those, six thousand had moved to other businesses across the country, many to start their own firms.

Explosive Growth of Computer Industry
- Grew from $1 bn to $15 bn per year during 1958–73, dominated by the magnetic core memory.
- Whirlwind and SAGE trained personnel migrated to industry, diffusing technology know-how.

Sources: Old 1981; Flamm 1988; National Research Council 1999; Defense Advanced Projects Agency 2008.

These closely connected Cold War projects demonstrate the influence of NSS technology procurement programs during the infant phase of computing. Whereas Whirlwind was conceived as part of a general-purpose flight simulator that evolved into a general-purpose digital computer, SAGE was launched as an air defense system intended to protect against Soviet bombers, which by mid-1945 had achieved the capability to reach the United States via the North Pole.

The private sector's capacity to exploit procurement for commercial market entry is well evidenced in the cases of IBM and Boeing. In entering the new field of computers, for example, IBM—which became the number one U.S. computer company in the 1950s—drew heavily on breakthroughs generated by the SAGE project and the ONR-sponsored Whirlwind computer program. At the start of the decade, IBM's founder, Thomas Watson, looked to the Defense Department for the market to drive IBM's entry into the computer business. "It seemed to me," Watson later wrote, "that if we could build a couple of one-of-a-kind machines under government contracts, we'd have a way of getting our feet wet" (Watson and Petre 1990, 215). Besides IBM's massive involvement in the actual SAGE system, the company extracted further benefits from the resulting technology in the form of the SABRE airline reservation system which it marketed in 1964, and which would later become the backbone of the airline industry (Edwards 1996, 101–2).

Similarly in the aircraft sector, Boeing and other aircraft manufacturers were able to apply the engine technology developed for large military cargo airplanes almost immediately in their wide-bodied passenger airplanes. As a major defense contractor, Boeing applied the expertise gained in building bombers and tankers for the U.S. Air Force to aircraft manufacturing in its civilian division. Breakthroughs achieved in jet engines and airframe technologies for the Air Force's Dash 80 prototype helped Boeing tool up for the 707, the first successful jet airliner for long-haul travel (Alic et al. 2003).

Thus, in the case of two of America's most important sectors, aerospace and information technology, it is clear that private actors were able to leverage public resources and support to bring their products to market. Commenting on the commercial impact of defense procurement, a 1978 contractor's report for the Congressional Office of Technology Assessment concluded that procurement had been "particularly important" in helping new firms get started by providing both the initial market and premium prices for major advances (U.S. Congress, Office of Technology Assessment 1978, 37).

Temporal diversity. Attention to changes over time highlights a third, and the most significant, limitation of the serendipity assumption—namely, its static picture of practices and policies that over several decades have taken significant new directions. Even by the late 1970s, Defense's practice of indirect encouragement of commercial innovation was under revision, as the Pentagon sought to contend with shortages of advanced items (more on this below). DoD concerns that inadequate supply could jeopardize its Offset Strategy meshed with broader fears that the United States might be losing the technological edge to Japan (and to some extent Germany), thus provoking a major Domestic Policy Review on industrial innovation. One of its recommendations was that federal procurement be used to enhance the links between military-led innovation and commercial spin-offs "to stimulate development of innovative items."[22] From the same source emerged the view that the United States needed to place more emphasis on dual-use ("generic") technology development and on government and industry working in partnership.

Thus began a policy shift under the Carter administration emphasizing direct programmatic support for commercial applications, at first gradually, then over the following decade more systematically throughout the NSS (including the national labs). By the late 1980s, the idea of commercial-military integration and dual-use technology development programs had come into its own in NSS practice, and was an emergent official policy. The markers of this transformation were various initiatives from the late 1970s onward. As demand for customized integrated circuits outstripped supply, two programs in particular were launched—Defense's Very High Speed Integrated Circuit (VHSIC) program; and not least the much more successful DARPA-led Very Large Scale Integrated Circuit (VLSIC) program, widely considered one of the most commercially influential in recent computer history. Both were largely connected with the DoD's strategically minded efforts to regain influence over the direction of technology by attracting innovative nontraditional suppliers (in many cases drawing them back) to defense projects.[23] Thus the idea of building the potential for dual-use applications into the program design took hold; in this respect, the notion of intended or anticipated spin-offs appears apposite.

To be sure, one must recognize the strong element of serendipity in all R&D—regardless of whether it takes place in the public or the private sector. At the start of a development project, scientists and engineers are normally only able to predict some of the difficulties they will encounter, and often they develop technologies that they never set out to create (McNaugher 1987, 66). By contrast, the act of finding or pursuing actual commercial applications of a breakthrough technology is more often a conscious process, reached less by accident than by focused effort. In this effort, there has always been a mix of direct, indirect, and stimulated innovation support from the NSS technology enterprise—even from the most unlikely sectors thereof, such as the Strategic Defense Initiative Organization. According to its successor agency, the SDIO's commercial spin-offs cited by the Reagan administration were "no accident."[24] Even spin-offs from large military contractors performing independent R&D under the IR&D program would often need long-term support to bring an innovation to the point of commercial readiness, as the case of a Honeywell spin-out, NVE Corporation (Non-Volatile Electronics), clearly illustrates. NVE develops and sells devices for medical, scientific, and industrial applications that incorporate a revolutionary "spintronics" technology. The technology is still being developed, largely with NSS-SBIR funding, which since the company's 1989 founding, has amounted to approximately $50 million.[25]

Such examples neatly illustrate the point that behind the happenstance of many a so-called technology spin-off lies a good deal of energy, effort, and enterprise backed by the resources of the NSS. Importantly, the emergent shift that we examine next is one that leads toward more direct support for commercial innovation and enterprise, even though motivated primarily by the national security mission.

Breaching the Wall: Edging toward Military-Commercial (Re-)Integration

Whereas the serendipity claim seeks to distance innovation outcomes from government influence (especially that of the military), a related claim implies that after the 1960s a "wall of separation" emerged between military and civilian industry so that even serendipitous spin-offs became less and less likely.[26] Wall of separation proponents argue that as a particular technology matured and as the services increasingly emphasized military specifications in their procurement contracts, technologies that were broadly applicable across industry sectors in their early phase took on highly military-specific characteristics over time (as with customized semiconductors for military satellite communications versus mass-produced semiconductors for video games and other consumer items). Together with other barriers, this development allegedly began to segregate military and defense-related markets from commercial markets.

Although the extent of segregation has never been empirically established, and has indeed been found to have been more recently the exception rather than the rule (Kelley and Watkins 1997),[27] nonetheless, by the late 1970s the DoD could no longer look to the prime defense contractors to supply all its critical needs in advanced technology. In the fast-moving field of information and communications technology in particular, the traditional contractors could not keep pace. Lengthy acquisition cycles meant that DoD was deploying technology that was sometimes a generation behind the commercially available version by the time it was integrated into a system. This indeed marked the beginning of the NSS's continuing quest for innovation outside the traditional circle of prime contractors conventionally associated with the military-industrial complex. The most innovative firms were not part of that traditional pool of defense suppliers. A good deal of the advanced work in electronics and communications was now being produced by the very commercial firms once nurtured on defense funding for technology development and procurement contracts. The problem was that these firms were no longer inclined to work as federal contractors. Several disincentives made working for the Pentagon in particular a less and less attractive proposition for those technology firms who were former or potential suppliers to the government market. However, as we shall see, instead of cementing in place a wall between military customers and civilian firms, the impediments to collaboration gradually drove measures designed to breach this divide.

Three impediments to civilian firms working with defense customers were targeted by policy reforms and programmatic approaches. First, the acquisition process had become too onerous; not only did firms have to comply with ponderous military specifications, but cumbersome rules put in place during the Kennedy administration by the McNamara reforms, designed to increase accountability and oversight in contracting, had inadvertently discouraged commercial technology companies from bidding for defense contracts.[28] Second, ownership of intellectual property arising from federally funded programs remained uncertain, subject to diverse agency approaches. In the view of the Government Procurement Commission, reporting in 1972, it was precisely these two disincentives that were "steering innovators away from the government market."[29] Third, and by no means least, the high-volume federal procurement market for microelectronics of the 1950s and 1960s was rapidly being overtaken by the growth of commercial markets.[30] The effect of all three obstacles combined to dramatically diminish the incentive for commercially innovative firms to do defense work.

An Innovation Crisis: Integrated Circuits

In some instances these problems led to shortages of strategically important supplies—chiefly, of customized integrated circuits. Acute shortages of customized chips in the mid-1970s posed a strategic risk for the space-defense sector, which relied heavily on these devices. Thus, although there is no evidence of a *generalized* division between military and civilian industry, one area where it began to make itself most strongly felt was in the strategically critical sector of integrated circuits. In spite of their pivotal role in the birth of the industry, space-defense agencies began to face shortages of customized integrated circuits in the course of the 1970s. Key semiconductor firms of Silicon Valley had begun shifting in the 1960s to high-volume production of standardized memory chips (DRAMs) in order to supply the growing consumer market.[31] Defense systems, however, relied on shorter runs of customized components. In this fast-moving microelectronics sector, the ability to attract firms outside the traditional defense-contracting network to supply customized circuits for mission projects emerged as a major concern.

However, the problem was that semiconductor manufacturers had grown reluctant to work on defense-related projects, an aversion that eventually sparked new inducement efforts. The defense and defense-related agencies effectively embarked on a path toward new procurement mechanisms that would increasingly emphasize commercial relevance of the required products.

From the Pentagon's perspective, the commercial sector was in some aspects more technologically advanced in microelectronics than the prime defense contractors, but its products were not suited to the defense market. The problem was being forcefully articulated in defense circles. As the then deputy under secretary of defense for research and technology, Edith

Martin, announced to a 1983 Defense Appropriations Committee, "We now find that existing commercial tech-based capabilities are no longer adequate for defense," which was leading to shortages of customized devices for both military and industrial users (Heinrich 2002, 273).

By the late 1970s, the Pentagon saw that a focus on common technological goals would be the only way to pull merchant semiconductor producers back to defense work and regain control of the technological agenda in microelectronics. Bringing this point home to the Senate Armed Services Committee in 1979, William Perry made clear the intention of the Pentagon to promote the concept of dual-use technology development (Stowsky 1991, 21). Domestically, then, the Pentagon's dual-use investment strategy was based on the understanding that a new effort would be needed to (re-)enlist commercial firms to respond to its technology needs. Geopolitically, policymakers and Pentagon planners were also concerned that Japan should not take the lead in commercial development of dual-use technologies, lest the U.S. military become dependent on foreign suppliers for key components. As we saw in Chapter 2, DoD concern would deepen over the coming decade as study after study showed Japan gaining the lead in semiconductor technology, notably in the manufacturing process, and outstripping U.S. industry in sectors deemed critical to national security. The Japan factor thus strengthened the emerging push for greater integration of security with commercial technology goals. However, given the primacy of the military mission, striking a balance between commercial and security goals in its technology policy was a challenge that Defense would take time to master.

Luring Industry with Commercial Payoffs

As the growth of bureaucratic and procedural impediments began to limit their access to the most advanced companies in the private sector, NSS actors would have to find ways to rekindle relationships with industry. In particular, the Pentagon would have to become more adept at luring (or reattracting) advanced technology firms—notably, with the promise of demonstrable commercial pay-offs. Two major technology programs launched in the late 1970s neatly illustrate this point—VHSIC and VLSIC.

These programs aimed to reassert NSS influence over the direction of technology development by offering industry the prospect of commercial payoffs, or what we might term intended spin-offs (see table 5.3). The VHSIC program was the first of these two efforts to exploit commercial capabilities in the semiconductor industry for defense-related applications.[32] Motivated by reports of Soviet advances in integrated circuitry, program planners sought the collaboration of semiconductor manufacturers to design circuits for DoD. Support of leading U.S. firms was won on the basis of extensive industry input into program planning, thereby holding out the hope of commercially relevant advances in a range of process technology areas, including lithography, circuit technology, and computer-aided design. Commercial spillover was expected in such areas as satellite communications, weather forecasting, and search systems. As Fong observes, "the civilian spin-offs were the hook to bring in the military deliverables" (2000, 166).

There is compelling evidence to suggest that the VHSIC program was in some respects a procurement success and in other ways a failure. These inconclusive assessments differ according to the varying goals that commentators have attributed to the project.[33] One of its originating missions, to reintegrate military and commercial work in integrated circuits, was not achieved. Some argue that pressure from the Pentagon and military services led to a downgrading of industry technology priorities and imposition of export controls out of fear that premature commercialization would be exploited by the Soviets. This, they claim, effectively reduced commercial applications (Stowsky 2004).[34]

For all its weaknesses, however, the VHSIC program was not without considerable commercial significance. Among several commercially important impacts, the program "drove development of CAD tools" (Defense Advanced Projects Agency 2008, xx).[35] This is important because CAD (computer-aided design) was instrumental in overcoming Silicon Valley's DRAM crisis of the 1980s (effectively its worst economic crisis) since these design tools offered a low-cost means of customizing chips for a variety of markets without sacrificing volume. In practical terms, the CAD advances effectively reduced the cost of chip design—costing anywhere between $100 and $200 per gate at the beginning of VHSIC—to around $1 for some chip designs at the end of the decade (Department of Defense 1990, 27–28). Although Silicon Valley had pulled away from customized chips for defense markets in the 1960s to become the world leader in DRAMs, strong competition from Japanese firms and "a drop-off in the quality and reliability of U.S. products" (Congressional Research Service 1998, 15) eroded that lead, causing U.S. market share to plunge from 90 percent in 1975 to 5 percent in 1986 and forcing all but two U.S. companies from the standardized memory market. VHSIC was among the key commercially relevant programs that helped to turn that situation around, arguably contributing to the Valley's renaissance at the end of the 1980s, as was also the case with the VLSIC program.[36]

By way of contrast with the more innovation-shielding approach of VHSIC (Stowsky 2004), the DARPA-led VLSIC program maintained a tighter focus on military-commercial technological complementarity and achieved no less than an "industry revolution." As several studies acknowledge, the VLSIC program was "a landmark success, not only in creating new technologies and revolutionizing the computer industry, but also in forming the basis for major new industrial technologies and a number of companies that have become major corporations" (National Research Council 1995, 19). DARPA'S approach, an important contributor to VLSIC's success, was to combine academic R&D funding with the demand pull of a federal procurement market.

As an instructive study of Silicon Valley's crisis and recovery has observed, an "often ignored factor" in the 1980s revival of chip producers was the Pentagon, which not only funded a variety of important R&D projects, but also "became a major customer of startups," including, inter alia, Silicon Graphics, Sun Microsystems, and Microlinear Corporation (Heinrich 2002, 274). DARPA, for example, financed university acquisition of workstations from Sun Microsystems, whose "meteoric rise" in the workstation market owed something to the fact that 80 percent of its output supplied academic institutions (Heinrich 2002, 276). Some aspects of VLSIC's broader commercial impacts are outlined in box 4.2.

BOX 4.2. DARPA'S VLSIC PROGRAM: SELECTED COMMERCIAL IMPACTS

VLSI began in the late 1970s with the vision that integrated circuit technology could be made available to system designers and that it would have enormous impact. The program funded academic research activities as well as the Metal Oxide Semiconductor Implementation Service. MOSIS (established by DARPA, then expanded by NSF) provided low-cost, fast-turnaround VLSI fabrication services to the research community. The DARPA VLSI program is widely regarded to have been a major success. Among its notable achievements are the following:

- Developed the concept of the multichip wafer, which allowed multiple designs to share a single silicon fabrication run. Together with tools developed to assemble the designs and provide services for digital submission of chip designs, this capability made the concept of a low-cost, fast-turnaround silicon foundry a reality.
- Stimulated development of the Geometry Engine and Pixel Planes projects, which used the capabilities of VLSI to create new capabilities in low-cost, high-performance three-dimensional graphics.
- Stimulated development of Berkeley UNIX, which was funded to provide a research platform for the VLSI design tools. This version of UNIX eventually became the basis for the operating system of choice in workstations, servers, and multiprocessors. UNIX went on to become the most widely used vendor-independent operating system, with the code developed at Berkeley being key to this development.
- Accelerated understanding of the importance of low-cost, high-quality graphics for VLSI design, inspiring the creation of the Stanford University Network (SUN) workstation project.
- Several companies were formed to market a product based on the VLSI project and Unix, examples of which include

- VLSI Technology.
- Sun Microsystems, whose workstations and software are now distributed throughout the DoD, received a 1996 multiyear contract from the Air Force for almost $1.4 billion. Its revenues were at the time $7 billion (2011 dollar value).
- Silicon Graphics, whose 1996 revenues were $2.9 billion, was founded to capitalize on the Geometry Engine project at Stanford University. Its machines are found throughout the DoD; as well as having been leading supplier to the Major Shared Resource Centers of DOD's High-Performance Computing Modernization Program, SGI is also a key provider of systems for defense and intelligence image analysis and fusion.
- Developed two of the three Reduced Instruction Set Computing (RISC) experiments at Berkeley and Stanford, whose technologies formed the basis for many RISC designs, including those of MIPS Computer Systems (now owned by Silicon Graphics) and Sun Microsystems.
- Sponsored extensive developments in computer-aided tool design, which led to revolutionary improvements in computer-aided design technology for layout, design rule checking, and simulation—tools used extensively in both academic research programs and industry. The ideas led to commercial implementations by companies such as VLSI Technology, Cadnetix, and more recently, Synopsis.

Source: National Research Council 1995, 19; Defense Advanced Research Projects Agency 1997, 42–43.

The evidence presented here shows a quite different picture from that of spin-offs becoming not just serendipitous, but also rare, either because of a wall of separation or because of a shrinking government market vis-à-vis expanding commercial sales. Rather, strategically driven (by the effort to offset the Soviet's numerical advantage) but domestically constrained (by limited access to advanced industry capabilities), the NSS begins to reorient itself toward the commercial sector. Over the coming decades, commercial viability takes on a significance for the NSS that insistently works its way into program design and informs new ways of procuring innovations from the private sector. Far from being serendipitous or segregated from government, commercial innovation comes into its own, commanding greater attention and support from the NSS in a host of new approaches.

In spite of these well-documented cases, the idea of serendipity retains its appeal—presumably because it resonates with the antistatist mindset explored so ably by Aaron Friedberg, among others. For some, it serves a useful political purpose. At the very least, by implying a disconnect between military and commercial innovation, the serendipity view maintains the idea of U.S. technology leadership as a state-free process and leaves intact the free-market understanding of major U.S. achievements in commercial innovation. The effect is to preserve the fiction of the United States as a liberal market political economy and the American state as a minimal influence in high-tech commerce.

5

Reorienting the Public-Private Partnership

We must seek a new civil/military partnership, not one in which we become simply purchasers of commercial products and processes, but a dynamic and vigorous engagement that, through R&D, creates advanced products and systems with common technological bases. Through flexible manufacturing, this new partnership would allow us to produce low-volume, defense-unique items on the same lines with high-volume commercial items.

Jacques S. Gansler, 1998

. . . national security is no longer thought of as strictly a defense matter . . . if you look at defense industry, and you open up the box . . . you see a lot of things in there that were being produced not by what we traditionally say was defense industry, but by all of the other elements of industry. And so you're seeing the civilianization of defense.

Vice Admiral Arthur Cebrowski, 2004

It is often claimed that the mission agencies of the NSS, because of reduced market and R&D spending power relative to the private sector, no longer influence commercial innovation; that on the contrary, the influence flows in the opposite direction in a unidirectional (spin-on) manner, with the private sector setting the course for the NSS to follow. In this chapter I show why this declinist assumption needs revision: rather than (relatively) reduced market and spending power simply diminishing NSS influence over technology development, the mission agencies have instead sought to become more commercially proactive. The growth of new partnerships that emphasize joint projects, dual-purpose applications, and commercially viable innovations become a means to attract private-sector collaboration to NSS projects and regain influence over the direction of technology.[1]

In advancing this argument, I discuss several nontraditional forms of fostering and acquiring innovative technologies that have been instituted since the early 1980s, and that highlight key aspects of the public-private relationship that diverge from the declinist assumption. They include the broadening of public-private innovation networks to embrace nontraditional sources (beyond the so-called military-industrial complex); the policy emphasis on developing NSS technologies with dual-use or commercial applications; and the inadequacy of simple one-way, spin-off, or spin-on concepts of the security-commercial technology relationship. All three aspects are woven together in the case studies presented below.

It is one thing, however, to show how the NSS has become increasingly entwined, directly and proactively, with the commercial sector; it is quite another to understand why this has occurred. In order to do that, we must get beyond the "industrial policy" assumption. Although it is sometimes asserted that U.S. defense spending supports a covert form of industrial policy, closer inspection suggests that there is quite a different, more complex argument to be made. The NSS pursues technological superiority in order to sustain U.S. primacy, not to gain commercial advantage; however, in support of its national security objectives and in response to structural change, the NSS has increasingly had to play a more direct role in stimulating commercial innovation. What was effectively a dual-use *practice* in the early postwar decades would thus eventually become also official *policy*.

In the discussion that follows, I examine how and why, especially from the 1980s onward, this policy shift was manifested inter alia in the building of commercial considerations into NSS programs for developing and commercializing technology. Three domestic (structural) changes in particular have a reorienting impact that sees a more commercially proactive NSS. To begin, I discuss these changes in some detail because they have become the basis for the declinist view. In that framework, they are more typically understood as changes that remove or dramatically reduce federal influence over commercial innovation. I then show in a series of case studies how the changes in question have served to reorient rather than diminish NSS influence in the commercial arena.

Structural Changes in the Domestic Arena

In weakening NSS influence over commercial technology, two structural changes are widely considered paramount: first, commercial markets grew quickly, involved higher-volume production than the government procurement market, and soon dwarfed federal demand; second, private R&D spending climbed steadily, significantly exceeding federal R&D spending (and thus its largest constituent, NSS spending) by the end of the 1980s.

Relative decline of government market. This trend is dramatically illustrated by the case of integrated circuits (figure 5.1). Whereas in the mid-1960s military and defense-related users accounted for more than 70 percent of total

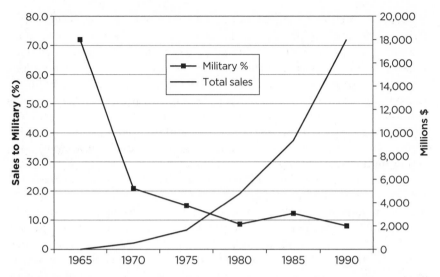

Figure 5.1 Integrated circuit sales to military as percentage of total sales, 1960–1990. Alic et al. 1992, 260, table 8-1.

sales of integrated circuits in the United States, by the 1980s their share hovered around 10 percent.

A closely related trend sees secular decline in procurement spending (aka "acquisition" spending) overall as the emphasis on offsetting the Soviet's numerical advantage with technological superiority drives up unit costs and lowers production runs of expensive weaponry. In reality, acquisition spending (for manufacturing and scaling up items)—as distinct from spending on technology procurement to create new technologies categorized as RDT&E (Research Development Test and Evaluation)[2]—fluctuates according to major strategic events such as the Korean War, the Vietnam War, the Reagan buildup, and Iraq-Afghanistan. Thus the Cold War peak of $231.4 billion in 1952 (FY11 constant dollars), was not even matched by the Reagan-era high of $155.2 billion in 1985, which in turn decreased over the following decade by almost 70 percent, reaching the Clinton-era low of $54.8 billion in 1997. By the turn of the century, the absolute size of defense procurement barely reached half of the 1985 Reagan-era high. Only after 9/11 did it begin a new upward trajectory, reaching the 1951 peak of $171 billion in 2008, thereafter again trending downward. By contrast, outlays for technology procurement (RDT&E) see a steady rise over the long haul (figure 5.2).[3]

Loss of NSS leadership in R&D spending. The second widely cited structural change involves the growth of private-sector R&D spending from the mid-1960s onward, which in the late 1970s begins to overtake and then, in the 1980s, to surpass federal R&D. As figure 5.3 shows, federal financing of

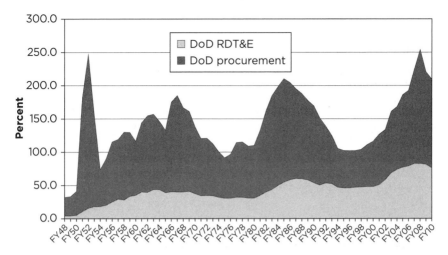

Figure 5.2 Acquisition budget compared with RDT&E budget, 1948–2010 (millions of FY11 constant dollars). Calculations based on data from DoD, Office of the Secretary of Defense (Comptroller), *National Defense Budget Estimates for FY 2011 (Green Book)*, March 2010, 61–66, Washington, D.C.

innovation remained substantial over the postwar period; it accounted for more than half of national R&D spending during 1953–78, then fell slightly below industry's share in 1980, dropping significantly after 1990. Even so, it is the relatively declining share of federal R&D spending—and by implication of defense-related R&D—that analysts emphasize in the context of debates over national innovation. Whereas in 1960 the federal government funded almost twice as much R&D as private industry, by 2000 industry's share was more than twice that of government.

Many accounts have cited these changes as evidence of the defense and defense-related sector's dwindling influence over commercial innovation. The reasonable presumption made is that via the change in the relative size of its procurement market, defense has lost the enormous leverage it once had in terms of market pull. Via the change in the relative share of R&D spending, it is assumed, the defense-related components have lost influence over the nature and direction of technology development and instead depend increasingly on spin-on from the private sector. Adding a competitive element to the mix, observers of the Japanese experience began to argue that America's military and economic security would henceforth depend on the ability to adopt a spin-on policy in the manner of its key economic rival (e.g., Borrus and Zysman 1992).[4] They were advocating not so much "dual-use," as Alic et al. proposed, but a more fundamental shift in an innovation regime that would henceforth be commerce-driven.

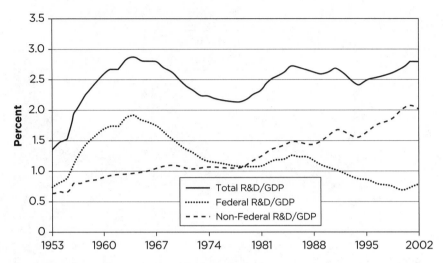

Figure 5.3 Total, federal, and nonfederally funded R&D as percentages of GDP, 1953–2002. B. Shackelford "Slowing R&D Growth Expected in 2002," NSF *InfoBrief,* NSF 03-307, December 2002, Arlington, Va.: National Science Foundation.

But consider an alternative outcome: What if the changes in question spurred NSS agents to a course of action designed to avoid declining influence? What if these very changes worked to alter innovation strategies and thereby strengthen the NSS-commercial relationship? The wide variety of cases examined here offer support for this proposition.

Reorientation: The Quest for Commercial Viability

As we saw in the previous chapter, by the late 1970s, the perception had grown that traditional contracting arrangements were no longer adequate to ensure the flow of innovations and their speedy transition to the armed services. The thicket of regulatory hurdles surrounding the system of defense acquisition, the reticence of prime contractors to work with advanced-technology companies, plus the uncertainty regarding rights to intellectual property had created significant barriers to collaboration. In addition to the hurdles keeping innovative firms away from the government market, by no means least was the pull factor of a rapidly expanding commercial market for high-technology products.

As the 1980s wore on, many voices argued that the traditional model of weapons acquisition was in crisis and in need of dramatic overhaul.[5] The demise of the Soviet Union, strong pressures on the federal budget, and the rapid advance of commercial technologies challenged U.S. officials to push more vigorously for new technology development and commercialization strategies that would give greater scope for commercially viable applications of mission-driven innovations. In the strategically vital and rapidly changing sector of information technology, for example, defense's highly specialized applications often fell behind the commercially available versions. Increasingly, as a result of long acquisition cycles and conservative investment preferences, the large traditional weapons contractors conventionally identified with the military-industrial complex could no longer deliver state-of-the art technology.[6] Indeed, the largest of these companies had consolidated significantly by the mid-1990s (from fifteen in 1993 to four in 1997) and the primary focus of the few remaining conglomerates was the integration of military-specific technology in defense systems.[7] By contrast, the trend toward commercial leadership in information technology and microelectronics was accelerating as semiconductor firms and much of Silicon Valley reemerged from their crisis (chapter 4). These converging trends, which mostly affected the military and intelligence communities, increasingly challenged the Pentagon to act more aggressively in finding ways to improve the ability and incentive for commercial companies to work in the national security arena.

At decade's end, an influential view proposed that military applications would need to rely more heavily on the commercial sector to develop and supply advanced technologies. Understanding the emerging trends, government executives over the course of the 1990s continued to make the case for broader and deeper engagement with the nation's commercial companies. John Alic and his collaborators were among the first comprehensively to articulate the new thinking of the time and to vigorously advocate an integrated dual-use strategy[8] (though its practice, as these authors acknowledged, had begun much earlier).[9]

The new Clinton administration endorsed a dual-use policy to promote defense conversion and reduce costs within a declining military budget. Such a policy, it was argued, would enable the pursuit of national security and economic strength as "mutually reinforcing goals." A dual-use policy would also allow the armed forces to better meet defense needs by exploiting what was now seen as a division of skills: on one hand, the innovation and market-driven efficiencies of commercial industry and on the other, the systems design and integration skills of its prime contractors. Conversely, such a strategy would better meet commercial needs by moving the innovations that originated in defense programs and laboratories more rapidly to the commercial sector. This rationale framed the Technology Reinvestment Program (TRP) which directed $800 million (with additional funds from commercial firms) to numerous dual-use projects before the program was terminated in 1996.[10] The program soon lost Republican support as it was seen to provide greater benefit to commercial firms than to the prime defense contractors and their military clients (chapter 2).

But an emphasis on the commercial viability of mission technologies had a longer history, and from 1980 onward found wider application in NSS programs (chapter 4). New approaches to producing innovation also called for more flexible contracting instruments, such as "Other Transactions." These were intended to bypass the lengthy and restrictive acquisition procedures of the Federal Acquisition Regulations.[11] A related step reformed the "defense waiver" system which imposed bureaucratic blockages. Responding to repeated criticisms of the acquisition system, Secretary of Defense William Perry issued a memorandum in 1994 proposing an overhaul of the use of waivers.[12] Whereas an acquisition manager in the past had to get a waiver in order to use commercial standards, henceforth these would be required wherever applicable. With the aim of lowering costs and most importantly, speeding integration of the latest technology, the acquisition system was thus effectively turned on its head with respect to military specifications and standards.

Beyond a Military-Industrial Divide: Innovating for Both Security and Commerce

But rather than seeing the development of new technology as one-way traffic—from commerce to the NSS—the new norm was to incorporate wherever possible the "intended spin-off" by creating technologies that could find markets in both government and commercial sectors and, conversely, by making "use, wherever possible, of components, technologies, and subsystems developed by commercial industry."[13] Much of the thinking behind these new "commercial leveraging" strategies, discussed shortly, embodies what I call the "Gansler principle" because it is so clearly articulated by Jacques Gansler (for example, in the epigraph to this chapter, drawn from his presentation to an international workshop on global security). As former Under Secretary of Defense for Acquisition and Technology, Gansler presents the strong case for pursuit of civil-military integration through deployment of commercial and dual-use technology. Yet he also makes clear that insofar as the commercial sector can sometimes better satisfy defense needs for advanced technology, this does not mean a passive one-way relationship in which commercial industry does all the innovation and defense does all the buying. On the contrary, it requires "vigorous engagement" with industry to create innovations with common applications that can be shaped into products for both markets.

Commercial viability has thus become a central criterion of government support for new and emerging innovation. Its institution required the adoption of new forms of technology development and commercialization—some that cultivate commercial expertise to produce innovations geared to both markets (such as the CIA's In-Q-Tel and the DoE's ASCI), others that stimulate entirely new initiatives and enterprise (such as Small Business Innovation

Research—SBIR), and others again that elicit breakthrough innovation by sharing with or shifting to the nongovernment sector some or all development risk (such as TRP and prize competitions, discussed below, which have recently been added to an expanding portfolio of technology procurement approaches).

I focus here on these nontraditional approaches, which seek to source technology applicable to both commercial and government markets. I use the term "dual-use" in the conventional sense to mean a technology that has both military and commercial applications. This category includes innovations that, though solicited originally to serve some military or security purpose, are at the outset of the conceptual process considered also sufficiently commercially viable to support production for industrial or consumer uses (SBIR being a typical example of the process); also included are technologies designed and developed jointly for military/security and commercial purposes (typified by the DoE's ASCI program).

Aspects of the reorientation of the national security state toward support for commercially viable technologies analyzed here[14] include myriad commercialization projects pursued through five major approaches: under the SBIR program by the DoD, NASA, NIH, NSF, and DoE; via large-scale, long-range procurement programs for information technology (ranging from integrated circuits in the late 1970s–1980s to supercomputers in the 1990s) led by DoD and DARPA, and then by DoE; through public-private consortia to build new commercial industries (such as hybrid electric trucks) that can supply both markets, led by the U.S. Army; by means of novel military-commercial partnerships to advance the technological frontier (such as a space-based internet); and by way of prize competitions sponsored by NASA, DARPA, DoD, and DoE in pursuit of revolutionary breakthroughs. All of these initiatives have reoriented the NSS agencies to align military and commercial goals, and helped bring the system to its present advanced state of technology development.

The Multiagency SBIR Program

The SBIR Program plays a much more significant role in the development-procurement complex than its low profile in the academic literature would suggest. It began in a small way in 1982, and thirty years later has grown to a massive program supporting startup firms of both military and commercial interest, having invested a total of some $30 billion in more than 100,000 separate projects.[15] No other public investment program anywhere in the world comes close to the SBIR in the scale and success of its operation. In addition to implementing its stated commercial objectives, the NSS impacts on the private sector via SBIR in three ways—as a catalyst for commercial innovation, as a source of new firm formation and entrepreneurship, and as a collaborative space for plugging network gaps critical to bringing innovations to market. In chapter 3, I discussed this program as a form of government-sponsored venture capital investing in early-stage technology development. However, SBIR is much more than a research program or even the world's most generous seed capital fund. It is also, at core, an innovation-led procurement program that promotes commercialization and seeks either to provide or to find a market for the technologies it sponsors. Charged with supporting private-sector commercialization of technologies developed with federal government funding, SBIR has incorporated planned spin-offs since inception (Wessner 2004, 13).

Thus, while remaining mission-oriented within the NSS, SBIR innovation programs also emphasize a company's need to market its technology to both public and private sectors. The funding agency in question will call for proposals, which it evaluates on the basis of technical merit, a firm's qualifications, and commercial potential in both markets. A typical call for proposals requires inclusion of a "commercialization strategy" to address intended commercial products, customers, financing, marketing expertise, and competitors. In certain cases, some funding is withheld until such a plan is forthcoming. Commercialization strategy has thus become a criterion for federal support.

A form of governed interdependence. Two aspects of the implementation process illustrate the SBIR-NSS relationship as a form of governed interdependence. The first (the "interdependence" aspect) is the input made by the private sector in response to NSS requirements. Rather than specifying technical solutions to be followed at the outset, agencies will often seek ideas and input from proposers; proposals are solicited in which NSS requirements are often expressed as problem sets or high-level problems to be tackled. The second ("governed") aspect of the relationship is the setting of performance conditions in exchange for support. These are enforced by making continuity of funding conditional on results, a function of the short time from proof of concept in phase I to production of a prototype in phase II (table 5.1). As a spokesman for high-tech SBIR companies put it to a recent Congressional committee, "the genius of the SBIR . . . programs is to force a down-select at the completion of the 'feasibility phase' before proceeding to the 'proto-type phase.' By selecting only the best 40 to 50 percent of the phase I projects, the maximum Federal R&D dollars are focused on the projects with the highest likelihood of success" (Squillante 2011, 17). Firms that make it to phase I through a rigorous selection process have six months to show proof of concept; if they make it through phase II by successfully developing a prototype, product, or service, they are deemed good bets for private and public investors. By tying funding to time-based results as well as a commercialization strategy, SBIR builds in performance standards. The biannual staging of dedicated SBIR conferences by individual agencies also establishes a co-ordinated networking space for regular dialogue and information sharing

TABLE 5.1
Three phases of the SBIR program: From concept to market

	Time frame, maximum budget	Maximum size of firm
Phase I * Proof of Concept	6 months Up to $150,000	500 employees
Phase II * Prototype/product/service (Potential for procurement)	2 years Up to $1,000,000	500 employees
Phase II Enhancement * Additional prototypes etc. * Letters of interest from potential customers-users	1 year Up to $500,000 (in matching funds)	500 employees
Phase III * Commercialization * Preferential procurement	Unlimited time Non-SBIR funding (public or private), unlimited	Unlimited

between public and private actors in the university, business, and venture capital communities.[16]

Transforming a prototype into a product for the market completes the process. In the words of one prominent defense authority speaking from the Navy's standpoint, "SBIR is all about Phase III"—commercialization.[17] Funding for commercialization efforts, however, must be pursued outside the SBIR program. In this final phase, NSS assistance takes the form of raising venture capital or direct funding from non-SBIR sources, federal or private, plus the prospect of an initial public market for the prototype, service, or final product.

Commercialization strategies. Since the program began, NSS agencies have taken several steps to increase the rate of commercialization and product acquisition. Such steps include coordinating meetings in which SBIR technology firms are introduced to potential investors, prime contractors, and commercial customers; fast-tracking transition of SBIR technology to production for the market by offering matching funds of between one and four dollars for every dollar from outside investors (Phase II Enhancement); and selecting the most promising firms for special commercialization support through dedicated programs implemented by NIH, DoD, and DoE.[18]

The prospect of selling to government agencies, "preferential procurement," is underwritten by an SBIR policy directive that states that "whenever practicable, an innovation or technology developed by an SBIR business will be used by the government" and that "Government owned, contractor operated facilities . . . give preference including sole source awards to the awardee that developed the technology."[19] The directive also requires the SBA "to report to Congress every instance when a firm creates an innovation or technology under the SBIR program, and yet the government goes to another business to develop and produce it" (National Research Council 2004a, section 4(c)3). For such firms, access to the procurement market is guaranteed for up to ten years under a special contracting arrangement, without the requirement to enter competitive bids (National Research Council 2009a, 32–4). Once a firm graduates from the program and enters the commercialization phase, no limit is placed on firm size or number of contracts possible. NSS agencies thus evolve long-term partnerships with former SBIR firms as they become large companies supplying both government and private markets.

In this way, not only are high-technology firms funded to develop the technologies for which they may not otherwise have obtained funding; they are also given preferential access to the federal market once their products have been developed. Preferential procurement also serves as a major investor-attracting device with which SBIR-backed firms effectively leverage investment from the private venture capital community. The case of MedShape Solutions, a medical device company that gained its start with SBIR funding, exemplifies the process whereby Phase III commercialization-cum–product development for public and private markets attracts preferential procurement and, ultimately, venture capital investment (box 5.1).

BOX 5.1. SBIR'S ROLE IN TECHNOLOGY PROCUREMENT AND COMMERCIALIZATION: THE CASE OF MEDSHAPE SOLUTIONS

SBIR concept → product → Preferential Procurement for Military and Commercial Markets → Venture Capital investment.

- Founded in 2005 in anticipation of SBIR funding in 2006.
- MedShape is a leading medical device company that has developed a novel shape-shifting polymer material to aid orthopedic surgeries. These devices help fuse bone to bone and soft tissue to bone and can be easily inserted in a temporary compressed shape, then triggered to deploy to the optimal functional shape. Initial applications of the technology involve the minimally invasive repair and reconstruction of injured or worn ligaments and tendons.
- The company's technology, a spin-off of the University of Colorado, is supported with more than $3 million in SBIR funding from NSF and NIH. Phase II work focused on prototype design and manufacturing processes for commercialization of a shape memory polymer device intended for knee reconstruction. With phase II Enhancement funding, MedShape commercializes the MORPHIX Shape Memory Suture Anchor.
- Launches the MORPHIX Anchor nationally at the American Academy of Orthopedic. Surgeons meeting in March 2010.

- Receives preferred vendor status in 2010 for its device at Veterans Health Administration hospitals and other Federally funded hospitals and health care facilities.
- Although MedShape is a niche firm producing small volumes, its high-priced products enable high profit margins and market impact in a $600 million shoulder and knee soft-tissue fixation market in the United States and Europe.
- In October 2010, MedShape receives venture funding from In-Q-Tel in an undisclosed financial round; reportedly has raised between $10 million and $15 million.
- Has several other SBIR-funded innovations currently on track for commercialization.
- The company's chief operations officer, Chris Fair, claims that SBIR funding was "critical to the development success and eventual commercialization of this innovative technology" and that its development with SBIR support was "a textbook case of how a partnership in development should occur."

Sources: MedShape Solutions press release, "Commercialization of SBIR Funded Technology," 5 March, 2010, http://www.medshape.com/news-events; National Science Foundation, *Phase II Grantee Abstracts*, Division of Industrial Innovation & Partnerships, SBIR/STTR Phase II Grantee Conference, Baltimore, May 17–20, 2010; SBIR data, https://www.inknowvation.com/node/16612.

Since Congress elevated "commercial" viability in justifying SBIR's 1992 reauthorization, several NSS agencies have regularly publicized SBIR success stories arising from their programs. If one Googles "SBIR Success Stories" almost 55,000 results come up (some of which are of course redundant). Even the military services publish "commercialization" (or "innovation") booklets on an annual basis, often displaying the names and technologies of firms that have launched new products. "Success" is measured in terms of innovative products reaching the market, and while it is conventional to count only SBIR "sales," this significantly underestimates actual commercialization outcomes.[20] Nevertheless, on this narrow metric, NRC surveys indicate that some 46 percent of SBIR-funded technologies (and some 50 percent of firms) reach the marketplace, which is considered a strong commercialization success rate for high-risk projects.[21] Indeed, selling into the nondefense and nongovernment markets has been a notable feature of the program: Surprisingly perhaps, DoD Phase II projects have generated almost as much nondefense as defense commercialization (National Research Council 2009a, 257). Similarly high rates of commercialization are reported by other

NSS agencies, notably NSF, DoE, and NIH, which aggressively promote SBIR companies seeking to bring their products to market.

Innovation and enterprise catalyst. As to how many important innovations result, no one has done the counting. DoD assessments claim that SBIR companies "are contributing to U.S. technological dominance," while case studies commissioned by the National Research Council indicate large impacts from some projects (National Research Council 2009a, appendix D). A conservative estimate comes from Defense's former SBIR program manager, Jon Baron, who suggests that in its first twenty-four years of existence the program spawned up to twenty major "breakthrough" technologies, such as excimer lasers, that is, "technologies which transformed their field and became major commercial successes" (Baron 2007, 19). In his testimony at the 2007 hearing for reauthorization of SBIR, Baron adds that the program has produced many "smaller but still important technological and commercial successes" (2007, 19–20). To be sure, Baron also mentioned a third category of SBIR projects that had produced no significant technology commercialization in either commercial or government markets, but he noted that this was entirely consistent with the nature of high-risk R&D, in which "only a fraction of projects will succeed, and fewer still will be breakthrough successes." Even so, it is also well recognized that commercial successes have been understated. Capturing outcomes from what can often be long lead times to wide diffusion and production for the market is inherently difficult. Indirectly, we have some inkling of this understating of commercial success in patenting results: SBIR is the largest single source of U.S. patents, its participant companies generating 50 percent more patents annually than the entire university sector.[22]

In addition to promoting commercially important innovations, SBIR is a strong catalyst for entrepreneurship and company formation. Again, we must rely on a variety of indicators rather than precise numbers. According to a National Research Council survey, most SBIR companies are spun out of universities and more than two-thirds of such companies at all agencies had at least one founder who was previously an academic. The same survey reports that one in four SBIR respondents acknowledged having founded their company because of a prospective SBIR award (National Research Council 2009a, 30). A cursory search through the SBIR awardee data, which show the interval between year of company formation and year of first SBIR award, suggests that the actual proportion of startups funded through SBIR is likely to be much higher, perhaps as high as two in three.[23] The latter estimate is consistent with the NRC finding that for 70 percent of the firms surveyed, the SBIR award was critical to initiation of research; and that for almost 50 percent, a good half of the firms' growth was directly attributable to SBIR (National Research Council 2009a, 31). These survey results, which applied to all the major funding agencies (DoD, NIH, NSF, DoE, and NASA), are consistent with earlier studies that found that SBIR induces scientists and engineers involved in research to shift career paths in order to become entrepreneurs and create startups (Audretsch et al. 2001; Feldman 2001).

But perhaps the broader significance of SBIR, working in conjunction with NSS contracts, lies in its role as an enterprise engine—pushing out innovations and new companies, and in turn generating further spin-off firms. As indicated in chapter 3, many of today's leading firms have roots in the SBIR program. Physical Optics Corporation for example, since its founding in 1985, has received more than 1,000 awards totaling more than $360 million (from DoD, DoE, NIH, NASA, NSF, and DHS), taken out more than ninety patents, and spawned at least six major spin-offs that themselves took root in SBIR contracts.[24] SBIR stars Amgen and Genzyme in biotechnology and Qualcomm in communications, which altogether currently employ a total of forty-four thousand people, benefited from multiple awards in their early startup phases. Qualcomm, which gained its start with SBIR funding in 1986, received awards totaling $1.6 million (from the Navy, Air Force, and NSF) when it had about thirty-five employees.

In sum, SBIR furthers the aims of the NSS by funding the creation of startup companies that develop promising and targeted technologies. It helps its graduates secure further development funding and product markets. Its endorsement strengthens the likelihood that graduate companies will secure preferential contracts from government and commercial sources. Its funding leverages further finance in the form of angel investing, bank loans, and ultimately IPOs. As a catalyst for commercial innovation, entrepreneurship, and company formation, SBIR appears to occupy a significant place in the NSS high-technology portfolio. Its contribution to innovation has become especially apparent now that major corporations have downsized their R&D facilities to focus chiefly on current product concerns.[25]

A key question, then, is why SBIR continues to enjoy strong bipartisan support from Congress when it offers such generous commercial payoffs for the private sector. The contrasting fate of the TRP makes this question especially pertinent. TRP was a multiagency program based on cost-sharing and flexible contracting that used "Other Transaction" authority. At close to $1.5 billion, TRP was one of the largest commercial investment efforts ever undertaken by the DoD, yet it soon fell victim to America's antistatist impulse. A recent history of DARPA recounts that "A new, Republican-dominated Congress decided that the program constituted more value for commercial industry than for the military" and in 1996 closed it down (Defense Advanced Projects Agency 2008, 35).[26] Lack of enthusiasm from prime defense contractors (newly buoyed by an economic upturn) no doubt put wind in the Republican sails. Instead of adapting defense technologies for commercial industry (the original defense conversion impetus), or developing dual technologies for both sectors, the smaller substitute program was refocused to emphasize military benefit, or spin-on (Potomac Institute for Policy Studies 1999, 20).

So what explains the difference? Why the antipathy toward TRP, but not SBIR? Antistatism is clearly not an absolute, an all-or-nothing mind-set; rather it has gradations that depend on political calculations. In this case, it would appear that opposition to interference in the political rather than the economic market was the motivating force that spelt the kiss of death. As some analysts have argued, Congressional Republicans fought to limit or block funding for civilian initiatives in order to prevent Democrats from wooing business allies with expanded technology programs (Block 2008, 185; Stowsky 1999). Wherever such initiatives entailed partnerships with prominent companies, as they frequently did during the Clinton administration, they failed the test of political viability and partisan antistatism kicked in.[27] This left bipartisan support for the NSS technology enterprise intact, provided that initiatives with clear and strong commercial payoffs could be delivered in hybridized forms (chapter 7).

The Department of Energy–Computer Industry Partnership: The Advanced Simulation Computing Initiative, 1995–2005

The ASCI program is one of the largest military-civilian technology development programs ever envisaged and carried out. It arose from the post–Cold War ban on nuclear testing, which required the United States military to be able to continue to maintain its nuclear arsenal in a state of readiness through extensive simulation. In effect, it was designed to enable the United States to switch from underground testing to computer-based testing of weapons. This required the design, production, and use of computers of a scale and power never before attempted.[28]

Under DoE leadership and coordination, three national labs were the drivers of the ASCI program: Los Alamos National Laboratory, Lawrence Livermore National Laboratory, and Sandia National Laboratory. The program spent no less than $5.2 billion in its first decade. These funds were expended in producing new platforms for computing, with a variety of totally new applications for simulating complex events; for handling and visualizing the vast amounts of data created by these simulations; for displaying the results of the simulations in high definition; and in developing programming and debugging tools. ASCI is a partnership between the DoE's laboratories, the universities, and industry. It builds on the massive capabilities in high-performance computing already achieved at the national labs such as Lawrence Livermore, where supercomputers able to perform hundreds of trillions of operations per second have been developed.

How ASCI was designed and executed, and the ensuing results, are of particular relevance to the argument of this chapter. First, it is a classic (and highly successful) case of dual-use technology innovation designed to produce major commercial innovations as well as meet mission-specific goals.

Second, the initiative is based on a relationship of governed interdependence between the industry of high performance computer manufacturers, smaller computer companies, and the Energy labs. Third, in drawing on, as well as contributing to, advanced commercial capabilities, the ASCI offers an important illustration of the dynamics behind the spin-around process and the Gansler principle.

Dual-use technology development: Mission-oriented, commercially attractive. As the Cold War was winding down, national labs were being financially assisted to commercialize their technologies by transferring them to U.S. companies. To access such finance, the labs had to meet the dual-use standard, so that funds would deliver advances for U.S. industry as well as the weapons testing program. ASCI leaders themselves, with an eye on the shrinking defense market at the end of the Cold War, stressed how important it was for computer companies to develop commercially attractive technology. Relying on systems suited to one major customer was no longer an option. "Keeping the industry viable" therefore became a central feature of ASCI's mission (Larzelere 2007, 82–83). Dual use offered benefits to both parties: the military gained from having a viable industry able to deliver the advanced simulation tools required, while the industry benefited from gaining access to advanced products that could become the next generation of advanced computing tools and packages.

Commercial partnerships. Consistent with its dual-use formulation, the ASCI program was required to work directly with commercial partners, in what must be one of the clearest examples in the United States of governed interdependence in action. Computer companies would not only produce the systems required, they would participate directly with the labs in all phases of the systems' design. Before the initiative was launched, program managers with DARPA experience stressed the importance of working with companies in a way that would enhance their commercial viability. At a preparatory 1994 ASCI workshop, this point was emphasized to the representatives of the nine computer companies in attendance: "It is important that industry tell DOE and the Laboratories what they think are their future directions."[29]

ASCI's needs entailed considerable risk for vendors. The national labs were pushing the high-performance computer industry far beyond its technology comfort zone in asking it to create brand new architectures and to rapidly achieve new performance levels. The labs were in effect contracting for computers and simulation capabilities that were not yet available or had not even been designed. Under such circumstances contracts could not be based on stable prices. And yet the computer companies would have to commit to achieving certain standards of performance and cost for systems that far exceeded existing technology horizons.

To deal with this challenge, contracting needed a fresh approach. Sharing the risks demanded a flexible arrangement that allowed for mutual give and take on both sides. The approach involved setting clear goals and timelines, accompanied by regular peer reviews. One interviewee relates that during the negotiations for ASCI Blue Pacific, Lawrence Livermore and IBM committed to "renegotiate a mutually acceptable solution in the future, if IBM had problems delivering on something," an understanding that became a formal clause (Larzelere 2007, 17).

Spin-around: Technical goals, commercial products, continuous innovations. ASCI's fundamental mission was to provide the tools needed to let weapons scientists conduct full-scale simulated testing of nuclear weapons. This meant developing the tools that collectively created a user environment, consisting of compilers, debuggers, operating systems, job schedulers, and data handling and storage controls—just as Windows creates a user environment on the PC consisting of word-processing, spreadsheet, display, and other applications, but on a much grander scale. As a dual-use program, the new tools would also be expected to become commercial products. Program participants concur that these objectives were achieved beyond expectation, resulting in simulation and visualization software to conduct the simulated explosions and weapons testing events, and then to make the data visually comprehensible; programming tools to construct and debug the simulation code; and displays to offer high-definition images of the processes.

Spin-around can be seen as intrinsic to the entire ASCI innovation process. For example, ASCI built new platforms and new tools and achieved major breakthroughs, but it also took advantage of existing commercial capabilities and innovations to achieve those breakthroughs. To visualize simulation results, for instance, "the labs worked with universities and industry to develop new, more scalable ways to visualize data, by taking advantage of the graphic cards developed for PC video games."[30] This in turn produced dramatic changes in how terascale visualization was done, well beyond what the laboratories could achieve alone. ASCI's procurement contract with Etnus to produce TotalView provides another illustration of the spin-around effect: "The ASCI contract helped Etnus do well, which further ensured they would be there to provide support for TotalView." Moreover, "Etnus continued to add new features and functions to the tool that benefit a host of customers, including the National Laboratories."

The success of several of the commercial applications resulting from ASCI within just a few years of its establishment point to the synergies of the program in achieving commercial as well as military goals. One striking aspect of the initiative is its promotion of ever higher-powered supercomputers, beginning with the ASCI-Red. Through its partnerships, the program yielded major results: ASCI achieved its accelerated goals; the once struggling high-powered computer industry recovered; and the computer companies built systems that they could make commercially viable.

Finally, ASCI is important because it illustrates the Gansler principle that DoD-NSS reliance on commercial technology should not be construed to mean simply buying readymade systems or technologies off the shelf. For, as this case demonstrates, the principle also involves working closely with industry to exploit existing or emerging advances, in order thereby to generate novel solutions that have complementary applications.

Creating New Industries for Future Military Supply: Hybrid Electric Trucks

In addition to new products and technologies, the changing missions of NSS components embodied aspirations for the creation of new industries that could offer a stable source of domestic supply. The NSS was very successful in its use of procurement to generate a semiconductor industry and a high-performance computing and computer graphics industry, The recent case of hybrid electric vehicles offers an interesting demonstration of the capacity of a specific branch of the NSS, in this case the Army, to jump-start a new industry without relying on massive R&D funding or direct procurement. The HEV initiative is part of a $4.5 billion investment program known as AVPI (Advanced Vehicle and Power Initiative). Nationally, medium- and heavy-duty trucks account for 4 percent of all vehicles and consume 20 percent of vehicle fuel. For the Army, these vehicles provide a quarter of its fleet and are regarded as "critical tactical assets." When the military first took an active interest in the sector a decade ago, no commercial industry for hybrid trucks existed in the United States. Most of the relevant engineering talent was focused on the challenge of emissions reduction and in spite of the emerging success of the Toyota Prius, no one in the industry perceived a market for heavier hybrids. By the end of the decade, however, the industry was capable of producing twenty thousand advanced vehicles. The steps leading up to this outcome offer an interesting variation on the NSS role as industry and innovation catalyst.[31]

The initial case for hybrid vehicles was made internally within the armed forces, which operate a fleet of some 200,000 nontactical vehicles (of which the Army has 40 percent), on the grounds of fuel savings. In this case, the key NSS player has been the U.S. Army which perceived that the medium/heavy duty truck sector offered "the greatest dual-use connection to the tactical fleet." In 2000, the Army's Tank Automotive Research, Development and Engineering Center's (TARDEC) National Automotive Center (NAC) formed a partnership with a nonprofit organization, CALSTART, to drive the development of a hybrid heavy vehicle industry with the long-term aim of military adoption.[32]

In a classic example of the spin-around idea, the calculation was that if successful, the fledgling industry would provide, at low cost to the Army, a vital demonstration and testing ground for the technology and a reliable low-cost source of supply for the future. By growing the initial market for an innovation that would be tried, tested, and improved in the commercial space, the military could serve its own longer-term acquisition needs with much less outlay of funds than would be required under conventional contracting. The Army may not call it thus, but it has a clear understanding of the spin-around effect: namely, that what goes back to the NSS has quite often, in the first place, emerged from public-private collaboration. In DARPA's words, "Often the best way to transition a technology into DoD is to transition it [first] to commercial industry so that it can be made available to DoD in the form of commercial off-the-shelf products and services (Defense Advanced Projects Agency 1998, 41). As a way of capturing and distinguishing the spin-around process, I outline the potential flows of influence in table 5.2, exemplifying responses to technology development challenges since the early 1980s.

The commercialization model. The approach taken by the Army-CALSTART partnership was to create a forum or association that would define and

TABLE 5.2
Public-private flows of dual-use innovations

NSS → commerce (Serendipitous spin-off)	Commerce → NSS (Spin-on)	NSS ← → commerce (Spin-around)
Commercial applications of defense technology are unplanned/ unsupported (no NSS influence or input)	COTS: products: "use of existing nondefense, commercially viable technologies in defense systems"[a] (with no NSS influence but some NSS adaptation)	(1) COTS (with early NSS development influence)[b] (2) Supported spin-off (via IR&D) (3) Supported spin-on (e.g., early development of integrated circuits via massive government demand driving up quality and driving down costs) (4) Purposeful spin-off/synergistic spin-on: —Promoting commercial applications of defense-originating capabilities for future NSS acquisition (e.g. national labs, DARPA. ONR) —Funding activities in the commercial sector to influence their development into capabilities that jointly meet needs of both sectors. (e.g. In-Q-Tel, SBIR, DARPA) —Co-funding joint S&T and product development to meet security and civilian needs (e.g. ASCI; CRADAs; TRP; technology consortia: nano, semiconductors, batteries, robotics)

Source: Author's own typology. See also White 1996.
   [a] Brandt 1994, 360.
   [b] "Notable examples of technology transitions to industry that resulted in products now purchased routinely by the Services and defense Agencies from the commercial sector" include computing technologies such as RISC microprocessors, and parallel processing and networking technologies such as packet switching and ATM systems (DARPA 1998, 41).

aggregate the needs of "the key players who could change an industry's direction," in this case the commercial users themselves.[33] Army sponsorship and seed funding established the Hybrid Truck Users Forum (HTUF) which brings together three different groups: major truck manufacturers such as Kenworth, existing military vehicle producers like Navistar and Freightliner, and fleet users such as UPS, FedEx, and Coca-Cola. The explicit goal was to catalyze the development and commercialization of hybrid technologies in heavier vehicles in classic dual-use mode—whereby the commercial producers were interested in creating new markets, and the commercial and military fleet users were looking to drive down energy costs and establish a reliable source of supply. Like the ASCI project, the program depends for its success on direct participation on the part of producers and users as they evaluate performance and build experience with newly developed versions of the hybrid vehicles.

The Users Forum coordinates user and producer interests through specialized working groups in which truck makers collaborate with committed users to develop "key performance requirements" (a concept adopted from the military). These requirements then serve as the basis of pilot deployments and preproduction manufacturing. The working groups also include military users whose emerging requirements can be taken into account in the design process. HTUF funds these activities with support from the Army's TARDEC and NAC as well as other NSS partners. Major industry gatherings and annual national conferences are held to create national momentum for the project.

In contrast to industry, which had abandoned earlier efforts, the Army retained a strong interest in exploring new technologies that would reduce fuel use: even before the Iraq invasion, the Army had been making key investments in hybrid technology and prototypes. But it was the Army's strong interest in making hybrid vehicles a core part of its future fleet that proved critical in convincing fleet users, and some manufacturers, "to reconsider hybrids." As senior vice president of CALSTART, Bill Van Amburg, observed, the military's involvement gave fleet users the confidence to participate in a process around hybrid vehicle commercialization. However, because of the high costs involved for units in small volumes, neither manufacturers nor fleet users were willing to take the first step and commit to preproduction vehicles. To reduce that risk, HTUF and the Army's National Automotive Center provided support funding of $1 million toward the cost of producing twenty-four test vehicles, while manufacturers and fleet users each contributed a total of $2.5 million to the pilot effort (Van Amburg n.d, 3).

As a model of commercialization, the key to the hybrid trucks initiative is market pull—but in this case, the pull of commercial fleet users. HTUF targeted dual-use applications, then aggregated demand by organizing first-mover fleets to collaborate with truck makers in defining common performance requirements. With a modest amount of funding on the part of the

Army, the HTUF has been able to steadily grow the market for hybrid vehicles without being attached to an explicit military procurement program.[34] Instead, it coordinates interested commercial parties, helping them to help each other in accelerating development and diffusion of the new technologies, thereby effectively creating a new industry sector while providing a test bed for the military and a commercial source of supply. As the military saw it, a commercial fleet could provide a critical demonstration project for the technology and allow for its continuous improvement and maturation. Within a decade, a base of commercial manufacturers and users had been established and costs reduced, so that the Army could begin trialing its first hybrid vehicles.[35]

As CALSTART's vice president explains, the core of the partnership is really the end stage of this multitiered strategy: "to allow the military to tap the industrial capabilities of the commercial industry" so that it can cost-effectively support military needs for advanced hybrids in combat and other rigorous applications. "The ultimate benefit of these efforts is a self-sustaining commercial capability, able to support commercial and military needs" (Van Amburg n.d., 8). It is assumed that large-scale adoption (procurement and conversion) will take place between 2016 and 2020 as the Army's nontactical fleet is replaced. A large proportion of the vehicles to be purchased will be supported by renewable power generation to charge the energy storage systems. The plan is to spend a total incremental amount of $150 million per year for fifteen years for this acquisition, amounting to more than $4.5 billion.[36]

The HTUF model is now being extended to other sectors. As a result of its perceived effectiveness, the commercial-military partnership has recently initiated a new Users Forum, this time for commercial construction equipment. Its mission is to foster advanced technology development in the heavy construction equipment sector (such as loaders, excavators, and bulldozers), using a similar approach to that involved in growing the market for hybrid trucks.

Advancing the Technological Frontier through Novel Military-Commercial Partnerships: Internet Routing in Space

The activities of the NSS in technology procurement now extend all the way to providing incentives to commercial companies to invent wholly new industries or applications for existing industries—in cases where this can serve an agency mission and where the commercial companies would be quite unable to develop the application or innovation on their own. A striking recent case—Internet Routing in Space (IRIS)—involves an unconventional partnership between the military and U.S. commercial firms, which has brought forth a new generation of internet and telecommunications satellite services.

The IRIS initiative represents the ability to merge ground and space communications infrastructure with internet protocol. It took shape in 2006 when the U.S. Strategic Command set industry the challenge to demonstrate internet protocol routing in space—within a three-year time frame. The procurement mechanism for the partnership was a Joint Capabilities Technology Demonstration (JCTD) project. JCTDs allow the military to try out a maturing technology with the aim of fast transition into service. For this reason JCTDs typically run no longer than three years and involve a relatively small outlay of $2–3 million per year. The IRIS JCTD was initiated in 2007. Under the agreement, industry would build, launch, and operate a space-based, radiation-hardened internet router, and the military would evaluate its capabilities in rigorous real-life scenarios. If successful, DoD would have the option to buy the commercial capability.

For the military, the stimulus for the JCTD-IRIS initiative comes from the increased congestion in earth-based internet connections and the possibility of leaping ahead to spaced-based systems where signals are transformed through a processing engine mounted on a satellite. In place of merely relaying the signal from one ground station to another via satellite connection (known as "bent-pipe" transmission) the IRIS concept puts the processor on board the satellite so that cross-network linkages are as easy to effect as center-to-periphery links, and time delays and other bottlenecks are almost eliminated, making real-time applications feasible. And the military was keen to develop an internet-based system of communication that would be flexible (allowing moving ships to communicate with each other, for example) and data-heavy (enabling roving tactical units access to criminal and immigration databases while at sea, for example). The JCTD-IRIS partnership is instructive in three ways.

Breaking innovation barriers: Mitigating risk. First, in spite of preexisting commercial capability and business interest, it took government involvement to mitigate the risk for commercial stakeholders and help bring the concept to fruition. Cisco, the dominant company producing routers for the terrestrial internet, was keen to develop a commercial version of IRIS, but was reluctant to engage in the private R&D that would normally be needed to underpin any technical advance of the magnitude of taking the internet into space. The third stakeholder, Intelsat, as the world's leading satellite service provider, was interested in a new kind of business for satellites that went beyond mainstream television broadcasting. Nevertheless, because the space sector is highly conservative, profitable, and capital-intensive, neither party was prepared to take the leap into the unknown. An alternative story is that big companies have become increasingly—and are now chronically—risk-averse because of the force of the "shareholder value" regime under which large corporations devote ever smaller sums to R&D of any kind (chapter 8).

Mitigating industry risk was where the military's involvement made the difference. It did so in two respects: by enabling rigorous demonstration of technical feasibility in real-world scenarios on land and at sea, and by providing a potentially high-volume customer for the critical launch market. Rather than using the commercial sector as a demonstration site for the military, as in the case of hybrid truck technology, IRIS relies on the demanding needs of the military as a proving ground for commercial viability. The IRIS satellite was launched in November 2009, with testing conducted in the first months of 2010. Subject to a further twelve months of testing, the DoD has the option of acquiring the IRIS capability for the armed services.

In both senses, the effect of government patronage has been likened to that of "anchor tenant" in a shopping center—whereby the prestige and clout of the first and leading tenant is able to attract other tenants and guarantee the stability of the enterprise. In this way, the JCTD IRIS process has "generated momentum for the commercial offering as well."[37] A recent assessment concurred on this point, noting that whether or not the current IRIS capability is ultimately judged suitable for the needs of the DoD user, "the successful on-orbit demonstration of IRIS represents the beginning of a new generation of commercial communication satellites" (Cuevas et al. 2011, 101).

The Gansler principle. The IRIS JCTD initiative is also an important example of the Gansler principle—"dynamic and vigorous engagement that, through R&D, creates advanced products and systems with common technological bases." The IRIS project illustrates the process whereby a military procurement mechanism to obtain commercially advanced technology requires NSS components to take an active role in the development process. IRIS is about the military acquiring commercially advanced general-purpose technology that is built upon several years of prior collaborative effort with industry. Following a chance encounter between a general at the DoD's Strategic Command and a group at Cisco, a small demonstration of the feasibility of taking internet routing into space was mounted at low cost. This 2003 demonstration was termed CLEO, for Cisco Router in Low Earth Orbit. It was then scaled up to a JCTD—the military's "stress testing" of a new technology—conducted in conjunction with commercial partners Cisco (for the internet router) and Intelsat (for the satellite hosting). In typical dual-use mode, this particular JCTD project departed from the normal procurement process whereby a specific product or service is developed for the DoD at a contracted price, and instead operated in what has been described as "collaborative concept exploration."[38] The DoD was an active participant in the development process: the project gave the government "an opportunity to influence the path and priorities of [commercial] technology innovation . . . to suit its needs."

Modest outlay, major breakthrough. Third, for a small investment, the JCTD procurement mechanism has brought forth a radical innovation.[39] For a modest outlay, the military and industry were able to come together and develop a payload that was hosted on a neutral satellite. The Cisco Space Router was launched in November 2009 on board Intelsat 14, a satellite built by Space Systems/Loral, in what is called "hosted payload" mode—meaning that the payload is shared with other parties. Some critics nevertheless fear that the proliferation of these shorter-term projects will displace the transformative advances that require long-term investment and thus threaten the DoD technology enterprise (chapter 8). In spite of these broader concerns, a recent assessment concluded that IRIS "represents the beginning of a new generation of commercial communication satellites" (Cuevas et al. 2011, 101). Having demonstrated the power of putting the internet into space, Cisco is now actively developing IRIS as a commercial product. According to at least one industry leader, "IRIS is to the future of satellite-based communications what ARPANET was to the creation of the Internet in the 1960s."[40]

Innovation Inducement Prizes: NASA, DARPA, DoE

A relatively new form of driving innovation in order to procure new technology shifts most of the up-front costs onto the private sector by running prize competitions that target tough problems and yield innovations intended to serve security and civilian markets. Although competitive prizes have a long history, their revival by the federal government is relatively recent. Under the America COMPETES Act (2007) federal agencies publish a challenge or problem they would like solved, then open a competition to individuals or teams. The program is meant to spur innovation, stimulate private-sector investment, and attract broad participation. Advocates claim that offering prizes has several advantages over traditional methods of inducing innovation. Sponsors get to see a variety of approaches to a problem, they pay less for an innovation by rewarding only those responses that are acceptable, and competitions accelerate the R&D process.[41]

The core aim of the competitions, recently run by DARPA, NASA, and the DoE, is to catalyze innovations that can meet mission needs without having to bear all the costs of development and possible failure—"paying only for what you get," as an OMB report put it, or rewarding only acceptable outcomes. Teams must be led by U.S. citizens, competitors must fund their own R&D, and the sponsoring agency pays out prize money only if there is a winning technology product. Prize money may be sourced internally (DARPA's Grand Challenge) or privately, as in the case of NASA's Centennial Challenge.

In the case of the defense agencies (specifically DARPA and the Army), provision for industry development is an integral component in evaluating the success of the competitions, while for NASA developing a commercial space industry has been one of the explicit goals. The incentives are generous enough to invite competitive innovation. DoD can offer up to $10 million in prize money per year. DARPA's three Grand Challenges since 2004 offered between $10 million and $20 million in prize money and required teams to build an unmanned vehicle capable of driving in traffic and performing complex maneuvers in difficult terrain over several hundred miles. In its report to Congress, the DARPA Prize Authority stated that the competition was essentially a "software race" and that its impact would be immediate and long-term across a broad array of technologies, leading to rapid advances in the areas of sensors, navigation, control algorithms, hardware systems, and systems integration. According to DARPA officials the competition "stimulated interest and excitement in a problem area important to DoD, broadened the technology base, and strengthened U.S. capability to develop autonomous ground vehicle technologies" (Defense Advanced Projects Agency 2006, 13). In financial terms, DARPA estimates that its "investment" of less than $20 million, returned almost sevenfold.

Other NSS prize contests include NASA'S Green Flight Challenge and DoE's Energy challenges. While the DoE is fostering the H-Prize in an endeavor to spur innovation in hydrogen fuel–related technology, NASA's 2011 Green Flight Challenge has already produced the first emission-free electric aircraft. The outcome has been hailed as a historic breakthrough in aviation which is likely to spur the growth of an electric aircraft industry. According to NASA's chief technologist, numerous companies have for years been quietly working away on electric and hybrid-powered aircraft, but it has taken the contest to move electric aircraft from the realm of science fiction to a new age of electric flight.[42]

It would be easy to dismiss such contests either as half-hearted efforts by governments to do innovation on the cheap or as what you do when you don't have in-house developmental capacity. But this would miss an essential formative effect of the technology challenge approach. As the DARPA director Tony Tether explained, the competitions play a critical role in breaking through the ideational barriers that often define what is and is not technically feasible: "Our job is to take the technical excuse off the table, so people can no longer say it can't be done."[43] In its report to Congress, DARPA endorsed the view of *Scientific American*, which pronounced the race "a resounding success" because it "has concentrated the minds of researchers, blown open the technological envelope and trained a whole generation of roboticists" (DARPA 2006, 13). By the end of the final autonomous ground vehicle competition in 2007, DARPA could confidently declare the results to be "truly groundbreaking."[44] If this is so, many technological breakthroughs, if not new industries, are likely to be advanced by this and similar ventures.[45] As a way of driving breakthrough innovations in a budget constrained environment, competition prizes seem destined to have a rosy future.

These cases of nontraditional ways of influencing innovation indicate how far the NSS has come in driving technological advances in the U.S. economy—far farther than timid steps entailed by resort to either "serendipity" or strict confinement to traditional contractors behind a wall of separation. The cases provide a window onto a new set of public-private relationships that underpin the NSS technology enterprise. The latter has shifted from being a largely security-centric activity, with both direct and indirect commercial payoffs, to an increasingly commerce-oriented undertaking—one that builds commercial considerations directly and explicitly into its development criteria. Innovation for the NSS is thus no longer an undertaking separate and apart from the commercial interests of the mainstream economy (if indeed it ever was). The variety of approaches examined here breaches the commerce-security divide by building in marketability right from the start of the technology development process and, in some instances, by shifting some of the costs onto or sharing the risks with the private sector. By reorienting the national security state, federal authorities have thereby made the relationship between mission achievement and commercial success purposefully symbiotic rather than accidental, occasional, or indirect.

We need not restrict this observation to the DoD. The "civilianization" effect evident in military acquisition strategy can be applied more broadly to the NSS technology enterprise. As we have seen, it is the outcome of several decades of efforts undertaken not just to counter the rising costs of weaponry, or to cope with the consequences of a smaller government market, but also to take advantage of commercial capabilities—and thereby strengthen those capabilities before they were lost to a strong competitor. As the federal market contracted relative to commercial sales, technology procurement emphasized greater complementarity between defense-related and commercial applications as an inducement to firms to work with the NSS, and thereby regain access and influence over the direction of technological innovation. In contrast to an influential assumption, the ability to influence commercial technology is not neatly reflected in the sum of defense spending on R&D or even the size of the government market. Although private R&D spending has indeed come to dwarf federal R&D outlays, the capacity of the U.S. government to influence commercial innovation, as the case studies demonstrate, has not thereby been curtailed.

Whereas the standard account suggests that the military adopts a dual-use approach because it now wields less influence over technology development than formerly,[46] I have argued that the military (more broadly, the NSS) deploys dual-use and other commercially viable strategies in order to reestablish its technological influence: the relative decline of the NSS procurement market and the technological advancement of the private sector have helped to change the way the NSS sources and develops technology—but not to curtail its commercial influence. Rather than the NSS being detached from commercial considerations, it now has extensive interest in serving security needs not only by acquiring, but above all by investing in and developing commercially viable innovations in partnership with the private sector. Rather than weakening the NSS as an S&T enterprise, the structural changes in question have instead strengthened the basis for military/security-civilian integration—as well as its practice. The result is more direct involvement of the NSS in how the commercial technology base develops, more public-private entwinement, and more spin-around of technology.

The larger question is whether this transformation has narrowed the scope for breakthrough general-purpose innovations. Has U.S. technological supremacy perhaps reached an impasse? In view of the changes examined here as well as the civilianization of the NSS, the question arises as to whether it can remain a source of revolutionary innovations into the future.

6

No More Breakthroughs?

The Owl of Minerva spreads its wings only with the falling of dusk.
G. W. F. Hegel, 1820

Like the Owl of Minerva, we usually recognize the moment of a historical shift or significant change only with hindsight—once it is fully under way. This chapter probes the basis for the claim that the United States can no longer look to the NSS for the high-tech innovations that have served its economic growth so well.

Some analysts have raised the concern that with the end of the Cold War and the focus on shorter-term asymmetric threats, the impetus for defense innovation may now lack the strength and sense of purpose needed to launch new breakthrough technologies in either the public or the private domain.[1] Vernon Ruttan, in particular, after examining how defense and defense-related procurement produced a host of general-purpose technologies that spawned key industries of the postwar period, concluded that the era of revolutionary innovations has very probably come to a close. Future U.S. technology development will instead be characterized by the incremental improvements that produce endless novelty rather than the general-purpose innovations that create new industries.[2] While this has consequences for military supremacy, Ruttan's concern was that the innovation deficit would diminish the capacity for sustained job-creating growth.

Post-9/11 Decline of the NSS Technology Enterprise?

So, are we witnessing the end of an era? Has U.S. technological superiority reached an impasse? Ruttan was led to this conclusion in part because of the weakening of government demand as a pull factor and in part because he perceived a post-9/11 shift away from long-term investments in big science and big technology toward shorter-term objectives designed to meet quick response tactical missions. And for all the well-rehearsed reasons—major technological breakthroughs require decades of support plus enormous sums of patient capital to reach the stage of commercial viability, while the gains are too diffuse for investing firms to capture—the private sector, he contended, would be most unlikely to undertake such innovations on its own (Ruttan 2006b).

General-purpose technologies are of course not the only alternative to endless novelty or incremental improvements.[3] But for those interested in where the NSS technology enterprise may be heading, they constitute a strong test of Ruttan's thesis. Are we witnessing the demise of the national security state's S&T enterprise and, with it, of the source of transformative innovations? Although one cannot avoid some element of speculation in reaching a conclusion, one can at least address the issue by asking a different question: Are there any areas or projects in which current NSS developmental investment and procurement offer potential for major breakthroughs?

At the outset, it should be noted that in the first decade of the twenty-first century, the NSS has been far from indolent in seeking to procure the kind of technologies that would meet Ruttan's concerns for the emergence of new growth sectors. Indeed, transformative innovations are the current focus of coordinated, well-focused investment and procurement initiatives in robotics, nanotechnology, renewable energy, as well as synthetic biology (biotechnology, life sciences), new materials, strategic computing, and new-generation semiconductors, to name some of the major growth sectors of the future.

In spite of these initiatives, the absence of quick payoffs does make us more like the Owl of Minerva, tending to develop understanding only with hindsight while overlooking or dismissing such efforts in the present. As we know from earlier patterns, however, the time lag between big technological breakthroughs and new sector growth can be anywhere between fifteen and twenty-five years—a factor that has confounded many studies seeking to measure the impact of defense R&D on economic performance. Instead I shall make a case for the continuing relevance of the national security innovation engine by examining three NSS-sponsored initiatives, in the fields of nanotechnology, robotics, and renewable energy. All three represent general-purpose technologies that are poised to serve strategic goals while also being capable of delivering transformative innovations to the commercial arena. Some of these initiatives have already begun to bear fruit in the commercial arena, although the most important anticipated developments are still to come. In some cases, commercial applications and innovations will be spurred by the volume of government demand as tended to occur in the past, but many more will emerge from "intended spin-offs" based on joint development projects, as discussed in the previous chapter.

Nanotechnology: A Coordinated Effort

Nanotechnology is the science and engineering of assembling materials and components at the atomic or molecular level to create large structures with fundamentally new properties. It is perceived as a transformative technology that will spark major advances in industries such as electronics, energy, environmental products, materials, medical, pharmaceuticals, sensors, manufacturing, and defense. Intertwined with parallel breakthroughs in the life sciences, computing, and industrial techniques, nanoscale developments pave the way for creating entirely new classes of products that exploit extreme miniaturization or yield extraordinary new properties. Although estimates vary significantly, one optimistic calculation suggests that global revenues from nanotechnology-enhanced products, estimated at $50 billion in 2006, are likely to reach around $3 trillion by 2015.[4] Most such products today offer only incremental improvements (in performance, cost, and weight), however the consensus within industry, government and the scientific community is that "nanotechnology is likely to have a significant economic impact and transformative effect on many industries" (Congressional Research Service 2011a, 3).

Perceiving its importance, the NSS (the Army in particular)[5] has made nanotechnology a national priority and a target of technology procurement for at least a decade, as evident from funding sources indicated in table 6.1 below. Three aspects of federal policy highlight the proactive nature of that effort. First, nanotechnology is the subject of a nationally coordinated initiative to bring research to the stage of commercial readiness; second, that initiative has directed increasing levels of federal investment to targeted priority areas; third, it has maintained that commitment in spite of a climate of federal budget constraints.

Coordinated and focused. In 2000 the United States launched the world's first national nanotechnology program, known as the National Nanotechnology Initiative. Broadly conceived, the task of the NNI is to "expedite the discovery, development, and deployment of nanotechnology in order to achieve responsible and sustainable economic benefits, to enhance the quality of life, and to promote national security."[6] Following a pattern established in other areas of interagency coordination (such as information technology), the NNI gathered together the preexisting nanoscale initiatives of key NSS agencies that had already begun their own coordinating efforts. Thus, although implemented as a presidential initiative of the Clinton administration, the NNI built on agency-level investments in nanoscale science, engineering, and technology development that had been under way for at least a decade.[7] By 2010, the original participants—NSF, DoD, DoE, NASA, NIST, and NIH—had increased to twenty-five agencies (of which around half conduct and/or fund nano projects).[8] However, it is the original six entities that account for more than 96 percent of the NNI's funding (Congressional Research Service 2011a, 9).

Large hopes are being entertained for nano, no less than "a revolution in information technology hardware rivaling the microelectronics revolution begun about 30 years ago."[9] Some believe that if microelectronics is to continue to achieve Moore's law improvements, this will come from breakthroughs in nanotechnology (Howell 2003, 51).[10] In addition to next-generation electronics, major nanotech breakthroughs are anticipated in renewable energy (solar energy collection and conversion) and sustainable nanomanufacturing (targeting scaling of carbon-based and cellulosic nanomaterials and optical metamaterials). Accordingly, the Office of Science and Technology Policy and the NNI member agencies have identified all three as priority areas. These so-called "signature initiatives" are conceived as part of "a new model of specifically targeted and closely coordinated interagency, cross-sector collaboration designed to accelerate innovation in areas of national priority" (Teague 2011, 3). For each signature initiative an interagency group—in collaboration with industry and other stakeholders—selects major research and development targets linked to near- and long-term expected outcomes, which allow for the monitoring of progress. The initial groundwork for the NNI itself similarly involved input from the private sector and research community (National Research Council 2002b, 11).

Funding. To this picture of a coordinated and focused investment initiative, we can add steadily increasing funding levels that have mostly withstood major constraints on the federal budget. From a 2001 base of almost $500 million invested by ten federal agencies, the NNI investment grew to a cumulative total of $14 billion by 2010.[11] Of the federal agencies actively sponsoring technology development over this period, three NSS agencies, NSF, DoD, and DoE, were allocated the largest block of federal money, with some 70 percent of the total funding directed toward university-based research in nanoscale science, engineering, and technology development. In spite of the severe fiscal circumstances, the Obama administration's 2012 budget provided for a further $2.1 billion for the NNI, an increase of $217 million over the 2010 funding level. U.S. companies and state governments have also invested billions. As a result of this sustained commitment, the United States has emerged as the global leader in nanotechnology, accounting for about one-quarter of global annual public investments.

Partnership pattern. Although conceived and initiated by the federal government in collaboration with NSS components, the National Initiative follows a time-tested partnership pattern. This entails multiple partnerships that mobilize the resources of industry, academe, and government in dedicated research and engineering centers and industrial consortia, in this case focused on accelerating the commercialization of NNI developments. Two such endeavors are the U.S. Army's $50 million MIT-based Institute for Soldier Nanotechnologies and the Nanoelectronics Research Initiative. The ISN is the collaborative umbrella for some 150 scientists, engineers and medical specialists from MIT, the Army, other S&T units within DoD, and companies with core competency in the field such as Dupont and Raytheon. For the Army, ISN will use nanotechnology to develop items that enhance protection and survival of the soldier, such as a uniform that is nearly invisible, soft clothing that can become a rigid cast when a soldier breaks a limb, and paper-light chain mail made of molecular materials. Turning laboratory innovations into scalable, affordable products is the challenge that falls to industry as the second ISN partner. Innovations arising from the collaboration are of course expected to serve both military and commercial markets, hence the requirement of financial co-investment as a basis for company participation in the ISN Industry Consortium.[12]

The Nanoelectronics Research Initiative also provides another classic instance of what I have called governed interdependence, rewarding industry in exchange for meeting performance standards. The initiative builds in commercialization potential by assuring industry of seamless transition of lab results from universities to NRI member companies and then, through competitive emulation, to broader industry sectors. Other benefits offered to consortium participants include the opportunity "for licensing ISN inventions"; the chance "to participate in research planning and to commission ISN research . . . of particular relevance to the industry sponsor"; "early access to technology commercialization opportunities"; and access to competitive peer reviewed Army funding for accelerating commercialization.[13] At the same time, the NRI insists on cost-sharing arrangements. The requirement that industry has "skin in the game" acts as a performance standard by ensuring a company's constant input, feedback, and close involvement in the outcome of a project.[14]

What results? As its implementation shows, the NNI was never intended as a purely research-centered initiative. After an early focus on nanoscale research and engineering, NNI investment shifted to applications, manufacturing, and commercialization.[15] A recent report on the state of nanotechnology observes that as understanding of the technology has matured, "the NNI has worked with a variety of industry organizations to facilitate the movement of research results from the laboratory bench to the marketplace in fields as disparate as semiconductors, chemicals, energy, concrete, and forest products" (Congressional Research Service 2011a, 15). As a result, by 2005, major U.S. corporations (including Intel, Motorola, Lucent, Hewlett Packard, and General Motors) had achieved substantial progress with several nanomanufactured products and had begun turning their attention toward overcoming obstacles to efficient mass production. Here too, the Obama administration has instituted an Advanced Manufacturing Partnership that is investing more than $500 million to help companies turn nano innovations into scaled-up products. At least three-fifths of the investment is for domestic manufacturing in critical national security industries with dual-use applications such as high-efficiency batteries and advanced composites.[16]

While the larger transformative impact of these and other developments is still some way off,[17] there is some evidence that federal nanotech investment and procurement initiatives are beginning to bear fruit in the form of new companies formed and significant breakthroughs achieved. Regarding new enterprise formation, numerous company spin-outs from earlier NSS-sponsored initiatives, and from later NNI-generated projects, have begun to commercialize advanced applications in a broad range of sectors, including electronics, medicine and medical diagnostics, energy, manufacturing, and new materials. A selection of such firms and their federal funding sources are indicated in table 6.1.

TABLE 6.1
Selected NSS-sponsored nano company spin-outs (life sciences, biodefense, medical care, energy, electronics)

Company[a]	Development contracts/ funding sources[b]	Products/applications
Cepheid (1996) Livermore license	NIH, DARPA SBIR: 7+ Army: 3+	Biodefense, life sciences research, clinical markets
Nanocomp Technologies (2004) Spun out of SBIR-backed Synergy Innovations	Army, Navy, USAF SBIR: 5.5+	Energy-saving materials, critical components
Nanosonic (1998) Virginia Tech (2011 winner "R&D 100")	Navy, Army DARPA, OSD, MDA, NIH, NASA, DoE, NSF SBIR: 60+	New materials
Nanosphere (2000) Northwestern University	Army, NIH, NSF SBIR: 3+ U.S. Government Technical Support Working Group: 5–6 (2003)	Medical diagnostics, biothreat detection, patient care, public safety
Nanosys (2001) Harvard University	DARPA, NIH, NSF, NASA, NASA, DoE SBIR: 5	Sensors for biodefense and medical services
NanoBio (2000) Michigan University	NIH, DoD: 10.2 SBIR: .6 DARPA: 11.8	Antimicrobial protection against biological agents and common infections
NanoScale Materials (1955) Kansas State University	U.S. Army Research Office contract, USAF, Army, NSF, DARPA, OSD, DoE, NASA SBIR: 13	Specialty chemicals for government, energy, pharmaceuticals, environment
Institute for Soldier Nanotechnology (2002) MIT (numerous company spin-outs)	U.S. Army sponsorship and industry co-funding	Nanomaterials, sensors

Sources: Individual company profiles compiled from company websites; SBIR database at www. inknowvation.com.
    [a] (Year founded), origin.
    [b] Millions of dollars, estimate.

To emphasize a familiar motif, in a majority of cases, the nanotech companies identified in the small sample in table 6.1 were formed by licensing an NSS-sponsored innovation. The company concerned then sought to refine and commercialize that innovation by drawing on SBIR funds or other NSS-based sponsorship. Consider the medical diagnostics company Nanosphere as a typical example. At a Congressional hearing, the company's CEO, William Moffitt, remarked with considerable candor that "Simply stated, without the National Nanotechnology Initiative, Nanosphere might not exist." As he went on to note, Nanosphere is "a product of university-based research" funded by the Army, NSF, NIH, and DARPA, among others. Further, since its formation the company had received about $5–6 million in government funding, which had been "leveraged to an additional $200 million in private and public equity financing, a 40 to 1 investment ratio." In short, he concluded, early federal funding played a "critical" role in securing "the long-term future and success of Nanosphere and the realization of significant advances in medical diagnostics" (Moffitt 2011).

Although the era of transformative innovation in nanotechnology is not imminent, recent breakthroughs at IBM would suggest that it is not obviously in the far distant future either.[18] The IBM achievement must be placed within its larger NSS context since it is a significant milestone for the DARPA-funded Carbon Electronics for RF Applications program.

Robotics: The Drive for Drones

Robotics, which has been designated by the Obama administration as a national priority with the formation of the National Robotics Initiative, is another general-purpose technology that has recently reached a tipping point of intense growth and is expected to generate new industries.[19] Development of the technology, which has multiple components and applications, is being driven by military demand in a focused effort to reduce pilot and soldier injury and mortality in battle, and expand capabilities through unmanned aerial vehicles (UAVs or drones). It is well known that the United States lags Europe and Japan in industrial robotics and the substantial manufacturing base that it requires. In a familiar American twist, however, unprecedented military demand for unmanned ground and aerial vehicles may soon change that commercial story. Current advances emerging from military interests indicate the potential to catalyze the growth of entire new industries serving civilian uses that range from crop dusting and environmental monitoring to health care and advanced manufacturing.[20]

Much of this effort is very recent. A major stimulus for the growth of a robotics industry has been the mandate, issued in 2001 under the National Defense Authorization Act, that one-third of operational ground combat vehicles be unmanned by 2015. Another stimulus comes from the U.S. Air

Force's heavy demand for unmanned aerial vehicles. Only ten years ago, the Pentagon had fewer than fifty UAVs; now it has at least seven thousand, effecting a revolutionary transformation in U.S. military operations by minimizing physical risk to troops on the ground.[21] In spite of cuts to the defense budget, USAF's technology procurement budget has not shrunk. Instead, it is mostly directed toward the creation and acquisition of high volumes of the less costly UAVs. These drones, ranging in size from large blimps to tiny hummingbirds, make up the largest procurement market in the current decade, following the USAF request to Congress for nearly $5 billion to support new drone programs in the 2012 budget. P. W. Singer, an authority on twenty-first warfare, notes that "the U.S. Air Force now trains more unmanned-systems operators than fighter and bomber pilots combined" (Singer 2011, 3). In addition to these aerial systems, the military now counts some twelve thousand unmanned ground vehicles in its inventory.

Military demand has also pushed the state of the art into new territory, for example, by combining robotics with innovations in solar energy conversion and energy storage technology. Presently under development are new generations of unmanned aircraft that will incorporate new energy sources, solar cells and fuel cells, destined for both military and commercial markets. Boeing, for instance, is under contract with DARPA to produce the SolarEagle unmanned aircraft that can stay aloft for exceedingly long periods, at very high altitudes, using solar power. The prototype is expected to fly in 2014. The full-scale version is designed to allow the kind of long-term surveillance that was previously the domain of satellites. Solar cells rather than batteries will store energy for twenty-four-hour use—a breakthrough achieved by the DARPA-funded VHESC (Very High Efficiency Solar Cell) consortium, a Dupont-Delaware University partnership, as part of an effort to raise the power efficiency of a new class of solar modules and deliver prototypes for ready manufacturing. Anticipated dual uses for the solar-powered UAV include surveillance, earth observation, and communications relay for both military and civilian purposes.[22]

As in the case of nanotechnology, so too in robotics, federal agencies are collaborating to coordinate their technology development projects. As part of a new SBIR initiative that encourages agencies to centralize technological efforts addressing areas of national priority, five federal agencies (DoD, DHS, NIH, NSF, and USDA) have recently issued a joint solicitation for topics in the area of robotics technology development and deployment.

Once again, public-private partnerships (technology clusters and consortia) are the preferred mechanisms for exploiting military and industrial advances in robotics. The Automotive-Robotics Cluster, for instance, fuses the commercial and production know-how of automotive companies with military robotics R&D initiatives in a two-way process designed to improve military products and transition these to the private sector.[23] Other DoD-led robotics clusters with different industry partners operate across the country.

In most such cases, firms participate in DoD research planning and benefit from accelerated transitioning of breakthroughs to commercial technologies.[24] In all cases, the broad approach is one that focuses on dual-use technologies, those developed originally for military purposes, which are commercially viable enough to support adaptation and production for industrial or consumer uses.

In contrast to the slower progress of nanotechnology, robotics is evolving at a fast pace on the back of public-private efforts. Of the fifteen finalists in DARPA's 2004 Grand Challenge, aimed at accelerating the development of robotic vehicles, none were able to complete the off-road course. One year later, five teams finished the race. The National Center for Manufacturing Sciences claims that the United States now has "the largest installed base of unmanned military systems," as well as "highly innovative roboticists" in academe and industry, and America's "first successful commercial robot companies."[25]

Following a typical pattern such as that of Genentech in biotechnology, the formation and growth of America's first major commercial robot producer, iRobot Corporation, has been intricately enmeshed with the projects of the national security state. As a university startup spun out of NSS-sponsored developments at MIT and expertise gained at NASA's Jet Propulsion Lab, iRobot is seen as the bellwether company for the emerging robot economy. According to its chairman and co-founder Helen Greiner, "iRobot is currently the leader in the mobile robotics field, an emerging high growth industry," which is "aggressively pursuing both the consumer and the military market."[26] Greiner grew the company initially by gaining military contracts, taking the business from a standing start in 1990 to participating in the massively funded Army procurement program for Future Combat Systems, which ran from 2003 to 2009. iRobot produces the famous military robot, the PackBot, a small tank-like unit that scopes out areas too dangerous for soldiers. It is also the maker of the world's first mass-produced consumer vacuum cleaner robot, the Roomba, which has sold more than six million units around the world. iRobot's co-founder has now launched a new startup, Heartland Robotics, which will develop next-generation robots for use in manufacturing. As a recipient of the SBIR Hall of Fame award in 2011, iRobot's CEO, Colin Angle, was quick to acknowledge the critical role of NSS venture backing for its innovation projects since 1996: "I can say with absolute certainty that without the help of the SBIR program, iRobot could not have become the industry leader we are today."[27]

Such cases suggest that in addition to saving the lives of military personnel, the robotics revolution is likely to impact more broadly in the commercial arena. In this regard, consider that Congress recently passed legislation that compels the Federal Aviation Administration to allow wider domestic use of unmanned aerial systems. These uses include many kinds of commercial endeavor, from crop dusting and selling real estate to monitoring oil spills and shooting films.[28]

It is of course my stated purpose in this context to appraise the Ruttan thesis and thus point to the "grand possibilities" that these developments in robotics open up for U.S. industry—and not least for the U.S. military. However, it is one thing to note how the NSS demand for UAVs has been pushing the state of the art and paving the way for new commercial ventures—the larger analytical purpose of my study. It is quite another to consider how, in typical two-edged fashion, the current use of that technology may ultimately be a self-weakening move. On this point, it would be unwise to ignore what P. W. Singer refers to as the great perils that are likely to accompany the widespread application of unmanned aerial vehicles, ranging from deeper public intrusions into domestic private space (through aerial surveillance systems), to making wars so much easier to start, and ultimately to what Chalmers Johnson famously called "blowback" by bringing war to one's doorstep.[29]

Clean Energy: From Laggard to Leader?

The United States once led the field in alternative energy innovations, but it has long dragged its feet as producer and user of those innovations. Although U.S. presidents have been calling for energy independence since the 1970s, the ability of fossil-fuel interests to dominate the energy policy agenda has meant that the United States now lags behind a number of European and Asian countries in the clean energy domain.[30]

All this, however, seems set to change now that the military has stepped into the picture and made renewable energy a national security priority. It is today commonplace to see headlines announcing a proactive energy strategy within the U.S. military: "DOD's Green Efforts to Reduce Combat Risks," "Defense-Energy Team Leads National Effort," "Department Makes Energy High Priority," "Biofuels Market to Cut Foreign Oil Dependence," "Army Embraces Solar Power," "Navy Solar Farm Construction Underway"—these and numerous other similar announcements on the DoD website give a flavor of the new energy activism now embraced by the U.S. military and its kindred agency, the DoE.

For a variety of strategic considerations that go to the heart of the military enterprise—such as assuring supply, eliminating vulnerability to attacks on refueling convoys and infrastructure, and maximizing operational preparedness in a budget-squeezing climate—the NSS is paving the way for a new energy paradigm. Thus, former Defense Secretary Robert Gates recently designated energy sources as one of the Department's Top 25 Transformational Priorities; the 2010 *Quadrennial Defense Review* addressed energy for the first time as a strategic issue; the military departments have established leaders and task forces to oversee all energy efforts;[31] and the DoD—mostly in partnership with startup firms, industry-university consortia, and other federal agencies—has invested in some five hundred projects in all energy-related fields. Some of this activity is mandated by legislation, but a good deal of the military effort is being driven by the services themselves, going beyond what the legislation calls for. The Navy, for example, has set itself a target of at least 40 percent of its total energy consumption to come from alternative sources by 2020.[32] Mandated or otherwise, there is an unmistakable policy shift underway that calls for new ways of generating, storing, and distributing power. As Defense partners with other agencies to develop and procure new sources of energy, many clean energy advocates anticipate revolutionary innovations that will create new commercial opportunities and give birth to a host of new industry sectors. The innovations range from solar-powered batteries and fuel cells to microgrids, waste-to-energy conversion devices, and next-generation (nonfood) biofuels—areas in which numerous technology investment and procurement programs are now under way.

The Military-cum-NSS as Energy Paradigm Changer

Although the Department of Energy is the major agency for energy R&D, and ARPA-E its flagship body focused on revolutionary advances, DoE has neither the scale of operations to act as a test bed nor the purchasing power to create products and markets. This is where interagency collaboration matters. Elaborating on the DoE partnership formed with DoD in 2010, Deputy Energy Secretary Daniel Poneman explained that "Through our national laboratory system, the [Energy] department brings tremendous scientific expertise to bear across a whole portfolio of national energy and scientific priorities. . . . Coupled with the scale of the Defense Department's operations and its potential to act as a test bed for innovative technologies, this partnership is a crucial vehicle to strengthen our national security and to build a clean energy economy for America."[33]

Making the market. The combined branches of the Defense Department form the single largest consumer of energy in the world, surpassing the overall consumption of more than one hundred nations. In 2010, the Pentagon consumed roughly 125 million barrels of oil annually and spent some $16 billion on energy to run its installations and conduct its missions ($5 billion and $11 billion respectively). Given the military's concerted shift away from conventional energy sources, federal spending on renewable energy to run military facilities and provide transportation fuel to the services is projected to rise rapidly over the next two decades, growing from less than $1 billion per year in 2010 to $10 billion by 2030.[34] Commercial opportunity appears largest for solar energy and liquid fuels, where much of the NSS investment (from DoD, DoE, and NSF) is concentrated. In the fuel domain, the focus is largely on biofuels (using, for example, advances in synthetic biology) to replace petroleum. Portable power for warfighters is also a top priority, in pursuit of which the DoD in particular is pursuing a variety of fuel cells and advanced battery technologies.[35]

The larger point is that the defense appetite for energy gives the U.S. military significant market- and industry-making capacity through its substantial procurement budget. As a former DARPA director observed, the Defense Department "is in the process of playing a catalytic role with renewable energy. . . . They won't be the biggest, most important market over time. But for the newest technologies, those first few percentage points of market share are tremendously important."[36] The ultimate technical challenge for the emerging energy innovations is to achieve economies of scale through a learning curve that will enable price parity with conventional energy. But the major challenge, discussed below, comes in the form of political opposition from Congressional Republicans who are hostile to nonconventional energy initiatives.

Track record. As well as market power, the U.S. military has acquired a track record in moving to new energy sources. The Navy, for instance, navigated the shift from sail to coal in the 1850s, and from coal to oil in the early twentieth century, prior to pioneering the transportation use of nuclear power in the 1950s. Navy Secretary Ray Mabus, known as the Green Hawk for having made ambitious renewable energy goals the keystone of his tenure, has regularly drawn attention to the Navy's historical record in leading the way in energy innovation. Mabus says, "And now, we're changing it again. And every single time, from the 1850s to today, you've got nay sayers, they say you're trading one form of energy that you know about, that's predictable, that's affordable for another that's not and you just shouldn't do it. And every single time, they've been wrong and I'm absolutely confident they're going to be wrong again."[37] Regardless of one's views on nuclear power, the Navy's experience in transforming the plant of a nuclear reactor to a size small enough to fit inside a ship from one that once filled the area of a city block, all within five short years, would seem to offer good grounds for Maybus's rejoinder to the naysayers.[38]

Nonetheless it is not only for technical reasons that critics question the military's ability to effect dramatic energy innovation. Indeed, some analysts claim that such an expectation is fundamentally mistaken, above all because it misunderstands the military approach to innovation and thereby underestimates the central importance of strategic benefit. In other words, unless the technology is critical to national security strategy, advocates are woefully misguided in placing their bets on the military model to promote renewable energy technologies. Thus for example, political scientist and defense analyst Eugene Gholz argues that appeals to "energy independence" and "energy efficiency" won't carry the day because they don't link directly to operational needs. A further challenge is that following the drawdown of troops and personnel in Iraq and Afghanistan, the operational rationale substantially diminishes (Gholz 2011).

The first of these observations carries weight. It is also consistent with one of the core arguments of this book, namely, that strategic issues—security, not competitiveness—are the driving motivation behind the military's commercial involvement. (And therefore, to reiterate, the minority conventional view that the Defense Department drives a "hidden industrial policy" is quite mistaken.) However, Gholz appears to underestimate the strategic intensity and intent of the military turn to clean energy. In short, while there are clearly hurdles ahead for energy innovation, none of them involve a lack of strategic relevance or military commitment. On the contrary, strategic motives seem to be altogether paramount in driving the new energy agenda. Let us see why.

Why the Military Interest?

One reason has to do with costs—in the broadest sense, costs that have strategic implications. The escalating costs of conventional fuel have been measured in terms of dollars spent, lives lost and injuries sustained, and diminished mission effectiveness. In recent operations in Afghanistan for example, it cost one mortality or serious injury for every fifty fuel convoys, up to four hundred dollars a gallon to deliver fuel to the troops, and the loss of one week in four out of combat operations just to manage the convoys.[39] It now takes more than twenty-two gallons of fuel per day to support one soldier on the battlefield, compared with one gallon during World War II. As Deputy Under Secretary of Defense, Installations, and Environment Dorothy Robyn explained in interview,

> What really grabbed peoples' attention were the convoys—the problem with getting fuel to theater. That's driving behavior. The Marines went to Helmand Province in October 2010 carrying solar equipment that folds up into a suitcase and tent shields and solar power communications equipment. They're doing amazing things with respect to expeditionary energy. And on the facilities side, for different reasons, similar things are happening. DoD is a big organization and it will take awhile, but once the policies are in place, it will have a lot of momentum.[40]

But beyond delivery vulnerabilities in any specific war theater, the military's vast energy needs make it extremely vulnerable to price increases. Every $10 increase in the price of a barrel of crude oil costs the DoD $1.3 billion. At the peak of oil and gas price hikes, in 2008, this meant that the Pentagon spent some $20 billion on fuel alone. More telling, whenever the DoD's standard price for a gallon of jet fuel rises by $1, this adds an extra $2.5 billion to its fuel bill.[41] Navy Secretary, Ray Mabus summed up the problem thus:

> We are too dependent on either potentially or actually volatile places on earth to get our energy. Now we're susceptible to supply shocks and even if we've got enough, we're susceptible to price shocks. I mean

when the Libya situation started and the price of oil went up $40 a barrel, that was almost a billion dollars additional fuel bill for the U.S. Navy . . . and the only place we've got to go get that money is operations or training, so our ships steam less, our planes fly less, we train our sailors and Marines less.[42]

But operational costs are not the only motivation for driving energy innovation. Even after the drawdown in Iraq and Afghanistan, there are robust reasons that energy innovation will continue to loom large in defense strategy. One is the increasing risk that instead of opponents attacking, say, U.S. carrier groups, they will take out the fuel infrastructure supporting the fleet. As a result, shoring up this area of vulnerability makes revolutionary energy sources such as solar-powered fuel cells increasingly attractive, since these can be contained within a surface combat vessel without significant external support.[43]

A further, perhaps more urgent, consideration is spelt out in a 2008 Defense Science Board report that calls attention to the fragile, ageing U.S. electric grid on which domestic military installations depend for most of their power. As the DSB task force concluded, the "fragility and vulnerability" of the commercial grid poses a serious risk to military operations should power become interrupted (Defense Science Board 2008, 65). Vulnerability to domestic blackouts and cyber attacks now impinges directly on defense strategy because the military relies more and more on the use of unmanned aerial vehicles and increasingly conducts remote warfare abroad from bases at home. Missions are therefore put at risk by the Pentagon's reliance on the commercial grid. As Dorothy Robyn pointed out to the Readiness Subcommittee of the House Armed Services Committee, "The changing role of the military's installations accentuates this concern. Although in the past fixed installations functioned largely to train and deploy our combat forces, they have an increasingly direct link to combat operations. . . . This means that power failure at a military base here at home could threaten our operations abroad . . ." (Robyn 2010, 44).

In response to the DSB report, energy officers at military bases have set about turning their facilities into "island microgrids" that can generate and store their own electricity independent of the commercial grid. The military is now partnering with industry to develop, test, and commercialize so-called "smart grids." Smart grids are considered the Holy Grail of the new energy revolution since they integrate a broad array of clean energy sources and offer a new decentralized model for energy production that boosts usage of local renewables. The military's interest in the technology has also spurred broader microgrid investments by defense, energy, and engineering firms. As Boeing Energy Vice President Tim Noonan stated on the occasion of his company partnering with engineering firm Siemens to work on military microgrids, "This is a market that's undergoing a transformation right now. . . .

We see DOD leading the way to commercialization. If we can get it right at the Department of Defense, we think we can drive it across and into other commercial markets."[44]

In sum, contrary to the claim that the military model of innovation does not apply to energy, there are cogent—and indeed urgent—strategic reasons for the military to change its energy profile and spur a revolution in clean energy technologies. We hear once again the voice of the Navy secretary driving home the point in a recent speech: "Seeking out some viable energy options isn't a fad. . . . We're doing it because we have to do it to be a more effective fighting force. The reasons are strategic, the reasons are tactical and the reasons are essential to our national security."[45] Acting on precisely those reasons, the Pentagon has launched an aggressive program to convert the oil-hungry military to renewable energy and at the same time spur creation of new industries that can supply the federal and commercial market at affordable prices. Let us briefly examine some of these initiatives.

How Is the NSS Driving Change?

A 2011 report by Pike Research on *Renewable Energy for Military Applications* enumerates the myriad of DoD initiatives that are being pursued to power military bases, vehicles, ships, and aircraft—and in the process are helping to kick-start emerging industries in renewable energy and related technologies.[46] The standout projects cover renewable fuel sources (wind, wave, solar, geothermal, biomass, biofuels, waste-to-energy conversion), as well as photovoltaics, advanced batteries and capacitors for energy storage, fuel cells, microgrids, smart meters, and energy efficiency devices. The military is advancing most of these initiatives in partnership with individual companies (including prime contractors like GE, Boeing, and Honeywell along with numerous nontraditional entrepreneurial companies), as well as industry-university-NSS consortia like the DARPA-funded DuPont-Drexel solar consortium or the various DoE-funded consortia for algal biofuels.

Collaboration with other agencies is also a key part of the mix, since this allows for different agency strengths to be mobilized. The recently created ARPA-E, for example, which was modeled on DARPA, focuses on transformational energy technology, where the risks and potential breakthroughs are greatest (Bonvillian and Van Atta 2011, 489). Under the rubric of promoting the nation's energy security, ARPA-E is tasked with the mission of rapidly developing and commercializing transformational clean energy technologies. As conceived, the energy agency seeks to emulate DARPA's agile organizational model and risk-taking culture in order to speed energy R&D into market-ready technologies. Although still in its infancy, by September 2011 ARPA-E had funded 180 projects in 12 program areas for an expenditure of $521.7 million; some of these projects had also attracted more than $200 million in follow-on private investment.

The key difference from DARPA, however, is that ARPA-E has no user-driven procurement mechanism with which to launch its technologies. ARPA-E can finance any number of smart energy breakthroughs, but without an ultimate user or assured demand for the innovations to help bring them to scale and reduce their cost, very little commercial uptake is likely. To compensate for its lack of market pull, the agency has set about building strong links with the military for test beds and initial markets. Under a memorandum of understanding between the Energy and Defense Departments, ARPA-E is collaborating with DoD on projects ranging from next-generation jet fuel, diesel fuel, and gasoline substitutes based on biological processes, to batteries for mobile energy storage based on alternatives to lithium, and smart grids incorporating multiple clean energy sources (Majumdar 2011). While the Navy secretary refers to ARPA-E as "a kindred spirit with the department of the Navy," ARPA-E director Arun Majumdar speaks of helping the DoD as "a win for our nation."[47] Addressing a recent appropriations hearing, Majumdar emphasized that breakthroughs in grid-scale energy storage, electric vehicle batteries, and power electronics will be deployed in the first instance by the military for use on its installations and by its mobile units, thus solving the initial problem of a ready market (Majumdar 2011, 3). A similar partnership has been struck between the U.S. Army Corps of Engineers and the DoE's Office of Energy Efficiency and Renewable Energy in order to accelerate deployment of fuel cell backup power systems at military facilities and to advance the technology via demonstration and testing.

In sum, through the departments of Energy (ARPA-E plus the national energy labs) and Defense, the federal government is advancing research and development on multiple renewable energy fronts. A 2011 Pew study found that DoD clean energy investments increased 300 percent between 2006 and 2009, from $400 million to $1.2 billion, and are projected to reach $3 billion in 2015, exceeding $10 billion annually by 2030. When DoE and related government spending are added, it is estimated, the federal government invests in the order of $4 billion dollars annually on clean energy programs.[48] Many have suggested that this sum is vastly inadequate. Nevertheless, this amount is close to DARPA's annual budget and higher than that of SBIR— both of which, though dispersed across many different technology fields, have fostered significant breakthroughs over the years.

Breakthrough Innovations? The Case of Sustainable Biofuels

If the U.S. military is leading the American version of the Green Energy Revolution this is because the very success of its mission is dependent on energy. Yet pathbreaking innovations are still some years away. According to the Information Technology Innovation Foundation, a green energy advocacy organization, there are currently in play some "potential game-changers," among them algal and waste-derived biofuels, advanced batteries based on new chemistries, and smart grids able to integrate multiple energy sources. But these are still some years from full-scale commercialization.[49] Indeed, during the Department of Energy's ARPA-E Energy Innovation Summit in February 2012, both Steven Chu and Bill Gates cautioned against basing expectations of early breakthroughs on the information technology experience, with the reminder that energy requires a much longer development time frame: "I worry that people underestimate the time to innovate," said Gates.[50]

Although there are other interesting cases and promising stories that could be told, I shall focus on just one—advanced biofuels. Liquid fuel for transportation, whether on the battlefield, at sea, or in the air, is the military's major energy requirement and the single largest item of expenditure in the U.S. energy mix (primarily for jet fuel for the air force and Navy). The United States depends on foreign sources for most of its crude oil supplies, and those sources are perceived as increasingly hostile and politically unstable regimes. This makes the military's biofuels initiative especially urgent. In another respect, however, aspects of the biofuels experience also apply more broadly to the emerging energy field. One is the critical role of NSS-industry collaboration in delivering innovation. Another is the general-purpose nature of the technology, which is fostering multiple applications and kick-starting new industries. Yet another is the political obstacle to overcoming the commercialization hurdles that lie ahead.

NSS-industry collaboration. For many people, biofuels mean corn ethanol, raising the contentious issue of "food versus fuel." However the newest generations of biofuel are considered sustainable since they do not rely upon or displace food crops. Major advances in synthetic biology and chemical engineering enable emerging firms to produce drop-in (i.e., requiring no modification to existing engines or infrastructure) jet fuels and gasoline alternatives made from feedstocks that do not compete with food crops— among them farming waste, prairie grasses such as switch grass, and inedible oil-rich crops such as jatropha, camelina, and algae that can grow on nonarable land. According to specialists, algae, for example, can provide a high-yield source of biofuel without compromising food supplies, rainforests, arable land, or potable water.

However, rather than betting on one particular technology, Defense together with the Energy and Agriculture has been sponsoring multiple technology pathways that use a variety of nonfood feedstocks and different conversion processes including photosynthetic and fermentation. In some cases, such as marine algae, which uses only CO_2, minerals in seawater, and sunlight, or algae engineered to consume CO_2 from smokestacks, even the use of feedstock is minimal. "We're looking at second and third generation biofuels made from algae, made from things like camelina . . . an inedible part of the mustard family and . . . from inedible grease," says Ray Mabus. ". . . we don't have a specific technology in mind, we just need the energy."[51]

The centerpiece of the Navy's fuels strategy is the Great Green Fleet, to be deployed by 2016. Its ambitious goal is to ensure that by 2020, at least 50 percent of the Navy's energy consumption comes from renewable sources—an estimated 8 million barrels of biofuel (336 million gallons).[52] After making the largest purchase of biofuels in American history the service has successfully certified its aircraft to use biofuels (made from algae and from camelina) and is doing the same with its surface fleet.

The air force too has certified its entire fleet to fly on biofuels and has flown test flights using a fifty-fifty mix of plant-based biofuel and jet fuel. It proposes to buy enough renewable fuel to power half of its domestic flights by 2016 (roughly 400 million gallons). Its ultimate goal is for 50 percent of annual fuel consumption for domestic aviation to come from renewable blends. Since it uses about 1.2 billion gallons of aviation fuel each year for domestic operations, this amounts to about 600 million gallons annually. Considerations of cost, however, will figure in USAF's final calculations, since it emphasizes the need for renewable aviation fuels to be "cost competitive" with petroleum. As an air force energy official put it, "It has to be a business consideration because we want competitively priced fuels for it to make sense to do it."[53]

As the centerpiece of its renewable fuels policy, the Obama administration took steps to ensure a military market for advanced biofuels. First, the administration invoked the 1950 Defense Production Act, issuing a presidential finding that designated advanced biofuels as a strategic resource vital to national security. As well as making biofuels a strategic commodity, this designation is intended to give them special privileges in contracting. In a connected move, the administration in 2011 announced a $510 million investment for a biorefinery to commercialize advanced biofuels for military purposes. To implement this initiative, the USDA, DoE, and the Navy announced that they would each commit $170 million to finance biorefineries, with the expectation that this would be matched by the private sector, thus providing $1 billion to bring advanced biofuels to commercial scale. By providing market opportunities now and promising more in the future, as well as by testing and certifying renewable fuels, the services intend to send strong signals to the venture community and provide an early stimulus for commercial production of renewable fuels. As we shall see, however, political blockages abound in this military endeavor.

Multiple applications, new industries. In the process of gearing up to meet military demand, a clutch of emerging companies have found many other applications for their biofuel technologies. A detailed review of twelve Unites States–based companies that are developing third- and fourth-generation biofuels shows how these ventures are also moving into bioindustrial and household chemicals, bioplastics, food supplements, and personal care products, using synthetic biology to produce engineered microorganisms and specialty enzymatic products.[54]

The SBIR-backed company Solazyme, for example, a leader in algal synthetic biology—and one of two companies recently invited by the Navy to fill the world's largest order of biofuels to date—has found that there are handsome prospects for algae to meet demands for products beyond biofuels. With the same technology, it is now making anti-aging creams, which command about one thousand times the price of fuel.[55] As one senior engineer from the Air Force Research Lab commented, "We're growing a whole new industry there. It's not just fuel . . ."[56]

Political Challenges to Commercialization

Once a biofuel has been developed, tested, and certified, a further challenge is to improve yield, scale up production, and bring down costs. Algal biofuels, for example, at a cost of more than five dollars per gallon, are not yet competitive with fossil fuels, though the price is rapidly falling as NSS-sponsored projects achieve new milestones.[57] To lower the cost will mean achieving simultaneous breakthroughs in various technical areas such as how to grow and harvest massive amounts of algae and how to maximize extraction of oil, and how to do it all at sufficient scale within the time frame of a decade.

But the largest hurdle to be mounted is likely to be a political one. A Catch-22 situation has arisen in that industry needs long-term purchase commitments in order to attract investors and scale up production. Without the ability to scale up, costs will not come down (as we saw, a time-tested pattern in the procurement of information technology). Fuel developers thus seek assurance of demand via longer contracts for fuel delivery. However, the military cannot commit to large volumes until prices fall—and prices cannot fall until large volumes can be produced. Moreover, the military's contracting authority is limited to a maximum of five years (and a total amount of less than $500 million), unless specifically authorized otherwise by Congress. The interagency effort to fund biorefineries was intended to kick-start the scaling-up process, but this came unstuck in the first half of 2012 with Congress's refusal to approve the Navy's use of existing appropriations to fund its commitment. (While the USDA had secured its share of funding, the DoE and the Navy were required to seek their shares in 2013 budget appropriations.) First, the House Armed Services Committee prohibited the Defense Department from purchasing alternative fuels that were more expensive than traditional fossil fuels. Then, in a subsequent (national security-weakening?) move, Republican leaders in the Democratic-majority Senate Armed Services Committee narrowly passed an amendment to the bill authorizing defense programs in 2013 that prohibits the Defense Department from building a refinery for biofuels unless authorized by law. "I don't believe it's the job of the Navy to be involved in building . . . new technologies," Republican Senator John McCain told the press, in a stunningly ahistorical statement.[58] Tellingly, however, the same Republican leaders (with support from an undisclosed number of Democrats) inserted a provision that exempts coal and gas from the costing prohibition applied to Defense purchases of alternative fuels.[59]

Although both legislative prohibitions on Defense's renewable fuel efforts have since been repealed,[60] Congressional Republicans have not given up their assault on DoD's energy security initiatives.[61] Indeed, the ups and downs of the biofuels story can be seen as exemplifying the (mainly, though not exclusively) partisan opposition to green energy initiatives more generally. One must therefore conclude that it is political blockages that are most likely to hold back commercialization and transition to new energy sources, as Congressional Republicans aided by powerful coal, oil, and gas interests, push back against the Obama administration's policies to promote renewable energy. The importance of political support, as one argument would have it, is precisely where the NSS-led green revolution comes up against a brick wall. The reasoning offered by Eugene Gholz is that since most of the innovative companies exist outside the traditional network of giant contractors, green tech is unlikely to get off the ground because its entrepreneurial companies lack the political influence and expertise of the primes "in helping the military lobby for its preferences" (2011, 3). In short, goes the argument, those most able to appeal to elected leaders for funding are not the key technology developers in the green energy arena. In this connection, Gholz makes the interesting observation that "Because the military is blocked by the professionalism that defines American civil-military relations from overtly lobbying for its preferences, its trusted relationship with key defense contractors provides a key link in developing political support for military innovation" (2011, 3).

One can of course accept this point without endorsing the zero-sum logic behind it. Although it is true that the primes are increasingly risk-averse and less adept at innovation than the nontraditional suppliers (chapter 5),[62] it is also true that they too are being drawn or nudged into the world of green technology, often through alliances with innovative clean-tech companies, and with full encouragement from the DoD. Honeywell, Lockheed, and Boeing, for example, have all begun green technology projects, working through their extensive network of innovative suppliers or through joint ventures with nondefense companies. At DARPA's instigation, for example, prime contractor Honeywell has teamed with algal specialist Solazyme to develop biofuel with Honeywell's jet fuel process technology. Lockheed too is jointly developing a green hybrid propulsion system running on renewable energy for small unmanned aerial systems. In short, it is not a case of prime contractors (the industry core of the so-called "military-industrial complex") versus the entrepreneurial (nondefense) companies, since both are being involved in DoD's renewable energy strategy.

Because of its politicization, what matters in the longer run for energy innovation is the leadership and commitment of the armed services, perhaps not least because the U.S. military has long been the most trusted institution in the nation.[63] On this point it seems fitting to conclude with the statement of Dorothy Robyn, who declared in early 2011 that "Many young people in the military get it, and there's commitment at the top. It's not just conversation; it's here to stay."[64] In March 2012, the Pentagon released the implementation plan for its Operational Energy Strategy, a broad effort by senior Defense officials to reduce the military's dependence on oil and expand its use of alternative energy. Outside in the commercial arena, the story is taking a more conventional turn as vested interests in fossil fuel mobilize strong Republican support for minimally regulated extraction of what Michael Klare (2012) has called "extreme energy," of which "fracking" (or hydraulic fracturing) for gas deposits is one such controversial instance.[65] Difficult political times ahead may retard the Pentagon plan, but it would be foolish to discount the signs of a DoD-led energy revolution in the making.

Caveat: A Faltering NSS Innovation Engine?

A cautionary note is warranted. The technology leadership of the NSS has long been a source of U.S. military superiority and industrial strength. However, there are some recent indications that the NSS innovation engine may be faltering as long-term S&T investment in broad-based revolutionary innovation is redirected to serve the more immediate needs of fighting asymmetric conflicts.

Specialists in the field have defined the problem as the loss of a long-term strategic vision, manifested, for example, in "the Pentagon shifting what it wants every couple of years."[66] Some attribute this indecision to internal management problems, especially within the Pentagon's S&T community.[67] Still others point to the intrusion of Congressional pressures in R&D funding decisions. Since the events of September 2001, the mission agencies appear to have been under increased pressure from Congress (and military commands) to demonstrate the relevance of R&D funding to warfighting exigencies. Exchanges between ONR and Congressional committees in 2005, for example, have been viewed as "typical" of the pressure to treat S&T activity "as part of an integrated product development scheme" that can show Congress and the wider public how expenditure on scientific research "saves lives and contributes to mission accomplishment in places like Afghanistan and Iraq" (Coletta 2009, 17). The JASON group also found that many funded projects that claimed to be for basic research were actually for short-term goals that met service needs. This finding led to their dramatic conclusion that "DoD has largely eliminated basic research and redefined 'product development' as the new, improved version" (MITRE 2009, 47).[68] As a result of these pressures, many voices proclaim the erosion of the long-term vision and funding

144

needed for revolutionary advances, portending a "mediocre future" for the DoD and the nation (MITRE 2009, 47)—a concern also expressed earlier, for different reasons, by Vernon Ruttan.

To the extent that the perceived impairments to the NSS innovation engine are structural rather than cyclical in nature, they would seem related to the much altered geopolitical environment. Not least important has been the disappearance from the scene of what the U.S. political and military leadership once perceived as an existential threat. During the Cold War the United States had a clear strategic priority of achieving military superiority over the Soviet Union. This hard-power threat from a well-matched rival was for a time intensified and to some extent superseded by the very different challenge from Japan—an emergent technology superpower whose superior commercial capabilities threatened to erode the U.S. defense industrial base. The Japanese commercial threat, which transmogrified into a national security one, has now been replaced by multiple less clearly definable threats from lesser adversaries. In turn, the need to respond to these many threats from many different sources has displaced the long-term strategic vision singularly focused on advancing the U.S. technological frontier. Under these circumstances, a coherent long-term strategy for the future becomes much less feasible.[69] What the disappearance of well-matched rivals also means is a reduction of the pressure on political actors to sustain a transformative project.

To clarify: the faltering in question does not imply an absence of transformative innovation. Nevertheless, it does provide some perspective on the concerns raised in various reports regarding an inconsistency of vision and wavering political support for the U.S. transformative project. The weakening of Congressional support has been especially pronounced in the case of renewable energy initiatives that connect innovation to production. Congressional Republicans have been particularly strong opponents of initiatives to extend or expand support for advanced energy manufacturing, for example, by dismissing tax credits as "spending programs."[70] Even the fact that the military supports such initiatives as part of its broader push for energy security has not won over those political opponents who are otherwise staunch defenders of national security. Are we witnessing an erosion of the bipartisan consensus that has long sustained the NSS technology enterprise? In view of the historically demonstrated importance of an external impetus to forge a consensus in a highly competitive political environment, it may well take another Sputnik moment to restore the political seriousness of purpose needed to reenergize the nation's transformative ambition.

To varying degrees, each of the cases I have touched on in this chapter seems to hold out more promise than that implied by Ruttan's conclusion—at least with regard to the NSS capacity for eliciting, conducting, and managing transformative innovation. Where that capacity is most likely to be thwarted is in the political arena. Can one explain this at some deeper level in structural terms? The end of the Cold War has, after all, removed the perception of an existential threat. Along with that, it has removed the persistent pressure that has made S&T innovation—even when it has meant fostering commercial industries—a national security priority for both sides in politics. We glimpsed the beginnings of this post–Cold War shift in the George H. W. Bush administration's sacking of DARPA's director, for doing what the agency had long been doing: promoting commercial innovation for spin-around purposes and in order to enhance the defense-security industrial base. The dismissal no doubt sprang from a mix of motives, but in a larger sense it also symbolized the transition to a different geostrategic environment in which the persistent pressure on both branches of government to support a broad version of security-relevant S&T with transformative aims had been well and truly lifted. Furthermore, as we have seen, in the pushback on renewable energy, the dismissal was a portent of things to come. Congressional Republicans, it seems, have grown more willing not just to push back on military projects like renewable energy, but also to sacrifice these if necessary to advance their own political preferences; hence the unexpected implementation of sequestration.

Even with the NSS's transformative potential largely intact, these observations thus give rise to a larger question, reserved for the final chapter. In the post-9/11 era of multiple asymmetric threats, vaguely defined adversaries, a hemorrhaging manufacturing industry, and budgetary uncertainty, is it likely that the NSS innovation enterprise can continue to deliver the golden eggs?

7

Hybridization and
American Antistatism

> Such is the power of the interpretive tendency to put things wholly
> in one category or another—public or private. But one of the more
> interesting things about American history is the degree to which it
> frequently resists such simple, bifurcated categorization.
>
> William J. Novak, 2009

The road traveled so far has taken us from the transformative technologies of the early Cold War years right up to the present quest for new
breakthroughs. Along the way, we have witnessed the emergence of a major
innovation engine in the form of the NSS—one that has evolved to influence and serve both government and commercial sectors. We can agree with
Aaron Friedberg that what we see is a far cry from a despotic garrison-style
state, in spite of the heavy focus on national security. However, we must also
conclude that the result is equally a far cry from the weaker or limited (passive?) state that, in his account, emerged in its stead.[1] This raises an obvious
question: Why is this innovation engine so invisible? Why don't Americans
see their state?

One response suggests that this is a result of decentralization: the state's
hand is hard to see because its innovation activism is so dispersed.[2] This is
plausibly part of an explanation, but it may well be only a small part. To this
we can add the much less observed tendency that I have called hybridization:
the state's activities are hard to see because they are often presented in—and
thus obscured by—forms that merge public and private institutions in novel
ways. The result is something that is neither wholly public nor wholly private,
but a fusion of the two—hence best described as a hybrid. This is an important
source of the confusion over the nature and extent of American state capacity.

What I am proposing, then, can be seen as a counterpoint to Friedberg's state versus market argument. In Friedberg's account, the postwar American state was kept weak while the private sector thereby grew strong, and this was because of America's robust tradition of antistatism. Within the American context, antistatism can be defined as "the body of ideas and arguments used by those who have opposed efforts to increase the size and strength of the executive branch of the federal government" (Friedberg 2000, 11).[3] As Friedberg argues, animosity toward government is a deep-rooted and long-standing tradition within American political culture, arising from rebellion against the colonial state.

Antistatism also has consequences for the story here. However, there is a clear divergence in the institutional outcomes we each highlight. Friedberg's analysis is designed to emphasize what antistatism helped to prevent. By contrast, I seek to show what it helped to create: a hybridized state and economy. Most Americans believe that the state has a responsibility for national defense, but many vehemently believe the state should not attempt to drive national economic developments unless it is essential to do so to fulfill that responsibility. This suggests why commercially focused policies such as the Advanced Technology Program are rarely long-lived, even when broadly dual-use technology policies have prospered. As a consequence, antistatism has a pervasive impact on the way the state gets involved in the private sector—even when the mission is security driven (Friedberg 2000, 13). The result is what I call a hybridization tendency—a merging or fusion of public and private resources.

The hybridization tendency, I further propose, is not an accidental or random outcome, but one that is organic to the American setting. As a historian of U.S. public-private governance observes, "one of the dominant characteristics of American policymaking over time has been the curious blending of public and private initiatives, techniques, and institutions" (Novak 2009, 26). One indicator of hybridization's organic fit, or what Max Weber would have termed its "elective affinity" with American political culture is an unusual level of bipartisan support for the creation of hybrid organizational forms, even where this may entail a continuing or higher level of government involvement than before the creation of the entity in question.

In this chapter I bring the hybrid political economy more sharply into focus. I seek to define and distinguish different types of hybrid organization, with an emphasis on what I call "innovation hybrids." We have already encountered such public-private entities in earlier chapters when examining the shifting dynamics and forms of NSS activism. Here their different forms, characteristics, rationale, and consequences provide the main focus. I propose that hybrids in the U.S. context are organizational innovations that—effectively if not intentionally—blunt the (national security) state's impact and blur its visible presence in economic governance, avoid political blockage, and promote the business of innovation. Long-standing, growing, diverse, often sui generis and hard to classify, U.S. innovation hybrids are more complex than mere public-private partnerships, outsourcing, or privatization. Their pervasive presence and importance give us a measure of the "hybrid state."

The Significance of Hybridization

Why are hybrids significant? One reason is that they confound the presumption of a public-private dichotomy that lies at the doctrinal core of economic liberalism. The institutionalized separation between public and private spheres has long provided a historic marker of modern society and a framework for the liberal intellectual tradition.[4] Although the boundaries have never been watertight, historically static, or drawn similarly across the modern map of nation-states, the public-private dichotomy has powerfully framed the discourse of the social sciences through the influential lens of liberalism and more recently neoliberalism. In political science and political economy in particular, for the past thirty years or so neoliberalism has provided the default perspective, shaping the framework within which the state's role in market economies has been widely understood and compared. A core assumption of this perspective, articulated in the idea of the rise of the so-called neoliberal state (most typically identified with the United States), is that the distinction between the state and the market must be drawn as clearly and sharply as possible (Weintraub 1997, 8). It is often assumed in discussions of neoliberal policies that the boundaries between the public and the private sector have not only been redrawn but also reinforced by various processes, such as privatization and outsourcing. According to this view, by shifting out to private economic actors the assets and activities that the state once owned, operated, or provided itself, the state has been hollowed out to the advantage of the private sector. In much of this discussion, questions of jurisdiction have thus tended to dominate—boiling down to disputes over which activities should be the business of the state and which should belong to the market.

However, an alternative literature highlights a number of developments, especially in the American context, that are poorly explained, let alone acknowledged, by the liberal (or neoliberal) perspective (Moe 2002; Koppell 2003; Congressional Research Service 2011b). Instead of producing clear delineations between the activities of state agencies and private economic actors, the era of neoliberalism has witnessed increasing fluidity of state-market boundaries, complex partnerships between public and private actors, and the widespread creation of new hybrid forms that belie the privileged state-market dichotomy at the conceptual core of liberalism and its "American model" counterpart in the comparative capitalism literature. A host of complex arrangements have emerged that do not simply breach the historic wall between public and private sectors; such arrangements replace these well-defined realms with a web of "partnerships" that are neither strictly public nor strictly private (Congressional Research Service 2011b, 40). Sometimes called the "quasi-government," hybrids perform a wide variety of functions that range from financing home purchases to commercializing technology to promoting U.S. exports. Quasi-governmental entities are by no means new on the scene; some date back more than a century.[5] The Federal Reserve system, for example, a public-private hybrid created in 1913, was designed out of a compromise between the competing advocates of privatization and government regulation (Stanton 2002, 68). Similarly, the famous Radio Corporation of America whose charter required it to be mostly American-owned, was founded in 1919 at the instigation of the Navy which saw commercial and military advantage in convincing General Electric to form the company.[6] What does seem relatively new, however, is the recent growth of quasi-government, with many public-private hybrids appearing, somewhat ironically (but not incidentally, one may suggest), in the period of economic liberalism's ideological ascendancy.[7]

Hybridization challenges the liberal (and comparative capitalism) perspective because it often involves integrating the state in the "private" economy, not removing it or limiting it to a regulatory capacity. The results of this integration in the postwar United States are of particular interest for conceptual and empirical reasons. First, hybrids play an important role in financing, creating, applying, transferring and commercializing new technologies and the startup companies that market the innovations. Thus the transformative form of hybridization I shall discuss can be seen as a very different process to that of privatization: where privatization involves getting the private sector to do what the state once did (or ought to do, as some accounts would contend), hybridization is about getting the state (qua NSS) involved in innovation-cum-developmental activities that, in the liberal economic system, are considered more typically the business of the private sector. Second, the confounding of public and private boundaries poses a challenge to the dominant conceptualization of the United States as the archetypal liberal state operating within a free market economy.

An American Tendency?

As well as considering the consequences of hybridization vis-à-vis state-economy relations, I shall pay some attention to the question of its sources. This entails two separate analytical issues. The first concerns the historical pattern alluded to earlier: Why the U.S. tendency to hybridize? Since we can assume that there are different ways of skinning a cat, the preference for creating a hybrid (rather than some other form) to meet some public policy goal is neither obvious nor universal, and hence calls for some explanatory effort. The second issue is one of impetus or drivers: Why the apparent growth of hybrids in recent decades, notably since the 1980s? Favored explanations tend to fall into the functionalist category: hybrids exist and multiply because of the functions they perform or because of the consequences that they allegedly produce, such as superior efficiency over traditional bureaucracies, improved operational flexibility, and insulation from democratic oversight. I propose, however, that no general explanation of this kind is possible because hybrids differ too widely in character and purpose. Rather, in order to make headway, we need to distinguish different types of hybrids—and particularly to grasp the character and purpose of innovation hybrids.

There are two strands to my argument. One concerns the general historical pattern of a hybridization tendency. This, I propose, has much to do with what we can call the domestic constraint: because of America's antistatist mindset, hybridization has become a preferred U.S. response to public policy problems that call for the state's presence in economic affairs. But when we turn to account for the second, more specific issue concerning the recent growth of innovation hybrids, antistatism by itself will not suffice. Here we must turn to the interaction of international pressures and domestic constraint. Specifically, since the 1980s at least, a combination of strategic and economic pressures in the international environment has called for an increased innovation effort, which must nonetheless be responsive to the antistatist constraint in the domestic political environment. Conservative antipathy toward government involvement in market processes reemerged with new vigor in the very period (the so-called neoliberal era) when such involvement was most called for—that is to say, when national security and economic pressures were converging. In both arenas, U.S. technology leadership was narrowing. On the national security front, from the late 1970s throughout the 1980s, the Pentagon sought to address what was to become a recurring problem—"the rush of commercial firms away from the defense business," particularly in the increasingly critical IT sector.[8] On the geo-economic front, U.S. firms were being pushed out of high-technology markets by foreign competitors. As U.S. firms faced falling profits and productivity at home and aggressive competition in markets abroad, a new competitiveness agenda gained ground. By the late 1980s, however, the push from Congressional Democrats for a more civilian-oriented technology policy encountered resistance from the George H. W. Bush administration, keen to assert its free-market credentials. Symbolic in this regard was the dismissal of high-profile DARPA director Craig Fields, who was both advocate for and party to a more active government role in dual-use projects with high commercial potential, such as high-definition television. In reality, the antistatist dividing line between (ideological) belief and (political) interest is not always clear and the much-publicized sacking may also have had a political motive.[9]

Beneath the surface of these political-ideological struggles and stalemates, a deeper shift was taking place as commercial viability became a hallmark of new NSS technology programs. As the meaning of commercially viable technology broadened over the following decades to encompass the technology interests of the defense and national security agencies, innovation hybrids came into their own. Thus what some have characterized as a shift toward a competitiveness regime was in reality more complex since that shift was overlaid with and stimulated by perceived weaknesses within the industries feeding the NSS industrial base. The shift toward a commercially viable technology policy—the context in which new innovation hybrids were created and existing ones modified—was manifested in more broadly defined missions, greater emphasis on creating dual-use technologies, and new forms of public-private partnerings. This shift was accompanied by a new narrative of commercial strength to complement the narrative of national security. It produced a cluster of legislative acts, markedly from 1980 onward, that established technological innovation—its promotion, protection, transfer, and commercialization—as key to national military and economic strength.[10] In the university sector, the shift involved not so much a new as a more explicit focus on universities as engines of innovation and potential growth,[11] leading to the creation of triadic partnerships among industry, universities, and government aimed at commercializing publicly funded R&D. In the defense and intelligence communities, as well as the national security laboratories, the shift entailed new forms of linkage and partnering with commercially focused enterprises as key innovators in the growing field of information technology. In this high-stakes context, it seems reasonable to propose that the creation of hybrid forms offered policy actors a way of circumventing ideological-political blockages—in particular, a robust antistatism—that might otherwise have retarded or stymied innovation activism.

My purpose is to inject some precision into the use of the term hybridization by contrasting it with privatization and public outsourcing. I discuss several cases of innovation hybrids with the aim of highlighting the varieties of state involvement in commercial processes that nevertheless have security as their sole or primary mission. Finally, I propose an explanation for the growth of the U.S. hybrid economy that integrates international pressures and structural economic changes with domestic political constraints.

Nature of the Beast: Neither "Privatization" nor "Outsourcing"

When thinking about hybrids and hybridization we need to establish limits beyond which these terms do not apply. Privatization, outsourcing, and public-private partnerships are sometimes used as synonyms for hybridization, but this is misleading. Partnerships are many and varied, some established as or bordering on hybrid creations, but many more retain distinct rather than merged public and private identities. Privatization, on the other hand, creates private companies, not hybrids (an assertion that will be later qualified). Outsourcing, understood here as the contracting out of services for which the state is the client, gives business to private contractors. Sometimes the two tendencies are combined: the rise of the private military industry, for example, owes its existence to both privatization and outsourcing. The U.S. military now relies on thousands of contractors to do everything from intelligence gathering to operating weapons systems to setting up base camps in far-flung places. The fact that there was one contractor employee servicing some fifty active-duty personnel in the 1991 Gulf War, but a ratio of one to ten by the time of the Iraq invasion in 2003, well illustrates the changing infrastructural reach of the federal government (Singer 2003, 260). The effects however are anything but straightforward, since outsourcing can not only hollow out state capacity, it can also be a force multiplier and a means to achieve foreign policy goals freed from the need to secure public approval (at least in the short term since there is an ultimate consequence in the budget process that constrains spending in this way).[12]

There is no question that the nature and extent of such contracting in the U.S. system does at times blur the boundaries between state and private actors. Lockheed Martin, for example, the nation's largest military contractor best known for its weapons systems, has also built a formidable information technology empire that "now stretches from the Pentagon to the post office."[13] Lockheed, it appears, does practically everything apart from collect taxes: as well as running interrogation programs and conducting security operations, it sorts mail and calculates taxes, cuts social security checks, runs space flights, and monitors air traffic. As a "one-stop-shop" for the federal government, it is virtually impossible to tell where Lockheed begins and the government ends. As a *New York Times* article summed it up: "Lockheed Martin doesn't run the United States. But it does help run a breathtakingly big part of it."

But there is no hybridization here, at least in the strictly formal-legal sense. Lockheed remains formally a private for-profit company, even if the great bulk of its business is conducted to service one client, the federal government. In this interesting case, it is as if the company were a giant arm of the U.S. government, with just a few toes in the private sector, sufficient to give it private-sector credibility. Sociologically speaking, the significance of private sector credibility should not be underestimated in a theory of hybridization, United States style, a point I shall return to below.

Similarly, when it comes to the operational activities of such "private" security companies as Blackwater or other military contractors, we may have to revise completely our ideas of public and private. As a recent *New York Times* article reported, Blackwater's secret missions for the CIA "illuminate a far deeper relationship between the spy agency and the private security company than government officials had acknowledged." As well as being highly profitable for the company, "Blackwater's partnership with the C.I.A . . . became even closer after several top agency officials joined Blackwater." According to a former top CIA officer, "It became a very brotherly relationship. . . . There was a feeling that Blackwater eventually became an extension of the agency."[14]

Such entanglement inevitably raises the questions: What is the state? What is the private sector? If ostensibly private institutions depend entirely or almost wholly on public contracts for their revenue and organizational survival (as do, for example, Halliburton and private military companies); if they are managed or staffed by persons socialized in public (read NSS) institutions and intimately connected to a national elite; if their operational staff receive their training in public institutions; and if they are directly involved in the provision of public goods—what then is "private" apart from the profit taking? Private military companies, and perhaps even a good number of armaments contractors fall into this shadowy no-man's-land—companies whose *raison d'être* is *raison d'état.*

These entities surely deserve to be called de facto if not de jure hybrids. If we imagine hybridization as a spectrum of greater and lesser degrees of government input or influence, we might assign the de facto hybrid to the lesser end and the de jure version to the greater end.

In distinction to privatization and outsourcing, hybridization is the process of combining, mixing, or merging public and private sector characteristics to create a new type of entity. American hybrids or "quagos," unlike the prolific British "quangos," for example, are a genuine blend of the public and private sectors in so far as they incorporate market-based mechanisms into their operations (Koppell 2003, 17). Koppell offers a useful definition based on two criteria, ownership and funding source. Here it will serve as a first cut:

> A hybrid organization is an entity created by the federal government (either by act of Congress or executive action) to address a specific public policy purpose. It is owned in whole or part by private individuals or corporations and/or generates revenue to cover its operating costs. (Koppell 2003, 12)

Deploying this framework, we can distinguish hybrids from the general population of organizations as set out in table 7.1.

TABLE 7.1
Typology of organizations: A first cut

Category	Ownership	Funding
Government agency	Public	Public[b]
Private entity	Private	Private
Hybrid	Public	Private[c]
Hybrid/Public-interest org	Private or mixed[a]	Public or mixed[b]

Source: Adaptation of Koppell 2003.

[a] Considered mixed if federal government shares ownership with private investors (e.g. Federal Home Loan Banks).

[b] Considered publicly funded or mixed unless the entity effectively covers all or most of its operating expenses with its own revenue in most years.

[c] Considered privately funded if the organization generates revenue that covers most of its operating expenses; those relying partly on revenue and partly on appropriations (or subsidies) are considered publicly funded. This latter category includes organizations whose viability is partly dependent on a government guarantee.

However, this typology takes us only so far. Since the entities we are dealing with have fluid boundaries, our typology requires some adjustment to accommodate this fluidity. It will be evident from our earlier discussion that this first cut excludes a sizeable group of hybrid-like entities, which we might situate at two ends of the ownership spectrum. At one extreme, we find formally private companies that have come into being either at government's request (like System Development Corporation and Innovation Services)[15] or through a mix of private initiative and public resources in order to provide a public good, and are almost entirely dependent on revenue derived from government (such as Draper Lab, divested from MIT; SAIC, a Los Alamos Laboratory spin-out; SRI-International, a spin-out from Stanford; and Sarnoff, an offshoot of RCA, now part of SRI). These we may call de facto hybrids. At the other extreme, we find formally government-owned companies serving a public policy goal and initially dependent on public appropriations—yet in their market operations and management, indistinguishable from a private company. These we may refer to as de jure hybrids. Focusing for the moment on innovation hybrids, this second cut would look as shown in table 7.2.

Even armed with clear criteria, it must be said that the apparently simple task of identifying which entities are hybrids is complicated by the Alice-in-Wonderland quality of the Congressional labels—corporations, agencies, foundations, institutes, and so forth—applied arbitrarily to different entities, both for-profit and nonprofit. Observing this bewildering array, Koppell comments that "Improbable as it may seem, in fact, no one knows just how many federal hybrids exist. This is a function of ambiguity, not secrecy" (2003, 8).

A recent Congressional Research Service report seeks to impose some order on this universe by identifying six main categories of hybrid created to carry out public goals (Congressional Research Service 2011b). These include government-sponsored enterprises (financial GSEs), such as Fannie Mae; Federally Funded Research and Development Centers (FFRDCs) such as the Energy Department's Argonne National Laboratory); government-sponsored venture capital funds (GVFs), quasi-official agencies, agency-related nonprofit organizations (such as national park administrations), and

TABLE 7.2
Innovation hybrids

Ownership	Funding (revenue)	Operation	Examples
Private	Private/mixed[a]	Private	SAIC; SRI; SBICs
Public	Public[a]	Private	FFRDCs; MITRE; SEI
Private	Public	Private	Rosettex
Public	Public	Private/mixed	In-Q-Tel; OnPoint, CCAT

[a] This category includes private organizations that rely either in part on appropriations (e.g. SBICs) or that depend on government for 80% or more of their revenue (e.g. SRI International, Lockheed Martin, SAIC).

Congressionally chartered nonprofit organizations, as well as other instrumentalities of an indeterminate character. These categories cover a very general universe, rather than (but including some of) the particular innovation hybrids I will discuss in a moment.

Embodied in this classification is a warning. The sheer variety of hybrid organizations in terms of labels, funding sources, ownership, and governance structures renders causal generalizations hazardous. The different periods of their creation, even within the same hybrid category, further complicates the task of constructing a general explanation. Take for example the six financial GSEs created by Congress to reduce the cost of capital for various borrowing sectors of the economy (mainly farmers, homeowners, and students). In this case alone, their emergence spans a seventy-year period from 1916 to 1987 (Stanton 2002). GSEs are privately owned, federally chartered financial institutions with specialized lending powers that benefit from subsidies and an implicit federal guarantee of all their obligations, which enhances their ability to borrow money. The federal government has attempted to direct GSE activities to sectors, such as housing and agriculture, deemed to be underserved by private capital.

Nonetheless, in spite of the differing circumstances of their creation, the GSEs do share one significant feature, namely, the public effort to manage and absorb high-level risk. In spite of America's famed antistatism and the dominant laissez-faire narrative, the U.S. government has a lengthy history as an active manager and absorber of risk in social and financial policy (Moss 2004).

In the case of innovation hybrids, we see not only this public underwriting and absorption of investment risk in the earlier more risk-exposed stages of activity (discovery, innovation, prototyping, testing) but also a more recent emphasis on bringing those innovations to market readiness.[16] In this respect, innovation hybrids complement the host of federal funding programs aimed at the higher-risk end of technology development.

Innovation Hybrids

Drawing on—and expanding upon—the CRS categories, I distinguish a specific population of innovation hybrids that combine public and private features pertaining to their ownership and/or their funding, operation and management. As we have seen, several hybrid arrangements exist for converting breakthrough inventions into market-ready innovations or products. In table 7.3, I group these diverse arrangements into four types of innovation hybrid. The representative examples should be taken as indicative rather than exhaustive. Perhaps this list only scratches the surface, for the task of tracking down the great diversity of hybrids and tracing their genealogy is a project in its own right.

Most innovation hybrids date from the end of World War II. Some were established in the Vietnam War era in an effort to dissociate universities from

TABLE 7.3
Selected innovation hybrids

Type of hybrid	Year of authorization
Venture capital funds	
SBICs (SBA)	1958
ARCH (DoE Argonne–University of Chicago)	1984
In-Q-Tel (CIA)	1999
OnPoint Technologies (Army: MILCOM)	2001
Rosettex Technology & Ventures (DoD-NGIA/SRI-Sarnoff)	2002
Federally funded research and development centers (FFRDCs) *(as commercialization/spin-out hubs 1980s–2012)*	
Los Alamos (DoE: Los Alamos National Security LLC)	1943
Oak Ridge NL (DoE/UT-Battelle LLC)	1943
Argonne NL (DoE/U Chicago)	1946
Sandia NL (DoE/Sandia Corporation-Lockheed Martin)	1947/1979
Lawrence Berkeley NL (DoE/UC Berkeley)	1931/1946
Lawrence Livermore NL (DoE/UC Berkeley)	1952
Lincoln Lab (US Air Force/MIT)	1951
MITRE Corporation (DoD)	1958
Jet Propulsion Lab (NASA/Caltech)	1943/1958
National Center for Atmospheric Research (NSF/UCAR)	1960/1986
Pacific Northwest NL (DoE/Battelle Memorial Institute)	1965
National Cancer Institute at Frederick (NIH/SAIC et al.)	1972
Software Engineering Institute (DoD/Carnegie Mellon)	1984
National Biodefense Analysis and Countermeasures Center (DHS)	2002
Technology Ventures Corporation (DoE-Sandia/Lockheed Martin)[a]	1993
Technology Maturation Funds (DoE labs)[a]	2002
Technology Commercialization Fund (DoE labs)[a]	2005
Venture Acceleration Fund (DoE–Los Alamos National Lab)[a]	2005
Commercialization consortia	
CCAT (Center for Commercialization of Advanced Technology/Navy)	1999
ACIN (Applied Communication and Information Networking/DoD)	2001
ISN (Institute for Soldier Nanotechnologies/Army)	2002
TeCC (Technology Commercialization Center: NIA/NASA)	1999
NTCI (NAVAIR Technology Commercialization Initiative: Navy)	
CTC Inc. (NASA)	1992
"Public interest" corporations	
SRI International	1946/1970
Sarnoff Corporation	1942/1997
Draper Laboratory	1973
SAIC	1969

[a] Venture funds created by the DoE National Laboratories

the war effort (such as Stanford's SRI and MIT's Draper Laboratories). Others were created much earlier but had their missions significantly revamped in the 1980s when directed to find new markets for the glut of NSS-sponsored innovations (among them the Energy Department's National Security Labs at Los Alamos and Sandia). Still others were created in the aftermath of the Cold War as rising technology costs and declining defense budgets inspired new ways of leveraging advanced commercial capabilities, whether by spinning in innovations or by fostering startups and new products (including In-Q-Tel, Rosettex, CCAT, and ISN).

Since it would be tedious to cover each and every hybrid listed in table 7.3, I shall confine my discussion to one case from each of three hybrid models—the "public interest" corporation, the national laboratory (the so-called Federally Funded Research and Development Center), and the commercialization consortium. I shall only briefly touch on the hybrid nature of the venture funds since these were treated in depth in chapter 3.

The "Public Interest" Corporation: The Case of SRI International

SRI International—formerly Stanford Research Institute—is a legendary hybrid that takes defense-inspired innovations from the lab to the market via the art of the spin-off. SRI was separated from Stanford University in 1970 at the height of the anti-Vietnam movement in response to vigorous protests over the university's work on military projects, and its establishment as a nonprofit corporation enabled military and other security-related work to continue (Leslie 1993b, 247, 250). This hybridization process was replicated in various other instances across the country, where university labs were seen to be too closely associated with the military.

Although SRI is technically independent—not affiliated with a company or public agency—its hybrid character is rendered explicit in several ways—not least by the statement of its vice president, Norman Winarsky, appearing before the House Armed Services Committee in 2012. Explaining the role of SRI and similar non-profits in the Defense Industrial Base, he declared that "non-profits"–in which he included SRI, universities, FFRDCs, and government laboratories—"exist to provide a public service," and that "maintaining their capabilities is in the best interest of national defense." In short, he continued, "nonprofits possess unique advantages over other organizations. For one, we have no shareholders. That means we can focus on providing the warfighter with the best possible solution, being unconcerned about bottom-line considerations such as profit margins, share price, and shareholder satisfaction . . ." (Winarsky 2012, 6).

In spite of SRI's claim to independence, it would not exist in its current form without the patronage and support of the NSS. By far the largest share of SRI's revenues ($585 million in 2011) comes from the federal government—and DoD is its single biggest client. As Winarsky confirms: "Almost four billion dollars in research and development has been sponsored at SRI in the past decade alone. . . . Government clients, primarily the Department of Defense, fund approximately ninety percent of our work" (Winarsky 2012, 3).

Several other aspects of SRI's operation and activities underline its character as an innovation hybrid. First, on the innovation side, SRI's work is widely associated with the creation of revolutionary new developments that include minimally invasive surgery, ultrasound, the first intelligent mobile robot, the computer mouse, the modem, personal computing, the birth of the internet, and much more. One should also note that these are virtually all NSS/DoD/DARPA-funded projects that have been researched, coordinated, or commercialized through SRI.

Second, SRI boasts a business model that "excel[s] at transitioning products from the laboratory to the assembly line" (Winarsky 2012, 44).[17] Indeed, SRI has been acclaimed as a spin-off engine, a commercialization machine, and in *Business Week*'s version, the "soul of Silicon Valley," famously licensing its technologies to create new startup companies.[18]

NSS funding is important, but it is not the only way the mission agencies achieve their goals by harnessing the power of hybrids. For instance, in addition to financing most of the innovations that SRI develops, the NSS also has a central role in orienting its research by virtue of formulating the problem sets that generate novel solutions.

As an example of this problem-setting role, consider the recent case of Siri, the mobile app that acts as a personal assistant, now installed on Apple's iPhone. The technology that underpins Siri originates in the DARPA-funded project CALO (Cognitive Agent that Learns and Organizes). CALO, derived from the Latin *calo*, meaning "soldier's servant," was an ambitious artificial Intelligence project which DARPA sponsored under its PAL (Personalized Assistant that Learns) program. In 2003, SRI International was awarded a five-year contract to lead the $200 million program (involving more than three hundred researchers from twenty-five universities and commercial organizations) and produce the prototypes.[19] In addition to the funding, DARPA provided the problem set: investigate the feasibility of a system that can help commanders and staff manage information more effectively in military command-and-control environments—specifically, personalized assistants that instead of having to be programmed anew "can reason, learn from experience, be told what to do, explain what they are doing, reflect on their experience, and respond robustly to surprise."[20]

In a typical process whereby an innovation originating in an NSS project becomes as it were "privatized," SRI then spun out Siri Inc., in order to shape the core technology into a product. Other Silicon Valley venture capital firms were then attracted to invest in the process; ultimately, Apple itself acquired the company and now controls the technology. Thus, a federal agency like DARPA will often be the instigator and financial sponsor of a specific SRI breakthrough. The sponsoring agency, however, "may not be the appropriate market for the resulting innovation. The SRI business model is designed to figure out the right markets for the federally funded innovation."[21]

The story of Siri's emergence reveals much about the undiminished role of NSS problem setting and technology sponsorship in the success of Silicon Valley. But it also reveals the prowess of a legendary hybrid, SRI, in finding new markets for national security–inspired innovations.

Federal Labs: The Transformation of R&D Hybrids into Spin-out Engines

The National Labs—predominantly attached to the Department of Energy— are widely considered the crown jewels of the nation's S&T enterprise (Hubry et al. 2011, 30). Known officially as Federally Funded Research and Development Centers, these hybrid entities formally partner federal labs with universities and industry to take later-stage research from the lab to the market. The labs engage in fundamental and applied research and technology development for the mission agencies. In seeking to commercialize federally funded and/or federally created innovations, they deploy a variety of mechanisms that include licensing innovations, sponsoring scientist-entrepreneurs, funding startups, and sometimes sharing development costs with industry partners. They are exclusively or mostly financed by the federal government, structured as not-for-profit, limited liability companies, and managed either by a university, a nonprofit organization, or an industrial firm.

Several labs stem from World War II when there was an urgent need to concentrate scientific expertise. After the war was over, their establishment as FFRDCs provided a means to retain this intellectual capital. As of 2009, there were thirty-nine such centers, deploying a budget of $15.2 billion to develop and commercialize innovations in everything from semiconductors and specialty materials to nanotechnology, robotics, and advanced batteries. The DoE and DoD have the most FFRDCs, with sixteen and ten respectively, followed by the NSF with four.[22]

Many advanced industrial countries have national institutions that work on applied research and seek to commercialize their results. Germany's famed Fraunhofer Institutes are perhaps the outstanding example. The Fraunhofer-Gesellschaft, however, is a public institution, not a hybrid. Another contrast with the NSS labs is that the Fraunhofer units are explicitly dedicated to applied research for commercial benefit; this is reflected in a funding model that makes them dependent on commercial success (and consequently on industry sponsors which account for 70 percent of their funding). By contrast, in the United States, mission success of the prime sponsor (for the most part, an NSS agency like the DoD or DoE) remains the highest priority. In this framework, commercial success is a means, not an end, to supporting or strengthening the security mission.

What then has changed? First, the understanding of mission success has broadened significantly since the 1980s; second, and as a consequence, so too has the role of the federal labs (Hubry et al. 2011, 30). After World War II, the labs' applied knowledge base served as a foundation for commercially relevant efforts in the private sector. In more recent times, however, these hybrid bodies have provided a much more direct boost to industry's commercialization efforts. Since the passing of the 1980 Stevenson-Wydler Act and subsequent amendments, the DoD-driven Federal Laboratory Consortium for Technology Transfer has used its Congressional mandate to deepen industry involvement in order to push lab inventions into the market (U.S. Congress, Office of Technology 1990a).

As a result of this sea change, a number of the most important national labs have become increasingly integrated into the entrepreneurial economy. Through mechanisms such as entrepreneurship training, exclusive licensing of lab inventions to startups, venture funding, and cost-shared industry partnerships (otherwise known as CRADAs, Cooperative Research and Development Agreements), the national labs have turned their hand to commercializing the results of research and technology development, spinning out innovations and new companies. Many FFRDCs now routinely deploy entrepreneurship training schemes for lab scientists, special leave schemes for staff to form startups, and venture funding to foster company spin-outs and product development.

The Department of Energy's Nuclear Weapons Labs

Consider two of the famed nuclear weapons laboratories, Los Alamos and Sandia. Both have a long history of innovation in everything from solar power and microelectronics to medical devices.[23] For the past two decades and more, they have been systematically turning their hand to entrepreneurial endeavors, marketing their innovations and creating startups. Los Alamos, for example, offers classes in commercialization and entrepreneurship, administers a formal Entrepreneurial Leave-of-Absence Program, and has developed a network of corporate and venture investors to help fund lab scientist startups. It also deploys a Technology Maturation Fund, as well as DoE enterprise funds, to help commercialize lab technologies. As the lab explains on its website, Los Alamos targets promising inventions that can be readily moved to the prototype stage in order "to attract potential licensees or investors interested in funding a startup company or commercializing a new technology." The Technology Maturation Fund is therefore "similar to a venture capital fund," but invests in internal technologies instead of start-up companies.[24] Funds come from a combination of licensing and royalty revenues and monies earmarked for this purpose under the laboratory's prime contract with Los Alamos National Security. Los Alamos National Security's Venture Acceleration Fund also provides modest investments (up to $100,000) to fund new or existing companies that commercialize lab technology.[25] As of 2008, Los Alamos had helped spawn at least fifty-four startups since 1997. Even the most esoteric projects, it seems may lend themselves to commercialization.[26]

In the same vein, Sandia, managed by Lockheed Martin's Sandia Corporation, combines its primary R&D mission—to manage DoD's nuclear stockpile—with sponsoring entrepreneurial ventures. Sandia runs its entrepreneurial training program through the nonprofit Technology Ventures Corporation which it established with funding from Lockheed and DoE. According to TVC's senior director, "We do sessions inside Sandia for their benefit" and in order "to find entrepreneurs from the scientific staff who may want to start their own commercial technology business."[27] TVC has started 114 companies, raising approximately $1.2 billion and employing over 13,000 people. Congress deems the model successful, providing the company with appropriations since 2002 in order to extend its commercialization services to other DoE laboratories.[28] Note that when labs partner with a company or startup to commercialize the technology involved, they typically deploy commercial license agreements, which specify payment either in license fees, or royalties on sales, or even equity in the licensee company.[29] In this and other respects, the labs have become quasi–business ventures, adding a further layer to their already hybridized nature.

One could easily extend such examples of entrepreneurial-cum-innovation hybrids beyond the DoE laboratories. For instance, Lincoln Laboratory, the DoD-sponsored lab run by MIT, which played a key role in developing the SAGE air defense system for the U.S. Air Force in the early 1950s, has spun out more than ninety companies since 1956. Most famous among them is Digital Equipment Corporation, which was started by staff at Lincoln Lab. MITRE Corporation, another important example of an innovation hybrid, is itself a spin-out of the MIT Lab as well as an FFRDC now sponsored by the departments of Defense and Homeland Security.

The Defense Department's Software Engineering Institute

Yet another important example is the DoD-Carnegie Mellon Software Engineering Institute (SEI), whose broad impact in the commercial arena is rarely a subject of scholarly attention. In contrast to other FFRDCs which became spin-out hubs in the 1980s, the SEI was expressly created to tackle the perceived threat of a strategic weakness in industry and military power involving software development. One year prior to SEI's establishment, Edith Martin, then Deputy Under Secretary of Defense for Research and Advanced Technology, clearly articulated the underlying motivation:

> The U.S. has lost its lead in many of the mature technologies from which our industrial base and military power were built. The threat of a similar strategic loss now faces the electronics, computer, and software industries and cannot be tolerated. The military and even the economic position of this country is inextricably tied to the ability

to exploit advantages of computer technology. The U.S. Department of Defense . . . which has consistently moved to ensure the vitality of the U.S. computer technology base . . . is preparing to launch a software initiative to complement the VHSIC and Ada programs. (Martin 1983, 53)[30]

The new hybrid's key objective was to advance software systems and techniques so that the United States could maintain its lead in this militarily important industry. SEI combined incentive programs that sought to build software expertise, introduce quality control measures, and diffuse technologies to industry. Bear in mind that programming in the early days was more an art than a science, and that there were no standards by which to evaluate software code. The SEI established the first quality control standards for software engineering (a fancy name for programming carried out in a systematic way), the Capability Maturity Model, which provides a graded series of quality assurance benchmarks that firms can aspire to reach. This was initially of importance to the military in making choices between software engineering firms bidding for military contracts, but then, as intended, it became more extensively used in industry and software-development organizations.[31] (With the latest version, CMM 5, the first companies to get certified were Indian software contractors like Infosys!) The SEI has also been playing a pivotal role in crisis recovery and security, for example, in response to cyber attacks—a major issue for both the NSS and private industry.

Twenty-five years ago none of the federal laboratories had extensive contact with industry from the point of view of commercializing innovations. Indeed, the managers of DoE's Defense Programs once viewed commercialization as a distraction from the agency's mission to supply the military's needs, but over time "it has come to believe that the military would benefit from stronger civilian industries" (U.S. Congress, Office of Technology Assessment 1990a, 187). Such considerations became more prominent during the 1980s as fears mounted that U.S. industries, battered by foreign competitors, were not sufficiently innovative. Thus another pressure for change, beyond—but overlapping with—the national security rationale, was the concern to exploit major discoveries before they could be developed by America's competitors (Trivelpiece 1988, 42).

But it would be a mistake to cast this or similar initiatives as a form of industry policy. This was no simple industry policy in the making, "hidden" or otherwise. Security issues kicked in even here insofar as commercial development was encouraged mostly where the DoD took a close interest in the military benefits of a discovery. An important example is the case of high-temperature superconductivity. When this phenomenon was discovered in 1986, Defense soon recognized the military and commercial potential of HTS materials and devices and called for pilot programs to be established. High-temperature superconductors are revolutionary materials that can be used in numerous ways, for example, to make lighter, smaller, more efficient, higher-capacity power devices; relieve congested power line networks; and increase power transmission capacity. The fear that this technology would be developed and commercialized elsewhere was the catalyst for the Reagan Administration's 1987 announcement of a cooperative HTS initiative to involve government, industry, and universities. In 1988, Commercialization Pilot Centers for Superconductivity were established at the DoE labs. Joint development projects with industry were supported on a fifty-fifty cost-shared basis with the express intent of developing stronger ties to industry and providing a test bed for new experiments in commercializing lab technology (U.S. Congress, Office of Technology Assessment 1990b, 66). In the same period, broader anxiety about the industrial base had generated "the concern that the United States might not have a sufficient opportunity to rapidly develop products or services based on this discovery" (Trivelpiece 1988, 42).[32] (Commercial applications of high-temperature superconductivity have since made possible dramatic improvements in cellular and satellite communications systems, for example, as well as greater accuracy of the Global Positioning System.) Moreover, the HTS project helped breathe new life into ailing labs like Argonne, whose funding for nondefense nuclear research had dried up. These converging concerns helped to move the national security labs into closer dealings with industry and ultimately, as Congressionally authorized incentives improved, to assume an entrepreneurial character. Simply focusing on the DoE's commercialization programs in superconductivity might lead one to classify the HTS initiative as industry policy. Linking them to Defense's prior interest in superconductivity enables us to see the strategic military driver and the synergies arising from this general-purpose technology.

Commercialization Consortia

A third hybrid arrangement for commercializing technology is the three-way consortium that brings industry and university researchers together with an NSS agency or its R&D lab. While there are many such consortia, not all are hybrids. Many are simple partnerships with a fixed- (usually short-) term objective after which the alliance is terminated (such as the advanced battery alliance or the robotics technology consortium). Those arrangements are genuine hybrids that have a more institutionalized character, such as CCAT, the Navy's Center for Commercialization of Advanced Technology.[33] Another case is the Army's Institute for Soldier Nanotechnologies (chapter 6). ISN is a three-way collaboration that brings MIT and industry together with the U.S. Army—as both problem-setting sponsor and hands-on R&D partner. The ISN venture is phrased in terms of a national security outcome—to expedite the mass-manufacture of products in order to serve "the customer—the individual soldier." Commercial companies collaborate because ISN is a dual-use technology program; it calls for cost-sharing from its industry partners and receives proposals from companies interested in developing MIT technologies for civilian as well as military markets.[34]

What we see in each of these commercialization ventures is a state whose innovation goals are neither mediated nor conducted at a distance by third parties. Rather, through the mission agencies, the state is closely integrated in innovation decisions and outcomes as funder, problem setter, catalyst, network node—and ultimate user.

Government Sponsored Venture Funds

One of the most innovative—and unusual—innovation hybrids that has gained ground since World War II is the government-sponsored venture capital fund (GVF). With the exception of ARCH (chapter 3)—these funds are quite different in purpose from the hybrid funds at the DoE laboratories. Unlike the latter, whose primary purpose is to spin out federal innovations from the labs to the private sector, government-sponsored funds typically invest directly in companies that have emerging technologies of interest to users within the mission agencies.

With some exceptions, the GVF is typically set up as a private, for-profit or nonprofit investment firm, which is funded either entirely or chiefly by a public agency. The CIA's In-Q-Tel is undoubtedly the best known. Less well understood is the wider role of the NSS in helping to kick-start the modern venture capital industry, or indeed its continuing significance in America's venture capital system—notably through the GVF's pivotal investment role in the high-risk end of the innovation chain. in chapter 3 I probed the great variety of GVF arrangements, examined how they emerged from or became enmeshed with the national security state, thereby highlighting their commercially significant influence. Here I focus on the case of In-Q-Tel, in particular the hybrid quality of the fund and its interfacing with the private sector.

When the George H. W. Bush administration sacked DARPA Director Craig Fields, the episode made headlines. Fields was ostensibly removed for appearing to stray too far into the commercial arena, after having taken DARPA into a series of new dual-use ventures. But the final straw came when he authorized a $4 million equity investment in a company making semiconductor devices with advanced materials.[35] In spite of what proved to be a well-judged investment, such an obvious breach of the state-market divide left the DARPA leader vulnerable to antistatist opposition, leading to his subsequent removal.

By contrast, when the CIA wanted to do the same thing that DARPA had attempted but on a much larger scale, it took the safer route by creating a hybrid—a venture capital company that looks for all the world like a wholly private venture. Just like a private venture capital company, the CIA's equity investment arm, In-Q-Tel, takes equity positions in private enterprise, and sells equity stakes to realize a profit; it interfaces on a regular basis with the private VC community to lead an investment round; it remunerates its private-sector managers in the manner of a VC company; and it funds technologies with significant commercial market potential.

The big difference is that In-Q-Tel is organized as a nonprofit vehicle, is wholly "owned" and funded by the CIA, though legally independent, and pursues a distinctive mission: to identify promising innovations in the private sector that can be modified or developed for use by the intelligence community. Since the aim was to attract the interest of the private sector, the decision was made to direct most investment to "areas where there was both an Agency need and private sector interest" (Yannuzzi 2000, 29). The CIA uses its VC fund to serve its mission while also sponsoring development of viable products for the private market. The reader may recognize at least one of them: Keyhole—a firm that develops interactive 3-D visualization technology, originally marketed as a real estate application, then following In-Q-Tel's involvement, used by the Pentagon and National Geospatial-Intelligence Agency in the Iraq war. The CIA led the investment round to develop the technology. Google, soon after, acquired Keyhole—which we now know as Google Earth.

Much has been written about In-Q-Tel's success and investment savvy. Rather less has been said about the thinking behind its formation. In a candid statement, In-Q-Tel's then CEO, Amit Yoran, opened a window onto that thinking, revealing a mindset that takes into account a kind of pragmatic antistatism at work in the broader community. The important thing for a VC company like In-Q-Tel, he emphasized, is to "avoid the trap of becoming bureaucratic." How is this ensured? "The short answer is we are not a government organization. . . . We make independent decisions. We pride ourselves on independent thought and being nimble. Part of our mission is to stay largely independent and unencumbered by bureaucracy. We look and act to the world as regular venture capitalists."[36]

So how is In-Q-Tel structured to make that happen? In the first place, the composition of its Board of Trustees straddles the worlds of commerce, academe, and national security. In-Q-Tel's founding CEO, credited as one of In-Q-Tel's founders, was former CEO of Lockheed Martin Norm Augustine. Second, In-Q-Tel is legally independent of the CIA and responsible for its own operations. Because it is designed to operate on an equal footing with its commercial peers it has license to undertake a range of deals—establish joint ventures, fund grants, sponsor open competitions, award sole source contracts, and so forth—without seeking agency approval. At the same time, however, the CIA needs continuous insight into In-Q-Tel's activities, and this task falls to a specially created Interface Center (QIC) within the Directorate of Science and Technology. QIC has the "day-to-day responsibility for guiding the CIA's relationship with In-Q-Tel, including the design and implementation of the contract and the problem set" (Yanuzzi 2000, 38). In-Q-Tel's success has not been without some controversy, which arises from these private-sector qualities.[37] Even so, the CIA model is widely admired, not least by the services and the DoD, which have set up their own different versions of the hybrid fund (see chapter 3).

There are many more variations on innovation hybrids examined, which I will not pursue here. My objective has been to highlight the way this fusion of public and private structures enables the U.S. government to foster new business ventures, undertake risky investments, broker new deals—in short, to actualize entrepreneurial activism more or less by proxy. Such patterns of course shine a clear light on the hybrid nature of the American state. One may also add that such endeavors appear incompatible with antistatism and are rarely associated with the U.S. government, least of all with its national security components. Working through hybrid structures no doubt helps to preserve that perception of "governance without government."

Three main patterns emerge from this analysis. First, the changes in public-private sector relations that innovation hybrids represent have effectively integrated the state into investment decisions and market processes. Whether one chooses to view this as "direct" or "indirect" state involvement makes no difference to this fact. Hybrid creations have become the federal government's preferred vehicle through which to pursue innovation and absorb risk across the investment cycle, from research and development all the way to commercialization.[38]

Second, rather than Congress strengthening and institutionalizing the innovation role of the civilian agencies, the agencies and laboratories of the national security state have instead had their missions broadened to include commercial strength. As a Congressional Research Service report put it, national security has been "redefined to include economic well-being in addition to weapons superiority" (2008, 16). In pursuit of its own strategic objectives, the national security state has thus emerged as a key source of "developmental" hybridization.

Third, hybrids take traditional "bureaucracy" out of state involvement in the market and thus create the appearance (illusion?) of an absent or passive state, of economic governance without government. This is plausibly the main source of their popularity. I do not dispute the claim that hybrids can effectively reduce transparency and minimize public accountability; but such effects are more consequence of than cause or motivation for creating hybrids in the first place. In this light, recall that the U.S. preference for hybrids goes back a long way—before such concepts achieved the political currency they have today.

Why Hybridization?

We began with two observations regarding the lengthy history of hybridization and the recent growth of innovation hybrids.[39] These give rise to two related questions: Why hybridization? And why the recent proliferation?

With regard to the first, historian William Novak writes that "public-private governance" is "a distinctive form of American policymaking with roots back to the earliest settlements and the constitutional foundations of the republic" (Novak 2009, 40). Indeed in the economic arena, some might say that hybrids began with Alexander Hamilton who created the nation's first public-private partnership, the Society for Establishing Useful Manufactures, to compete with Great Britain (National Research Council 2007, 153). So, what accounts for the U.S. preference for hybrids, or as Novak (2009, 32) puts it, a "preference for balancing public direction with private initiative"?

Neoliberal preferences? One hypothesis is that hybridization arises from a neoliberal preference for institutional insulation from democratic oversight and from a strategy "to integrate state decision-making into the dynamics of capital accumulation and the networks of class power that are in the process of restoration" (Harvey 2005, 77). However, as an explanation for a hybrid-ization tendency, the neoliberal preference only makes sense under three conditions: if all those involved in the decision-making are neoliberal in pol-icy preferences and/or suspicious of democracy; if neoliberalism has been the ascendant policy paradigm since the emergence of hybrids in the U.S. system, that is to say well before the 1980s; and if all such hybrids escaped Congressional oversight. None of these statements stands up to scrutiny. As already noted, scholars have documented hybridization as a well-established pattern in U.S. history, dating back several centuries. Equally inconvenient for the "neoliberal preference" hypothesis is the inability to account for why hybridization has been driven and supported by both sides of the political spectrum. This suggests the influence of something more deeply entrenched than a focus on actor preferences would imply.

Domestic institutions and ideology? A plausible hypothesis must be able to account for continuity—the persistence of the tendency in question right up to the present. This reconnects my argument to the role of antistatism—understood not just as a dominant constitutional tendency to divide and dis-tribute power, but most importantly as an ideological/normative mind-set that self-interested groups can also exploit to advantage.[40]

Thus we return to the role of hybrids. Earlier discussion showed how in-novation hybrids focus in one way or another on assisting the private sector to develop and commercialize innovations for the marketplace. Their primary motivation, however, is to attract the private sector to undertake innovative activity of interest to the military and NSS generally. Their creation and con-tinuing operation therefore generally involve substantial government input and influence in business and market outcomes, modifying and absorbing investment risk on behalf of the private sector. The puzzle remains why these entities find favor with the nation's lawmakers in a country famous for its antistatism.[41] The answer, I suggest, lies in the nature of these entities them-selves. As Amit Yoran pointed out in seeking to give In-Q-Tel a positive spin, the fund does not look like a government agency and does not act like one.

That is something that resonates positively with a broader American constituency. One might therefore conclude that the GVF's unconventional focus on commercializing technology collaboratively with private-sector firms is well suited to the U.S. context because it "serves to lessen the ideological objection" to what might otherwise seem to be a government-driven innovation program.[42]

Phrased in more theoretical language, one might posit that innovation hybrids are organic to the U.S. institutional environment in which antistatist political norms flourish. Because such hybrids address the demand for state activism in a variety of ways that sidestep traditional bureaucracy, they are more likely to emerge in a context shaped by certain institutional constraints, specifically, one in which strong conventions exist against the use of state power to achieve economic goals. To this extent, we would expect to find a greater reliance on nonstate and hybrid forms of intervention to address policy goals in the U.S. setting. This would help also to explain why hybrids find broad support from both Democrats and Republicans, interventionists and market fundamentalists.[43] As suggested earlier with regard to the creation of the Federal Reserve system, hybrids are favored because they have cross-partisan appeal: for laissez-faire conservatives they are a form of privatization, for progovernment liberals a form of public intervention. As one early observer of America's hybrid economy put it, "They found in this hybrid economy a confluence of interests and a new consensus."[44]

Why the Recent Profusion of Hybrids?

To answer this question, we must look for changes in the environment that may have created a greater demand for hybrid responses in more recent times. Establishing timelines for the growth of hybrid organizations does not lend itself to precision. Some authors start the clock ticking in the 1980s, but they have in mind a much broader idea of the hybrid economy than my own (which does not include privatization or simple partnerships). Although innovation hybrids are dotted right across the postwar period, the post-1980 period does mark a high water point for the remodeling of existing and the formation of new hybrids. As I have already indicated, this period was not only marked by "fears of American industrial decline and fiscal crisis" (Sternberg 1993, 11). It was also prefaced by the gathering innovation crisis of the late 1970s and early 1980s. Importantly, it was this concern that impinged directly on U.S. military strategy. Since the U.S. strategic goal was to depend on superior technology rather than quantity of materiel to best the Soviet Union, the growing flight of innovators from the NSS portfolio threatened its success. Superimposed onto this strategic issue was the more contingent geopolitical challenge from America's major high-technology competitor. The fear of losing the race in microelectronics to Japan, and the need to access capabilities in the commercial domain led to major rethinking of the incentive structure.

In this reformulation, NSS technology policy would increasingly offer the private sector the carrot of commercial viability and dual-use applications of NSS innovations. It is important to stress this strategic point in order to understand why the NSS has become more commercially proactive, since it diverges from the claim that the United States pursues a hidden industrial policy via Defense.

If we take the period since the late 1970s as our point of reference, we can therefore note three important structural changes—one in the domestic arena and two in the international system—that challenged federal authorities over the next decade or so to refocus policy priorities. One outcome of this policy shift has been a more commercially proactive NSS. Another outcome—closely related to that shift and examined in this chapter—has been the process of institutional fusion that I have called hybridization. So what were the changes orienting that shift?

The first change, although domestic in origin, impacts directly on military strategy and gives primary impetus to the shift in technology policy—namely, the need to find a solution to the problem of reconnecting defense and related NSS components with the more innovative nontraditional suppliers in the burgeoning information technology sector. These firms had veered (or stayed) away from the government market. Reattracting them was essential for the military strategy of technological superiority to succeed. Recharging the incentives structure connected with NSS projects—in particular, by holding out the promise of commercially viable innovations and granting ownership of federally funded intellectual property—was the end result of this process.

A second overlapping change was the Japanese "technonationalist" challenge, experienced most intensely in the domestic arena through falling productivity and profits, loss of market share to the new giant from Asia, and, in particular throughout the 1980s, Japan's emerging dominance in high technology. It was during this period that a "competitiveness coalition" took form, espousing a new national narrative focused on American economic renewal—much as we are witnessing today as a result of the Great Recession. Some date the legislative beginnings of the "competitiveness agenda" between 1980 and 1983, and trace its effects in institutional changes that reshaped the rules governing ownership of publicly funded research (such as patent reforms), and that promoted new collaborative partnerships (e.g., Slaughter and Rhoades 1996, 323). State responses to economic contingencies such as declining competitiveness weave in and out of the NSS innovation story and frequently piggyback on strategic imperatives, making it sometimes difficult to disentangle motivations for government responses. Nevertheless, it should be evident from earlier discussion that NSS actors viewed Japan's rising prominence in high-tech industry as a threat to the United States' technological supremacy; from their perspective—however seamless the commerce-security connection was becoming—addressing that threat was thus a national security imperative. Combined with the need to expand the domestic network of technology innovators, these pressures gave some urgency to the reforms and public-private mergers in question. As we saw, the 1970s DoD-sponsored company surveys, for example, revealed that uncertainty over patent rights was acting as a key disincentive against working with the NSS, and contributed to patent reform in the 1980s. The important point about geo-economic change in this context is this: it calls forth pressures for government action in the very era when the state (qua federal government) is being stigmatized in the official narrative as "the problem, not the solution." This antistatist constraint, whether pragmatic, self-interested, or ideological in origin, tends to find some resolution in hybridized responses.

The third major change was also geopolitical in origin, namely the demise of the Soviet empire, the dismantling of the Cold War machinery and the much-anticipated peace dividend. The resulting shift in federal funding priorities, and the rise of asymmetric threats that prioritize radical innovation in information technology, have combined to place a premium on access and affordability in NSS technology policy. This has had the effect of institutionalizing dual-use practice as policy. Thus although the new competitiveness regime was politically contested and short-lived as the economy bounced back,[45] from the 1990s onward, the national security agencies would seek to incorporate commercial considerations both in their mission goals and in their technology sponsorship.

It follows that both the pressures and the opportunities for a larger role for the state are therefore substantial in this period. But there is one further situational influence that we must factor in, which goes counter to that outcome (and to which I have already alluded): namely, the rise of a neoliberal coalition poised to take the state out of the economy and to take public assets out of the public sector. The broadening of agency missions and the massive deployment of the public science and technology infrastructure for commercial achievement as well as national security needs was the outcome.

In sum, I conclude that the efflorescence of America's hybrid economy, while sourced from earlier developments, is a product of an unusual confluence of structural, situational, and institutional factors. Changes in the domestic arena, the international economy, and the geopolitical environment tested both military strategy and, intermittently, U.S. competitiveness. These changes, in turn, created pressing demands as well as new opportunities for state activism at the very time that neoliberal dictums have been in the ascendant,[46] embodied in President Ronald Reagan's much cited slogan: "Government isn't the solution, government is the problem." Republicans, and then Democrats, seized on the ideology of public-private partnership. When irresistible force meets immoveable object, hybridization comes to the rescue.

8

Penetrating the Myths of the Military-Commercial Relationship

Myths which are believed in tend to become true.
George Orwell, 1947

The central proposition of this study is that the NSS is the originating source of America's commercial prowess in high-technology. Without the NSS and the strategic stimuli that have sustained its existence, the United States would probably be an innovator much like Germany or Japan, but it would not generate the revolutionary multipurpose innovations that give rise to whole new industries. In short, it would not be a high-tech hegemon.

In the course of advancing this proposition, I have also challenged several influential ideas and assumptions that have framed conventional thinking about the relationship between defense and commercial industry—concepts that ultimately have the status of myths. In so calling them, I do not intend to suggest that they are mere fictions; rather, I use the term "myth" to mean a foundational or influential narrative that has become the conventional view, or part of an ideology, or is considered to illustrate a cultural ideal—two examples of the latter being the myth of American individualism, and the myth of the free market. There are often grounds of some sort for the beliefs in question, but these look far from robust when examined with two eyes rather than one.

Readers will already be aware from earlier discussion of the key myths regarding the defense-commerce relationship that I have christened "serendipitous spin-off," "hidden industry policy," the "wall of separation," and "quantity of R&D spending creates innovation leadership." My purpose here is to provide both a general overview and individual criticism of these myths. In addition, I examine a quite different aspect of the military-commercial relationship which, while also distinguishing my approach, lies more in the realm of controversy than myth. This turns on the continuing controversy that surrounds the issue of defense spending. I aim to clarify why it is that efforts to quantify the economic impacts of R&D spending (specifically defense R&D) remain controversial, and more important, why different appraisals of defense spending—both positive and negative versions, "military Keynesian" and "depletionist" respectively—remain extraneous to the arguments of this book.

Four Myths Laid Bare

The first myth in our series, that of serendipitous spin-off, assumes that such spin-offs are the key feature of the relationship between mission-oriented technology development and commercial innovation. In this view, spin-offs from the defense-NSS enterprise have occurred mostly by chance, rather than by choice, intent, or influence. As an account of how major NSS-sponsored breakthrough innovations have kick-started high-tech industries, serendipity is congenial to U.S. policymakers because it complements rather than contradicts America's free-market identity. By creating the impression that the innovations occurred without the anticipation, influence, or support of defense and related agencies, the serendipity myth serves as the conceptual twin of the laissez-faire construction of American capitalism.[1]

The industrial policy myth can be seen as the counterpart of the serendipity view. Its central claim is that America practices a de facto or hidden version of industrial policy through its national defense establishment. The myth's adherents contend that, although often pursued with considerable success, America's industrial policy is piecemeal and inchoate, "irrational and uncoordinated" because it lacks a coherent plan.[2] Industrial policy proponents have thereby sought to convert skeptics and opponents of government involvement in the economy. Rather than pretending it does not exist, they reason with all good intent, better to admit it and craft a coherent version of industrial policy that will work to the nation's advantage.[3]

The wall of separation myth is the conceptual twin of the notion of the military-industrial complex. Recalling President Eisenhower's 1961 speech, wall of separation proponents see a dichotomy between commercial and military technologies and defense-related production, the latter being an activity that takes place in highly specialized firms isolated from the rest of the economy. Because the kind of firm fostered by the defense market is viewed as fundamentally different from the commercial firm, there is very little scope for overlapping technologies.[4]

The spending determines leadership view assumes that mission-oriented programs have drastically weakened NSS leverage over technological development as a result of reducing its share of the nation's R&D investment. Once the leading sponsor of the nation's R&D, contributing 67 percent of U.S. funds in 1964, the federal government had seen its share fall to

26 percent by 2008. Conversely, business provided more than two-thirds of the total.[5] This reversal is widely used to suggest a before-and-after picture in which military-related R&D once mattered to the wider economy but has barely counted since being overtaken by private-sector spending. Since the U.S. private sector now dominates in R&D funding, many believe that this translates into technological leadership and conversely, that it renders the NSS largely irrelevant to commercial innovation.[6]

Serendipitous Spin-Off

In the serendipity story, defense technology produces commercial spin-offs without the need for any government assistance or planning. More than two decades ago, Alic et al. provided a compelling critique of this view's underlying assumptions. In particular, they challenged the policymaker's conception of the spin-off as the easy, inexpensive unplanned gift of defense-led technology. On the contrary, they argued, spin-off was often complex, time-consuming and costly for industry. Indeed, it might entail considerable support from the mission agencies. Moreover, the more similar or general-purpose the technologies and the more co-involved the mission and industrial communities (through such factors as R&D cooperation, technology procurement and demonstration, and personnel mobility) the more likely that firms will reap commercial benefits from mission-oriented innovation.

Most critically, as the discussion of specific NSS technology procurement programs here has shown, the serendipity myth misses a key shift within the DoD's approach itself: from less to more purposeful spin-offs, and from narrow to broad commercial support. Of course an element of serendipity inheres in all technology development conducted at the frontier. Being unable to fully anticipate outcomes, producing new widgets often in the process of solving unrelated problems—this is the stuff of all R&D that works at the edge of what is known. What, after all, is the nature of radical innovation if not this very uncertainty, this risk that cannot be calculated?[7] Even if R&D is for a military goal, one cannot predict whether the outcome will be military or commercial. Those involved in a large-scale multifaceted R&D program are likely to produce a whole range of technologies applicable to many uses—so-called "technological surprises." The Navy's funding of research on microwaves, to take one example, had something very different in mind than the multiple cutting, targeting, and telecommunications applications that eventually resulted.

The important point is, however, that spin-off and technological surprise have become to a large extent institutionalized—that is, well anticipated and planned for. For several decades, NSS technology procurement programs and venture funds, for example, have favored both mission-oriented and commercial applications at the outset. We can note a similar process of institutionalization by shifting our gaze from the NSS to large defense contractors, where we find the creation of "commercialization engines" dedicated to spinning mission technologies into new companies, for instance Raytheon's military work in optical (transparent) ceramics.[8] More generally, hybrid public-private institutions have been expressly designed for that "translation" purpose, equipped with business models that seek to capitalize on that very same spin-out process (as we saw in the case of SRI International). In all these cases and more, we observe cross-fertilization between the two domains and an institutionalized preparedness to reap whatever commercial benefits inhere in, or can be extracted from, co-involvement in the mission-oriented space.

But there is an even more significant point to make in this connection. The conventional focus on defense spin-offs has not only averted attention from spin-around; it has masked the reality of a much richer, more complex relationship between the NSS and commercial innovation.[9] As I have sought to show throughout the present study, this relationship runs from the generation of problem sets, which catalyze multipurpose revolutionary advances, to the reduction of business risk through early-stage funding, the sharing of discovery and invention with the private sector, the creation of entirely new industries, and the early acquisition of innovations by technically demanding users in the mission agencies. Such actions by no means exhaust the commercial scope of NSS activism, but they do caution us against the oversimplification that has resulted from the idea of serendipitous spin-off. To the extent that the idea has persisted, one suspects this is because it appeals to a sizeable number of policymakers who balk at the idea of a civilian technology policy.

Hidden Industrial Policy

The notion that America practices an industrial policy largely through its national defense establishment has found favor among two different groups: on one hand, policy advocates who wish to "civilianize" U.S. technology policy, and on the other, policy critics who seek to play up the existence of a gap between the U.S. government's free-market advocacy and its actual practice. While recognizing the cues that might point one in this direction (having myself entertained the industrial policy hypothesis when commencing this study), I have since come to reject it. Instead, I have found that although the military, along with other NSS components, has evolved an explicit commercial orientation in its approach to innovation, the underlying principle and intent differ significantly from those that drive an industrial policy, hidden or otherwise.

Industrial policy arguments tend to emerge during periods of pronounced economic downturn when governments are most under pressure to ease the pain. For example, both the Reagan and the George H. W. Bush administrations undertook significant policy initiatives to strengthen industry's technological capabilities. In spite of their professed rejection of intervention in the market, the security as well as commercial implications of intense foreign competition eroding the high-tech industrial base could not be ignored. This led federal policymakers to promote closer collaboration between industry, universities, and the national laboratories, and to see the merits of subsidizing the semiconductor consortium Sematech.

However, when applied to the more commercially proactive agenda of the mission agencies, the hidden industrial policy characterization misses two important cues that combine to drive that agenda. Examining changes in the domestic context as well as pressures from the international strategic environment offers an enhanced, more accurate understanding of government involvement than the proxy industrial policy view. Importantly, this understanding also meshes with the DoD's own account of its commercial activism.

Moving beyond the industrial policy framework, I identify four motivations that drive the NSS to directly encourage industrial innovation. First and most important has been the intention to provide the private sector with an attractive incentive that would counter the flight from defense-related work where the government market has contracted relative to the much larger commercial markets, chiefly in the critical information technology sector. Second is the desire to secure a sustainable domestic supply of items by ensuring their suitability for larger commercial markets. Third is the effort to reduce costs to the services and other NSS components by taking advantage of the much greater commercial scale and R&D resources available to the private sector. A final, if less common ambition, is to enhance NSS user confidence in innovations by having them seen first of all widely deployed in commercial applications. We have already seen most of these motivations at work in earlier chapters; nonetheless it is fruitful to review them here, noting how they relate to changes in domestic structures and the broader strategic environment. Above all, however commercially oriented the mission agencies may be, their motivations remain fundamentally different from those that orient an industrial policy.

Stemming the flight from defense-related R&D is a most important driver. As we saw, the DoD (and broader NSS) shift toward encouraging commercially relevant innovation initially took shape as a means to stop the flight of innovative firms from the defense-related market. As early as 1972, it was known that ponderous procurement practices and uncertainty surrounding patent policy for government-sponsored R&D were steering innovative firms away from the government market, paving the way for shortages of critical customized devices (such as integrated circuits). This problem was emerging just when the United States was defining its dominance of the battlefield in terms of superior technology as opposed to the Soviet emphasis on quantity of armaments.

The flight of private firms from government R&D would prove to be a recurring issue creating difficulties mostly for Defense and the intelligence community. In the second half of the 1980s, several studies articulated the need to address the "eroding industrial base." This was code for industry's rejection of NSS work in favor of more profitable commercial markets, which was found to be affecting not only product innovation but also the manufacturing process. In 1989, a major report co-sponsored by members of the House Armed Services Committee drew attention to "the rush of commercial firms away from the defense business" in addition to the erosion of manufacturing capacity and process innovation, and called for new legislation, policies, and programs to deal with the problem (Bingaman et al. 1989, 5). A decade of reforms and programmatic changes later, the problem had once again resurfaced among the nation's leading seventy-five or so information-technology companies, the majority of which would not conduct R&D for the military. Top officials at the Pentagon linked this domestic issue to DoD's strategic interests, emphasizing how the U.S. military's future technological superiority—"a battlefield dominated by information technology"[10]—was in jeopardy if it failed to access and influence commercial innovation.

Thus, from the late 1970s and through the 1980s into the 1990s, as the national security supply base for information technology and microelectronics began to shrink, and as budget pressures increased, it became a matter of strategic importance to improve the capacity of and incentive for commercial companies to support the NSS.[11] Recognizing this problem, executives within the NSS called for greater investment in emerging commercial technologies that could be put to use in both markets, and by the same token, improve the incentives for commercial firms to work with government.

As for reining in escalating costs and increasing returns on R&D investment, in a growing number of areas, the development of commercial applications for advanced military technologies has become "a way to increase use and thus to lower the cost to DoD."[12] To illustrate, in the 1980s DoD pursued an important integrated circuit technology, microwave monolithic integrated circuits (MIMICs—advanced gallium arsenide semiconductors used for radar) as a strictly military development. However, the high cost of the devices prohibited their widespread use. The lesson was not lost on Defense and by the 1990s, it had turned things around by encouraging MIMIC contractors "to pursue commercial applications—in collision-avoidance systems for automobiles, satellite communications, and air traffic control signal processing." "The payoff to defense," as a study from the Office of Technology Policy reported, "is the world's best radar at a lower cost by leveraging commercial production."

NASA is another mission agency with a long and active history of producing technologies that have found widespread use—and not by chance. "It's something we do to create a return on investment," states one of NASA's technology transfer program executives under the Office of the Chief

Technologist. Of course, as the same official reasons, from an industrial policy perspective this makes little sense because "If you wanted to create a miniaturized heart pump, building a space shuttle main engine wouldn't be the most efficient way to go about doing that."[13] Although the innovations are not designed with the marketplace in mind, NASA officials see the value of commercial uptake for the agency not merely in the form of royalties, but also in the form of public support. Having watched its budget steadily decline since the 1970s, NASA took the decision to justify its value to the Treasury by publicizing the broader commercial applications emerging from its R&D investments.

Exploiting the synergies of spin-around, such as sustaining supply and enhancing confidence in a technology, highlights a final motivation. We have seen many examples in earlier chapters of the spin-around process, whereby an innovation that originated in an NSS project migrates into the commercial arena where it is refined and scaled up, then comes back to the NSS as if it were an actual creation of the private sector. Although the process is well known to NSS practitioners, it is rarely articulated in this manner, or indeed as a strategy for developing and diffusing commercial innovations. One of the clearest statements comes from DARPA: "Often the best way to transition a technology into DoD is to transition it to commercial industry so that it can be made available to DoD in the form of commercial off-the-shelf products and services (Defense Advanced Projects Agency 1998, 41). It is worth repeating the spin-around logic here, since it offers yet another rationale for the NSS to support commercial innovation, which is at odds with the industry policy assumption. Promoting general-purpose technologies that can be spun back to government agencies ensures a source of supply that is sustainable and affordable. DARPA's aspirations for restarting "a robust and competitive supercomputing industry" through its High-Productivity Computing Systems project illustrate the intent: "to prime the industrial pump so that the technologies will be honed and made more affordable—and therefore more likely to be adopted."[14] In the words of the project's manager, "We didn't want to design a machine that would only work for us, and be very expensive. We really wanted a machine that would be more broadly useful. This would be cheaper and more sustainable in the long run." Designing technologies that will have both military and commercial applications is clearly an effective way to make government-funded technology available in commercial venues so that the technology can be further developed and eventually spun back to government. As a DoD program manager of the cost-shared Dual Use Science and Technology Program explained, "That's really the key. You can develop the technology, incorporate it into commercial products which support an industrial base, and then DoD can tap into it."[15]

In the case of other NSS components, such as the DoE weapons laboratories, spinning out new companies with lab technology is also framed as a means to advance mission goals. The nuclear lab at Sandia, for example, envisaged its commercialization of microelectromechanical systems devices and products that sense, think, act, communicate, and self-power—not just as a source of future income for the lab, but also as a vehicle for widespread usage that would "boost the confidence needed to deploy it in critical defense applications."[16] Following a similar logic, the Missile Defense Agency (a legacy of Reagan's defense buildup) puts effort into commercializing mission innovations through its Technology Applications Program. The agency claims that this effort "reduces costs" and "improves the reliability of the ballistic missile defense system" by expanding the military market to encompass commercial applications.[17]

Stemming the flight from defense work, reducing costs and sustaining supply, boosting returns on agency investment, and enhancing confidence in the technology—all these efforts lead the NSS to boost commercial innovation in a deliberate and purposive manner. The basic underlying principle, however, is not the promotion of economic competitiveness, as industrial policy proponents would claim. It is rather that these efforts buttress the primary NSS endeavor, which has been to ensure the superior technology essential to sustaining American primacy (however contested that status may currently be).

Wall of Separation and Military-Industrial Complex

The key focus of the wall of separation myth is defense contracting. Its central assumption is that defense-related procurement is dependent on a manufacturing base substantially isolated from commercial activities; that peculiarities of the defense-contracting relationship—such as special military requirements and separate accounting practices—have created a system of captive suppliers able to satisfy only defense-unique needs, hence having little potential for overlap with commercial activities, skills, or markets. Prominent exponents of this idea thus posit an unbridgeable divide between commercial and military production that weaves its way right through the various subcontractor layers, leaving little scope for cross-fertilization (Markusen 1991, 400, 404; Markusen and Yudken 1992).

Earlier chapters have shown why the wall of separation has operated more as warning device than generalized constraint. Whereas many see the impediments and disincentives to working with defense as erecting permanent barriers, in fact these very disincentives stimulated an effort within the NSS that was designed to draw commerce and security closer together, and a variety of NSS approaches deliberately breach the commerce-security divide by building in the marketability of technologies from the very start of the development process.

The findings of three different survey-based studies undertaken at roughly ten-year intervals confirm this analysis. First is the influential 1986

Packard Commission report which examined defense procurement practices and how to improve them. This study was motivated by the poor image that surrounded the Pentagon-contractor relationship and by public alarm at cost overruns and allegations of abuse and fraud. In the course of its extensive analysis of the problems besetting defense contracting, the study drew the opposite conclusion to the one implied by the idea of a military-commercial divide.[18] It highlighted instead the existence of a "dual commercial-military product base": "DoD makes only a small percentage of its equipment. It depends primarily on the nation's industrial companies to develop weapons and to manufacture everything from belt buckles to aircraft carriers. In general, these companies do not work solely on defense contracts . . . in this way, the technological base developed for commercial products can be effectively applied to military products, and vice versa" (Packard Commission 1986, 43). Indeed, the extent to which the nation's companies engage in production for both sectors was later adduced in the commission's recommendations as justification for Defense to expand its use of commercial products in lieu of customized military ones. As we saw, this was not simply a matter of plucking existing commercial products off the shelf. The commission envisaged that the DoD would have to be drawn more fully into developing and diffusing civilian technology, if it were to increase its reliance on off-the-shelf technologies.

In the following decade, as conversion to a post–Cold War era loomed large in public debate about defense-led technology, a second study set out to identify if any barriers existed to converting the bulk of defense plants to further serve commercial markets. Just how specialized and isolated from the rest of the economy were defense-contracting firms? Kelley and Watkins's (1995) study, unusual insofar as it actually subjected the wall of separation claim to empirical testing, provides the most comprehensive demolition to date of that thesis. They surveyed a random sample of 973 U.S. manufacturing plants in 21 capital goods industry sectors.[19] Their findings overturn the influential belief that little overlap exists between defense and commercial activities. On the contrary, the authors demonstrate that in the capital goods sector,

- Defense spending reaches a broad segment of manufacturing, affecting nearly one-half of all establishments.
- Commercial-military integration was largely the normal practice at the end of the Cold War.
- The vast majority of defense contractors manufacture military products in the same facilities using the same workforce and equipment employed in producing items for commercial customers. Indeed, commercial customers dominate the sales of most defense contractors.
- Firms engaged in defense contracting invest more than their strictly commercial counterparts in modern, productivity-enhancing technologies

that are relevant to nonmilitary production. This is explicable, Kelley and Watkins point out, when one considers that DoD has provided a more supportive environment for long-term investments and the diffusion of advanced technology than occurs for firms engaged in strictly commercial customer-supplier relations.[20]

Regarding this last finding, it is worth pausing to take note of how it qualifies the varieties of capitalism theory of the U.S. model of capitalism. For here we see yet another way in which the NSS appears to plug institutional gaps in the U.S. model of capitalism—not only with regard to the market for patient capital, including early-stage venture funding, but also with regard to the market for intermediate goods, as indicated by the last finding concerning interfirm relations. In other words, in distinction to the spot-market approach of U.S. companies to their subcontractors, the NSS (qua DoD) encourages its primes to engage in longer-term relational contracting with their suppliers. This illustrates the principle of institutional compensation that was sorely missing from earlier analysis of comparative capitalism with its emphasis on institutional congruence and complementarity.

It seems then that the idea of a great divide in the organization of military and commercial production was built less on solid evidence than on "too much attention" being paid "to a few high profile cases" (Kelley and Watkins 1995, 529). That conclusion was reaffirmed roughly a decade on when a third study reported similar findings across four different high-technology sectors. The 2004 survey, commissioned on behalf of the U.S. Air Force by the Department of Commerce's Bureau of Industry and Security, included companies in advanced composites, power electronics, batteries, and wireless broadband.[21] That study found that almost 94 percent of companies used "the same employees, facilities, and equipment to manufacture commercial and DOD products." Of the firms that were already defense contractors, only 7.6 percent had a "separate business unit, subdivision, or office . . . devoted exclusively to providing R&D services to the federal government"; and only 8.9 percent had a "separate business unit, subdivision, or office . . . devoted exclusively to providing manufacturing products for the federal government." As the report concluded: "Most defense contractors also have sizeable commercial sales, which make isolation of the defense market very difficult" (Department of Commerce, Office of Strategic Industries and Economic Security 2004, 8). In stark contrast to the claim that defense contractors struggled to operate in commercial markets, the survey found that the chief reason that most high technology companies ceased contracting for the Defense Department was simply that the commercial market was more profitable.

As a final blow to the idea of a divorce between military and commercial technology, one might take stock of the number of dedicated venture capital funds that have sprung up specifically to invest in companies operating at the intersection of the commercial and defense/security markets.[22] To the extent that a wall of separation ever existed, there is little question that it has been well and truly ripped down. The image of defense production taking place in a specialized set of firms detached from the rest of the economy conjured up (if not necessarily intended) by President Eisenhower's warning against the military-industrial complex is not simply outdated, but has been firmly laid to rest.

R&D Spending Creates Innovation Leadership

For some time now it has been a core feature of the U.S. innovation story to emphasize how much more the private sector invests in R&D than the federal government, and how this reverses the relationship that obtained up to the 1980s.

The standard story goes something like this. For many years, the federal government was the largest contributor to R&D funding, developing society-transforming technologies such as communication satellites, biotechnology, computers, the internet, and many others. However, a dramatic shift in R&D funding has taken place since the 1980s when industry's share surpassed that of government. Since then, federal R&D funding has remained fairly flat in constant dollars (declining as a share of GDP and the federal budget, though increasing in absolute and real dollar value), while industry's contributions have grown in most years. By the 1990s, it was the commercial sector— predominantly in information technology—that took the lead in creating innovative products. So far so good. But the conclusion to this standard story is that private-sector dominance in R&D spending must mean that the NSS is now largely irrelevant to commercial innovation.

So how well does the commercial leadership and NSS irrelevance assumption hold?' Our lengthy earlier discussion shows that using the quantity of R&D funding as a proxy for influence over the nature of technology development involves two basic errors. First, it confuses different kinds of innovation being pursued by private corporations on one hand, and by NSS actors on the other; second, it assumes rather than investigates the effects of the shift in R&D contributions.

Different kinds of innovation. Since at least the 1960s, many specialists have regularly observed that corporate actors in the private sector mostly pursue a different kind of innovation from that funded by federal agencies. To capture these differences in technological orientation, analysts have used a variety of different terms, such as "radical versus incremental," "product-specific versus technology-focused," and "short-versus long-term horizons." Common to each is the perception of a profound difference in the nature of R&D that is being conducted in each sector.

Consider the case of microelectronics, a sector much vaunted for its rapid commercial advances and high expenditure on R&D. Technology specialists have found that although the leading U.S. semiconductor manufacturing firms spend 10 to 15 percent of revenues on R&D, most of these outlays are directed toward the more immediate or short-term goals of new product development. Thus, in a statement whose implications for the identification of R&D spending with technology leadership went unremarked, technology specialists reported in 1998 that "None of the new leaders in digital communications perform any fundamental research or maintain much internal semiconductor R&D, instead focusing their efforts on the development and marketing of next-generation semiconductor products" (Macher et al., cited in National Research Council 2003, 203).

Far from unique to semiconductor companies, the short-term, product-improvement nature of private R&D is well established for all high-technology sectors. As Alic and his co-authors explained two decades ago, the relentless pressure to produce short-term profits means that, excepting the labs of a few leading firms, American industry "pays little for R&D with intermediate or longer-term horizons" (Alic et al. 1992, 51). In 2000–2001, corporations interviewed across eight major high-technology sectors cited "increased pressure on R&D to deliver measurable results" as a key force that "has driven corporations almost entirely away" from R&D activities that do not support existing lines of business. Most companies interviewed channeled R&D funds to existing technologies and markets rather than aiming for breakthrough innovations that might enable entry to new markets. The study of eight industry sectors found that "Projects that did not have demonstrable financial benefits were not funded, and the R&D portfolio shifted dramatically toward product development," a trend that transcended all of the industries covered.[23]

Whether the R&D habits of industry have actually shifted quite so dramatically, however, is none too clear. Well before the massive expansion of commercial markets and the rapid growth of corporate R&D, prominent researchers pointed to the incremental nature of most commercial research and development. In 1967, a study co-sponsored by RAND and the Brookings Institution found that "Outside defense and space related R&D . . . and possibly some segments of the civil electronics and chemical industries, the bulk of corporate R&D is modest design improvement work not reaching very far—the type of work that results in yearly changes in automobile design, gradual improvements in refrigerators . . . rather than radically new products and processes" (Nelson et. al., 1967, 54).[24]

In contrast to the national security state which focused on rapid state-of-the-art advances, most commercial firms were found to direct their R&D to what science policy analyst Harold Orlans called "humdrum activity aimed at small changes . . . in products or processes, or the introduction of new variants of old products." Although these words were written in 1973, Orlans was making the larger point that R&D statistics are a lamentable instrument for determining which research and development does or does not advance useful knowledge and technology. After all, he asked, "what sense does it make to equate the dollars spent on high energy physics and on a new kind of toothpaste, or the work of a test pilot, a sanitary engineer, and a geneticist?" (Orlans 1973, 119–20).

The main point is that we need to factor into our reliance on R&D expenditures the recognition that the national security agencies have a risk appetite that is fundamentally different from that of the private sector. In contrast to the commercial world, the military and other national security actors are focused on obtaining qualitative superiority vis-à-vis rivals. As a result, they value performance above all other goals, and will accept very high costs to achieve it (MacKenzie 1986, 365–66). The payoff from such a high risk appetite goes well beyond national security since it breaks barriers that the commercial world can then exploit—and which it is reluctant to tackle on its own.

Risk appetite has major implications for how we interpret R&D spending levels. Public-sector R&D dominates those high-risk ventures relevant to the cutting-edge innovations that benefit the private sector—and public-sector R&D is where more of the breakthroughs originate precisely because of their high-risk nature. By contrast, the risk-averse nature of commercial industry is well documented and well understood, given the annual and quarterly pressure for shareholder returns. Research that is expected to take more than five years to produce a marketable product is seldom funded. GE's ten-year project for a digital X-Ray (the Digital Detector System) is one of the exceptions that prove the rule. It was also the largest development project in the company's history. Tellingly, corporate headquarters had rejected funding the project. It took DARPA's backing and collaboration with the company's medical division to overturn that decision. After "11 years and $130 million in investments," GE was profiting handsomely from marketing the device to military and civilian hospitals around the globe (Defense Advanced Projects Agency 2008, 31–32). In short, there is irrefutable evidence that the bulk of the private sector's R&D is biased toward late-stage product development and known markets—hence unlikely to constitute a source of the transformative innovations that sustain technology leadership.

In this way, a concentration on who funds most U.S. R&D has often precluded a probing discussion of what lies behind the spending. It is simply assumed that endless variation and novelty—currently symbolized in the triple treat of FIG (Facebook, iPhone, and Google)—sit perfectly at home in the same category as the revolutionary general-purpose innovations (computers, aerospace, communications satellites, internet, biotechnology, and so forth) that established a slew of new high-technology industries. Aside from the fact that even the FIG innovations build on prior breakthroughs that were sponsored by the NSS, there is a strong element of "paradigm maintenance" in the focus on R&D spending. Above all, it reinforces the standard view that the United States owes its leadership in transformative innovation to a sui generis private-sector capacity that is constantly being replenished by an unstoppable flow of entrepreneurial individuals tinkering away in their garages. The main point, then, is that aggregate data about relative shares of national R&D spending in the U.S. economy tell us little about what is being done with that expenditure. This makes R&D expenditure a poor indicator of who is leading transformative innovation in the American economy.

A new NSS approach to innovation: Building in commercial incentives. The second major shortcoming of the R&D funding shift myth is the tendency to deduce rather than empirically investigate the behavioral effects of the funding shift in question. That shift is substantial: already in 2001, the commercial investment in information technology (then a trillion dollars annually) was "three orders of magnitude larger" than DoD's "budget for information systems technology" (National Research Council 2001b, 4). But it is because of that very repositioning that the mission agencies have had to rethink how to benefit from commercial capabilities. In particular, as the same NRC report explained, "DoD cannot forgo its own investment in information systems S&T. Commercial hardware is normally not rugged enough for military use. Commercial software is frequently not reliable enough to use for mission-critical systems nor secure enough against determined adversaries. Commercial technology also spreads rapidly, which eliminates military advantages" (National Research Council 2001b, 4). However, instead of examining how the weaker R&D funding position of government vis-à-vis industry may have changed the approach of the mission agencies, many analysts have simply posited only one possible outcome, namely, that it has turned the NSS into a technology taker rather than a technology maker, drastically diminishing its influence in national innovation.

In contrast to this understanding, I examine the extent to which the R&D funding shift has served as a pressure for change within the mission agencies, especially the DoD. This focus goes to the heart of how the NSS innovation enterprise has evolved. I find that rather than driving the NSS out of the commercial innovation picture, the growth of private R&D spending (together with the shrinking volume of government demand) has motivated the mission agencies to find new ways of maintaining influence and access to private-sector capabilities.

Among the (relatively) new approaches to procuring new technology, the common NSS pattern is one of support for innovations that will appeal to both commercial and government markets, in an effort to attract the more technologically sophisticated firms to work with the mission agencies. These findings inform my argument concerning the NSS promotion of venture capital schemes, which is fully developed in the case studies of the commercial reorientation of the mission agencies as well as in the most recent iterations of that dual-market focus evident in the emerging fields of nanotechnology, robotics/artificial intelligence, and renewable energy.

To conclude, the higher R&D spending of the private sector compared with that of the federal government serves as a poor proxy for influence in effecting transformative innovation. A focus on quantity of R&D spending not only fails to distinguish the different kinds of innovation that prevail in each sector; it also entirely overlooks the behavioral effects of that spending shift on the mission-oriented agencies most concerned to harness the capabilities of the private sector. Instead of sidelining the mission agencies' role in innovation, it motivates them to devise new ways of procuring technology in order to regain access to and influence over commercial capabilities.

The Defense Spending Question: In Search of the Holy Grail?

The standard question that has guided much research on the defense-commercial relationship is one that has produced inconclusive answers: What is the economic impact of U.S. defense spending? I discuss it here by way of making clear the different approach in the present study.

Which question? Effects of military spending versus sources of transformative innovation. The two main approaches to this question—the "military Keynesian" and "the depletionist"—have been amply discussed elsewhere, so I shall not repeat the arguments in any detail.[25] In briefly presenting these quantitative approaches, I am less concerned to defend or reject them than to explain why they are inappropriate for my own explanatory aims.

One major reason is that existing approaches are concerned to explain the link between military spending and economic performance. In this vein, some studies examine the effects of military spending in general (the focus of military Keynesianism), while others concentrate more narrowly on military R&D spending (some versions of the depletionist argument). By contrast, the present study sets out to explain America's unusual capacity for transformative innovation: rather than on the relationship of military spending and economic performance, it focuses on the link between NSS high-technology activism and U.S. commercial innovation. While certainly related to economic performance, the capacity for breakthrough innovation cannot be reduced to standard measures such as GDP growth or productivity gains—the stuff of quantitative analysis. Nor will measuring a simple input such as R&D spending offer adequate insight. For as I have argued extensively, NSS activism in science and technology—my *explanans*—necessarily encompasses a good deal more than military R&D spending.

Existing Approaches to the Military Spending Question

Military Keynesianism is the idea that certain forms of military spending—mostly the kind that produces quick results—can be used to stimulate economic activity during times of severe economic downturn. It therefore offers an expansionist view of the economic effects of the military budget.

Economic historians applying this idea have compared changes in U.S. military spending with changes in GDP and found that large spending increases have coincided with strong growth, and conversely that reduced spending has been followed by pronounced output decline.[26]

Whatever the general merits of this approach when applied to shifts in the defense budget, military Keynesianism remains a blunt instrument for my particular purposes. It is not too hard to see why. Consider, for instance, the following statement in which Harvard economist Martin Feldstein is advocating a form of military Keynesianism to stimulate demand and escape from the Great Recession following the 2008 financial crisis:

> If rapid spending on things that need to be done is a criterion of choice, the plan should include higher defense outlays, including replacing and repairing supplies and equipment, needed after five years of fighting. . . . Infrastructure spending on domestic military bases can also proceed more rapidly than infrastructure spending in the civilian economy. . . . In addition, a temporary increase in military recruiting and training would reduce unemployment directly, create a more skilled civilian workforce and expand the military reserves.[27]

Note the forms that such military spending is expected to take: "replacing and repairing supplies and equipment" (off-the-shelf procurement), "infrastructure spending on domestic military bases," "a temporary increase in military recruiting and training." The main point to emphasize is that there is nothing in military Keynesianism qua explanatory concept to indicate a preference for investing in high-tech innovation—in fact quite the opposite, since innovation is a long-term proposition that would do little to meet the more immediate need for a demand stimulus.

Perhaps an even bigger problem with the expansionist argument, as David Gold observes, is the fact of a declining military burden. It is true that Pentagon spending has been growing fast since 9/11. According to OMB, the national defense budget, not including supplementary war costs and funding for nuclear weapons, has grown 35 percent over the last decade, adjusted for inflation. Taking the longer view, however, produces a different picture. Outlays for national defense for the entire period 1947–2011 show that the inflation-adjusted defense burden has declined substantially, as a share of both GDP and total government outlays (figure 8.1). Even including the war-intensive period since 2001, we find the defense burden averaging 4 percent of GDP for the decade, less than half the Cold War peak of 10 percent in the second half of the 1950s, the Vietnam peak of 9.4 percent, or the 6.2 percent reached at the height of the 1980s buildup. As a share of the federal budget, defense spending fell by more than half—from 52 percent in 1960 to 23 percent in 1980 to 20 percent in 2011 (figure 8.2). That this is still a very large share is not in question, but the basic tendency, as David

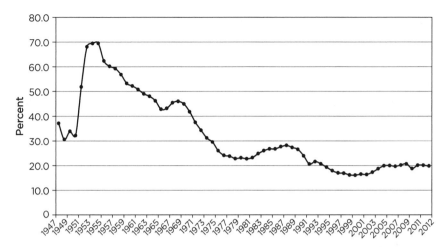

Figure 8.1 National defense expenditure as a percentage of total federal outlays, 1947–2012. Calculations based on data from DoD, Office of the Secretary of Defense (Comptroller), *National Defense Budget Estimates for FY 2012* (Green Book), 238–40, March 2011 Washington, D.C.

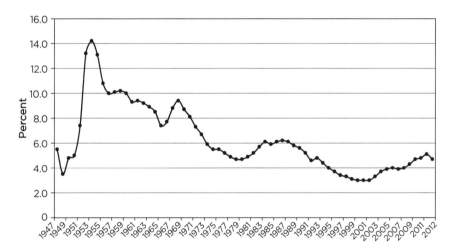

Figure 8.2 National defense expenditure as a percentage of GDP, 1947–2012. Calculations based on data from DoD, Office of the Secretary of Defense (Comptroller), *National Defense Budget Estimates for FY 2012 (Green Book)*, 238–40, March 2011, Washington, D.C.

Gold puts it, is that "U.S. military spending has gone through a series of cycles but has not grown, in real terms, for more than fifty years. As a share of the economy and as a share of government spending, military spending has declined substantially over the same period" (2005, 9).

Whilst a declining military burden sits uneasily with expectations of military Keynesianism, it is also inconvenient for the depletionist case. Depletionist accounts emphasize the "opportunity cost" and "crowding out" effects of military spending, with a particular focus on defense R&D. Seymour Melman's influential work exemplifies this line of argument. A key claim is that the technology-intensive defense industries rob the private economy of resources needed for innovation. By crowding out private-sector investment and recruitment, by appropriating government funds for defense projects rather than, say, infrastructure investment, military R&D spending has a predatory effect on the economy, sapping productivity, draining technological talent, and weakening national competitiveness.[28] These ideas have deeply influenced the way that many Americans think about the relationship between defense and the private sector. Much of the 1980s commentary over the Reagan buildup was saturated with depletionist claims (sparked by the alarming proposal to militarize space) and the military response to 9/11 has made them once again current. Yet the actual trends in defense R&D spending, as a share of both national income and federal outlays, give some room for doubt (figures 8.3 and 8.4).

It is true, as Roland has noted, that America's commitment to qualitative superiority in weaponry kept expenditures high as a percentage of the federal budget throughout the Cold War. But because "economic growth absorbed the impact of this spending," defense R&D investment has consumed

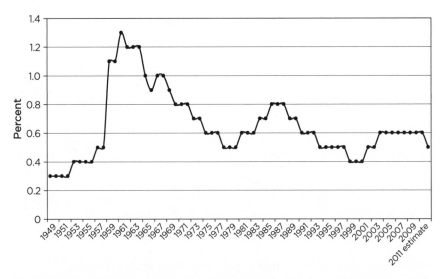

Figure 8.3 R&D outlays for national defense as a percentage of GDP, 1949–2011. Calculations based on data from Office of Management and Budget, n.d., "Historical Tables," table 9.7, http://www. whitehouse.gov/omb/budget/Historicals.

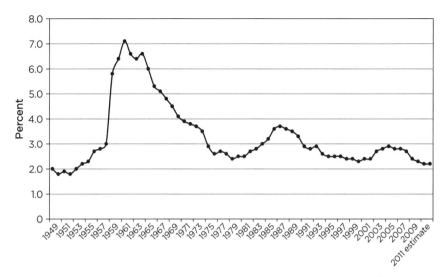

Figure 8.4 R&D outlays for national defense as a percentage of federal outlays, 1949–2011. Calculations based on data from Office of Management and Budget n.d. "Historical Tables," table 9.7, http://www. whitehouse.gov/omb/budget/Historicals.

a declining share of the budget, as well as GDP (Roland 2007, 357). In 1962 defense R&D outlays reached 6.6 per cent of the federal budget (1.3 per cent of GDP), but in 1986 at the height of the Reagan defense buildup, the proportions were just 3.6 per cent of the budget (0.8 per cent of GDP), and in the decade after 2001, defense R&D never exceeded 2.9 per cent of the budget (0.6 per cent of GDP).

Leaving the R&D data to one side, there is something about the depletionist argument that seems intuitively correct—give a company federal R&D funds and it will reduce its own contribution accordingly. However, the so-called opportunity costs and crowding out effects may not necessarily translate as a loss for transformative innovation. Consider two reasons. First, it might actually mean that the company engages in fewer tweakings of existing products (for which it uses its own R&D funds), and instead achieves more breakthroughs down the road (using federal funds, either alone or jointly with matching private funds, to tackle NSS problem sets). Second, opportunity costs are much less likely when federal R&D projects enjoin participating firms to develop technology with both mission and commercial applications.

A more serious objection, however, is that no one has demonstrated that defense spending on R&D either saps a nation's productivity, reduces economic growth, or drains scientific and engineering talent away from the private sector. Whether positive, or negative, or neutral, the economic effects of defense spending have not been established.[29] The fundamental problem, it seems, is not that defense spending is necessarily incompatible with robust economic performance, but rather that there are so many variables to the performance equation: Because defense spending does not occur in isolation, but in conjunction with several other policies that can produce negative consequences, one's measurement techniques may not be up to the mark (Fordham 2007).

Staying with the measurement issue for a moment, consider briefly some further reasons that efforts to relate spending inputs to innovation and industry outputs have yielded inconclusive results.

First, identifying causal relationships between defense/R&D spending and growth or productivity gains creates huge difficulties when the development and sale of new products incorporating federal R&D occurs long after the relevant investment. "Often, the delays run into decades, making it difficult to tell midcourse how effective a particular program has been" (Congressional Research Service 1986b, 4).

Second, the benefits of a particular technology development program may not become visible until complementary advances in other areas are achieved. For example, "advances in computer graphics did not have widespread effect until suitable hardware was more broadly available for producing three-dimensional graphical images." In this way, it took thirty years of federal support before virtual reality was commercialized (National Research Council 1999, 137).

Third, the synergistic interaction between the commercial sector of an industry and its corresponding defense sector means that advances in one sector may contribute to advances in the other in ways that are not well captured via R&D spending. A key example is the software industry, which grew out of federally supported research, manpower, and major advances funded by the defense sector; the latter then benefited in turn from industry innovations.

Finally, econometric studies that relate military R&D inputs to productivity outputs assume a close connection between innovation and production. The problem is that this connection has weakened significantly since the 1980s as many companies have moved manufacturing offshore. Innovation has thus become increasingly disconnected from production (the implications of which I return to in the final chapter)—and without the direct link to production you cannot reliably measure, either at the firm or industry level, the productivity gains that flow from technological innovation—since the gains are likely to be reaped not at home but offshore (Triplett 1999, 322).

Nobel Prize–winning economist Robert Solow encapsulated all these measurement problems in his now famous aphorism: "You can see the computer age everywhere but in the productivity statistics."[30] Similarly skeptical of econometric efforts, Vernon Ruttan expressed the view that "we do not yet have, and perhaps cannot have, a body of rigorous econometric evidence against which to evaluate the economic impact of defense and defense-related R&D and procurement" (Ruttan 2006a, 170). While Ruttan advocated "careful narrative analysis of individual cases" as a more reliable way to evaluate economic benefits, his approach would not satisfy those who seek answers to quantitative questions like: What was the overall net commercial payoff to the government's defense expenditures? Yet it must be said that for some purposes such questions make little sense because they apply a simplistic accounting standard, net payoff (like profit and loss), to a quintessentially qualitative problem—in this case, the sources of America's unusual capacity for transformative innovation.

Existing approaches are motivated by different concerns to those of the present study and accordingly deliver up different responses. Military Keynesianism focuses on the ability of broadly defined defense spending to stimulate relatively quick results in economic growth and employment, thus circumventing or moderating the effects of an economic slump. As such, it has little to say about the sources of America's unusual capacity for transformative innovation, and much less light to shed on either the efforts or the outcomes of sustaining high-technology leadership. By contrast, depletionist accounts seek to demonstrate the damaging and draining effects of the national defense budget and related R&D spending. It has not been my purpose to detail the pros and cons of this literature, though it seems fair to point out that a long-term decline in the U.S. defense burden, relative to national income and federal outlays, does little to bolster either expansionary or contractionist views of military spending. Moreover, since military spending is the international norm, but transformative innovation is relatively rare, it is hard to see the explanatory relevance of this kind of focus.

Although this study tackles quite a different question, it can nonetheless be seen as countering the bald depletionist case. It has shown that the NSS puts more into U.S. innovation and enterprise than is either generally understood or acknowledged. Problem setting, procuring new technology, providing an end market, funding IR&D, training scientists and engineers, sharing S&T facilities, licensing inventions, commercializing technology, sponsoring new company formation—all these add up to a much more complex array of activities than a focus on either the defense budget in general or defense R&D spending in particular can hope to capture.

There is nonetheless broad agreement that defense- and national security–led innovation is an inefficient route to commercial innovation. But since commercial innovation is not its primary purpose, this is beside the point. Indeed some have been tempted to conclude just the opposite: that to the extent that NSS-led innovation enables two bites at the cherry—both national security and commercial innovation—it delivers double the value for (a lot of) money.[31] There is no need to enter into this fruitless debate in order to extract the important point that a compelling critique of defense-led innovation must be directed at *strategy*: it must be able to show that the RDT&E and procurement spending—or some substantial part of it—is *strategically* neither necessary nor useful. The oft-repeated claim that it is an inefficient way to promote civilian innovation is undoubtedly true; but it is also beside the point—for this has never been its primary intention. To argue on nonstrategic grounds against the NSS technology enterprise is thus to aim the arrow at the wrong target. Stephen Walt's striking statement hits closer to the mark: ". . . in some ways America's strategic position is actually more favorable than it used to be, which is why its bloated military budget is something of a mystery."[32] At least one thing is clear: in the absence of a political judgment as to the objectives of U.S. military strategy, people will continue passionately and seriously to argue both sides of the key question: How much is enough?[33]

Finally, we should note that as the nation is forced to contend with its ballooning deficit, the "bloated military budget" looks set for a substantial trim. Under the 2011 Budget Control Act, defense spending is to be capped each year through 2021. In addition, the act mandates steep automatic cuts in discretionary spending (including defense), so-called sequestration, unless Congress agrees on a deficit-reduction budget. At the time of writing, the extent of future cuts is unknown since this depends on the outcome of fierce political wrangles over fiscal policy. Capping is a means of reducing budget growth—by some $400 billion over ten years, and by about $900 billion should sequestration continue.[34] Tellingly, the threat of sequestration was premised on the Obama administration's confident calculation that it would never be implemented because support for the NSS enterprise was built on such a robust bipartisan consensus from which the Republicans would be least likely to defect. As sequestration proceeds, however, it appears that not even the prospect of compromising military preparedness can modify the conservative take-no-prisoners approach.

How heavily might this financial squeeze impinge on the U.S. technology enterprise? While the reduction is significant, three considerations suggest that its material impact is likely to be moderate rather than dramatic. First, the proposed reductions (caps plus sequestration) are not unprecedented. Defense spending declined, after adjusting for inflation, by a third between 1985 and 1998 (Congressional Research Service 2012, 16) and the drawdowns projected for the postsequestration era are smaller than the drop in spending after the Korean, Vietnam and Cold wars.[35] Second, what matters for the NSS innovation engine is not defense spending per se (two-thirds of which goes to operations and maintenance) but the budget for RDT&E and procurement. Whereas procurement has been subject to oscillation, RDT&E spending has historically been preserved; the Defense *Green Book* projects reductions that are relatively small. To remain within the limits mandated by the budget caps, however, Defense spending plans will have to be trimmed, so there is some uncertainty surrounding the technology enterprise. Nonetheless, it deserves reemphasis that budget size is not a neat predictor of innovation capacity: a significant number of innovations have come from agencies or programs with relatively modest budgets such as DARPA and SBIR). Finally, the NSS is larger than defense as such, and all its components' budgets should be part of the calculation. Clearly, defense and the NSS more generally are entering a period of significant spending constraints and major budgetary uncertainty—relative to the relaxed post-9/11 environment (which saw the base budget balloon by more than 40 percent after adjusting for inflation). This thickens the fog that has gathered around the technology enterprise since 9/11. But for all the reasons that I have outlined, a shrinking budget may be one of the lesser challenges that lie ahead for the NSS innovation engine.

Hybrid State, Hybrid Capitalism, Great Power Turning Point

Americans today consume more goods manufactured overseas than ever before, and yet they are less likely to be employed in manufacturing than at any time in the last 100 years. . . . This has potentially significant implications for defense, because to protect, we must produce.

Regina Dugan, 2011

The rise of China does not necessarily imply slowdown or demise for the United States. But if they specialize in making things and we specialize in finance, they will eat our lunch.

Simon Johnson, 2009

Concluding chapters traditionally invite reflections on the larger implications of a work, both theoretical and practical. Before tackling that task, however, let me start by recalling the key substantive issue. My orienting question focused on the unusual capacity for transformative innovation that has underpinned America's postwar dominance in high technology. Why, in particular, has the United States, more than any other country on the planet, been the source of so much high-tech industry, and why after, but not before, World War II? And is this pattern likely to continue into the future?

I have set my story within the evolving geopolitical landscape in which perceived threats to U.S. leadership helped forge a bipartisan consensus over the NSS technology enterprise. In a domestic context marked by intense political competition—often expressed in antistatist terms—this broad consensus has endured for more than half a century. Furthermore, when the NSS enterprise has appeared to stray too far or too obviously into the commercial arena—namely in nonhybridized forms—that consensus has at times worn thin, most notably in the period since the Cold War's end. As we have seen in the case of the Republican pushback on the military's renewable energy strategy (and as happened more spectacularly in the case of sequestration, a calculated gamble that went awry), the technology enterprise of national security is not immune to the wrenching partisan conflict that increasingly rends American politics.[1]

However, the core of the story involves the creation and activities of a central new player, the national security state. The main arguments and evidence I have advanced can be summarized as follows.

America's propensity for radical innovation is not a "stateless" story and free-market capitalism is not how the United States achieved high-technology leadership. Through an extensive array of public-private alliances and innovation hybrids, technology development programs and investment funds, the United States has created not a liberal, but a hybrid political economy—one that is shaped by a national security state deeply entwined with the commercial sector.

Pursuit of defense preparedness, driven by Cold War exigencies and threat perceptions, produced a national security state much broader and more encompassing than the "defense sector," responsible for mobilizing the nation's science and technology resources.

The technology activism of the national security state—though of inestimable benefit to the nation's industry and innovation—was not motivated by economic ambition (industry policy) but by the pressure to sustain American primacy through technological dominance.

Nevertheless, challenges to technology leadership deriving from international rivalry and domestic structural changes have had the effect of reorienting the public-private partnership toward closer integration of security and commerce in the American economy. This has significantly broadened the reach of the NSS beyond the military-industrial complex as traditionally understood.

By privileging commercial viability in its investment strategies, the NSS has not only extended its technological influence outside the security arena; it has also ventured into economic activities that are more typically associated with the private sector. But by channeling its activities into hybrid structures that merge public and private resources, the breadth and depth of NSS involvement acquire low visibility and high (in other words bipartisan) political appeal.

In drawing out the implications of these arguments, I touch on two areas of political science, the first concerned with varieties of capitalism (theories of comparative political economy), the second dealing with American political development (specifically, understanding the American state as an economic actor). I then take up the substantive question of whether the NSS innovation engine is still working to the benefit of the United States and draw out its implications for the recent debate on American power and U.S. decline.

Comparative Institutions and Varieties of Capitalism

Thanks to an ample critical literature, there is no need to belabor the point that comparative institutional analyses have often overstated the degree of congruence across different spheres of the national political economy. In the varieties of capitalism literature, for example, state activism is incongruent with, and thus absent from, depictions of the typical liberal market economy. While drawing attention to institutional discrepancies, the most advanced critiques nonetheless refrain from drawing the banal (and unhelpful) conclusion that all political economies are therefore simply "mixed." More profoundly, by deploying the concept of institutional compensation, VOC critics enjoin the analyst to focus on, rather than dismiss, those apparently incongruent institutions.[2] Specifically, one should consider the extent to which nonconforming institutions may instead offset certain deficiencies or shortcomings of the dominant institutional complex.

The NSS Innovation Enterprise as a Compensatory Institution

Applying this conceptual framework allows a different perspective on the national security state (qua technology enterprise). Neither anomaly nor parasite, the NSS can be seen as an institution that (inadvertently or otherwise) compensates for certain shortcomings (failures?) of the free market for capital, goods, and services. The NSS's compensation mechanisms take the following forms.

First of all, *the freedom to take a long-range view of investment in innovation:* in contrast, the private sector, with a constant eye on the bottom line, is constrained by the pressures of realizing shareholder value that rewards short-term value-extraction over long-term productive investment.[3]

Second, *an appetite for risk that is fostered by the drive for technology leadership and military preparedness:* such a risk tolerance promotes transformative innovation by focusing resources on achieving a desired goal with strategic importance.

Third, *provision of patient capital* (risk-tolerant, medium- to long-term investment): this enables pursuit of innovation with delayed payoffs, thus compensating for the more risk-averse behavior of private capital markets. The NSS provides several sources of patient capital, from technology procurement contracts to venture capital funds. As we saw in chapter 3, beginning with the galvanizing event of Sputnik, the federal government has created a network of government venture capital funds which fill a significant gap in the investment infrastructure for high-risk innovation.

Fourth, *cultivation of relational contracting and longer-term supplier relationships in producing new equipment:* this compensates for the short-term focus of the spot market for goods and services. Essentially, NSS contracting for new equipment provides a counterbalance to the arms-length approach that Hall and Soskice see as the sine qua non of U.S. capitalism. As research on capital goods industries has found (chapter 8), compared with firms engaged in strictly commercial customer-supplier relations, companies participating in defense contracting operate in a more supportive environment for long-term investment and the diffusion of advanced technology. As a consequence, they invest more than their strictly commercial counterparts in long-term supplier relations and modern, productivity-enhancing technologies that are relevant to nonmilitary production.

Regarding this last finding, it is worth pausing to take note of how it qualifies the varieties of capitalism theory of the U.S. model of capitalism. Here we see yet another way in which the NSS appears to plug institutional gaps in the U.S. model—not only with regard to the market for patient capital, including early-stage venture funding, but also with regard to the market for intermediate goods. This stands in contrast to the typical transactional approach of U.S. companies to their subcontractors.[4] This of course illustrates the principle of institutional compensation that was sorely missing from earlier analysis of comparative capitalism with its emphasis on uniformity and coherence.

Finally, *cultivation of networks that plug gaps in the innovation ecosystem:* as we have seen throughout this study, the NSS is populated by a large number of units that routinely connect industry, investors, research labs, and program managers in networking arrangements with broad commercial reach. In this respect, the CIA's In-Q-Tel is typical in cultivating a vast network of private venture capital firms, labs and research organizations, technology transfer offices, and NSS–funded program managers. In this and many other cases, the NSS provides a coordinated, "collaborative public space" for plugging network gaps, which is critical to bringing innovations to market (Breznitz 2005). In this respect too, the NSS can be seen to fill in certain institutional gaps in the workings of U.S. capitalism.

In sum, the NSS does not complement the institutions of a liberal market economy so much as it compensates for them. As an actor with long-time horizons, a high tolerance for risk, and extensive networking capabilities, the national security state offsets well-described features of U.S. markets. The unremarkable point, of course, is that all political economies are a blend rather than a homogenous mix of institutional arrangements. Yet it must also be said that this does not automatically make them hybrid political economies. The United States, I conclude, is a genuine hybrid in the strong sense of the term—both at the macro level, because of the extraordinary scale, scope, and integration of its government-driven NSS with the workings of the broader market economy, and at the micro level because of the way it has organized its active involvement in the delivery and commercialization of innovation. My study therefore provides further support for the critique of the varieties of capitalism framework and demonstrates conclusively that the characterization of the U.S. political economy as a liberal market economy needs urgent revision.

The American State

My analysis of the NSS technology enterprise also joins a substantial body of work that throws fresh light on the American state. This literature, usually identified with "unconventional approaches" to American political development, has paid particular attention to how national political institutions have been substantially shaped by international events and processes, and not least to the centrality of the military to early state building.[5] Its findings in different domains of public policy at different periods have challenged an influential conception of the American state that emphasizes weakness, fragmentation, and ineffectiveness.

Inasmuch as the present study of the largely neglected field of innovation and technology development overturns the idea of an American state removed from significant economic involvement and influence, it strengthens this challenge. It is of course ironic that just as these fresh understandings of American political development began to emerge in the post–Cold War era, the fascination with neoliberalism, deregulation, and privatization also reached its peak (Novak 2008, 756).

Centralization versus coordination. In contrast to many other countries in which one agency or a few entities control funding for science and technology, the United States divides responsibility among multiple, mission-oriented agencies. Fragmented authority, decentralized decision-making, and policy pluralism are of course well-known features of administrative power in the U.S. polity. A common argument against government's economic involvement is that the American administrative structure is too fragmented and the political system too "pluralistic, disorderly, and open at so many places to influence from special interests that rational government decisions on technology or industry policy are next to impossible" (U.S. Congress, Office of Technology Assessment 1990, 72).[6]

These features of American political institutions evoke a certain "messiness," a lack of coherence, that sits uneasily with presumptions about what it takes to pursue strategy or make an effective state. For whatever else that recipe entails, centralized policymaking is widely considered an essential ingredient of state capacity. But is centralization perhaps overrated? In the innovation arena one might well conclude the reverse: that the decentralized, pluralistic character of the national security state has been a source of strength, not weakness. By creating a good deal of slack in the mission-led environment of the NSS, dispersed authority has allowed different technology bets to be placed, diverse experiments to be tried, multiple sources of patient capital to be accessed—and not least, complementary agency strengths to be harnessed in bringing innovations to maturity (famously, DARPA, NSF, and the internet). Here, a reminder from Roland of the significance of the National Research Council's "landmark study" of U.S. computer development, *Funding a Revolution* (1999), is appropriate. As he puts it succinctly, the

NRC study concluded that "computer technology advanced in the United States because it enjoyed multiple models and sources of government support." DARPA, he emphasizes, was "just one of several federal agencies . . . that made a difference" by playing "more or less critical roles at various stages." (Roland 2010, 10). If, as Nathan Rosenberg states, "technological innovation is so uncertain that it cannot be planned, then encouraging diversity is the best 'planning' we can do" (cited in Holbrook 1995, 161).

One might venture further that a certain level of policy and program heterogeneity, by generating a variety of technology options, works something like the trial and error of the market. John Alic and his fellow innovation specialists concur with this proposition, concluding that "Despite the heterogeneity in federal policies—or perhaps because of it, given the high levels of uncertainty that characterize innovation—government actions have been remarkably effective" (Alic et al. 2003, 15).

Pluralism yes, but within limits. While the absence of centralization has been widely noted, and often lamented, the role of coordination has perhaps been underplayed. In addition to smaller initiatives such as alternative energy, there is now a well-established pattern of interagency coordination in national priority areas that include information and communication technology, bioinformatics, renewable energy, and nanotechnology. We have seen how this flow of R&D investment runs all the way from basic research to technology development to commercialization of results, and covers a wide range of innovations from artificial intelligence and digital libraries to virtual reality and the next generation of the internet.[7] Indeed, compared with its reputation for dispersed policymaking, the United States is a relatively impressive practitioner of interagency coordination, which includes formal and informal mechanisms, bottom-up and top-down approaches, and bilateral as well as multilateral initiatives.

Prior to the 1980s, interagency coordination would often be carried out in an informal, bottom-up fashion as program managers from different agencies came together to create a joint agenda such as the Federal Laboratory Consortium. Over time, as technology ambitions and spending needs have grown, the tendency has been for the budget and general directions to be set through federal offices like those of Management and Budget and Science and Technology Policy.[8] Most notably, the major High Performance Computing and Communications program,[9] now part of a larger multiagency IT initiative,[10] as well as the National Nanotechnology Initiative, bear the characteristics of this top-down coordination process that originated in informal interagency exchanges.[11] Indeed the NNI is one of the clearest examples of this process, having built on the initiatives of key NSS agencies, which had already begun their own coordinating efforts. In the words of the director of the National Nanotechnology Coordination Office, this "closely coordinated interagency, cross-sector collaboration" forms part of "a new model," which aims "to accelerate innovation in areas of national priority."[12]

In sum, NSS agencies and components have long used a variety of formal and informal mechanisms to coordinate their shared interests in a particular field of technological innovation. Whether to mitigate areas of duplication and overlap or to bring complementary strengths to bear on common problems, federal agencies collaborate over projects large and small. Fred Block and Matthew Keller's take on the federal approach to innovation, captured in the phrase "let a hundred flowers bloom," is only half the story (2010, 168). For the full picture, the take of Andy Grove, the highly regarded former CEO of Intel, on the company's approach seems closer to the mark: "Let chaos reign, then rein in chaos."[13] Grove's saying brings to mind President Eisenhower's description of the new DoD structure for managing research, development, engineering, and acquisition as the "decentralization of operations, under flexible and effective direction and control from the center."

A relationship of governed interdependence. I have argued that national security is the main motivator of transformative innovation in the U.S. economy and that the national security state is a vital actor in that enterprise. Clearly, the national security state needs the private sector and nonstate actors to carry out its projects, and because of the myriad ways it pursues its goals, neither state- nor society-centered frameworks make much sense. On one hand, the NSS innovation enterprise has been built to pursue public purpose and mission-oriented problem sets; on the other hand, it has also been increasingly required to satisfy private goals, by absorbing risk and appealing to commercial viability.

The perspective I have emphasized seeks to capture the key features of this two-way relationship in the concept of governed interdependence. In this framework, we see quite clearly that the national security state is not just standing at a distance, mediating between private actors; nor is it delegating its powers in some sort of corporatist set-up. On the contrary, the NSS is project-oriented, proactive, and performance-driven. In the disciplining of private-sector performance, imperfect though it is in practice, we glimpse a standard imposed through multiple mechanisms, from cost sharing to time-limited support, that is conditional on designated milestones achieved. The NSS is in all these respects, and more, deeply integrated with the private sector to achieve its goals. Through a relationship of governed interdependence, the NSS thus expands its commercial reach while giving the commercial sector a stake in implementing its projects. This concept applies whether the partnership is controversial (NSA and Google) or classical (the Department of Energy's nuclear labs and the supercomputer industry).

Using this framework, my analysis does not invert the original narrative about American inventiveness (clever folks, energetic entrepreneurs, tons of initiative)—on the contrary, it embraces them. These are all necessary ingredients for a high-risk project to work. Many more could be added. But a list of ingredients produces a recipe, not an explanation. My explanation emphasizes the point that the critical actor in the transformative story is the NSS—but not for statist reasons. Statism tries to control initiative—bound it, monitor it, direct it; in a relationship of governed interdependence, by contrast, the state tries to motivate initiative—frame it, discipline it, reward it. As Margaret O'Mara has observed in her history of Silicon Valley, the "tactics of private-sector persuasion—not government mandate—are often the way the U.S. state gets things done" (2005, xi). In the pursuit of technology leadership for national security, this relationship has produced industrially significant consequences.

Conceptually, the notion of governed interdependence thus accords with what King and Lieberman depict as the emerging understanding of the state in which "American state building, strength, and institutional capacity form through links with society, not necessarily by virtue of autonomy from society." (2009, 549). In the NSS technology enterprise, governed interdependence is a way of conceptualizing those links with society: a relationship that involves considerable collaboration, negotiation, and partnering with private actors for mutual benefit, but which is ultimately governed by NSS objectives that prioritize security, not commerce. Quite often this relationship goes beyond mere partnering to create the fusion with nonstate actors and institutions that I call hybridization.

Hybridization. As we have seen, there are several ways of organizing links with society for the technology enterprise. Some of these links entail straightforward partnerships with private actors, such as ASCI, SBIR, Sematech, and the nanotechnology and battery consortia, while others involve the privatization of formerly public functions, among them the post–World War II replacement of the military arsenal by private contracting with industry, engendering the so-called military-industrial complex. But there are many more partnerings that fit neither of these forms, and that have their own logic. Rather than "privatizing the public," these innovation hybrids mostly do the reverse: they draw the state into economic pursuits that are conventionally viewed as the "business of business"—hence a hybrid state.

Hybridization is a preferred American way of organizing the state-society link. Above all, hybridization comes to the rescue in a context where a robust antistatist ethos prevails and when a task calls for a strong state presence in economic ventures. What we have seen in the case of numerous investment and commercialization ventures is a state whose actions are neither mediated nor conducted at a distance, but closely integrated with innovation and investment decisions—and commercial outcomes. Hybridization is why I conclude, contra Aaron Friedberg, that American antistatism has not restricted the state's economic activism but simply changed its form of engagement, and thus helped shape its innovation enterprise. As a result of its bipartisan appeal, hybridization compensates for the antistatist constraint by neutralizing or sidestepping institutional and, not least, political blockage. In that respect, the American state's forays into the innovation arena accord with the findings from many other domains of public policy, thus indicating a distinc- . tive American way of achieving public purpose.[14]

On a more general note, students of American history would want to remind us that the American state (both subnational and federal) has always engaged in the development of its economy, whether in providing infrastructure and transportation technology or in promoting agriculture.[15] In these and other pre–twentieth-century nation-building activities, the state centered on Washington was no different from—and certainly no less capable than—many of its peers. The emphasis of this study, however, has been on the distinctiveness of the American experience. Where it has differed, going a good deal further and faster than anyone else, is in pioneering and leading a high-tech innovation economy, propelled by a national security imperative. Owing to America's antistatist taboo, immensely fortified by Cold War rivalry with a command economy, the legitimacy of that project could only be assured if the security rationale remained paramount.

Old Shibboleths. Any discussion of the American state cannot avoid the phalanx of readymade phrases regularly launched at government efforts to shape economic outcomes. Spearheaded by terms like "picking winners" and "government failure," the presumptive bias seems to be that state effectiveness in a given arena must be measured by freedom from error and absence of failure.

But a fear of failure would be fatal to any form of transformative innovation, whether embarked on for security or for commercial reasons. Indeed, acceptance of failure is the operating principle in a number of NSS ventures. Take DARPA, for example. Its approach emphasizes "a complete acceptance of failure" if the payoff of success is high enough. Alex Roland (2010, 10) estimates no more than a 15 percent success rate. This makes for a long list of failures. Yet, rightly or wrongly, DARPA is widely discussed, admired, and known best for its successes including the internet, the GPS, and stealth technology. The CIA's venture capital fund operates on much the same principle. In-Q-Tel's inaugural CEO, Gilman Louie, put it like this: "The best thing about In-Q-Tel, to me, is that it's risky. . . . The CIA's new venture may fall flat, but so what. Washington has been a zero-defect culture for too long. If we want a CIA that performs better, we'll need to take more risks—and give our government freedom to fail."[16] Moving well beyond the national security arena, we find a similar view being articulated by the president of Pixar Animation Studios and Walt Disney Animation Studios, Ed Catmull: "We need a more risk-tolerant environment. . . . I always wince when I hear politicians attack a government-funded R&D program that's slow to produce results or has suffered a failure as a boondoggle. They'll say, 'We're going to prevent that from happening again,' when their reaction should be, 'Oh, good, we were trying something new and we learned from the failure.' "[17] It is precisely the freedom to fail that is deemed crucial to the pursuit of high-risk, high-return research and technology development. As the founder of one of the handful of large corporations that still engages in this kind of activity, put it: "If you want to succeed, raise your error rate."[18]

What does this discussion mean for an understanding of the American state? Most generally, in concert with studies in American political development focused on other policy domains, it means that as an economic actor, the state is far more effective—or if you prefer your glass half-empty, is much less ineffective—than our presumptions about distributed power and fragmentation tend to allow. As the U.S. experience shows, to produce results in the economic innovation arena, a state need not have centralized powers, dispensing policies in a highly orchestrated effort from the top. A less centralized, bottom-up but agency-directed process could deliver better results. Three conclusions follow. First, the larger the territory and the more advanced the economy, the more a form of "coordinated pluralism" is advantageous (and conversely, the more centralization is harmful). Second, to the extent that the American state has the ability to access, establish, and tease out desired performance from nonstate actors, this comes not from statism, but from a relationship of governed interdependence. Third, if the state often uses private actors to do its business, it also does business while appearing as a private actor—hence, a hybridized state. This at least is how I have come to view the NSS role in advancing the technological frontier.

On an equally general, but slightly different note, state activism is quite possibly the least of the threats that face a struggling U.S. economy. If anything, it may well be the weakness of the state's response that matters most as the United States enters more troubled waters in the coming decade.

Great Power Turning Point

Since I have spent the major part of this book building a case that links technology leadership and the capacity for transformative innovation to the quest for American primacy, there are two obvious questions that remain to be addressed. Is the NSS innovation engine still working for the United States? And if not, why not? Even if entirely satisfactory answers remain elusive at this stage, I will try to show why the issue is important to consider. Specifically, the status of the NSS innovation enterprise has a strong bearing on the future of American power that is often overlooked in discussions of so-called "U.S. decline."

I have argued that, in the post-9/11 era, the NSS innovation engine no longer has the laser-like focus that the intensity of the Soviet threat and Japanese rivalry encouraged. Wavering political support for the U.S. transformative project has also been evident in the period of asymmetric threats, manifested not only in Congressional pressures for short-term payoffs from military S&T spending, but also most powerfully in Republican opposition to those energy initiatives from the military that clash with a preference for the incumbent energy producers. Most of all, the breadth and depth of polarization in the political arena is strikingly revealed in the extent to which not even the prospect of a weakened military could prevent sequestration. And if this new era of budgetary uncertainty is unlikely to sharpen the U.S. strategic focus, one might still ask why China has not yet metamorphosed into a rival that spurs innovation like the Soviet Union and Japan.[19] The question deserves further consideration because, although it is still a good way from the technology frontier, China's rising status as a manufacturing superpower may well provide that launching pad, especially if the Japanese experience offers any guide.

To be clear, the NSS still has the ability to deliver technology leadership, which after all is the currency of U.S. military power. But what of its ability to continue delivering broader commercial-economic benefit? If this is in jeopardy does this mean that U.S. technology leadership, qua military superiority, is also compromised? My sense is that something disquieting is indeed taking place which, if not arrested, will unravel the technology enterprise and, along with it, the strategic and commercial benefits it has delivered.

These questions lead on to further questions connecting the debates about financialization, the offshoring of U.S. production, and American preeminence. What happens if U.S. technology leadership fails to translate into domestic production for commercial benefit? How long can a great power sustain its military leadership while leaking domestic manufacturing capacity to overseas locations? These, I grant, are large questions without easy answers. But that does not make them any the less essential to consider.

Let me emphasize that even if the United States is militarily overstretched or challenged by rising new powers on the horizon, it is not a great power in decline. It is true that Washington's international influence has waned, that its economic and strategic agenda has a diminished global impact. It is in that specific sense that one can speak of the "end of the American era." As Stephen Walt lucidly argues, this means that the United States is likely to "remain the strongest global power but be unable to exercise the same influence it once enjoyed" (Walt 2011, 7). Despite the many circumlocutions that play with terms such as "polarity," "primacy," "dominance," "preeminence," and the like, the United States is not about to fall from its perch as a great power. Who needs reminding that its military primacy is still uncontested or that its capacity for innovation and high-value economic output, however unevenly distributed in national income, has no peer? The question is: Can the United States remain, well into the future, *the preeminent power*? Its economic strength has undoubtedly taken a heavy beating as a result of the 2008 financial meltdown and the massive indebtedness, fiscal crisis, and unemployment thereby created. Many thinkers, both conservative and liberal, have linked the origins of this debacle to the "financialization" of the U.S. political economy, whereby a financial oligarchy—or plutocracy—has wreaked systemic and social havoc by tilting the policy space and all other playing fields in its favor.[20] Here I wish to focus on a trend that is closely related to financialization, namely offshore outsourcing.

To begin with, it is well to knock on the head any possible confusion of innovation capacity with competitiveness. Surely, one is inclined to ask, if U.S. industry has been so effective in helping to turn out new widgets, why then is it lagging, with a manufacturing base that is now running on empty and job creation at an-all time low? A nutshell response is that competitiveness depends on many different factors, not just technology—among them productivity, currency fluctuations, and corporate strategy. To complicate matters, recent data on comparative performance show that a country—notably Germany—can score high on competitiveness while lagging in innovation capacity and technology leadership.[21] Conversely, some industries may lose competitiveness even if they are innovators because they lack the necessary "complementary assets," such as the capacity to manufacture and market, that imitators may access (Teece 1986, 303). As if to confirm that point, a 1991 Carnegie Commission report observed that "Our strengths in technology and innovation have not prevented an erosion in market shares of U.S. companies in many industries. As new products mature, the advantage quickly shifts from the innovator to the efficient producer."[22]

This last statement goes to the heart of the matter—production (as distinct from innovation) also counts a great deal for competitiveness. This fact in turn reveals the primary reason for anticipating diminishing returns from the NSS innovation engine, both for the U.S. economy and for the NSS itself: that a pronounced disconnect between innovation and manufacturing has come about as a result of downsizing production at home and distributing it to offshore suppliers. This disconnect is largely a consequence of financialism, not militarism or the national security state. By financialism, I mean not just the preponderant power of the financial sector in the political economy, but also the broad institutionalization of its value set throughout the industrial system, encapsulated in the primacy of shareholder value and the preference for financial investments over productive assets. Let us turn to see how this bears on the technology leadership issue.

The disconnect: Innovation without production. Most of the current challenges to the NSS technology enterprise are worrying rather than critical. But there is one challenge that bothers many close observers. It is the fact that NSS innovation now confronts a dramatically changed domestic environment, one in which the bulk of U.S. manufacturing is increasingly conducted in foreign locations. U.S. industry has for a long time prospered as a result of the transformative general-purpose innovations shepherded into existence by the NSS. Companies have taken those innovations and designed new products. The difference now is that they have those products increasingly manufactured abroad. We come then to the most important reason why the NSS technology enterprise is likely to produce diminishing benefits for the U.S. economy (and ultimately for the NSS itself)—namely, the divorce between innovation and production. As a recent study conducted by the National Research Council concludes, "it no longer follows that discoveries and inventions flowing from research conducted by America's universities, corporations and national laboratories will naturally lead to products that are commercialized and industrialized on U.S. shores . . . the U.S. is finding it increasingly difficult to capture the economic value generated by its tremendous public and private investments in R&D" (National Research Council 2012, 2).

The problem, now widely recognized, is that innovation has become increasingly disconnected from its manufacturing base—and thus from the industry development, productive investment, and job creation that have formed an essential part of nation and economy building. Let us also include the tax revenue derived from that base that helps sustain the NSS technology enterprise. Taking advantage of globally integrated production chains is of course now de rigueur for companies in many parts of the world. However, U.S. companies seem to have gone further than most, arguably creating an extreme form of the process. For example, as well as leading the way to become the "largest offshoring procurer" (Aspray et al. 2006, 29), they have also increasingly pushed the "downsize and distribute" process to the limits so that all the bits of a project may now be executed outside the country, including the most knowledge-intensive parts of the value chain (Government Accountability Office 2006, 2). For this reason, offshoring is widely perceived as the enemy of productive vitality at home. Although the trend began earlier, it has accelerated since the 1980s.[23]

As one indicator of this trend, the China-located Taiwanese computer and mobile phone manufacturer, Foxconn, which figures prominently in the U.S. supply chain, now employs more people in China than Apple, Dell, Microsoft, Cisco, Intel, and Hewlett-Packard combined employ in the United States.[24] Another indicator is the state of U.S. investment. Whether in new production, or in product and process innovation, U.S. business investment at home ranked lower than in every other advanced country, just ahead of Burma at 135th position, according to CIA data.[25] This accords with William Lazonick's findings that the large U.S. corporations that make up the S&P 500, while making very substantial profits, are reinvesting only a tiny fraction, if any, preferring instead to pay out the overwhelming share of their net income (94 percent) in dividends (40 percent) or for share buybacks (54 percent). Lazonick calculates that from 1997 through 2008, a total of 437 companies in the S&P 500 "expended $2.4 trillion on stock repurchases, an average of $5.6 billion per company, and distributed a total of $1.6 trillion in cash dividends, an average of $3.8 billion per company" (Lazonick 2011, 6). This practice, known as "maximizing shareholder value," is integral to the operational logic of financialization—the shift "away from productive investment and into financial investments where quick and larger profits can be realized" (Milberg and Schöller 2008, 5). In a survey by the National Bureau of Economic Research of 401 senior financial executives, almost 90 percent believed "building credibility with [the] capital market" took priority, hence a good 80 percent reported that they would slash or forgo spending on research and development to meet their quarterly projections; they also deferred company investment in valuable long-term projects to meet earnings targets.[26] Needless to say, this preference for consumption of profits over their productive reinvestment would have startled Max Weber for its ruthless cutting of the link between the "Protestant ethic and the spirit of capitalism."

Why the disconnect? What is the source of the drive to abdicate production to foreign suppliers? A key part of the puzzle is that U.S. innovation now takes place in a highly financialized environment. Its "downsize and distribute" business model is one in which increasing a company's share price has become the supreme value for corporate management, so U.S. executives tend to base their investment decisions on increasing corporate earnings in order to boost the company's stock price. This explains why it is that almost all S&P 500 companies devote so much of their income to repurchase their own shares.[27] Both offshoring and share repurchasing are favored because they boost stock prices and thereby increase returns to shareholders and to the top executives themselves who benefit when cashing in their own stock.

The two trends, financialization (especially share repurchasing) and offshoring, have grown together in a self-reinforcing manner. Lazonick's analysis suggests a three-step process whereby manufacturing is downsized and distributed to suppliers abroad. It begins with mass layoffs at home. Second, the layoffs release extra funds for the company and these funds are then used to make massive stock repurchases.[28] As the company's stock price increases, shareholders gain in dividends, and top management gains an income boost from realizing its stock options. Finally, what was once produced onshore with U.S. plant, labor, and equipment is now moved to suppliers in cheaper or more flexible locations. Hewlett Packard's actions exemplify the process: in September 2008, the computer company announced that it would lay off almost 25,000 workers; it then announced another $8 billion share buyback (adding to an $8 billion buyback program started in the previous November). Its stock price went up. A few weeks later, in October, Hewlett Packard announced its intention to build a new computer plant in China.[29] Whatever the benefits that offshoring produces, companies are diverting the gains to the acquisition of financial assets—as evidenced in the combination of a falling U.S. investment rate and a rising share of company profits in national income—hence sustaining financialization (Milberg and Winkler 2009, 2, 13).

Ashton Carter observes a similar financializing impact at work on defense companies, which face the same short-term pressures to justify themselves to investors as commercial companies (Carter 2001, 10). Thus, even the large defense contractors have joined the offshoring and share repurchasing practices, often conducting production for DoD through their foreign subsidiaries. For a decade at least, according to a survey conducted by the

Government Accountability Office, prime contractors have been relocating manufacturing abroad to avoid payroll taxes and related expenses at home.[30] William Bonvillian (2009, 73) adds the striking observation that the relocation of U.S. industry abroad is dissolving the long-standing "triangular innovation alliance" between industry, universities, and the defense sector.

Whether to reduce costs, to avoid labor regulations, to be closer to the global market, or to access supply chains, the decision to farm out production is a choice that has been aided by America's public officials who have rewritten the rules to encourage the process.[31] As the institutional embodiment of the financialization process, financialism cultivates that choice, driving it further in the United States than almost anywhere else. A writer for *Computerworld* who covers offshoring practices in the IT sector put it most starkly: "We have lost manufacturing because Wall Street has rewarded short term solutions, like outsourcing. . . The financial services industry, including banking and insurance, is already the most aggressive industry in the U.S. when it comes to offshore outsourcing."[32]

When the pressure to relocate production comes directly from U.S. companies themselves, rather than from an abstraction called "globalization," we might see in this a pattern of "extreme offshoring" at work. Consider for example, the Congressionally mandated 2007 study, *Rising above the Gathering Storm*, which reported that "For several years, U.S. companies that outsource information-technology jobs have all but ordered their contractors to send some portion of the work overseas . . ." (National Research Council 2007c, 27). Equally telling of financialism's grip on the American entrepreneur's imagination is the description of venture capital's "exit-to-China strategy" for the U.S. computer industry. Andy Grove offers an illuminating example of the individually rational but collectively suicidal strategy to drive production offshore: "Five years ago a friend joined a large VC firm as a partner. His responsibility was to make sure that all the startups they funded had a 'China strategy,' meaning a plan to move what jobs they could to China. He was going around with an oil can, applying drops to the guillotine in case it was stuck."[33]

In short, there is no dearth of innovation startups in the United States, but many of these no longer make anything. With some exceptions, the key products and services of the all-important ICT sector, including the high-value, highly engineered components—are increasingly made offshore, usually by Japanese, Taiwanese, Korean or German companies. Apple's iPhone, a leading exponent of the "distributed" or "modularized" manufacturing model, exemplifies the problem.[34] As Grove went on to argue, innovation will hardly matter in keeping America in the lead if its inventions do not result in U.S. production.

Why should this matter to U.S. preeminence? Why is manufacturing important? The general argument, made by many scholars over the years, is that research, development, design and manufacturing need to exist side by side, that manufacturing matters for preserving hard-to-rebuild capabilities, for sustaining an ecosystem of industries, for future innovation, and not least, for creating skilled jobs. The pioneering study by Cohen and Zysman (1987) advanced a compelling argument that "manufacturing matters"—for job creation, competitiveness, and not least for technological progress, and that (*pace* the myth of a "postindustrial" society) services could never fill the gap created by the exit of manufacturing. Indeed, these and other researchers at the Berkeley Roundtable on the International Economy had been pressing the case since the early 1980s. Motivated by the Japanese challenge, they argued that the U.S. lead in R&D would count for little if the nation lost the edge in production.

In addition to severe economic consequences, many voices express fear of national security casualties of this manufacturing migration, including trustworthiness and supply assurance for critical components, especially regarding the strategically important microelectronics sector. In a startling declaration, a recent Defense Science Board task force on high-performance microchip supply had this to say about the relocation of critical microelectronics manufacturing capabilities from the United States to countries with lower-cost capital and operating environments: "From a U.S. national security view, the potential effects of this restructuring are so perverse and far reaching and have such opportunities for mischief that, had the United States not significantly contributed to this migration, it would have been considered a major triumph of an adversary nation's strategy to undermine U.S. military capabilities" (Defense Science Board 2005, 4).

As the epigraphs to this chapter reveal, there is a growing awareness that changes in the U.S. industrial base provide little basis for complacency. Redressing the disconnect that has been fostered by an extreme version of financialization would seem critical to recapturing the outputs of innovation on which so much else depends.[35] As the National Research Council study *Rising to the Challenge* concludes, "America's economic and national security future depends on our succeeding in this endeavor" (National Research Council 2012, 12).

When institutional strengths become fetters. Mounting such an endeavor will be challenging, for in order to be effective it will have to confront America's most powerful nonmilitary institution, the financial world. In particular, reconnecting innovation to production would require remaking the rules that currently tilt all playing fields in finance's favor—whether the game is derivatives trading or high-tech offshoring and share repurchasing, and whether the locale is Wall Street or California. It is not hard to appreciate that any such reconnecting effort would require a degree of federal reregulation and intervention that would likely bump up against America's pervasive distaste for government.

These observations can be linked to a theory of why countries lose their preeminence, if not necessarily their great power status. Essentially, the argument is that all countries institutionalize the features that make them strong, but when circumstances change, those very institutional strengths can turn into fetters that hinder efforts at reform to meet new challenges. By preventing effective adjustment to new circumstances, today's strengths become tomorrow's weaknesses. Countries thus get trapped in the very conditions that led to their success.[36] It does not take too much effort to see how such a framework applies to the U.S. experience. In America's case, the power and values of finance—politically, economically, and institutionally—have become all-encompassing. A politically powerful financial elite has neither interest nor stake in the fortunes of the nation's domestic industrial base. The dominance of financial capitalism in national priorities has weakened not only the domestic economy but also Washington's global ideological influence. Having once contributed to the United States' great power status, financialism has become a fetter that now threatens its preeminence by aiding and abetting the dramatic loss of industry abroad and by standing in the way of a reversal of this trend. Although using different language and addressing different questions, the recent analyses of the U.S. experience mentioned earlier reach a similar conclusion.

We can add to this institutions as fetters analysis. Aaron Friedberg ingeniously argued that American antistatism helped win the Cold War. It was the ace up the institutional sleeve that prevented the "most stifling excesses of statism" and "made it easier for the United States to preserve its economic vitality and technological dynamism" compared with its "supremely statist rival" (Friedberg 2000, 4). But now that circumstances have altered and there is a need to reconnect breakthroughs with followthroughs, distaste for government action can easily turn from asset to liability.[37] As Friedberg himself acknowledges in a prescient statement, antistatism can become self-destructive if unchecked: "Institutions that are perpetually deadlocked will be unable to generate workable solutions to the new problems and challenges that history inevitably presents" (Friedberg 2000, 351). Whether manifest as institutional or politico-ideological deadlock, antistatism now keeps company with financialism, making remedial action by government a challenging task of high order.

In closing, it would be fair to say that there are doubtless more desirable innovation models than one centered on national security. But telling the U.S. story of transformative innovation as it is, rather than as one might wish it to be, deserves to be understood as an important task in its own right. For one thing, it confirms the more general point advanced in several existing studies, namely that the state remains a vital actor in helping to shift the economy up the technology ladder—a principle that clearly applies to the world's most advanced political economy, *pace* its foundational narrative.[38] In addition, the story makes clear that even the most avant-garde innovation does not consistently translate into broader benefits if the disconnect from production is taken to an extreme, as the U.S. experience demonstrates. As for broader lessons, it is also evident that the U.S. approach to that continual ladder-climbing process is highly specific to its great power status and therefore unlikely to work for (or appeal to) others. The NSS innovation engine would be difficult to adopt or emulate because it is highly embedded in a national security logic that stems from the quest for strategic superiority. No other state has instituted such an NSS-driven innovation enterprise and there are very few candidates for such a model.[39] Given its size and military ambition, China might be a candidate for building a more statist version in the not too distant future. But for those very statist reasons, it is unlikely to achieve the transformative heights of the U.S. experience.[40]

Finally, a key policy question is whether cutting the umbilical cord that connects U.S. industry and enterprise to the NSS by drastically scaling back its contribution to the technology enterprise would increase commercial innovation payoffs. From the perspective offered in this book, cutting the cord would be akin to killing the goose that laid the golden egg. Like the goose, some parts of the NSS, have a tendency to overeat and put on weight; they can sometimes make a lot of noise, act extremely aggressively, and even lose their way; yet over time they have also produced some pretty fine eggs for U.S. consumption (and some would say, for all the world). Moreover, if the foregoing analysis is accepted, a dismantling or further weakening of the NSS technology enterprise will not by itself provide the economic boost anticipated by advocates of a "civilian" technology policy. Restoring economic strength would require a concerted effort to reconnect innovation with onshore production, and thus a dislodging of the preponderant power of financialism that is presently part of the problem and hampers a solution.

Notes

1. The National Security State and Technology Leadership

1. On a much larger terrain Peter Katzenstein (2005) has charted a similar course in his magisterial study of Asian and European regionalism, there examining how the links between culture, security, and technology shape the behavior of core states in world politics. Richard Samuels's (1994) definitive study of Japanese "technonationalism"—the belief that technology must be indigenized and nurtured to make a nation rich and secure—also fits into this general comparative frame.

2. "Breakthrough," "radical," and "revolutionary" are terms frequently applied interchangeably to the kind of innovation in which the United States is seen to dominate (in contrast to "incremental" innovation said to be more typical of Germany). I shall use the term "transformative" in lieu of these terms.

3. It is one thing to agree with the claim that defense spending needs significant scaling back; it is quite another to agree that such spending (either as a whole or just that part allocated to technology development) is a cause of U.S. economic decline. In this long-running and contentious debate, passions run high and diametrically opposing conclusions abound; see chapter 8 for an overview.

4. These include the Central Intelligence Agency, Department of Energy, the National Aeronautics and Space Administration, the National Science Foundation, the National Institutes of Health, and the more recently created Department of Homeland Security. It also includes the federally owned and funded laboratories attached to specific federal agencies (administered either by those agencies, private firms, or universities), as well as the numerous not-for-profit companies created, sponsored, or operated by various NSS agencies. Arguably, other bodies not included here perform national security functions, for example, the Department of Agriculture, or even the National Institute of Standards and Technology, both of which have served military requirements. I will not defend the selection of agencies included here, but instead refer the reader to chapter 2.

5. For the geopolitical argument applied to Korea and Taiwan, see Woo-Cumings 1998 and Zhu 2002, also Weiss and Hobson 1995.

6. For the argument that the Pentagon pursues a "closet" industrial policy, see for example, Markusen 1986. Some of the more considered analyses within this industry policy genre can be found in Hooks 1990, Hart 1992, Vogel 1996, and Fong 2000.

7. The industrial policy claim implies that the initiatives in question are designed to improve the competitive position of an industry or to change its structure. To take a typical example, the motives behind DoD's unsuccessful effort to catalyze an industry in flat-panel

displays have been framed as driven by competitiveness rather than security concerns. This mis-specifies the security rationale, as Flamm explains at some length (1994, 27–32). That industry has benefited commercially from a variety of measures taken over the years is not in question. But these measures have, with few exceptions, been motivated by security concerns. Since overall the underlying principle has not been the boosting of economic competitiveness, it is something of a stretch to label the measures as industrial policy.

8. The ATP was the first explicitly commercially focused technology development program, initiated in 1991 under George H. W. Bush, then enacted and implemented under Clinton's presidency. After a decade of repeated dismantling attempts by a Republican-led Congress, plus opposition from the George W. Bush administration, it was finally suspended in 2005.

9. Earlier instances of the military's role in technological innovation go back to the Civil War (Smith 1985), but the war-technology connection is a more general historical pattern (McNeill 1982). To nail down our orienting question—why the United States?—we need to start with something new on the scene that is larger than the military and more enduring than war as such.

10. If conducted for directly commercial benefit, which they are not, these measures would amount to an industrial policy for the advanced knowledge economy.

11. Alex Roland's enlightening essay (2007) discusses the events that inspired Eisenhower's use of the term and the subsequent meanings it has since acquired as both "lobby" and "trope."

12. For expressions of this widely held view see, for example, Jay Stowsky, who writes in *American Prospect* that "The commercial benefits of America's defense-driven technology development strategy were pervasive if unintended," http://prospect.org/article/conversion-competitiveness-making-most-national-labs.

13. Richard Nelson's work has been the bible of understanding in this vein, asserting that "Although American dominance of the frontiers of military technology gave the United States significant civilian technological advantages during the 1950s and 1960s, today that dominance buys very little outside the military sphere. . . . For the most part since the late 1960s, advances in military technology have had very few spillover effects into civilian technology" (1990, 18).

14. This consensus is well articulated in the work of Charles Wessner, National Academy Scholar and director of the Program on Technology, Innovation, and Entrepreneurship. See, e.g., his essay section on "The Myth of Military Spin-offs" (2005, 72–73) and especially his presentation to European officials seeking to learn from U.S. innovation policies: "The Military R&D Myth about U.S. Innovation," www.6cp.net/downloads/04brussels_wessner.ppt.

15. For a critical perspective on the defense-commercial relationship, see Stowsky 1999.

16. Scholars note that a good number of the sectors that Hall and Soskice deem radically innovative (e.g., microelectronics, semiconductors, and biotechnology) were beneficiaries of substantial federal support in their infant stages. Moreover, if the United States is the only liberal market economy that has a high incidence of radical innovation, it cannot be the liberal market itself that accounts for this outcome. See Taylor 2004.

17. Vivien Schmidt (2002) observes that the Hall and Soskice two-model view of capitalism leaves out a third state-guided variety such as the East Asian and, arguably, the French model.

18. For a penetrating critique along these lines, see Crouch 2005a.

19. Comments made by Block as discussant on the panel "Return of the State: Learning from the BRICs?" Conference on New Economic Thinking, Teaching, and Policy Perspectives: A Brazilian Perspective within a Global Dialogue, Rio de Janeiro, November 7–9, 2011, http://www.minds.org.br/fordconference2011/.

20. Harold Sapolsky is one of the few to put the matter candidly, albeit writing with specific reference to medical innovation: "Wars, of course, are a major spur to medical innovation although as I have discovered no one likes to dwell much on this unhappy truth" (1992, 2).

21. For a sample of the critical literature, see Melman 1974, DeGrasse 1983, and Wirls 1992. On the 2008 financial crisis, Simon Johnson's electrifying analysis in *The Atlantic* (2009) leaves little doubt as to the key protagonist, and gains credence from the fact that Johnson until recently occupied the position of chief IMF economist.

22. On the distinction between authoritarian and liberal militarism, see Mann 1996.

23. Exemplary works include William McNeill's *The Pursuit of Power* (1982), and Merritt Roe Smith's *Military Enterprise and Technological Change* (1985).

24. In this tradition, see Chalmers Johnson's important trilogy examining the consequences of American empire (*Blowback, The Sorrows of Empire, Nemesis*), and Andrew Bacevich's critical examination of sixty years of American militarism in *Washington Rules* (2010).

25. Markusen and Yudken (1992) have set the standard on this topic.

26. See also Mann's preface to his volume of essays (1988), written between 1976 and 1986, in which he comments on social science's long neglect of war and militarism as a society shaping influence.

27. By the same token, we cannot ignore the merits of the argument that permanent defense preparedness helps to maintain peace—something that even neutral countries, such as Sweden, understand very well.

28. On the private sector's reluctance to cooperate in war production, see the writings of Georges Doriot, World War II director of the U.S. Army's Military Planning Division, in Ante 2008. More recent difficulties in getting leading IT firms to do defense work are discussed in Carter 2001 and Gansler 2011.

29. Likewise, scholars dissatisfied with both top-down and bottom-up frameworks in governance studies have argued that rather than positing them as mutually exclusive approaches, their combination can be more effective for explaining policy outcomes in public/private networks (e.g., Peters and Pierre 1998).

30. The complete formulation is "war makes the state, and the state makes war" (Tilly 1975, 42).

31. See the essays in Katznelson and Shefter 2002.

32. For a recent application of this argument to the post-9/11 era, see Kroenig and Stowsky 2006.

33. One of the few studies in this vein is Margaret O'Mara's (2005) fine analysis of the Pentagon's role in the making of Silicon Valley during the early Cold War period.

34. For the seminal distinction, see Mann's 1984 article "The Autonomous Power of the State . . ." reprinted in Mann 1988.

35. As he succinctly puts it in an earlier article: "the openness of American political institutions to interest group pressures and the content of American ideology combined to place very real limits on the power of the state over society and the economy" (Friedberg 1992, 110).

36. Although still tied to the language of "garrison state," the work of both Andrew Grossman and Michael Sherry leans in a similar direction, indicating the emergence of a new kind of state power that is not readily quantifiable (Sherry 2003, 164) and that collapses the public-private divide (Grossman 2002, 475).

37. Similar public-private patterns have been documented for France (Coleman and Chiasson 2002); Israel (Breznitz 2007); Korea (Kim 2010); and Denmark (Daugbjerg and Halpin 2010). For the more general argument, with application to European and East Asian cases, see Weiss (1998; 2003, chap.14).

38. In short, there are two theories of complementarity; in the first, institutions reinforce each other's incentives; in the second, they compensate for each other's shortcomings. For an interesting attempt to adjudicate this debate, with application to the U.S. financial crisis, see Campbell 2011.

2. Rise of the National Security State as Technology Enterprise

1. The classic treatments of the early postwar years include Hogan 1998, Hart 1998, Stewart 2009, and Friedberg 2000. For an account of the evolution of the NSS up to the present era (emphasizing its secrecy and intelligence aspects), see Nelson 2007.

2. Mowery and Rosenberg (1998, 6) observe that "the technological position of the U.S. economy before the Second World War bore more than a superficial resemblance to the situation of Japan in the 1960s and 1970s"—a flair for making improvements to technologies created elsewhere.

3. Citations in this paragraph, unless otherwise specified, are from Hart 1998, 174. In this large-scale history of S&T policy, Hart devotes only one chapter to the NSS, but it is a standout for its elegance and insight.

4. For an extended discussion of the forms and influence of antistatism in the development of the NSS, see Friedberg 2000, chap. 1.

5. For details of these organizations and their inability to withstand the "intense bureaucratic competition that characterized the initial shake-out period" (1947–53), see Stewart 2008, 9.

6. In addition, the government built civil defense shelters, conducted drills for schoolchildren, founded think tanks like RAND "to ponder the new security dilemma," and set about hunting down communist sympathizers (Carter 2001, 15).

7. On the close collaboration of the NIH with the NSS, see, for example, NIH/NIAID press release, http://www.niaid.nih.gov/news/newsreleases/2002/pages/usamriid-niaid_partner ship.aspx.

8. This paragraph draws on Halvorson 1992.

9. George W. Merck, president of pharmaceutical giant Merck & Co. and chair of the War Research Service, the wartime body responsible for the nation's biological warfare program, used his government contacts and contracts to initiate secret work in some twenty-eight elite universities.

10. See Special Committee on Technical Information Research and Development Board 1951.

11. For the broader argument based on archival research see Hurt 2010.

12. Hart (1998, 224) remarks, without elaborating, that "there are intriguing parallels between . . . national security and health security" and that the NIH is an area "ripe" for further research.

13. *An Overview of the United States Intelligence Community for the 111th Congress*, 2009, http://www.ncirc.gov/documents/public/ODNI_Overview_of_US_Intell_Community.pdf.

14. See DoE's website, http://www.energy.gov/about/index.htm.

15. All the elements of modern nuclear medicine, argue Lenoir and Hays (2000, 62), sprang from the programs of the AEC and the Veterans Administration, direct descendants of the Manhattan Project.

16. I draw here on the historian John Krige (2010, 124, 132), who applies Joseph Nye's concept of "soft power," arguing that national security ideas during the Cold War were often understood as a struggle for hearts and minds, not just about military preparedness.

17. The shift toward high-technology weapons systems began under Truman during the Korean War (Hart 1998, 195).

18. Eisenhower's memo, "Scientific and Technological Resources as Military Assets" (April 27, 1946) is reprinted in Melman 1970, app. B, 1235.

19. The Munitions Board, the Research and Development Board, the Defense Supply Management Agency, and the office of Director of Installations were abolished and their functions vested in the Secretary of Defense.

20. The principal service agencies responsible for scientific research and technology development are discussed in Peck and Scherer's pioneering study of weapons acquisition (1962, 71). On the Office of Naval Research in particular see Sapolsky 1990. On the centralization of authority within the armed services, see Allison 1985, 299–300.

21. On the AEC, see Orlans 1967, 6. On the NIH, see Congressional Research Service 1986a, 29–30.

22. National aviation was the partial exception, for which the armed services assumed prewar developmental responsibility (Danhof 1968, 24).

23. On the role and evolution of MIT and Stanford as Cold War universities, see Leslie 1993b; also O'Mara 2005.

24. Robert Watson, official historian of the Office of the Secretary of Defense, quoted in Stuart 2008, 321. On the psychological and cultural impact of the Sputnik launches see McDougall 1982.

25. See figure 2.2 for data source.

26. See Alex Roland's (2010, 10) response to efforts to model DARPA's "success," in which he presents a nuanced picture of DARPA's achievements and "jewel in the crown" status.

27. On the role of technology procurement (as distinct from research) in creating new sectors see chapter 5.

28. Hurt (2010, 39–40) also claims that the NSS sought to use the private sector as "a shield" to protect its interests in a "new underground arms race" as détente ended.

29. The rationale for declaring a "War on Cancer" in the early 1970s remains intriguing rather than obvious. At the time, there was no clear escalation in national cancer rates. Moreover, the leading cause of death in the United States is cardiovascular disease, not cancer;

yet cancer research has received the lion's share of funding. See Congressional Research Service 2006, table 1.

30. Washington Correspondent, "Biological Warfare: Relief of Fort Detrick," *Nature,* November 28, 1970, 803.

31. On the complementarity of biotech projects funded by both DOD and NIH, see Feldman 2001.

32. See the special article by S. Young-McGaughan and other researchers at the U.S. Army Medical Research and Materiel Command, Fort Detrick, "The Department of Defense Congressionally Directed Research Program: Innovations in the Federal Funding of Biomedical Research," *Clinical Cancer Research* 8 (April 2002): 957–62.

33. The 1976 report of the Defense Science Board, *Summer Study Panel on Industrial Responsiveness,* was one of a series through the 1970s and early 1980s that warned of a drop in preparedness.

34. The government accounted for 100 percent of the U.S. market for integrated circuits in 1962, but little more than 10 percent by 1978 (Alic et al. 1992, 260).

35. On the intensity of United States–Japan rivalry in microelectronics, see Borrus, Millstein, and Zysman 1984.

36. In the critical information and communications technology sector, for example, these defense-intensive contractors were engaged in incremental innovation for the services, often integrating the more radical innovations developed by nontraditional suppliers (National Research Council 1999, 101).

37. This act also created technology transfer offices in the federal labs and established a National Technology Medal.

38. Lab descriptions and quotes in this paragraph are from Stowsky 1992, 91, 92.

39. As Japanese firms began conquering U.S. technology markets notably in chip production from the mid-1970s, numerous U.S. semiconductor firms exited the market, giving rise to Silicon Valley's worst crisis (Heinrich 2002; see also chapter 4 below).

40. By achieving substantially higher yield rates (hence fewer defects) per wafer, Japanese producers were able to outcompete U.S. firms on quality and price, leading many to exit the DRAM business.

41. On the Microsoft campaign, see Richard Clark and Robert Knake's *Cyber War,* cited in Etzioni 2011.

42. Fareed Zakaria, "Fareed's Take: U.S. Has Made War on Terror a War without End," *Global Public Square* (CNN), http://globalpublicsquare.blogs.cnn.com/2012/05/06/national-security-state/.

43. GAO's observations, consonant with those of several other bodies, are reported by the Panel on Business Challenges in the Defense Industry (U.S. House, Committee on Armed Services 2012, vii).

44. The need to do more with less has been a persistent theme of Jacques Gansler's work, including his latest book (2011).

3. Investing in New Ventures

1. SBA website, http://www.sba.gov/aboutsba/sbaprograms/inv/INV_SUCCESS_STO RIES.html.

2. Although definitions vary, most would agree with Bruce Held's view that the concept of venture capital covers "a broad category of investment schemes targeted at new or young companies that have a concept or technology but lack the resources to develop and market it." Other features include a high risk of failure and potentially high returns, and in most cases a "fairly high degree of investor involvement" both in managing and promoting the young firms being backed. Moreover, not all venture capital is equity capital in which funding is provided in exchange for a stake in the enterprise. Royalties on future profits or interest on loans offer other types of VC investment mechanism (Held 2002, 41).

3. The entire May 2008 edition of ejournalusa, "Venture Capital Meets Hi-Tech," tells the story of how the modern U.S. venture capital industry developed as a wholly private-sector initiative, http://www.america.gov/publications/ejournalusa.html.

4. RAND analyst Krishan Kumar reported in 2009 that "high-growth early-stage entrepreneurial activity in the United States is more than twice that of Germany and more than three times that of Japan," http://www.rand.org/commentary/2009/09/17/PPG.html.

5. The following section is based on Spencer Ante's (1980) illuminating biographical study of Doriot. See also Lightbody 2004.

6. For similar cases of east coast VC firm formation linked to war reconversion, see Reiner 1991, 207.

7. The study reported a shortage of financing as the chief obstacle to the development of "entrepreneurial businesses" (Board of the Federal Reserve System 1958, 329); see also Noone and Rubel 1970.

8. The SBIC manages both a debenture program and a participating securities program. Debenture SBICs mainly provide debt or debt-with-equity features and focus on companies mature enough to meet interest payments; participating securities SBICs typically make pure equity investments.

9. Small Business Investor Alliance, "SBIC Program History," http://www.sbia.org/?page=SBIC_Program_History.

10. According to Gompers (1994, 10), prior to the 1980s, annual flows into new venture funds rarely exceeded $200 million.

11. The following section, with quotations, is based on the UC Berkeley Oral History Interviews with early venture capitalists of the Silicon Valley area, this one conducted on April 14, 2008 (Draper 2008, 1–95, at 38ff). Draper was one of the first professional west coast venture capitalists, now running a number of VC funds. Tellingly, he and several of the pioneers who established SBICs were students of Doriot.

12. "Fund-Raising? Make Mine an SBIC," *Wall Street Journal,* October 15, 2010.

13. All data from the SBA website, "The U.S. Small Business Investment Company Program," http://www.sbia.org/?page=sbic_program_history.

14. Hudson Ferry Press Release 2010, http://www.prnewswire.com/news-releases/hudson-ferry-capital-forms-100-million-sbic-100330984.html.

15. "Small Business Investment Act of 1958 (P.L. 84-699 as amended)," http://www.sba.gov/sites/default/files/tools_resclib_lr_sbinvact.pdf.

16. Reported by Stephen Merrill, then member of the Senate Committee on Commerce, Science, and Transportation (Merrill 1979, 11–12). The 1977 OMB report cited above also found that the small business sector of the U.S. economy compiled "a striking record of innovation," firms with under 1,000 employees "accounted for almost 1/2 of major U.S. innovations during 1953–73" (Office of Management and Budget 1977, i).

17. All quotes in this paragraph are drawn from U.S. Senate, Select Committee on Small Business 1979, 9–10.

18. See the DoD's Program Solicitation Number 84, Small Business Innovation Research Program, Washington, D.C., October 15, 1983, p. 1, http://www.acq.osd.mil/osbp/sbir/solicitations/sbir1984/preface84.pdf. Likewise, the NSF piloted an early version of the SBIR in 1978, reporting considerable success.

19. Jacques Gansler 2002, "Interview with Andrew Butrica, Defense Acquisition History Project," U.S. Army Center of Military History, September: www.history.army.mil/acquisition/research/int_gansler.html.

20. The varying figures depend on whether one adjusts for the inflation stemming from the 1999–2001 dot.com bubble. See National Science Board, *Science and Engineering Indicators 2010,* appendix, table 6-72.

21. Data from National Science Board (2010: appendix, table 6-72).

22. SBIR invested approximately $2.5 billion in technology companies, "while the venture capital industry only put $1.7 billion into early-stage investments." See SBA website, http://www.sbir.gov/content/announcing-sbir-20.

23. Inknowvation is a database of SBIR awardees (1983–present) that helps put large firms in touch with startups and innovative companies working on technologies of interest to them. See http://www.inknowvation.com/sbir-techbase/sbir-companies.

24. MIT engineering Ph.D. graduate cited in Maureen Farrell, "How To Get Uncle Sam To Fund Your Start-Up," *Forbes,* July 25, 2008, http://www.forbes.com/2008/07/25/small-business-grant-ent-fin-cx_mf_0725governmentgrant.html.

25. The program has received frequent assessments from the GAO, all largely positive. For samples, see Government Accountability Office 1987, 1995.

26. See e.g Audretsch et al.'s (2002: 188) findings based on case studies and data from a survey of twenty firms.

27. These were the findings of the Defense Industrial Base Panel, reported as recently as 2012 in *Challenges to Doing Business with the DoD* (U.S. House, Committee on Armed Services 2012). Three decades of similar complaints give them a déjà vu quality.

28. However, Bernard Chachula, author of an instructive VC report (2004) commissioned by the U.S. Air Force, points out that the DoE had already shown the way more than a decade earlier with the creation of the ARCH venture fund, a partnership between Argonne National Laboratory and the University of Chicago. I discuss ARCH below.

29. See Held and Chang 2000.

30. Quoted in Kimberley Palmer, "Agencies Start Their Own Investment Funds to Bring New Technologies to Government," *Government Executive*, May 15, 2006, http://www.govexec.com/magazine/2006/05/government-executive-vol-38-no8/21872/.

31. Statement by then Deputy Under Secretary of Defense for Acquisition Reform Stan Soloway, prior to the launch of a new DoD fund (Rosettex), discussed below (quoted in Chachula 2004, 9).

32. With an average deal flow at least as high as, and sometimes double that of the typical VC firm (which may complete a dozen deals in any one year), In-Q-Tel's investments are estimated to range in value from $500,000 to $5 million. Although the fund's budget is classified, it reportedly grew from about $27 million to $60 million just in the first six years of operation. See S. Lacy, "Meet the CIA's Venture Capitalist," *Business Week*, May 10, 2005.

33. The following two paragraphs and quotations are based on Cotell's 2006 statement (Cotell 2006, 102, 104).

34. A further benefit of the QIC filter, whose members must hold security clearances, is that it allows the fund to be staffed by personnel without security classifications.

35. Data reported in Cotell, 2006.

36. Basis Technology CEO Carl Hoffman, cited in Kashmir Hill, "Startups Backed By The CIA," November 22, 2010, http://www.forbes.com/2010/11/19/in-q-tel-cia-venture-fund-business-washington-cia.html.

37. Of the forty In-Q-Tel alumni portfolio companies listed on its website as of July, 2013, thirty-seven have been acquired by other companies, including IBM, Oracle, Symantec, and Google, http://www.iqt.org/portfolio/alumni.html.

38. Noah Shachtman, "Google, CIA Invest in 'Future' of Web Monitoring," July 28, 2010, http://www.wired.com/dangerroom/2010/07/exclusive-google-cia/.

39. See OnPoint's website, http://www.onpoint.us/about-us/index.shtml.

40. Kimberley Palmer, "Agencies Start Their Own Investment Funds to Bring New Technologies to Government," *Government Executive*, May 15, 2006, http://www.govexec.com/magazine/magazine-news-and-analysis/2006/05/venture-capital/21878/.

41. This may take the form of suggesting modalities of use that could find a willing customer and making relevant introductions. On the DoD initiative, see "Officials to Begin Testing 'Venture Catalyst' Solutions," http://www.defense.gov/News/NewsArticle.aspx?ID=60853. On the Navy VC Panel, see Maryann Lawlor, "Sea Service Recruits Venture Capitalists," December, 2003, http://www.afcea.org/content/?q=node/52. For a useful survey of the main GVFs discussed here, see the Homeland Security Institute report (2005).

42. The term "spin-out" is widely used to refer to the creation of a new company that comes "out" of a research institution or national laboratory, or from an existing company that does not wish to deviate from its business model. The term spin-off is usually reserved for technologies.

43. ARCH takes the first two letters from its two principals, Argonne and Chicago.

44. See the presentation by the vice president of ARCH Development Corporation, Teri Willey, at a 1998 workshop on Overcoming Barriers to Collaborative Research (National Research Council 1999, 26, 35).

45. Data in this paragraph are from ARCH Vice President Teri Willey's presentation (National Research Council 1999, 27, 35).

46. Michael Hardy, "CIA Funds Not-So-Secret Investment Operation," *Federal Computer Week*, August 4, 2003, http://fcw.com/articles/2003/08/04/cia-funds-notsosecret-investment-operation.aspx.

47. In 2005, OnPoint had $40 million invested in eight portfolio companies (Homeland Security Institute 2005, 31). Eight years on, its portfolio counted twelve companies, http://www.onpoint.us/portfolio/index.shtml.

48. The NTA is an initiative of the intelligence community that seeks to foster relationships with critical commercial sectors in order to broaden and deepen access for the Defense R&D community into the nation's commercial technology base.

49. See Sarnoff Corporation press release, "Joint Business Venture of SRI International and Sarnoff Corporation Will Lead Team to Develop Next-Generation Information Systems for Military and Private Sector Use," October 21, 2002, http://www.thefreelibrary.com/Rosettex+Signs+Five-Year,+$24+Million+Contract+With+U.S.+Army...-a093082615.

50. In-Q-Tel President Mike Griffin, quoted in Michael Hardy, "CIA Funds Not-So-Secret Investment Operation," August 4, 2003, *Federal Computer Week*, http://fcw.com/articles/2003/08/04/cia-funds-notsosecret-investment-operation.aspx.

51. As venture capitalist Lee Buchanan, partner at Paladin Capital Group, puts it, "VC is not an institution meant to reward innovation. Venture Capital Funds are in the business of making money, which they do by investing in companies that do well." the quotation summarizes his comments at the Prize Summit at London Business School, April 8, 2011. See http://theprizesummit.com/Prize_Summit_Summary_key_debates.pdf.

4. Beyond Serendipity

1. *Beyond Spinoff* was a Harvard project initiated in 1987; its findings influenced legislation that introduced the important but ill-fated dual-use Technology Reinvestment Program (chapter 5).

2. Alic et al. 2003, 16. Ruttan's 2006a study is perhaps the most explicit effort to differentiate and prioritize technology procurement as against the more passive conception of R&D.

3. For the original and important distinction between technology procurement and R&D, see Edquist 2005.

4. The only use is by the DoE's Office of Energy Efficiency and Renewable Energy, which has a technology development program focused on buyers' needs in the commercial space. See the Pacific Northwest National Laboratory website: http://tpd.pnnl.gov/capabilities/tp.stm, and their 'Building Technologies Program' http://readthis.pnl.gov/MarketSource/ReadThis/B2815_not_print_quality.pdf.

5. It was the relative absence of such attention that inspired the late economic historian, Vernon Ruttan (2006a), to attempt the first comprehensive statement of the commercial impact of defense-led technology procurement.

6. It also authorized the use of advance payments during the performance of a contract and the furnishing of government-owned facilities to privately owned plants.

7. As opposed to a fixed-fee contract, a cost-plus contract pays a contractor all allowed expenses to a set limit, plus a predetermined fee to allow for a profit. While this was initially important, critics pointed to the abuse of cost-plus contracting, which has subsequently declined.

8. On the computer and information technology industries, see Flamm 1988 and National Research Council 1999; on aerospace, see Mowery and Rosenberg 1982.

9. In the late 1950s, NSS agencies accounted for some 70 percent of the semiconductor market.

10. These innovations are civilian technologies originating in defense-related applications and/or directly supported in the high-cost phases of development, testing, and marketing. Examples drawn from Congressional Research Service 1986b, 427–30, and Office of Science and Technology Policy *Fact Sheet on How Federal R&D Investments Drive the U.S. Economy*, June 15, 2000, http://www.math.utk.edu/~vasili/va/files/federalR+D.html.

11. In addition to the cost of the integrated circuits and the production lines, Flamm notes that from the late 1950s to the early 1970s "defense customers ended up paying for nearly half of all semiconductor research and development" (1988, 18).

12. For a representative statement, see Wessner 2004, 2005. Wessner is director of the National Academies Program on Technology, Innovation, and Entrepreneurship.

13. For this interpretation see Wessner 2004, 2005.

14. MIMICs are advanced gallium arsenide semiconductors used for military radar; commercial uses include collision-avoidance systems for automobiles, satellite communications, and air traffic control.

15. Al Romig, Sandia's chief technical officer, cited in "Sandia Spin-off Company to Commercialize Labs-Developed Microsystems Technology," *Sandia LabNews*, October 6, 2000, http://www.sandia.gov/LabNews/LN10–06–00/MEMX_story.html.

16. Through its Office of Technology Utilization, for example, NASA sought to ensure that its technologies made their way quickly into industry's hands. DARPA too drove revolutionary advances in IT through broad-based programs that encouraged diffusion of technologies to industry and university as well as military users. As well as its early role in building a nuclear power industry, the AEC/DoE led initiatives that established a radioisotope industry for nuclear medicine.

17. The DoD is the largest user of IR&D. As its website explains, contractors are allowed "to claim a portion of their IR&D costs as part of the overhead in 'cost plus'' contracts. By reimbursing these costs, DoD encourages industry to explore new technologies with potential application to military systems." See http://www.dtic.mil/dtic/stresources/researchinprogress/ird_desc.html.

18. Data from DoD Technical Information Community webpage, http://www.dtic.mil/ird/stats/; see also DoD's summary of recent IR&D costs, http://www.acq.osd.mil/dpap/cpic/cp/docs/Summary_IRD-BP_2009-2010.pdf.

19. DoD Directive (DDR&E) No. 3204.1, *Independent Research and Development and Bid and Proposal Program*, May 10, 1999 (replacing the 1983 Directive); see www.dtic.mil/dtic/pdf/customer/STINFOdata/DoDD_32041.pdf.

20. Based on Goldstine's analysis of the minutes of a meeting at the Ballistic Research Laboratory in October 1945, cited in Alic 2008, 27.

21. For the history of military- and NSS-sponsored advances in computer development see Flamm 1988 and Stefik 1985. For an overview of the federal government's impact on commercial innovation in a variety of sectors see the contributions in DARPA's fiftieth anniversary history (Defense Advanced Projects Agency 2008).

22. See the Domestic Policy Review procurement report in National Academy of Engineering 1981, 63; this work reproduces all the DPR Committee reports.

23. The VHSIC program fed directly into the NSS strategy of technological superiority, which placed a premium on quality and performance standards.

24. According to this source, SDIO's commercialization efforts also resulted in fifty startup companies and over three hundred commercial products (Department of Defense 2000, 14).

25. National Research Council 2008, 326–28. See also www.inknowvation for updated SBIR funding amounts and sources.

26. On the so-called military-industrial divide, see Markusen 1991 and Markusen and Yudken 1992. Both authors contend that key industries in aerospace, communications, and electronics fostered by Pentagon patronage grew behind a "wall of separation" shaped by military demands and isolated from civilian markets. Mowery and Rosenberg (1998, 32–34) articulate a softer version of this claim, arguing that spillovers in aircraft, computers, and semiconductors occurred in the 1950s when military and commercial requirements (such as for performance, cost, and ruggedness) did not diverge dramatically, but did so to an increasing extent thereafter.

27. Heinrich writes that numerous firms in Silicon Valley moved between the two arenas of technology development and production without setting up separate divisions and that when Intel began manufacturing chips for the military in 1980, it was producing in the same facility microelectronics for telecommunications, automobile, and military applications (2002, 272).

28. A 1979 report reiterated the view of the 1972 Commission on Government Procurement that ponderous procurement practices and bureaucratic requirements (plus inexpedient patent policies for government-sponsored R&D) were retarding innovative enterprise and "steering innovators away from the Government market" (Government Accountability Office 1979, iii). Federal policies adversely affecting the defense industry during the 1960s and 1970s are discussed in Gansler 1980.

29. Cited in Government Accountability Office 1979, iii–iv, which reiterates the view of the 1972 commission.

30. Whereas in 1962, government sales accounted for 100 percent of the market for integrated circuits, by 1969 its share had dropped to 36 percent, reaching a bare 1 percent by the mid-1990s.

31. The work of business historian Thomas Heinrich provides an illuminating argument detailing the DoD contribution to the renaissance of Silicon Valley at the end of the 1980s (Heinrich 2002, 272–4). See also O'Mara 2005, chap. 5 on Silicon Valley's move into commercial markets following the 1960s shift in defense procurement pursuant to the McNamara reforms.

32. See Fong 1991 for details of the program's inception and appeal to industry. It was initially projected to cost $750 million by 1989, but the final sum was closer to $1 billion.

33. Larry Sumney, commenting on the VHSIC legacy as president of Semiconductor Research Corporation, formerly DoD Director of the VHSIC Program Office, cited in Department of Defense 1990, 26–27. This report contains a comprehensive account of the military and commercial outcomes a decade on from the program's inception.

34. Industry's initial enthusiasm for the project and subsequent disappointment is detailed by Fong (1991). A perhaps less disinterested view is that of the program's chief architect, Larry Sumney, who emphasizes that VHSIC has been an "outstanding success" when measured against the "actual intentions and goals of the DoD. . . . That it has not solved the major defense system development cycle challenge nor the competitiveness problems of the U.S. commercial semiconductor industry is not surprising. It was neither intended, directed, nor funded to do either" (Department of Defense 1990, 29).

35. Fong (1991, 77) notes that in its initial design, due to industry pressure, CAD accounted for 40 to 45 percent of VHSIC's budget.

36. For the detailed argument, see Heinrich 2002, 274. The much studied Sematech program, jointly funded by DoD and industry, was another contributer to the Valley's revival (Howell 2003).

5. Reorienting the Public-Private Partnership

1. From a quite different perspective, Dombrowski and Gholz 2006 also argue against the view that progress in commercial technology will determine military innovation.

2. The terms "acquisition" and "procurement" are often used interchangeably. Up to now, I have used the term procurement to refer to the creation of new technologies (i.e., technology procurement) and acquisition to refer to expenditures that include the cost of purchasing ready-made items as well as the scaling up, production, and insertion of new technologies. When discussing the spending data, I will revert to the standard classifications of "procurement" and "RDT&E" to refer to acquisition and technology procurement, respectively.

3. By 2010, procurement spending had declined to $133.1 billion.

4. In particular, Japan scholars drew attention to the way in which Japanese firms leveraged commercial technologies to create military equipment. This version of a dual-use approach (viewed as spin-on) was one that they recommended for the United States since it appeared to contribute to Japan's superior economic performance. On Japan's military use of commercial technology as a form of spin-on, see Vogel 1992. For an extended historical treatment of Japan's approach which draws lessons for the United States, see Samuels 1994.

5. Chief among them was the president's Blue Ribbon Commission on Defense Management, known as the Packard Commission (1986).

6. For the view that "the vast majority of innovative and revolutionary components, systems, and approaches that enable and sustain" the U.S. technological advantage lie outside the prime defense contracting circle, see the 2010 *Quadrennial Defense Review* (Department of Defense 2010), pp. 105–6.

7. In 1993, Secretary of Defense William Perry, at a gathering famously known as the "Last Supper," warned the Pentagon's prime contractors to prepare themselves for lean times ahead by consolidating. In the course of a decade, fifty or so prime contractors consolidated into six. See John D. Banusiewicz, "Lynn: U.S. Must Preserve Its Defense Industrial Base," May 12, 2011, http://www.defense.gov/News/NewsArticle.aspx?ID=63913.

8. Due to its endowment "with passionate overtones" by competing constituencies with different institutional and political objectives, there is no universally accepted definition of dual use (White 1996, 21–22).

9. As noted earlier, their stance thus contrasts with that of Samuels 1994 and the Berkeley scholars, Borrus and Zysman 1992, who saw Japan's dual-use approach more in terms of spin-on from commerce than as jointly developed or general-purpose technology.

10. For background on the TRP see Stowsky 1999; also White House press release, August 12, 1993, http://www.ibiblio.org/darlene/tech/TRP.html.

11. "Other Transactions" allow government agencies to advance R&D and prototypes (but not product acquisition) by designing agreements outside the Federal Acquisition Regulations and intellectual property requirements under Bayh-Dole.

12. *Acquisition Reform: A Mandate for Change,* http://www.library.dau.mil/PerryWJ_Acq Reform_Feb94.pdf.

13. See the White House document *Defense Acquisition Reform,* http://clinton4.nara.gov/ WH/EOP/OSTP/nssts/html/chapt2-2.html.

14. For a different perspective on reorientation that focuses on the changing mission of defense, see Fong 2000 who introduces an economic–industry policy argument.

15. As the program marked its twenty-fifth year in 2007, over $22.3 billion had been invested in more than 100,016 projects (Congressional Research Service 2010, 4). By the turn of the decade, the cumulative SBIR investment figure was closer to $30 billion.

16. Since SBIR is an interagency program (in which Defense and Health have the largest presence), agency differences arise, mainly in the use of external versus internal evaluation, broad versus focused topics, type of award (contract versus grant), and focus on technology procurement.

17. Deputy Assistant Secretary of the Navy McGrath, National Research Council 2007a, 61.

18. See the SBA's webpage on the SBIR program: http://www.sba.gov/sbir2/; and the DoD's SBIR webpage on acceleration of commercialization: http://www.acq.osd.mil/osbp/ sbir/sb/process-acceleration.shtml.

19. See National Research Council 2004a, section 4(c)(7).

20. Commercialization may take the form of insertion in the acquisition process; direct sales to government or the private sector; licensing of innovations; and acquisition of SBIR firms by large defense contractors in the private sector. By these metrics, "commercialization" is significantly underestimated (National Research Council 2009a, 4).

21. See the multiagency survey results reported by National Research Council (2009a, figure 4.1).

22. SBIR patent database, Innovation Development Institute: www.inknowvation.com.

23. A rigorous analysis of the www.inknowvation.com database might also indicate a higher proportion of such firms in the engineering and IT sectors than in biotech.

24. Physical Optics' website lists as its funding sources the following agencies: DoD (Army, Navy, Air Force, DARPA), DHS, HSARPA, Special Operations Command, DoE, NIH, NSF, NASA, and six smaller agencies.

25. See http://www.inknowvation.com/home/techseeker-registry. This database is geared to assisting large corporations find relevant technologies among the SBIR community.

26. Products from the DARPA-managed program, which held its last of three solicitations in 1995 and selected 133 technology development consortia, "continued to emerge for years to follow." See "Revolutionizing the Commercial Marketplace" in the DARPA's 50-year history (Defense Advanced Research Projects Agency 2008, 35).

27. Other examples being the Advanced Technology Program and the Partnership for a New Generation of Vehicles.

28. The details in this section are based on the history of the ASCI program commissioned by the Department of Energy's Lawrence Livermore lab, aptly titled *Delivering Insight* (Larzelere 2007).

29. Victor Reis, former DARPA director, here addressing industry as Assistant Secretary for Defense Programs (Larzelere 2007, 67).

30. Quotations in this paragraph are from Larzelere 2007, 121.

31. This and the next paragraph are based on the Advanced Vehicle and Power Initiative' (AVPI), a Government, Industry and Academia White Paper, TARDEC, draft 4, May 25, 2010, available from CALSTART, http://www.calstart.org/Libraries/HTUF_Documents/AVPI.sflb. ashx; and the final report of July 29 (McGrew and Skalny 2010).

32. CALSTART (not an acronym) was itself founded in 1992 to kick-start clean technologies for transportation. NAC is the Army's outreach arm to the commercial industry. Its mission is defined as "understanding the capabilities of the commercial transportation industry, and working to increase the capabilities of the commercial industry to build advanced technologies that can support emerging Army and military needs." See Van Amburg 2009, 2.

33. This section, and the data that follow, are drawn from Bill Van Amburg 2009, 2–3.

34. The director of the Army's TARDEC-NAC, Paul Skalny, is frequently singled out for his long leadership in driving the shift to hybrids in military and commercial vehicles.

35. After a decade, there were about 9,000 hybrid heavy vehicles in use in the United States. Market research firm Pike estimates that more than 100,000 units will be on the road by 2017: http://www.greencarcongress.com/2011/09/pike-20110907.html.

36. This sum includes $1 billion for renewable energy systems according to McGrew and Skalny (2010, 24).

37. See Szajnfarber and Weigel 2009, 6. Under the IRIS JCTD, the DoD commitment included funding its own project management team for the development period and conducting three months of operational testing, ending with a formal assessment and option to acquire.

38. This and the subsequent quotation are from Szajnfarber and Weigel 2009, 7.

39. IRIS has been described as "a radical innovation in the communication satellite market" because it changes fundamentally how to conceive and allocate capacity (Szajnfarber and Weigel 2009, 3).

40. Don Brown, vice president of hosted payloads for Intelsat General, one of the companies that built the platform. See news item "Net reaches out to Final Frontier," April 13, 2007, http://news.bbc.co.uk/2/hi/technology/6551807.stm. See also JCTD Fact Sheet, http//www. acq.osd.mil/jctd/ iris.html.

41. For an overview of federal prize competitions, see Congressional Research Service 2009.

42. See the comments by Joe Parrish, NASA's acting chief technologist, in J. Welsh, "Electric Plane Flies 200 Miles, Wins NASA Prize," *Wall Street Journal*, October 4, 2011; also the home page of the Comparative Aircraft Flight Efficiency Foundation, http://cafefoundation.org/v2/main_home.php.

43. Cited in Aaron Hoover, "UF's Robotic Car, NaviGATOR, Competed in the Race for a $2 Million Prize," 2006, http://www.research.ufl.edu/publications/explore/v11n1/story2.html.

44. See DARPA's archived "Urban Challenge" webpage, http://archive.darpa.mil/grand challenge/.

45. While some autonomous ground vehicle owners have transitioned the technology to conventional military applications, new applications have also been developed for industry and the broader procurement communities of national security and homeland defense.

46. The literature is discussed in Cohen 1999.

6. No More Breakthroughs?

1. Ruttan (2006a) was the first to fully articulate this concern. For his most concise statement, see Ruttan 2006b; see also Bonvillian and Van Atta 2011.

2. The terms "platform," "enabling," and "generic" are often used interchangeably to indicate general-purpose technologies that support a broad range of applications and industry sectors.

3. Between these two extremes lies a range of innovations one could characterize as cutting-edge, in that they advance the state of the art or produce breakthroughs in a particular field.

4. See Congressional Research Service 2011a, 3, which notes the wide discrepancy between this and the lower estimate of $5 billion.

5. Nanotech is a significant target for military procurement, in part because of the potential to further miniaturize military electronics and drastically lighten the load carried by soldiers in the field, hence the mission of the Institute for Soldier Nanotechologies, one of the many "innovation hybrids" discussed in chapter 7.

6. National Science and Technology Council 2004, 1.

7. Efforts to coordinate nanoscale work began in 1996 when staff from several NSS agencies began a series of meetings to discuss their programs and projects for nanoscale science and technology.

8. See also the White House press release "National Nanotechnology Initiative: Leading to the Next Industrial Revolution," January 21, 2000, http://clinton4.nara.gov/WH/New/html/20000121_4.html.

9. See *The National Nanotechnology Initiative: The Initiative and Its Implementation Plan,* http://nano.gov/sites/default/files/pub_resource/nni_implementation_plan_2000.pdf. More information on the nano program can be found at http://www.nano.gov/.

10. Moore's law is the idea, ascribed to Intel's co-founder Gordon Moore, that computing power will double every two years, based on the capacity to continually increase the number of transistors on a silicon chip.

11. This paragraph is based on Congressional Research Service 2011a, 2, 3, T.1, 16.

12. MIT Institute for Soldier Nanotechnologies, web.mit.edu/isn/partners/industry/index.html.

13. See MIT's ISN website, http://web.mit.edu/isn/partners/industry/benefits.html.

14. See the House Testimony of the NRI director Jeffrey Welser (2011, 38), who emphasizes that industry representatives are consequently "more engaged, providing feedback during the course of the research and taking results back to others in the company."

15. See the NNI website, http://nano.gov/initiatives/commercial; also U.S. Army, RDECOM-ARDEC 2008, 9 for an overview of the Army's novel business approach for nanotech.

16. S. Rickert, "The Nano-Economy," January 20, 2012, http://www.industryweek.com/articles/the_nano-economy_time_to_reap_the_rewards_26408.aspx.

17. It is also claimed that nanomaterials and nanotechnology-based products carry inherent health and safety risks that are poorly understood and are not being effectively addressed as an increasing number of commercial products incorporating synthetic nanoparticles are released onto the market (Congressional Research Service 2011a, 37).

18. One such advance involves a new class of semiconductor material made of nanocarbon tubes, set to replace silicon chips and revolutionize microelectronics. See *Mobile Industry & Wireless Technology News,* http://mobile.eweek.com/c/a/Mobile-and-Wireless/IBM-Delivers-PinheadSized-Nanotechnology-Circuits-for-Wireless-Devices-237031/.

19. Although launched by Obama, the National Robotics Initiative piggy-backed on earlier NSS achievements and grew out of a 2006 NSF-sponsored initiative that called for the formation of a national Computing Community Consortium. Between 2008 and 2009, the CCC generated a roadmap for robotics research and applications; it also called for a national strategy for robotics growth and presented a White Paper on robotics to a newly established Congressional Robotics Caucus. See, e.g., "From Internet to Robotics: The Next Transformative Technology," http://www.cra.org/ccc/visioning/visioning-activities/robotics; for the updated version, http://robotics-vo.us/sites/default/files/2013%20Robotics%20Roadmap-rs.pdf; see also the White Paper, *Robotics,* by Rodney Brooks, March 17, 2009, http://www.cra.org/ccc/files/docs/init/Robotics.pdf.

20. See National Center for Manufacturing Sciences, http://www.ncms.org/index.php/programs/robotics-technology-consortium/.

21. M. Russell, "Unmanned Systems: Can the Industrial Base Support the Pentagon's Vision?" *National Defense Magazine,* July 2010, http://www.nationaldefensemagazine.org/archive/2010/July/.

22. N. Clark, "Betting on a Wing and a Sunbeam," *International Herald Tribune,* June 20, 2011.

23. Patrick Pinter, "Robotics Cluster Initiative Builds Road Map for the Future," *GVSET News* 6 (10), on Dr. Jim Overholt, director of TARDEC Joint Center for Robotics, addressing an Automotive-Robotics Cluster Initiative in Michigan in 2009, http://www.tardec.info/GVSETNews/article.cfm?iID=0610&aid=13.

24. Joint Ground Robotics Enterprise, 13 September, 2007, http://www.ndia.org/Divisions/Divisions/Robotics/Documents/Content/ContentGroups/Divisions1/Robotics/E.Purdy_JGRE_Update_13-Sept-07.pdf; and http://www.ncms.org/index.php/programs/robotics-technology-consortium/.

25. National Center for Manufacturing Sciences, http://www.ncms.org/index.php/programs/robotics-initiative/.

26. See Massachusetts Technology Leadership Council, http://76.12.40.240/abo/trustees/HelenGreiner.aspx.

27. See iRobot's press release, http://www.irobot.com/en/us/Company/Press_Center/Press_Releases/Press_Release.aspx?n=021611.

28. See, e.g., N. Wingfield and S. Sengupta, "Drones Set Sights on U.S. Skies," *New York Times,* February 17, 2012.

29. In a discussion of the ethical issues involved, Singer (2011) observes that opening U.S. civilian airspace to allow more widespread use of drones by 2015 paves the way for a massive increase in surveillance of U.S. citizens. Military ethicists also fear that in turning war into a low-risk video game that disconnects the American citizenry from its wars, the United States

will be drawn more easily into conflicts. For a starker view of a drone-filled future, see Turse and Engelhardt 2012. The argument for reforming U.S. drone strike policies is made in Micah Zenko's (2013) special report for the Council on Foreign Relations.

30. A 2009 Pew report shows that the United States ranked eleventh among G20 nations in intensity of clean energy investment (i.e., as a percentage of GDP)—behind China, Brazil, Germany, and Spain, where feed-in tariffs, financial incentives for investment and production, and in some cases ambitious targets for wind, biomass, and solar energy have been instituted (Pew Research 2009).

31. For a concise statement of the Navy's energy roadmap, see Alexander Stoyen, "The New Dawn of Naval Energy," *Phase III Commercialization*, Spring 2010, http://www.dawnbreaker.com/about/phase3_spr10/energy.php.

32. For its part, the air force has developed a strategy called the Renewable Energy Game Plan that aims to add thirty-three renewable energy projects on installations over a five-year period, providing up to 27 percent of electric supply in renewable form by 2016 (thereby exceeding the federal mandate of 16 percent). See the USAF website, http://www.af.mil/news/story.asp?id=123289489.

33. See http://www.defense.gov/news/newsarticle.aspx?id=63699.

34. Data from the 2011 Pike Research report "Renewable Energy for Military Applications," http://www.pikeresearch.com/research/renewable-energy-for-military-applications.

35. American Council on Renewable Energy (ACORE), *U.S. Department of Defense & Renewable Energy*, p. 22, www.aee.net/files/dmfile/DoDRenewableEnergyPrimer.pdf.

36. Statement by Arati Prabhakar, former director of microelectronics for DARPA, who now chairs the Energy Department's Efficiency and Renewables Advisory Committee, cited in C. Davenport and Y.J. Dreazen, "The Green Lantern," *National Journal*, May 26, 2011, http://www.nationaljournal.com/magazine/the-clean-energy-military-20110526.

37. *Q&A*, Interview with Ray Mabus, February 5, 2012, http://q-and-a.org/Transcript/?ProgramID=1377.

38. Alexander D. Stoyen, "The New Dawn of Naval Energy," *Phase III Commercialization*, Spring 2010, http://www.dawnbreaker.com/about/phase3_spr10/energy.php.

39. The toll since the start of the war in Afghanistan exceeds three thousand U.S. troops and contractors who were either killed or injured protecting convoys; 80 percent of these were transporting truck fuel. See Annie Snider, "Battlefield Energy Plan Aims to Spark Major Changes in the Pentagon," *New York Times*, June 15, 2011.

40. Rosemary Calvert, "DOD's Evolving Energy Revolution: An Interview with Dorothy Robyn, PhD, Deputy Under Secretary of Defense, Installations & Environment," *livebetter*, March/April 2011, http://www.centerforabetterlife.com/eng/magazine/2011_back_issues.lasso.

41. USAF Assistant Secretary Terry Yonkers (2011, 13).

42. *Q&A*, Interview with Ray Mabus, February 5, 2012, http://q-and-a.org/Transcript/?ProgramID=1377.

43. ONR, for example, is supporting the development of fuel cell technology that can be integrated with solar photovoltaic panels for alternative power generators. ONR has contracted Lockheed Martin in collaboration with an SBIR-backed company, Technology Management, to design and integrate the generator sets. See Lockheed Martin's press release, Aug 8, 2012, http://www.lockheedmartin.com.au/us/news/press-releases/2012/august/ms2-0808-lockheed-martin-to-integrate-fuel-cells-solar-power-for-military.html.

44. Quoted by A. Snider, "Pentagon Still Can't Define 'Energy Security,' Much Less Achieve It," *Greenwire*, January 16, 2012, http://www.eenews.net/public/Greenwire/2012/01/16/1.

45. American Council on Renewable Energy (ACORE), "U.S. Department of Defense & Renewable Energy" 2012, p. 4, www.acore.org/wp-content/uploads/2012/01/DoD-Renewable-Energy-Primer.pdf.

46. Pike Research report, *Renewable Energy for Military Applications*, http://www.pikeresearch.com/research/renewable-energy-for-military-applications.

47. Statements at the March 2011 ARPA-E Forum, reported in "ARPA-E and DOD Advance Partnership for Storage Solutions," *Greentech Media*, March 2, 2011, http://www.greentechmedia.com/articles/ read/arpa-e-and-dod-advance-partnership/.

48. See the Pew study *From Barracks to the Battlefield* (2011). The Energy Innovation Tracker calculates total federal energy innovation–related spending (including nuclear fission and coal) at around $4 billion for 2011, http://energyinnovation.us/data/analysis/gaps-analysis/.

49. See the ITIF website, http://www.innovationfiles.org/category/green-innovation/.

50. Quoted at http://energy.aol.com/2012/02/29/energy-technology-could-go-viral-if-prices-fall/?icid=related4.

51. Quoted in Biofuels Digest, http://www.biofuelsdigest.com/bdigest/2012/02/08/aviation-and-military-biofuels-new-thinking-on-finance-fuels/.

52. The Great Green Fleet is a thirteen-ship carrier battle group composed of nuclear ships, surface ships, and aircraft powered by fifty-fifty blends of biofuel.

53. Citation and data from *National Defense Magazine,* http://www.nationaldefensemaga zine.org/archive/2011/January/Pages/AirForceTellsBiofuelsIndustrytoBringIt.aspx.

54. http://greeneconomypost.com/synthetic-biology-biofuel-biochemical-company-17244. htm#ixzz1oZcvUazz.

55. The company is now branching into health and skincare, human and animal nutrition, household chemicals, and biodegradable plastics.

56. Tim Edwards, senior chemical engineer leading the Air Force Research Laboratory's alternative fuel program, cited in http://www.nationaldefensemagazine.org/archive/2011/January/Pages/AirForceTellsBiofuelsIndustrytoBringIt.aspx.

57. DARPA, for example, has recently claimed one of its projects is on track to achieve large-scale refining of algal oil for jet fuel at a cost of less than three dollars per gallon: http://www.algaeindustrymagazine.com/darpa-closes-in-on-2gal-algae-fuel/.

58. Cited in Erik Slavin, "Mabus: Congress Hasn't Derailed Navy's Plan to Increase Use of Biofuels," *Stars and Stripes,* July 16, 2012, http://www.stripes.com/news/navy/mabus-congress-hasn-t-derailed-navy-s-plan-to-increase-use-of-biofuels-1.183064.

59. As Democrats hold a fourteen-to-twelve edge in committee seats, at least two switched to vote with the Senate minority proposal. For details, see Roberta Rampton and Susan Cornwell, "Senators Gird for Fight over U.S. Navy's 'Green Fleet,' " July 17, 2012, http://www.reuters.com/article/2012/07/17/us-usa-navy-senate-idUSBRE86G1BZ20120717.

60. For details of the 2012 legislative activity related to DoD's renewable fuel efforts, and the DoD's response to the restrictive provisions, see Congressional Research Service 2012a, 9–11.

61. See Jim Lane, "Operation Free Critique US House Action in Restricting DoD Energy Security Investments," June 6, 2013, http://www.biofuelsdigest.com/bdigest/2013/06/06/operation-free-critique-us-house-action-in-restricting-dod-energy-security-investments/.

62. Zachary Fryer-Biggs, "DoD Wants Innovation, Firms Want Less Risk," *Defense News,* February 6, 2012, http://www.defensenews.com/article/20120206/DEFREG02/302060005/DoD-Wants-Innovation-Firms-Want-Less-Risk.

63. According to Gallup polls on "Confidence in Institution," http://www.gallup.com/poll/1597/confidence-institutions.aspx.

64. Rosemary Calvert, "DOD's Evolving Energy Revolution: An Interview with Dorothy Robyn, PhD, Deputy Under Secretary of Defense, Installations & Environment," *livebetter,* March/April 2011, http://www.centerforabetterlife.com/eng/magazine/2011_back_issues.lasso.

65. Extreme energy refers to the extraction of fossil fuels under ever more extreme conditions that pose greater risks and costs for the human and natural environment. Daniel Yergin (2011) presents the most influential case for such extraction.

66. Peter Singer, senior fellow at Brookings, quoted in Fryer-Biggs, "DoD Wants Innovation, Firms Want Less Risk," *Defense News,* February 12, 2012, http://www.defensenews.com/article/20120206/DEFREG02/302060005/DoD-Wants-Innovation-Firms-Want-Less-Risk. In an even-handed account of strengths and weaknesses in the U.S. defense industrial base, Brookings Institution's defense analyst, Michael O'Hanlon (2011, 10) similarly observes that "we do not have a national security strategy with clear priorities," and that the "main customer, DoD, is often unsure of its clear wants and needs."

67. The Defense Science Board reported that the DoD S&T workforce has "limited capability and expertise to manage emerging technologies, such as biotechnology, nanotechnology, and IT that are evolving outside the traditional defense industrial base" (2008, 43). The military's influential scientific advisory group, the JASONs, in a study commissioned by MITRE Corporation (2009, 47) found that there has been an exodus of technically literate program managers and scientific and technical experts, who have traditionally underpinned the DOD research enterprise.

68. There is little purity behind these R&D labels: most "basic" research conducted in universities is "directed" toward some goal (Crow and Tucker 2001); and NSS-sponsored research has rarely been "undirected," even if not aimed at getting to a specific product. We need not

pursue this line of argument too far, because funding for basic research is not about to fall through the floor; indeed, it was already restored to former funding levels by 2012.

69. For an argument consonant with this reasoning, see Barry Watts's (2008) instructive discussion of the difficulties of framing long-term strategy for the U.S. industrial base.

70. See Roger Cohen's piece in the *New York Times*, "America, Awaken," June 27, 2011.

7. Hybridization and American Antistatism

1. Referring to the consequences of antistatist forces in the early Cold War decades, Friedberg concludes that "state weakness and national strength went hand in hand" (2000, 349).

2. Block (2008; 2010) makes this argument.

3. Friedberg distinguishes two main branches of American antistatism—an "antipower ethic" conceived as "a generalized suspicion of power in all its forms and of government power in particular" and a philosophy of "economic liberalism" conceived as a "widely shared presumption in favor of the market over the state, the private sector over the public sector" (2000, 11, 14). In addition to these institutional and ideological manifestations, Friedberg's analysis points to opportunistic or political antistatism, which occurs when specific interests are at stake.

4. In the discourse of political economy, this distinction refers to the boundaries between the state and the market, the political and the economic, the governmental and the nongovernmental.

5. For examples of public-private governance in the eighteenth and nineteenth centuries, see Novak 2009.

6. The RCA was formed explicitly as a patent pool to break the patent logjam that was holding back U.S. innovation in radio technology; generous incentives included antitrust waver and equity contributions (National Research Council 2007b, 153).

7. Several studies refer to the recent growth of hybrids, e.g. Seidman 1988, 23; Koppell 2003; Moe 2008; and Congressional Research Service 2011b, 2.

8. The Center for Strategic and International Studies reported this finding in a major study of the industrial base, co-sponsored by Senators Bingaman and McCain (Bingaman, McCain, and Blackwell 1989, 5). Similar findings have been reported recently and in earlier surveys (chapter 2).

9. For example, it is said that Fields mixed well with leaders of high-tech companies and "found favor on Capitol Hill with Democrats who had economic competitiveness high on their political agenda." See Evelyn Richards, "Should Uncle Sam Get Involved in Technology as a Venture Capitalist?" *Washington Post*, May 3, 1990.

10. "Protection" here refers to the patent reforms under Bayh-Dole and subsequent amendments (chapter 2).

11. Crow and Tucker (2001, 2) observe that U.S. universities have long been engines of innovation and applied research but that for politically expedient reasons, this has not been explicitly acknowledged as such in R&D funding policy.

12. On the use of private contractors to circumvent international legal constraints, see Brayton 2002. On privatization as a force multiplier for the U.S. government, enabling it to augment its influence in foreign jurisdictions, see Avant 2005.

13. Citations in the paragraph from T. Weiner, "Lockheed and the Future of Warfare," *New York Times*, November 28, 2004.

14. J. Risen and M. Mazzetti, "Blackwater Guards Tied to Secret C.I.A. Raids," *New York Times*, December 10, 2009.

15. SDC was spun off from RAND in 1957 "to work in the public interest on research, development, and application of information technology and the system sciences associated with computers." In addition to its main customer, the U.S. military, it was also a consultant to large private businesses. See http://www.cahighways.org/aboutme/sdc.html. Innovation Services was established in 1989 as a key technology transfer resource for agencies within the DoE and DoD. See *Fact Sheet No. 1, Innovation Services, Inc.—The Story behind Innovasan Corporation*, http://www.innovasan.com/fact-sheets/innovation-services-inc-the-story-behind-innovasan.

16. As an example of the relatively risk averse nature of the private VC sector, of the $20 billion or so in rounds of private venture-capital investment in 2004, "only $105 million represent seed rounds, a constant trend in recent years." Instead, the federal government steps in where venture capitalists fear to tread. NIST director, March Stanley, quoted in National Research Council 2007, 154.

17. Thanks to the Bayh-Dole Act (1980), SRI (like other nonprofits, universities and small firms) has the right to inventions arising from federal funding, enabling it to license the results of its work to others.

18. SRI claims to have started more than forty spin-off companies to leverage technologies in new commercial applications. In Winarsky's own words: "We bring our innovations from the laboratory to the marketplace through technology licensing, new products, and spin-off ventures. Our innovations have created entirely new industries, billions of dollars in marketplace value, and lasting contributions to society" (2012, 4).

19. Data based on interviews with SRI staff, reported in SemanticWeb.com, http://venture beat.com/2008/10/13/shadowy-government-project-spins-off-siri-to-help-direct-your-affairs/.

20. SRI International, http://www.ai.sri.com/project/CALO.

21. Wade Roush, "The Story of Siri, from Birth at SRI to Acquisition by Apple," *Xconomy*, http://www.xconomy.com/san-francisco/2010/06/14/the-story-of-siri-from-birth-at-sri-to-acquisition-by-apple-virtual-personal-assistants-go-mobile.

22. See the NSF master list of FFRDCs at http://www.nsf.gov/statistics/ffrdclist/agency.cfm.

23. Data and citations in this paragraph are from Pete Engardio, "Los Alamos and Sandia: R&D Treasures," *Business Week*, September 11, 2008.

24. See http://www.lanl.gov/orgs/tt/tips/tech_mat_tip.shtml.

25. See Los Alamos National Security, LLC Venture Acceleration Fund flyer, www.lanl.gov/source/orgs/tt/pdf/vaf_short2.pdf.

26. One of Los Alamos's spin-off start-ups, APJeT (founded in 2000), has commercialized a lab invention developed to kill anthrax spores. The company now uses the application process to treat multiple surfaces, from plastics to paper and textiles, including making fabrics water-resistant.

27. Personal communication from TVC's George Friberg.

28. See the TVC website, http://techventures.org/about-us/our-vision/.

29. See SNL's partnership brochure for a summary of corporate partnership agreements and funding options, http://www.sandia.gov/news/publications/partnerships/_assets/documents/PartnershipBrochure.pdf.

30. Ada refers to a high-level computing program language designed for the DoD in the late 1970s and early 1980s in order to replace hundreds of existing programming languages.

31. On the interlacing of military and commercial objectives in the original sponsoring agreement, see the NSF website, http://www.nsf.gov/statistics/nsf02317/indffrdc.htm#sei.

32. On the centrality of the defense interest in superconductivity programs, see U.S. Congress, Office of Technology Assessment 1990b, 4.

33. On CCAT's history see http://www.ccatsandiego.org/history.html.

34. See MIT's ISN website, http://web.mit.edu/isn/partners/index.html. For an overview of each company, see "MIT's Institute for Soldier Nanotechnologies Adds New Industrial Partners," http://www.azonano.com/details.asp?ArticleID=600.

35. The company, Gazelle Microcircuits (now TriQuint) has since become a world leader in gallium arsenide semiconductors, a dual-use technology. Electronic components made with gallium arsenide operate at faster speeds and are more resistant to radiation than silicon chips, making them indispensable for high-performance weapons. At the time of Fields's investment, most of the gallium arsenide used by the military had to be imported.

36. A. Sternstein, "Risky Business: Government-funded Venture Capital Firms Spark Agency Innovation," *Federal Computer Week*, April 24, 2006, http://s.tt/1d5uj.

37. In-Q-Tel's remuneration policies, for example, provide generous compensation for its executives as well as profit sharing for its employees when shares sold in fund-owned companies yield returns above the initial investment. In one reported case, forty-five of In-Q-Tel's employees made substantial profits (many more than fifty thousand dollars each) from the private sale in 2005 of the fund's holdings in fledgling laser weapons maker Ionatron. See Mark Kaufman, "NASA Invests in Its Future with Venture Capital Firm," *Washington Post*, October 31, 2006.

38. As one study of the legislative changes promoting commercialization of academic science and technology similarly concludes: "These changes integrated the state into the production process more directly than before and to some extent rendered problematic the older distinctions between the state and the economy" (Slaughter and Rhoades 1996, 324).

39. I am grateful to Herman Schwartz for encouraging me to make this distinction.

40. For the definitive statement, see Friedberg 2000, 6.

41. Moss (2004) asks a similar question of the federal government's historical role in risk management in a range of social policies. He concludes that such policies required little in the way of invasive bureaucracy and were thus well accommodated by a society suspicious of state activism.

42. Here I am adapting an insight from Etzkowitz 2003.

43. Some would argue of course that the implied partisan division is misleading because administrations of both colors have presided over a small government regime since President Reagan.

44. For an interesting early attempt to make sense of the growth of hybrids, mostly from a "new public management" perspective, see Sternberg 1993.

45. See, e.g., the comments by Burton, as President of the Council on Competitiveness, who cautions against relaxing policy vigilance just because the U.S. is "once again the unrivaled economic leader of the world" (1996, 100); see also Burton 1993.

46. For an original argument about the rise of neoliberalism and its role in the great recession, see Mann 2013, chapters 6 and 11.

8. Penetrating the Myths of the Military-Commercial Relationship

1. On the serendipitous spin-off's appeal to policymakers, see Alic et al. 1992, 81.

2. For a representative statement, see Bingham 1998, and Magaziner and Reich 1982, 255.

3. See, for example, Graham 1992, chap. 8. Block's work (2008, 2010) is similarly oriented, however he emphasizes the "civilian-ness" rather than the security/mission-intensity of federal support for innovation. A similar view of the U.S. government as an effective industry policy actor can be found in Mariana Mazzucato (2013).

4. For the classical statement of the wall of separation view, see Markusen and Yudken 1992.

5. Data based on National Science Board 2010.

6. Both strong and weak versions of this idea run throughout the academic and government literature on technology policy.

7. On the difference between risk and "primary uncertainty" applied to the state's effort to seed an industry at the technological frontier, see Wong 2011.

8. Raytheon Commercial Ventures Inc. is likewise a case in point, established in 2001 to spin out new companies that could commercialize defense-led innovations. See DoD TechMatch Success Stories, http://www.dodtechmatch.com/DOD/SuccessStories/View.aspx?id=60133.

9. A point well made by Alic et al. (1992), though with a focus on defense rather than the broader NSS agency complex.

10. Stan Solaway, then Pentagon head of acquisition reform, quoted in "Pentagon Finds Fewer Firms Want to Do R&D," *Wall Street Journal*, October 22, 1999.

11. Asymmetric threats have redoubled the importance of keeping DoD "at the forefront of the IT revolution," argues Ashton Carter, who emphasizes three reasons for DoD's sponsorship of commercial innovation in this field: promoting breakthrough innovations rather than the near-term advances of much commercial IT R&D; evincing the higher quality, reliability, and security that commercially available technology cannot provide; and remaining a smart buyer by participating in the information revolution (2001, 18).

12. Quotations in this paragraph from Department of Commerce, Office of Technology Policy 1996, 32.

13. Daniel Lockney, cited in T. Michael "For NASA, Tech Transfer Is Old Hat," *Innovation*, February/March, 2012, http://www.innovation-america.org/nasa-tech-transfer-old-hat.

14. Quotes in this paragraph from the Defense Advanced Projects Agency 2008, 95.

15. Dan Petonito, Program Manager of DUST, cited in L. Kozaryn, "All Benefit From DoD-Industrial Dual-Use Partnerships," American Forces Press Service, May 17, 2000, www.dau.mil/pubscats/PubsCats/PM/articles00/afps3-a.pdf.

16. See Sandia news release, "Sandia Spins Off Company to Commercialize Microsystems Technology," http://www.sandia.gov/media/NewsRel/NR2000/MEMX.htm.

17. "The Success of the MDA Technology Applications Program," MDA Technology Applications Report, 2007, http://www.mdatechnology.net/update.aspx?id=a5299.

18. For example, John Tirman led a team of authors who applied the wall of separation perspective emphasizing the "damaging effect" of military procurement on "the vitality of commercial high-technology" (1984, xiii). This view was influenced by the fear that the Reagan defense buildup would place U.S. high-tech industries at a competitive disadvantage.

19. Their survey covered almost the entire capital goods sector, but excluded computers and some consumer goods. Some forty thousand plants or 50 percent of all manufacturing establishments had defense contracts as of 1991, and the vast majority produced items for commercial markets in the same establishments, underscoring the overblown status of the wall of separation idea.

20. There is a substantial literature on the broader impact of DoD's advanced manufacturing program for defense contractors. See the study "National Security and the Industrial Policy Debate" by Charles E. Beckwith, Thomas D. Smith, and Robert Latiff, USAF, *National Security Program Discussion Paper Series 91–03*, U.S. Army War College, May 1991, www.dtic.mil/dtic/tr/fulltext/u2/a246619.pdf.

21. Surveys were sent to 1,022 companies in these four technology fields, as well as 47 "special category" companies in aerospace and electronics. Of the 491 respondents, 158 were already "defense contractors" (Department of Commerce, Office of Strategic Industries and Economic Security 2004, i).

22. For example, Arsenal Venture Partners, Battelle Ventures, CVP, and Four Seasons Ventures.

23. The survey was originally conducted under the auspices of the NSF and later reproduced for a DoC-sponsored report. See "Annex I. Summary of Report by Booz Allen Hamilton" (authored by a BAH team), in Branscomb and Auerwald 2002, 86.

24. Whether a similar profile applies to European or Japanese corporations is not relevant since I am not claiming that U.S. corporations are unique, but rather to the contrary: they are not typically high-risk or focused on the radical breakthrough innovations that come from longer time horizons.

25. For two instructive sources, see Gold 1991, 2005, and Friedberg 1989.

26. Relevant studies include those by Almunia et al. 2010, examining the effects of remilitarization in 1930s Europe, and Hall's (2009) analysis of U.S. military procurement in the period 1929–62. For a brief discussion, see also Paul Krugman, "How to End This Depression," *New York Review of Books*, May 24, 2012.

27. Feldstein, "The Current Stimulus Plan: An $800 Billion Mistake," *Washington Post*. January 29, 2009.

28. Melman developed several iterations of this argument during the Cold War and again in response to the post-9/11 buildup. For the original version, see *The Permanent War Economy* (1974).

29. Those who have reviewed the evidence find serious weaknesses in each approach. For an even-handed treatment see Gold 2005, also Chan 1985; see also Friedberg 1989 for a rebuttal of Paul Kennedy's (1987) depletionist argument.

30. Robert Solow, "We'd better watch out." *New York Review of Books*, July 12, 1987, p. 36.

31. Alic et al. (1992) aimed much of their critique at precisely this assumption, which they found to be widespread within policymaking circles and Congress.

32. For example, the U.S. and its allies account for nearly 70 percent of military spending while all its adversaries combined total less than 15 percent (Walt 2011, 16).

33. Here I am adapting an observation of David Gold (2005, 9).

34. The CBO notes that although facing an 11 percent reduction in 2013 (adjusted for inflation), the Defense department's budget "will increase by a cumulative total of 2 percent more than inflation between 2013 and 2021 . . . about what it was in 2007." See Congressional Budget Office, March 18, 2013, "Approaches for Scaling Back the Defense Department's Budget Plans," http://www.cbo.gov/publication/43997.

35. The Center for Strategic and International Studies calculates that under sequestration, annual DoD spending would drop 31 percent from its 2010 peak, compared with a 33 percent decline after Vietnam, a 36 percent drop after the end of the Cold War, and a 43 percent plunge after the Korean War. See Bennett, *Defense News*, "How Big Would DoD Budget be Under Sequestration? Historically Big, It Turns Out," February 8, 2013, http://blogs.defensenews.

com/intercepts/2013/02/how-big-would-dod-budget-be-under-sequestration-pretty-big-it-turns-out/.

9. Hybrid State, Hybrid Capitalism, Great Power Turning Point

1. The impact of partisan politics, for example, in the domain of grand strategy is examined by Trubowitz (2011).

2. See the discussion in chapter 1.

3. Notwithstanding a recent emphasis on shortened time frames for S&T projects, as Congress has called on DARPA and other agencies to meet more immediate "warfighting needs."

4. In the United States, the norm for the half-century since World War II has been "adversarial relationships with suppliers"; this began to change in the 1990s, in some sectors like autos (Helper and Levine 1992, 561).

5. The work of Balogh (2009), King and Lieberman (2009), and Novak (2008), as well as that of several other authors, highlights strengths within the American state, as well as the state-building role of the armed forces.

6. The same source also recognizes that this view is not consistent with the fact that the two technology leaders (and generators of trade surpluses), aerospace and IT, have been the most heavily supported by the U.S. government.

7. On interagency coordination in these areas, see the National Research Council's *Funding a Revolution* (1999, 149).

8. A fourteen-page Office of Science and Technology Policy/Office of Management and Budget memo outlines this top-down budgeting process. See OSTP/OMB, "FY2004 Interagency Research and Development Priorities," May 30, 2002, http://www.hsdl.org/?view&did=464736.

9. The 1991 HPCC Act grew out of the Office of Science and Technology Policy's 1989 interagency plan for high-performance computing that initially involved DoE, NASA, and NSF, with informal but influential input of the National Security Agency; though focused on highest-end computers and applications, its impacts have been very broad, as supercomputer advances migrated to the desktop (chapter 5).

10. Known as National Information Technology Research and Development (NITRD).

11. On the interagency character of key computing initiatives, see National Research Council (1999, 130–132).

12. Teague 2011.

13. This became the title of a paper that Grove co-authored with Robert Burgelman in a 2007 issue of the *Strategic Management Journal*.

14. See, for example, Novak's suggestive essay on "The Myth of the Weak American State" (2008, 770), in which he emphasizes "interpenetration" and "convergence" of public and private authority in everyday policymaking.

15. See, for example, Ferleger and Lazonick (1993) on the government's early involvement in developing and disseminating productive resources for U.S. agriculture.

16. Cited in Ignatius, "The CIA as Venture Capitalist," *Washington Post*, September 29, 1999.

17. "Pleasing Wall Street is a Poor Excuse for Bad Decisions," October 20, 2009, http://blogs.hbr.org/hbr/restoring-american-competitiveness/2009/10/outsourcing-in-and-of-it self.html.

18. The statement is widely attributed to Thomas Watson, founder of IBM, although the original context is unclear.

19. Is it because China's production networks are organized as much offshore as onshore, making its strides less visible (hence less threatening)? Or is it because Chinese firms seem far from mastering the design of semiconductor technology, which the Pentagon views as the litmus test of technology leadership? However real (and shortsighted) such perceptions may be, the issue deserves further inquiry.

20. A growing literature from a distinguished group of economists and political scientists examines the harmful role of America's financial plutocracy: see, for example, Simon Johnson, "China Rising, Rent-Seeking Version," *Baseline Scenario*, August 11, 2009, http://baselinescenario.com/2009/08/11/china-rising-rent-seeking-version/; also Kurth 2011, 16.

The entire January/February 2011 issue of *American Interest* is devoted to the question of American plutocracy.

21. Recent evidence on comparative performance suggests a more tenuous connection between competitiveness and innovation capacity. See Ezell, "The Atlantic Century II: Benchmarking Asian, EU, and U.S. Innovation and Competitiveness," July 2011, http://www. itif.org/publications/atlantic-century-ii-benchmarking-asian-eu-and-us-innovation-and-competitiveness.

22. Carnegie Commission on Science, Technology and Government, *Technology and Economic Performance: Organizing the Executive Branch for a Stronger National Technology Base* (1991), 48, http://www.ccstg.org/pdfs/EconomicPerformance0991.pdf.

23. As a share of GDP, manufacturing output declined from 21.2 percent in 1979 to just 11.7 percent three decades later (Cordesman 2012, 55).

24. Andy Grove, "How America Can Create Jobs," *Business Week*, July 1, 2010, p. 4.

25. Based on 2008 estimates from the *CIA World Fact Book*. The Bureau of Economic Analysis estimates gross U.S. private domestic investment as a share of GDP (inflation-adjusted) as 12.3 percent in 1990 and 13.1 percent in 2010, well below Korea (about 30 percent), China (almost 50 percent)—and even much-embattled Japan (20 percent).

26. J. Graham, C. Harvey, and S. Rajgopal, "Value Destruction and Financial Reporting Decisions," September 6, 2006, http://dx.doi.org/10.2139/ssrn.871215.

27. For example, over the 2000–2007 period, leading nonfinancial corporations (including but not confined to Microsoft, Cisco, Hewlett-Packard, Dell, Texas Instruments, Intel, and Boeing) purchased financial assets and distributed dividend payments whose value often exceeded their net income by up to 60 percent (Milberg and Winkler 2009, 15, table 3).

28. The data on corporate buybacks tell a startling story (see Lazonick 2009).

29. For the buyback details, see http://www.stocktradingtogo.com/2008/09/22/stock-buyback-plans-flood-wall-street/.

30. See the Government Accountability Office's 2010 report based on its survey of defense contractors.

31. One such rule is the 1982 SEC Rule 10b-18 which gave companies a "safe harbor" against manipulation charges being filed "if each day's open-market repurchases were not greater than 25 percent of the stock's average daily trading volume and if the company refrained from doing buybacks at the beginning and end of the trading day"; the rule was simplified even further in 2003 (Lazonick 2011, 7).

32. Patrick Thibodeau, "Bailout Won't Keep Wall Street from Sending Jobs Offshore," September 26, 2008, http://www.computerworld.com/s/article/9115638/Bailout_won_t_keep_Wall_Street_from_sending_jobs_offshore.

33. Grove, "How America Can Create Jobs," *Business Week*, July 1, 2010, p. 4.

34. For a discussion of how the IT sector lends itself to modularity—slicing and dicing the product into component parts that can be outsourced to global production networks, see Sturgeon 1997.

35. Threats to the U.S. industrial base from manufacturing decline are well recognized within the defense environment. See, e.g., Watts and Harrison 2011; also O'Hanlon 2011, 10.

36. For the original argument applied to Britain's rise and fall as a great power, see Mann 1988, chap. 8. However, I am using it to explain why U.S. preeminence, not its great power status, may be at stake.

37. See O'Hanlon 2011 on the need to overcome antigovernment influences as a matter of politics, political choice, and coalition building for change.

38. The historical role of government in effecting industrial and technological transformation is examined in Reinert 2007, Breznitz 2007, and Wade 1990.

39. A possible exception (that proves the security rule) is the case of Israel. For interesting parallels that highlight the important role of the defense industry in Israel's science-based industry, see Breznitz 2005, 2007.

40. Ironically, where the adoption of renewable energy is concerned (and resulting new industries and exports), Chinese statism may prove less of a hindrance to a "green-growth strategy" than American plutocracy. See, e.g., Mathews and Tan 2013.

References

Abrahamsen, Rita, and Michael C. Williams. 2008. "Selling Security: Assessing the Impact of Military Privatization." *Review of International Political Economy* 15 (1): 131–46.

Alic, John A. 2008. "A Weakness in Diffusion: U.S. Technology and Science Policy after World War II." *Technology in Society* 30: 17–29.

Alic, John A., M. Branscomb, H. Brooks, A. B. Carter, and G. I. Epstein. 1992. *Beyond Spinoff: Military and Commercial Technologies in a Changing World.* Boston: Harvard Business School Press.

Alic, John A., David C. Mowery, and Edward S. Rubin. 2003. *U.S. Technology and Innovation Policies: Lessons for Climate Change.* Department of Engineering and Public Policy Paper 95, http://repository.cmu.edu/epp/95.

Allison, David K. 1985. "U.S. Navy Research and Development Since World War II." In Merrit Roe Smith 1985.

Almunia, M., A. Bénétrix, B. Eichengreen, K. O'Rourke, and G. Rua 2010. "From Great Depression to Great Credit Crisis: Similarities, Differences and Lessons." *Economic Policy* 62 (April): 219–65.

Ante, Spencer E. 2008. *Creative Capital: Georges Doriot and the Birth of Venture Capital.* Cambridge, Mass.: Harvard Business School Press.

Aspray, William, Frank Mayadas, and Moshe Y. Vardi, eds. 2006. *Globalization and Offshoring of Software: A Report of the ACM Job Migration Task Force,* http://www.acm.org/globalizationreport/.

Atkinson, Robert D. 2010. "Role the U.S. Government Can Play in Restoring U.S. Innovation Leadership." Statement of Robert D. Atkinson, president, Information Technology and Innovation Foundation, before the House Committee on Science and Technology, Subcommittee on Technology and Innovation, 111th Cong., 2d sess., serial 111-90. March 24. Washington, D.C.

Audretsch, David B., Albert N. Link, and John T. Scott. 2002. "Public/Private Technology Partnerships: Evaluating SBIR-Supported Research." *Research Policy* 31 (1): 145–58.

Audretsch, David B., J. Weigand, and C. Weigand. 2001. "Does the Small Business Innovation Research Program Foster Entrepreneurial Behavior? Evidence from Indiana." In Wessner 2001.

Avant, Deborah D. 2005. *The Market for Force: The Consequences of Privatizing Security.* Cambridge, UK: Cambridge University Press.

Bacevich, Andrew J., ed. 2007. *The Long War: A New History of U.S. National Security Policy Since World War II.* New York: Columbia University Press.

———. 2010. *Washington Rules: America's Path to Permanent War.* New York: Henry Holt.

Baldwin, Peter. 2005. "Beyond Weak and Strong: Rethinking the State in Comparative Policy History." *Journal of Policy History* 17: 12–33.

Balogh, Brian. 2009. *A Government Out of Sight: The Mystery of National Authority in Nineteenth-Century America.* Cambridge, Mass.: Cambridge University Press.

Baron, Jon. 2007. Statement at the hearing on SBIR Program Reauthorization, House Committee on Science and Technology, Subcommittee on Technology and Innovation, 110th Cong., 1st sess., serial 110-43, April 26. Washington, D.C.

Berkowitz, Marvin. 1970. *The Conversion of Military-Oriented Research and Development to Civilian Uses.* New York: Praeger.

Bernstein, Barton J. 1987. "The Birth of the U.S Biological Warfare Program." *Scientific American* 256 (6): 116–21.

Bingaman, Jeff, John McCain, and James Blackwell. 1989. *Deterrence in Decay: the Future of the U.S. Defense Industrial Base. Final Report of the CSIS Defense Industrial Base Project.* Washington, D.C.: Center for Strategic and International Studies.

Bingham, Richard D. 1998. *Industrial Policy American Style: From Hamilton to HDTV.* New York: M. E. Sharpe.

Block, Fred. 2008. "Swimming Against the Current: The Rise of a Hidden Developmental State in the United States." *Politics and Society* 36 (2): 169–206.

———. 2010. "Innovation and the Invisible Hand of Government." In Block and Keller 2010.

Block, Fred, and Matthew R. Keller, eds. 2010. *State of Innovation: The U.S. Government's Role in Technology Development.* Boulder, Colo.: Paradigm.

Board of the Federal Reserve System. 1958. *Financing Small Business: Report to the Senate Committee on Banking and Currency and the Select Committees on Small Business,* vol. 1, 85th Cong., 2d sess., April 21. Washington, D.C.

Bonvillian, William B. 2009. "The Innovation State." *American Interest* 4 (6): 69–78.

Bonvillian, William B., and Richard Van Atta. 2011. "ARPA-E and DARPA: Applying the DARPA Model to Energy Innovation." *Journal of Technology Transfer* 36 (5): 469–513.

Borrus, Michael, James Millstein, and John Zysman. 1984. *Responses to the Japanese Challenge in High Technology: Innovation, Maturity, and the U.S.-Japanese Competition in Microelectronics.* Berkeley Roundtable on the International Economy, BRIE Working Paper 92A. BRIE Working Paper No. 6. University of California, Berkeley.

Borrus, Michael, and John Zysman. 1992. "Industrial Competitiveness and American National Security." In Sandholtz et al. 1992.

Brandt, Linda. 1994. "Defense Conversion and Dual-Use Technology: The Push Toward Civil-Military Integration." *Policy Studies Journal* 22 (2): 359–70.

Branscomb, Lewis M., and Philip E. Auerswald. 2002. *Between Invention and Innovation: An Analysis of Funding for Early-Stage Technology Development.* Washington, D.C.: National Institute of Standards and Technology, http://www.atp.nist.gov/eao/gcr02-841/gcr02-841.pdf.

Branscomb, Lewis M., and George Parker. 1995. "Funding Civilian and Dual-Use Industrial Technology." In *Empowering Technology: Implementing a U.S. Strategy,* edited by Lewis Branscomb. Cambridge, Mass.: MIT Press.

Brayton, Stephen. 2002. "Outsourcing War: Mercenaries and the Privatization of Peacekeeping." *Journal of International Affairs* 55 (2): 303–29.

Brewer, Elijah III, and Hesna Genay. 1995. "Small Business Investment Companies: Financial Characteristics and Investments." *Journal of Small Business Management* (July): 38–56.

Breznitz, Dan. 2005. "Collaborative Public Space in a National Innovation System: A Case Study of the Israeli Military's Impact on the Software Industry." *Industry and Innovation* 12 (1): 31–64.

——. 2007. *Innovation and the State: Political Choice and Strategies for Growth in Israel, Taiwan, and Ireland.* New Haven, Conn.: Yale University Press.

Brookings Institution. 2009. *Energy Discovery-Innovation Institutes: A Step Toward America's Sustainability.* Policy Brief, February 2009.

Brooks, Harvey. 1987. "What Is the National Science Agenda, and How Did It Come About?" *American Scientist* 75 (5): 511–17.

Burton, Daniel F. 1993. "High-Tech Competitiveness." *Foreign Policy* 92 (Autumn): 117–32.

——. 1996. "Competitiveness: Here to Stay." *Washington Quarterly* 17 (4): 99–109.

Business Executives for National Security. 2001. *Accelerating the Acquisition and Implementation of New Technologies for Intelligence: Report of the Independent Panel on the Central Intelligence Agency In-Q-Tel Venture.* Washington, D.C.

Campbell, John L. 2004. *Institutional Change and Globalization.* Princeton, N.J.: Princeton University Press.

——. 2011. "The US. Financial Crisis: Lessons for Theories of Institutional Complementarity." *Socio-Economic Review* 9: 211–34.

Carter, Ashton B. 2001. "Keeping the Edge: Managing Defense for the Future." In *Keeping the Edge: Managing Defense for the Future,* edited by Ashton B. Carter and John P. White. Cambridge, Mass.: MIT Press.

Center for Naval Analysis, Military Advisory Board. 2009. *Powering America's Defense: Energy and the Risks to National Security.* Arlington, Va.

Chachula, Bernard M. 2004. *Evaluate Initiation of An Air Force Venture Capital Fund.* Dayton, Ohio: Wright Brothers Institute.

Chan, Steve. 1985. "The Impact of Defense Spending on Economic Performance: A Survey of Evidence and Problems." *Orbis* 29 (2): 403–34.

Cohen, Linda R. 1999. "Dual-Use and the Technology Reinvestment Project." In *Investing in Innovation: Creating a Research and Innovation Policy That Works,* edited by Lewis M. Branscomb and James H. Keller. Cambridge, Mass.: MIT Press.

Cohen, Stephen S., and John Zysman. 1987. *Manufacturing Matters: The Myth of the Post-Industrial Economy.* New York: Basic Books.

Coleman, William D., and Christine Chiasson. 2002. "State Power, Transformative Capacity and Adapting to Globalization: An Analysis of French Agricultural Policy, 1960–2000." *Journal of European Public Policy* 9 (2): 165–85.

Coletta, Damon. 2009. *Science, Technology, and the Quest for International Influence.* Colorado Springs, Colo.: Institute for National Security Studies, U.S. Air Force Academy.

Congressional Budget Office. 1985. *Federal Financial Support for High-Technology Industries,* http://www.cbo.gov/sites/default/files/cbofiles/ftpdocs/94xx/doc9456/85-cbo-011.pdf.

———. 1987. *The Benefits and Risks of Federal Funding for Sematech,* http://www.cbo. gov/sites/default/files/cbofiles/ftpdocs/62xx/doc6205/doc14b-entire.pdf.

———. 2012. *How Much Does the Federal Government Support the Development and Production of Fuels and Energy Technologies?* http://www.cbo.gov/publication/43040.

Congressional Research Service. 1978. *Industrial Innovation and Its Relation to the U.S. Domestic Economy and International Trade Competitiveness.* Analysis of the Hearings Held by Subcommittees of the Senate Committees on Commerce, Science, and Transportation; and Banking, Housing, and Urban Affairs; and the House Committee on Science and Technology, February 14, April 26, and May 16 (prepared by Mary Ellen Mogee), Report No. 78-204 SPR, October. Washington, D.C.

———. 1986a. *Science Policy Study Background Report No. 1,* A *History of Science Policy in the United States, 1940–1985.* Report to the Task Force on Science Policy (prepared by Jeffrey K. Stine), House Committee on Science and Technology, 99th Cong., 2d sess., serial R, September. Washington, D.C.

———. 1986b. "Economic Impacts of Defense R&D." Chapter 13, *Science Policy Study Background Paper No. 8: Science Support by the Department of Defense.* Report to the Task Force on Science Policy, House Committee on Science and Technology, 99th Cong., 2d sess., serial II, December. Washington, D.C.

———. 1998. *Cooperative Research and Development Agreements and Semiconductor Technology: Issues involving the "DOE-Intel CRADA."* CRS Report 98-81 (Wendy H. Schacht and G. J. McLoughlin). Washington, D.C.

———. 2006. *The National Institutes of Health (NIH): Organization, Funding, and Congressional Issues.* CRS Report, October 19 (Pamela W. Smith). Washington, D.C.

———. 2007. *Energy Independence and Security Act of 2007: A Summary of Major Provisions.* CRS Report, December 21. Washington, D.C.

———. 2008. *Technology Transfer: Use of Federally Funded Research and Development.* CRS Report, August 25 (Wendy H. Schacht). Washington, D.C.

———. 2009. *Federally Funded Innovation Inducement Prizes.* CRS Report, June 29 (Deborah D. Stine). Washington, D.C.

———. 2010. *Small Business Innovation Research (SBIR) Program,* CRS Report, August 4 (Wendy H. Schacht). Washington, D.C.

———. 2011a. *The National Nanotechnology Initiative: Overview, Reauthorization, and Appropriations Issues.* CRS Report, March 25 (John F. Sargent). Washington, D.C.

———. 2011b. *The Quasi Government: Hybrid Organizations with Both Government and Private Sector Characteristics,* CRS Report, January 31 (Kevin R. Kosar). Washington, D.C.

———. 2011c. *Defense: FY2012 Budget Request, Authorization and Appropriations.* CRS Report, November 25 (Pat Towell). Washington, D.C.

———. 2012a. *DOD Alternative Fuels: Policy, Initiatives, and Legislative Activity.* CRS Report, December 14 (Katherine Blakeley). Washington, D.C.

———. 2012b. *FY2013 Defense Budget Request: Overview and Context.* CRS Report, April 20 (Stephen Daggett and Pat Towell). Washington, D.C.

Connell, David. 2006. *Secrets of the World's Largest Seed Capital Fund: How the United States Government Uses Its Small Business Innovation Research (SBIR) Programme and Procurement Budgets to Support Small Technology Firms.* Cambridge, UK: Centre for Business Research.

Cordesman, Anthony H. 2012. *The U.S. Defense Budget and Changes in U.S. Strategy,* Pre 2013 Budget Submission Report, Center for Strategic & International

Studies, January 23, http://csis.org/files/publication/120123_us_new_strategy_budget_med.pdf.

Cotell, Catherine. 2006. "Strategy, University, and Early Stage Investments." Statement before the House Science Committee, Should Congress Establish 'ARPA-E,' The Advanced Research Projects Agency-Energy? 109th Congress, 2d sess., serial 109-39, March 9. Washington, D.C.

Covert, Norman M. 1993. *Cutting Edge, A History of Fort Detrick, Maryland, 1943–1993.* Fort Detrick, Md.: Public Affairs Office:.

Crouch, Colin. 2005a. *Capitalist Diversity and Change.* Oxford: Oxford University Press.

———. 2005b. "Three Meanings of Complementarity." *Socio-Economic Review* 3: 359–63.

———. 2010. "Complementarity." In *The Oxford Handbook of Comparative Institutional Analysis,* edited by G. Morgan, J. L. Campbell, C. Crouch, O. Pedersen, K. Pedersen, and R. Whitley, 117–37. New York: Oxford University Press.

Crow, Michael M., and Christopher Tucker. 2001. "The American Research University System as America's *de facto* Technology Policy." *Science and Public Policy* 28 (1): 2–10.

Cuevas, Enrique G., H. A. Esiely-Barrera, H. Warren Kim, and Zhuangbo Tang. 2011. "Assessment of the Internet Protocol Routing in Space—Joint Capability Technology Demonstration." *Johns Hopkins APL Technical Digest* 30 (2): 89–102.

Danhof, Clarence H. 1968. *Government Contracting and Technological Change.* Washington, D.C.: Brookings Institution.

Daugbjerg, Carsten, and Darren Halpin. 2012. "Generating Policy Capacity in Emerging Green Industries: The Development of Organic Farming in Denmark and Australia." *Journal of Environmental Policy and Planning* 12 (2): 141–57.

Defense Advanced Projects Agency. 1997. *Technology Transition.* Washington, D.C.

———. 2006. *Report to Congress: DARPA Prize Authority, FY 2005.* 109th Cong. Washington, D.C.

———. 2008. *DARPA: 50 Years of Bridging the Gap.* Tampa, Fla.: Fairmount.

Defense Industry Daily. 2011. "Frontline Commanders Requesting Renewable Power Options." March 11.

Defense Science Board. 1980. *Report of the Defense Science Board Summer Study on the Defense Industrial and Technology Base.* Washington, D.C.

———. 1987. *Report of the Defense Science Board Task Force on Defense Semiconductor Dependency.* Washington, D.C.

———. 2005. *Report of the Defense Science Board Task Force on High Performance Microchip Supply.* Washington, D.C.

———. 2008. *Report of the Task Force on DoD Energy Strategy: "More Fight—Less Fuel."* Washington, D.C.

DeGrasse, R. W. 1983. *Military Expansion, Economic Decline: The Impact of Military Spending on U.S. Economic Performance.* New York: M. E. Sharpe.

Department of Commerce, National Institute of Standards and Technology. 1977. *The Influence of Defense Procurement and Sponsorship of Research and Development on the Development of the Civilian Electronics Industry.* Washington, D.C.

Department of Commerce, Office of Strategic Industries and Economic Security. 2004. *Assessment of Industry Attitudes on Collaborating with the U.S. Department of Defense in Research and Development and Technology Sharing.* Washington, D.C.

Department of Commerce, Office of Technology Policy. 1996. *Effective Partnering: A Report to Congress on Federal Technology Partnerships.* Washington, D.C.

Department of Defense, SBIR Program Office. 1983. *Program Solicitation Number 84: Small Business Innovation Research Program.* Washington, D.C.

——. Office of the Secretary of Defense (Acquisition). 1990. *Very High Speed Integrated Circuits—VHSIC, Final Program Report 1980–1990.* Washington, D.C.: Defense Technical Information Center.

——. 2000. *Harnessing the Power of Technology: The Road to Ballistic Missile Defense from 1983 to 2007.* Washington, D.C.

——. 2009. "Department of Defense Energy Security Efforts," http://wstiac.alion science.com/pdf/WQV9N1_ART01.pdf.

——. 2010. *Quadrennial Defense Review Report.* Washington, D.C.

——. 2011. *Energy for the Warfighter: Operational Energy Strategy.* Washington, D.C.

Dombrowski, Peter, and Eugene Gholz, 2006. *Buying Military Transformation: Technological Innovation and the Defense Industry.* New York: Columbia University Press.

Draper, William H. 2008. Interview conducted by Sally Smith, *Early Bay Area Venture Capitalists: Shaping the Economic and Business Landscape.* Regional Oral History Office, The Bancroft Library, University of California, Berkeley, http://digitalassets. lib.berkeley.edu/roho/ucb/text/draper_william.pdf.

Edgerton, David. 2004. " 'The Linear Model' Did Not Exist: Reflections on the History and Historiography of Science and Research in Industry in the Twentieth Century." In *The Science-Industry Nexus: History, Policy, Implications,* edited by K. Grandin, N. Wormbs, and S. Widlmalm. New York: Science History Publications.

Edquist, Charles. 2005. "Government Technology Procurement as an Instrument of Technology Policy." In *Technological Infrastructure Policy: An International Perspective,* edited by M. Teubal, D. Foray, M. Justman, and E. Zuscovitch. Boston: Kluwer Academic.

Edwards, Paul. 1996. *The Closed World: Computers and the Politics of Discourse in Cold War America.* Cambridge, Mass.: MIT Press.

Eisenhower, Dwight D. 1953. "Special Message to the Congress Transmitting Reorganization Plan 6 of 1953 Concerning the Department of Defence." Online by Gerhard Peters and John T. Woolley, *The American Presidency Project,* http://www. presidency.ucsb.edu/ws/index.php?pid=9831.

Etzioni, Amitai. 2011. "Cybersecurity in the Private Sector." *Issues in Science and Technology* 28 (1): 58–62.

Etzkowitz, Henry. 2003. "Public Venture Capital: The Secret Life of US Science Policy." In *Innovation Policies in Europe and the US: The New agenda,* edited by P. Biegelbauer and S. Borras. London: Ashgate.

Feldman, Maryann P. 2001. "Role of the Department of Defense in Building Biotech Expertise." In Wessner 2001.

Ferleger, Louis A., and William Lazonick. 1993. "The Managerial Revolution and the Developmental State: The Case of U.S. Agriculture." *Business History* 22 (2): 67–98.

Flamm, Kenneth. 1988. *Creating the Computer.* Washington, D.C.: Brookings Institution Press.

——. 1994. "Flat Panel Displays: Catalyzing a U.S. Industry." *Issues in Science and Technology* 11 (1): 27–32.

Fohlin, Caroline. 2005. "Creating Modern Venture Capital: Institutional Design and Performance in the Early Years," http://dx.doi.org/10.2139/ssrn.2197840.

Fong, Glenn R. 1991. "The Future of Pentagon-Industry Collaboration in Technology Development." In *The Political Economy of Defense: Issues and Implications,* edited by Andrew L. Ross. New York: Greenwood Press.

———. 2000. "Breaking New Ground or Breaking the Rules: Strategic Reorientation in U.S. Industrial Policy." *International Security* 25 (2): 152–86.

———. 2001. "ARPA Does Windows: The Defense Underpinning of the PC Revolution." *Business and Politics* 3 (3): 213–37.

Foote, Susan Bartlett. 1992. *Managing the Medical Arms Race: Innovation and Public Policy in the Medical Device Industry.* Berkeley: University of California Press.

Fordham, Benjamin O. 2007, "Paying for Global Power: Costs and Benefits of Postwar U.S. Military Spending." In Bacevich 2007.

Freeman, Eva C., ed. 1995. *MIT Lincoln Laboratory: Technology in the National Interest.* Lincoln Laboratory, Massachusetts Institute of Technology, Lexington, Mass.

Friedberg, Aaron L. 1989. "The Political Economy of American Strategy" *World Politics* 41 (3): 381–406.

———. 1992. "Why Didn't the United States Become a Garrison State?" *International Security* 16 (4): 109–42.

———. 2000. *In the Shadow of the Garrison State: America's Anti-Statism and Its Cold War Grand Strategy.* Princeton, N.J.: Princeton University Press.

———. 2002. "American Antistatism and the Founding of the Cold War State." In Katznelson and Shefter 2002.

Fukuyama, Francis. 2011. "Left Out." *American Interest* 6 (3): 22–28.

Gansler, Jacques S. 1980. *The Defense Industry.* Cambridge, Mass: MIT Press.

———. 1998. "Military and Industrial Cooperation in a Transformed, NATO-Wide Competitive Market." *15th International Workshop on Global Security—Vienna, 19–23 June, 1998,* http://www.csdr.org/98Book/gansler98.htm.

———. 2011. *Democracy's Arsenal: Creating a Twenty-First-Century Defense Industry.* Cambridge, Mass.: MIT Press.

Geiger, Roger. 1992. "Science, Universities and National Defense, 1945–1970" *OSIRIS,* 2d ser., 7: 26–48.

———. 1997. "What Happened after Sputnik? Shaping University Research in the United States." *Minerva* 35 (4): 349–67.

Gholz, Eugene. 2011. "How Military Innovation Works and the Role of Industry." Paper prepared for the American Political Science Association Conference, Seattle, September.

Gold, David. 1991. "Military R&D—A Poor Scapegoat for Flagging Economy." *Bulletin of Atomic Scientists* 47 (1): 38–43.

———. 2005. *Does Military Spending Stimulate or Retard Economic Performance? Revisiting an Old Debate.* International Affairs Working Paper 2005-01. The New School.

Gompers, P. 1994. "The Rise and Fall of Venture Capital." *Business and Economic History* 23 (2): 1–26.

Gompers, Paul A., and Josh Lerner. 2004. *The Venture Capital Cycle.* 2d ed. Cambridge, Mass.: MIT Press.

Government Accountability Office. 1972. *Means for Increasing the Use of Defense Technology for Urgent Public Problems: Department of Defense, Office of Management and Budget, and Other Civil Agencies* (GA 1.13:D 36/11). Washington, D.C.

———. 1974. *Independent Research and Development Allocations Should Not Absorb Costs of Commercial Development Work* (B-164912). Washington, D.C.

———. 1979. "Government-wide Patent Policy—Concerted Executive-Legislative Action Needed." Chapter 11 in *Recommendations of the Commission on Government Procurement: A Final Assessment.* GAO-PSAD-79-80. Washington, D.C.

——. 1987. *Federal Research: Small Business Innovation Research Participants Give Program High Marks.* GAO-RCED-87-161-BR. Washington, D.C.

——. 1989. *Federal Research: Assessment of Small Business Innovation Research Program.* GAO-RCED-89-39, Washington, D.C.

——. 1992. *Federal Research: Small Business Innovation Research Shows Success but Can Be Strengthened.* GAO-RCED–92–32. Washington, D.C.

——. 1995. *Federal Research: Interim Report on the Small Business Innovation Research Program.* GAO/T-RCED-95–154. Gaithersburg, Md.

——. 1997. *Federal Research: DoD's Small Business Innovation Research Program.* GAO-RCED–97–122. Washington, D.C.

——. 1998. *Federal Research: Observations on the Small Business Innovation Research Program.* GAO-RCED-98–132. Washington, D.C.

——. 2006. *Offshoring: U.S. Semiconductor and Software Industries Increasingly Produce in China and India.* GAO-06–423. Washington, D.C.

——. 2010. *Defense Contracting: Recent Law Has Impacted Contractor Use of Offshore Subsidiaries to Avoid Certain Payroll Taxes.* GAO-10–327. Washington, D.C.

——. 2012. *The Department of Energy's Office of Science Uses a Multilayered Process for Prioritizing Research.* GAO-12–410R. Washington, D.C.

Graham, Otis, L. 1992. *Losing Time: The Industrial Policy Debate.* Cambridge, Mass.: Harvard University Press.

Grossman, Andrew D. 2002. "The Early Cold War and American Political Development: Reflections on Recent Research." *International Journal of Politics, Culture and Society* 15 (3): 471–83.

Gummet, Philip, and Judith Reppy, eds. 1988. *The Relations Between Defence and Civil Technologies.* Boston, Mass.: Kluwer Academic Publishers.

Hall, Peter A., and David Soskice. 2001. *Varieties of Capitalism: The Institutional Foundations of Comparative Advantage.* Oxford: Oxford University Press.

Hall, Robert. 2009. "By How Much Does GDP Rise if the Government Buys More Output?" *Brookings Papers on Economic Activity* 2: 183–231.

Halvorson, Harlyn O. 1992. "Civilian Control of Biological Defense Research." *Annals of the New York Academy of Sciences* 666 (December): 191–201.

Hart, David M. 1998. *Forged Consensus: Science, Technology, and Economic Policy in the United States, 1921–1953.* Princeton,N.J.: Princeton University Press.

Hart, Jeffrey 1992. *Rival Capitalists: International Competitiveness in the United States, Japan, and Western Europe.* Ithaca, N.Y.: Cornell University Press.

Harvey, David. 2005. A *Brief History of Neoliberalism.* Oxford: Oxford University Press.

Havelock, R. G., and D. S. Bushnell. 1985. *Technology Transfer at the Defense Advanced Research Projects Agency: A Diagnostic Analysis.* Fairfax, Va.: Technology Transfer Study Center, George Mason University.

Heinrich, Thomas. 2002. "Cold War Armory: Military Contracting in Silicon Valley." *Enterprise and Society* 3 (2): 247–84.

Held, Bruce J. 2002. *Seeking Nontraditional Approaches to Collaborating and Partnering with Industry.* Rand Monograph Reports, MR-1401-A. Santa Monica, Calif: RAND Corporation.

Held, Bruce J., and Ike Chang. 2000. *Using Venture Capital to Improve Army Research and Development.* Santa Monica, Calif.: RAND Corporation.

Helper, Susan, and David I. Levine. 1992. "Long Term Supplier Relations and Product-Market Structure." *Journal of Law, Economics, and Organization* 8 (3): 561–81.

Hirschberg, Rona, John La Montagne, and Anthony S. Fauci. 2004. "Biomedical Research—An Integral Component of National Security." *New England Journal of Medicine* 350 (21): 2119–21.

Hogan, Michael J. 1998. *A Cross of Iron: Harry S. Truman and the Origins of the National Security State, 1945–1954*. New York: Cambridge University Press.

Holbrook, Daniel. 1995. "Government Support of the Semiconductor Industry: Diverse Approaches and Information Flows." *Business and Economic History* 24 (2): 133–65.

Holl, Jack M. 1997. *Argonne National Laboratory, 1946–1996*. Urbana: University of Illinois Press.

Homeland Security Institute. 2005. *Venture Capital Concept Analysis: Final.* Arlington, Va.: Department of Homeland Security.

Hooks, Gregory. 1990. "The Rise of the Pentagon and U.S. State Building: The Defense Program as Industrial Policy." *American Journal of Sociology*, 96 (2): 358–404.

Howell, Thomas R. 2003. "Semiconductors." In National Research Council 2003.

Hubry, Jill M., Dawn K. Manley, Ronald E. Stoltz, Erik K. Webb, and Joan B. Woodard. 2011. The *Evolution of Federally Funded Research and Development Centers*. Public Interest Report, Spring. Washington, D.C.: Federation of American Scientists.

Hurt, Shelley. 2010. "Military's Hidden Hand: Examining the Dual-Use Origins of Biotechnology, 1969–1972." In Block and Keller 2010.

Johnson, Chalmers. 2004. *Blowback: The Costs and Consequences of American Empire.* 2nd ed. New York: Henry Holt.

——. 2004. *The Sorrows of Empire: Militarism, Secrecy and the End of the Republic.* New York: Henry Holt.

——. 2006. *Nemesis: The Last Days of the American Republic.* New York: Henry Holt.

Johnson, Simon. 2009. "The Quiet Coup." *The Atlantic,* May, 46–57.

Kadlec, Robert P., and Alan P. Zelicoff. 2000. "Implications of the Biotechnology Revolution for Weapons Development and Arms Control." In *Biological Warfare: Modern Offense and Defense,* edited by Raymond A. Zilinskas. Boulder, Colo.: Lynne Rienner.

Kaminski, Paul G. 1995a. Testimony before the House Committee on National Security, Subcommittee on Military Research and Development, hearings on National Defense Authorization Act, FY 1996-H.R. 1530, 104th Cong., 1st sess., March 28. Washington, D.C.

——.1995b. Department of Defense Authorization for FY96. Statement before the Senate Committee on Armed Services, Subcommittee on Acquisition and Technology, 104th Cong., 1st sess., S. 1026, Part 5 Acquisition and Technology, March 14. Washington, D.C.

Katzenstein, Peter J. 1996. *Cultural Norms and National Security: Police and Military in Postwar Japan.* Ithaca, N.Y.: Cornell University Press.

——. 2005. *A World of Regions: Asia and Europe in the American Imperium.* Ithaca, N.Y.: Cornell University Press.

Katznelson, Ira, and Martin Shefter, eds. 2002. *Shaped by War and Trade: International Influences on American Political Development.* Princeton, N.J.: Princeton University Press.

Kelley, Maryellen, and Todd A. Watkins. 1995. "In from the Cold: Prospects for the Conversion of the Defense Industrial Base." *Science* 268: 525–32.

——. 1997. "Are Defense and Non-Defense Manufacturing Practices All That Different?" Second Klein Symposium on the Management of Technology,

Smeal College of Business Administration, Pennsylvania State University, January 1998.

Kendall, Frank. 2011. "The Health and Status of the Defense Industrial Base and Its Science and Technology–Related Elements." Hearing of the Senate Committee on Armed Services, Subcommittee on Emerging Threats and Capabilities, 112th Cong., 1st sess., serial 112-256, May 3. Washington, D.C.

Kennedy, Paul. 1987. *The Rise and Fall of the Great Powers.* New York: Random House.

Kenney, Martin, ed. 2000. *Understanding Silicon Valley: The Anatomy of an Entrepreneurial Region.* Palo Alto, Calif.: Stanford University Press.

Kenney, Martin, Martin Haemmig, and W. Richard Goe. 2008. *Venture Capital: Innovation in Global Industries: U.S. Firms Competing in a New World.* Washington, D.C.: National Academies Press.

Kevles, Daniel J. 1975. "Scientists, the Military, and the Control of Postwar Defense Research: The Case of the Research Board for National Security, 1944–1946." *Technology and Culture* 16 (1): 359–78.

Killian, James R. 1977. *Sputnik, Scientists, and Eisenhower.* Cambridge, Mass.: MIT Press.

Kim, Sung-Young. 2010. "Transitioning from Follower to Innovator: The Institutional Foundations of the Korean Telecommunications Sector." *Review of International Political Economy* 19 (1): 140–68.

King, Desmond, and Robert C. Lieberman. 2008. "Finding the American State: Transcending the 'Statelessness' Account." *Polity* 40: 368–78.

——. 2009. "Ironies of State Building: A Comparative Perspective on the American State." *World Politics* 61 (3): 547–88.

Klare, Michael T. 2012. *The Race for What's Left: The Global Scramble for the World's Last Resources.* New York: Picador.

Koppell, Jonathan G. S. 2003. *The Politics of Quasi-Government: Hybrid Organizations and the Dynamics of Bureaucratic Control.* Cambridge, UK: Cambridge University Press.

Krige, John. 2010. "Technology Leadership and American Soft Power." In *Soft Power and U.S. Foreign Policy: Theoretical, Historical and Contemporary Perspectives,* edited by Inderjeet Parmar and Michael Cox. New York: Routledge.

Kroenig, Matthew and Jay Stowsky. 2006. "War Makes the State, but Not as It Pleases. *Security Studies* 15 (2): 225–70.

Kurth, James. 2011. "The Foreign Policy of Plutocracies." *American Interest.* 7 (2): 5–17.

Larzelere, Alex R. 2009. *Delivering Insight: The History of the Accelerated Strategic Computing. Initiative (ASCI).* Lawrence, Calif.: Lawrence Livermore National Laboratory.

Lazonick, William. 2009. "The New Economy Business Model and the Crisis of U.S. Capitalism." *Capitalism and Society* 4 (2): Article 4.

——. 2011. "Reforming the Financialized Business Corporation" Academic-Industry Research Network, http://www.employmentpolicy.org/sites/www.employment policy.org/files/Lazonick%20Reforming%20the%20Financialized%20Corpora tion%2020110130%20(2).pdf.

Lécuyer, Christophe. 2006. *Making Silicon Valley: Innovation and the Growth of High Tech, 1930–1970.* Cambridge, Mass.: MIT Press.

Lenoir, Timothy, and Margaret Hays. 2000. "The Manhattan Project for Biomedicine." In *Controlling Our Destinies: Historical, Philosophical, Ethical, and Theological Perspectives on the Human Genome Project,* edited by P. R. Sloan. South Bend, Ind.: University of Notre Dame Press.

Lenoir, Tim, and Henry Lowood. 2005. "Theaters of War: The Military-Entertainment Complex." Manuscript, Stanford University.

Lerner, Josh. 1999. "The Government as Venture Capitalist: The Long-run Effects of the SBIR Program." *Journal of Business* 72 (3): 285–97.

——. 2009. *Boulevard of Broken Dreams: Why Public Efforts to Boost Entrepreneurship and Venture Capital Have Failed and What to Do about It.* Princeton, N.J.: Princeton University Press.

Leslie, Stuart W. 1993a. "How the West was Won: The Military and the Making of Silicon Valley." In *Technological Competitiveness: Contemporary and Historical Perspectives on the Electrical, Electronics, and Computer Industries,* edited by William Aspray. New York: IEEE Press.

——. 1993b. *The Cold War and American Science: The Military-Industrial-Academic Complex at MIT and Stanford.* New York: Columbia University Press.

Lightbody, Marcia L. 2004. "Building a Future: World War II and the Quartermaster Corps." In *The First Venture Capitalist,* edited by Udayan Gupta. Calgary: Gondolier.

Mackenzie, Donald. 1986. "Science and Technology Studies and the Question of the Military." *Social Studies of Science* 16 (2): 361–71.

Magaziner, Ira, and Robert Reich. 1982. *Minding America's Business.* New York: Harcourt Brace Jovanovich.

Majumdar, Arun. 2011. "ARPA-E Catalyzing Energy Breakthroughs to Secure America's Future." Statement before the House Committee on Appropriations, Subcommittee on Energy and Water Development, 112th Cong., 1st sess, March 31. Washington, D.C.

Mann, Michael. 1988. "The Autonomous Power of the State: Its Origins, Mechanisms and Results." In Mann 1988.

——. 1988. *States, War, and Capitalism.* Oxford: Basil Blackwell.

——. 1996. "Authoritarian and Liberal Militarism: A Contribution from Historical Sociology." In *International Theory: Positivism and Beyond,* edited by S. Smith, K. Booth, and M. Zalewski. Cambridge, UK: Cambridge University Press.

——. 2013. *The Sources of Social Power, Volume 4: Globalizations, 1945–2011.* Cambridge: Cambridge University Press.

Markusen, Ann. 1986. "Defense Spending: A Successful Industrial Policy?" *Journal of Urban and Regional Development* 10: 103–21.

——. 1991. "The Military-Industrial Divide." *Environment and Planning D: Society and Space* 9: 391–416.

Markusen, Ann, and Joel Yudken. 1992. *Dismantling the Cold War Economy.* New York: Basic Books.

Martin, Edith W. (Office of the Secretary of Defense). 1983. "Strategy for a DoD Software Initiative." *Computer* 16 (3): 52–59.

Mathews, John A., and Hao Tan. 2013. "The Transformation of the Electric Power System in China." *Energy Policy* 52: 170–80.

Matthews, William. 2011. "Bio Fleet: The Navy's Pursuit of an Ambitious Alternative Energy Program. *Government Executive* (January): 26–30.

Mayer, Kenneth R. 1991. *The Political Economy of Defense Contracting,* New Haven, Conn.: Yale University Press.

Mazzucato, Mariana. 2013. *The Entrepreneurial State: Debunking Public vs. Private Sector Myths.* London: Anthem Press.

McDougall, Walter A. 1982. "Technocracy and Statecraft in the Space Age—Toward the History of a Saltation." *American Historical Review* 87 (4): 1010–40.

McGrew, Dean Z., and Paul F. Skalny. 2010. Advanced Vehicle Power Initiative. Final Report, July 29. US Army-TARDEC, https://www.researchgate.net/publication/235196317_Advanced_Vehicle_and_Power_Initiative.

McKenna, Regis, Michael Borrus, and Stephen Cohen. 1984. "Industrial Policy and International Competition in High Technology." *California Management Review* 26 (2): 15–32.

McNaugher, Thomas L. 1987. "Weapons Procurement: The Futility of Reform." *International Security* 12 (2): 63–104.

McNeill, William H. 1982. *The Pursuit of Power: Technology, Armed Force, and Society Since A.D. 1000.* Chicago: University of Chicago Press.

Melman, Seymour. 1970. *Pentagon Capitalism: The Political Economy of War.* New York: McGraw Hill.

———. 1974. *The Permanent War Economy: American Capitalism in Decline.* New York: Simon & Schuster.

Merrill, Stephen A. 1979. "The Political Nature of Civilian R&D Management." In *Federal R&D and Scientific Innovation,* edited by Leonard A. Ault and W. Novis Smith, 3–19. ACS Symposium Series, vol. 105. Washington, D.C.: American Chemical Society.

Milberg, William, and Deborah Schöller. 2008. "Globalization, Offshoring and Economic Insecurity in Industrialized Countries." Paper prepared for UN Department of Economic and Social Affairs, March 11.

Milberg, William, and Deborah Winkler. 2009. "Financialisation and the Dynamics of Offshoring in the USA." *Cambridge Journal of Economics* 3: 1–19.

Miller, Zachary. 2012. *Enhancing the Defense Industrial Base: Strategic Analysis for National Security Policy.* Washington, D.C.: American Security Project.

MITRE Corporation. 2009. *S&T for National Security.* JASON Program Office, JSR-08-146. Washington, D.C.

Moe, Ronald C. 2002. "The Emerging Federal Quasi Government: Issues of Management and Accountability." *Public Administration Review* 61 (3): 290–312.

Moffitt, William. 2011. Statement to the House Committee on Science, Space and Technology, Subcommittee on Research and Science Education, hearing on Nanotechnology: Oversight of the Nanotechnology Initiative and Priorities for the Future, 112th Cong., 1st sess., serial 112-15, April 14. Washington, D.C.

Moss, David. 2004. *When All Else Fails: Government as the Ultimate Risk Manager.* Cambridge, Mass.: Harvard University Press.

Mowery, David C. 2009. "National Security and National Innovation Systems." *Journal of Technology Transfer* 34: 455–73.

Mowery, David C., and Nathan Rosenberg. 1982. "The Commercial Aircraft Industry." In *Government and Technical Progress: A Cross Industry Analysis,* edited by R. Nelson. New York: Pergamon Press.

———. 1998. *Paths of Innovation:Technological Change in 20th-Century America.* Cambridge, UK: Cambridge University Press.

National Academies of Sciences and Engineering. 2007. *Rising above the Gathering Storm.* Washington, D.C.: National Academies Press.

National Academy of Engineering. 1978. *Industrial Innovation and Public Policy Options: Background Papers for a Colloquium.* Washington, D.C.: National Academies Press.

———. 1981. *Industrial Innovation and Public Policy Options: Background Papers for a Colloquium.* Washington, D.C.: National Academy Press.

National Academy of Science and National Academy of Technology. 1992. *The Government Role in Civilian Technology: Building a New Alliance.* Washington, D.C.: National Academies Press.

National Research Council. 1995. *Evolving the High Performance Computing and Communications Initiative to Support the Nation's Information Infrastructure.* Washington, D.C.: National Academies Press.

———. 1996. *Conflict and Cooperation in International Competition for High-Technology Industry.* Washington, D.C.: National Academies Press.

———. 1997. *Energy-Efficient Technologies for the Dismounted Soldier.* Washington, D.C.: National Academies Press.

———. 1999. *Funding a Revolution: Government Support for Computing Research.* Washington, D.C.: National Academies Press.

———. 2001a. *The ATP Program: Assessing Outcomes.* (Edited by Charles W. Wessner.) Washington, D.C.: National Academies Press.

———. 2001b. *Review of the U.S. Department of Defense Air, Space, and Supporting Information Systems Science and Technology Program.* Washington, D.C.: National Academies Press.

———. 2002a. *Government-Industry Partnerships for Development of New Technologies* (Edited by Charles W. Wessner.) Washington, D.C.: National Academies Press.

———. 2002b. *Small Wonders, Endless Frontiers: Review of the National Nanotechnology Initiative.* Washington, D.C.: National Academies Press.

———. 2003. *Securing the Future: Regional and National Programs to Support the Semiconductor Industry.* Washington, D.C.: National Academies Press.

———. 2004a. "SBIR at the Department of Defense." In *SBIR Program Diversity and Assessment Challenges: Report of a Symposium.* Washington, D.C.: National Academies Press.

———. 2004b. *An Assessment of the Small Business Innovation Research Program: Project Methodology.* (Edited by Charles W. Wessner.) Washington, D.C.: National Academies Press.

———. 2007a. *SBIR and the Phase III Challenge of Commercialization. Report of a Symposium: An Assessment of the Small Business Innovation Research Program.* (Edited by Charles W. Wessner.) Washington, D.C.: National Academies Press.

———. 2007b. "Evolution of Technology Partnerships in the United States." In *Innovation Policies for the 21st Century: Report of a Symposium.* Washington, D.C.: National Academies Press.

———. 2007c. *Rising Above the Gathering Storm: Energizing and Employing America for a Brighter Economic Future.* Washington, DC: The National Academies Press.

———. 2008. *An Assessment of the Small Business Innovation Research Program.* (Edited by Charles W. Wessner.) Washington, D.C.: National Academies Press.

———. 2009a. *An Assessment of the Small Business Innovation Research Program at the Department of Defense.* (Edited by Charles W. Wessner.) Washington, D.C.: National Academies Press.

———. 2009b. *Venture Funding and the NIH SBIR Program.* (Edited by Charles W. Wessner.) Washington, D.C.: National Academies Press.

———. 2012. *Rising to the Challenge: U.S. Innovation Policy for Global Economy,* Washington, D.C.: National Academies Press.

National Science and Technology Council. 2004. *The National Nanotechnology Initiative: Strategic Plan*. December, http://www.nsf.gov/crssprgm/nano/reports/sp_report_nset_final.pdf.

National Science Board. 2010. *Science and Engineering Indicators 2010* (NSB 10-01). Arlington, Va.: National Science Foundation.

Nelson, Anna Kasten. 2007. "The Evolution of the National Security State: Ubiquitous and Endless." In Bacevich 2007.

Nelson, Richard R. 1990. "What Has Happened to US Technological Leadership?" In *Technological Competition and Interdependence*, edited by G. Heiduk and K. Yamamura. Seattle: University of Washington Press.

Nelson, Richard R., Merton J. Peck, and Edward D. Kalachek. 1967. *Technology, Economic Growth, and Public Policy*. Washington, D.C.: RAND and Brookings Institution.

Noone, C., and S. Rubel. 1970. *SBICs: Pioneers in Organized Venture Capital*. Chicago: Capital Publishing.

Novak, William J. 2008. "The Myth of the 'Weak' American State." *American Historical Review* 113 (3): 752–72.

——. 2009. "Public-Private Governance: A Historical Introduction." In *Government by Contract: Outsourcing and American Democracy*, edited by J. Freeman and M. Minow. Cambridge, Mass.: Harvard University Press.

O'Hanlon, Michael. 2011. *The National Security Industrial Base: A Crucial Asset of the United States Whose Future May Be in Jeopardy*. 21st Century Defense Initiative Policy Paper. Brookings Institution.

Office of Management and Budget. 1977. *Small Firms and Federal Research and Development*, Report to the Office of Procurement Policy by an ad hoc interagency panel, February 24. Washington, D.C.

——. 2010. *Memorandum on the Use of Challenges and Prizes to Promote Open Government*. OMB M-10–11. Washington, D.C.

Old, Bruce S. 1981. *Return on Investment in Basic Research—Exploring a Methodology: Report to the Office of Naval Research, Department of the Navy*. N00014–79-C-0192. Arlington, VA: ONR.

O'Mara, Margaret Pugh. 2005. *Cities of Knowledge: Cold War Science and the Search for the Next Silicon Valley*. Princeton, N.J.: Princeton University Press.

Orlans, Harold. 1967. *Contracting for Atoms*, Washington, D.C.: Brookings Institution.

——. " 'D&R' Allocations in the United States." *Science Studies* 3 (2): 119–59.

Paarlberg, Robert L. 2004. "Knowledge as Power: Science, Military Dominance, and U.S. Security." *International Security* 29 (1): 122–51.

Packard Commission. 1986. *A Quest for Excellence: Final Report of the Presidential Blue Ribbon Commission on Defense Management*. Washington, D.C.

Peck, Merton J., and Frederick M. Scherer. 1962. *The Weapons Acquisition Process*. Boston: Division of Research, Harvard Business School.

Perry, William J. 1994. *Acquisition Reform: A Mandate for Change*. Washington, D.C.: Department of Defense.

——. 2003. "Technology and National Security: Risks and Responsibilities." Stanford University Conference on Risk and Responsibility in Contemporary Engineering and Science: French and U.S. Perspectives, France-Stanford Center for Interdisciplinary Studies, April 7–8.

Peters, Guy, and Jon Pierre. 1998. "Governance Without Government? Rethinking Public Administration." *Journal of Public Administration Research and Theory*, 8 (2): 223–43.

Pew Research. 2009. *Who's Winning the Clean Energy Race?* Washington, D.C.

——. 2011. *From Barracks to the Battlefield: Clean Energy Innovation and America's Armed Forces.* Pew Project on National Security, Energy and Climate. Washington, D.C.

Potomac Institute for Policy Studies. 1999. *Technology Reinvestment Project (TRP) Development Study.* Washington, D.C.

Reiner, Martha L. 1991. "Innovation and the Creation of Venture Capital Organizations." *Business and Economic History* 20: 200–209.

Reinert, Erik S. 2007. *How Rich Countries Got Rich . . . and Why Poor Countries Stay Poor.* New York: Carroll & Graf.

Reppy, Judith. 1979. "Military R&D: Institutions, Output, and Arms Control." *Policy Studies Journal* 8 (1): 84–92.

Robyn. Dorothy. 2010. "Energy Management and Initiatives on Military Installations." Hearing before the Readiness Subcommittee of the House Committee on Armed Services, 111th Congress, 2d sess., serial 57-834, February 24.

Roland, Alex. 1995. *The Technological Fix: Weapons and the Cost of War.* Carlisle Barracks, Pa.: Strategic Studies Institute, U.S. Army War College.

——. 2007. The Military-Industrial Complex: Lobby and Trope. In Bacevich 2007.

——. 2010. "Cloning DARPA," (FORUM), *Issues in Science and Technology* 26 (2): 10.

Ruttan, Vernon W. 2006a. *Is War Necessary for Economic Growth?* New York: Oxford University Press.

——. 2006b. "Will Government Programs Spur the Next Breakthrough?" *Issues in Science and Technology* 22 (2): 55–61.

Samuels, Richard. 1994. *Rich Nation, Strong Army,* Ithaca, N.Y.: Cornell University Press.

Sandholtz, Wayne, Michael Borrus, John Zysman, Ken Conca, Jay Stowsky, Steven Vogel, and Steve Weber, eds. 1992. *The Highest Stakes: The Economic Foundations of the Next Security System.* New York: Oxford University Press.

Sapolsky, Harvey M. 1990. *Science and the Navy: The History of the Office of Naval Research.* Princeton, N.J.: Princeton University Press.

——. 1992. *Comparing Health and Defense.* DACS Working Paper, MIT Center for International Studies.

Schmidt, Robert N. 2007. "Reauthorization of the Small Business Innovation Research Programs and 'Unleashing American Innovation.'" Testimony before the House Committee on Science and Technology, Subcommittee on Technology and Innovation, 110th Congress, 1st sess., serial 110-43, April 26. Washington, D.C.

Schmidt, Vivien. 2002. *The Futures of European Capitalism.* Oxford: Oxford University Press.

Scranton, Philip. 2006. "Technology, Science, and American Innovation." *Business History* 48: 311–31.

Seidman, Harold. 1988. "The Quasi World of the Federal Government" *Brookings Review* 6 (3): 23–27.

Shefter, Martin. 2002. "International Influences on American Political Development." In Katznelson and Shefter 2002.

Sherry, Michael S. 2003. "A Hidden-Hand Garrison State?" *Diplomatic History* 27 (1): 163–66.

Singer, Peter W. 2003. *Corporate Warriors: The Rise of the Privatized Military Industry.* Ithaca, N.Y.: Cornell University Press.

——. 2011. "Military Robotics and Ethics: A World of Killer Apps." *Nature* 477: 399–401.

Slaughter, Sheila, and Gary Rhoades. 1996. "The Emergence of a Competitiveness Research and Development Policy Coalition and the Commercialization of Academic Science and Technology." *Science, Technology & Human Values* 21 (3): 303–39.

Small Business Administration. 2003. *State of the SBIC Program—Fiscal Year 2002, Special Report,* Exhibit 8. Washington, D.C.

Smith, Bruce L. R. 1990. *American Science Policy since World War II.* Washington, D.C.: Brookings Institution.

Smith, Merritt Roe. 1985. *Military Enterprise and Technological Change: Perspectives on the American Experience.* Cambridge, Mass.: MIT Press.

———. 1994. "Technological Determinism and American Culture." In *Does Technology Drive History? The Dilemma of Technological Determinism,* edited by Leo Marx and Merritt Roe Smith. Cambridge, Mass.: MIT Press.

Special Committee on Technical Information Research and Development Board. 1951. "Technical Information Activities of the Department of Defense." *Science* 114 (2973): 653–61.

Squillante, Michael R. 2011. "Spurring Innovation and Job Creation: The SBIR Program." Testimony of Chairman, Board of Directors, Small Business Technology Council, before the House Committee on Small Business, 112th Cong., 1st sess., serial 112-06. March 16. Washington, D.C.

Stanton, Thomas H. 2002. *Government-Sponsored Enterprises: Mercantilist Companies in the Modern World.* Washington, D.C.: AEI Press.

Stefik, Mark. 1985. "Strategic Computing at DARPA: Overview and Assessment." *Communications of the ACM* 28 (7): 690–704.

Sternberg, Ernest. 1993. "Preparing for the Hybrid Economy: The New World of Public-Private Partnerships." *Business Horizons* 36 (6): 11–15.

Stowsky, Jay. 1991. *From Spin-Off to Spin-On: Redefining the Military's Role in Technology Development.* Berkeley Roundtable on the International Economy, BRIE Working Paper 50. University of California, Berkeley.

———. 1992. "Conversion to Competitiveness: Making the Most of the National Labs." *American Prospect* 3 (11): 91–98.

———. 1999. "The History and Politics of the Pentagon's Dual Use Strategy." In *Arming the Future: A Defense Industry for the 21st Century,* edited by A. R. Markusen and S. S. Costigan. New York: Council on Foreign Relations.

———. 2004. "Secrets to Shield or Share? New Dilemmas for Military R&D Policy in the Digital Age." *Research Policy* 33: 257–69.

Stoyen, Alexander D. 2010. "Secretary Maybus' Goals for Reducing the Navy's Dependence on Fossil Fuel." In special issue, *Phase III Commercialization,* "Powering the Navy: The Energy Roadmap for the Future of the Fleet" (Spring): 6–7.

Stratton, Julius A. 1992. *Karl Taylor Compton 1887–1954: A Biographical Memoir.* Washington, D.C.: National Academies Press.

Stuart, Douglas T. 2008. *Creating the National Security State: A History of the Law That Transformed America.* Princeton, N.J.: Princeton University Press.

Sturgeon, Timothy. 1997. *Turnkey Production Networks: A New American Model of Industrial Organization?* Berkeley Roundtable on the International Economy, BRIE Working Paper 92A. University of California, Berkeley.

Swain, Donald. 1962. "The Rise of a Research Empire: NIH, 1930 to 1950." *Science* 138 (3546): 1233–35.

Szajnfarber, Zoe, and Annalisa L. Weigel. 2009. "Enabling Radical Innovation through Joint Capability Technology Demonstrations (JCTD): The Case of the

Internet Routing in Space (IRIS) JCTD." American Institute of Aeronautics and Astronautics, MIT, http://www.seas.gwu.edu/~zszajnfa/docs/Space09_Szajnfar berWeigel.pdf.

Taylor, Mark Zachary. 2004. "Evidence against Variety of Capitalism's Theory of Technological Innovation." *International Organization* 58 (3): 601–31.

Teague, E. Clayton. 2011. Statement before the House Committee on Science, Space and Technology, Subcommittee on Research and Science Education, hearing on Nanotechnology: Oversight of the National Nanotechnology Initiative and Priorities for the Future, 112th Cong., 1st sess., serial 112-15, April 14. Washington, D.C.

Teece, David J. 1986. "Profiting from Technological Innovation: Implications for Integration, Collaboration, Licensing and Public Policy." *Research Policy* 15 (6): 285–305.

Tibbetts, Roland. [1979] 1999. "The Small Business Innovation Research Program and NSF SBIR Commercialization Results." In *The Small Business Innovation Research Program: Challenges and Opportunities*, edited by Charles W. Wessner, Annex B, 128–67. Washington, D.C.: National Academies Press.

——. 2006. "SBIR, Renewal and U.S. Economic Security." Reauthorization letter to Congress, June 28, 2006, http://www.sbircoach.com/files/tibbetts_sbir_reaut horization%202006%20letter.pdf.

Tilly, Charles, ed. 1975. *The Formation of National States in Western Europe*. Princeton, N.J.: Princeton University Press.

Tirman, John, ed. 1984. *The Militarization of High Technology*. Cambridge, Mass.: Ballinger.

Triplett, Jack E. 1999. "The Solow Productivity Paradox: What Do Computers Do to Productivity?" *Canadian Journal of Economics/Revue canadienne d'Economique* 32 (2): 309–34.

Trivelpiece, Alvin W. 1988. "View from a National Laboratory" In *Technology Commercialization: Russian Challenges, American Lessons*, edited by National Research Council. Washington, D.C.: National Academies Press.

Trubowitz, Peter. 2011. *Politics and Strategy: Partisan Ambition and American Statecraft*. Princeton, N.J.: Princeton University Press.

Turse, Nick, and Tom Engelhardt. 2012. *Terminator Planet: The First History of Drone Warfare, 2001–2050*. TomDispatch Books (Kindle edition).

U.S. Army RDECOM-ARDEC. 2008. "Nanotechnology and Innovation Enterprise." Presentation to the Nano Valley Consortium, Armament Research Development and Engineering Center, Picatinny, N.J, 4 November.

U.S. Congress, Office of Technology Assessment. 1978. *Government Involvement in the Innovation Process: A Contractor's Report to the Office of Technology Assessment*. Washington, D.C.

——. 1981. *U.S. Industrial Competitiveness: A Comparison of Steel, Electronics, and Automobiles*. Washington, D.C.

——. 1985. *Information Technology R&D: Critical Trends and Issues*, OTA-CIT 268. Washington, D.C.

——. 1990a. *Making Things Better: Competing in Manufacturing*, OTA-ITE-433. Washington, D.C.

——. 1990b. *High-Temperature Superconductivity in Perspective*, OTA-E-440. Washington, D.C.

U.S. House, Committee on Armed Services. 1980. *The Ailing Defense Industrial Base: Unready for Crisis: Report of the Defense Industrial Base Panel*. 96th Cong., 2nd sess., December 31.

———. 2012. *Challenges to Doing Business with the Department of Defense: Findings of the Panel on Business Challenges in the Defense Industry*, 112th Cong., 1st sess., serial 112-66, March 19. Washington, D.C.

U.S. House, Committee on Science and Technology. 2008. *A History of the Committee on Science and Technology, 85th–110th Congresses, 1958–2008*. Washington, D.C.: National Academies Press.

U.S. Military Advisory Board. 2010. *Powering America's Economy: Energy Innovation at the Crossroads of National Security Challenges*, CNA Report, 27 July.

U.S. Senate. 2002. "Small Business Investment Company Amendments Act of 2001," 107th *Congress*, 1st sess, *Congressional Record* 147, pt. 16 (November 15, 2001). Washington, D.C.

U.S. Senate, Select Committee on Small Business. 1979. *Small Business and Innovation: Report on Underutilization of Small Business in the Nation's Efforts to Encourage Industrial Innovation*, 96th Cong., 1st Sess., June 14. Washington, D.C.

———. 1981. *Small Business Research Act of 1981*, 97th Cong., S. Rep. 194, September 25. Washington, D.C.

———. 1999. *Small Business Innovation Research (SBIR) Program*, S. Rep. 106-330, August 4. Washington, D.C.

Utterback, James, and Albert Murray. 1977. *The Influence of Defense Procurement and Sponsorship of Research and Development on the Development of the Civilian Electronics Industry: Final Report of U.S. National Bureau of Standards, Experimental Technology Incentives Program*. Cambridge, Mass.: MIT Center for Policy Alternatives.

Van Amburg, Bill. Undated. *Effective Heavy-Duty Hybrid Market Development: The HTUF Commercial-Military Model*, http://www.calstart.org/Libraries/HTUF_Doc uments/HTUF_Market_Development_Model.sflb.ashx.

Van Atta, Richard. 2008. "DARPA: Fifty Years of Innovation and Discovery." In DARPA 2008.

Vogel, David. 1996. *Kindred Strangers: The Uneasy Relationship between Politics and Business in America*. Princeton, N.J.: Princeton University Press.

Vogel, Steven. 1992. "The Power behind 'Spin-Ons': The Military Implications of Japan's Commercial Technology." In Sandholtz et al. 1992.

Wade, Robert. 1990. *Governing the Market*. Princeton, N.J.: Princeton University Press.

Walt, Stephen M. 2011. "The End of the American Era." *National Interest*, November/December, 6–16.

Watson, Thomas J. Jr., and Peter Petre. 1990. *Father, Son & Co.: My Life at IBM and Beyond*. New York: Bantam Books.

Watts, Barry D. 2008. *Strategy for the Long Haul: The U.S. Defense Industrial Base, Past, Present and Future*. Washington, D.C.: Center for Strategic and Budgetary Assessments.

Watts, Barry D., and Todd Harrison. 2011. *Sustaining Critical Sectors of the U.S. Defense Industrial Base*. Washington, D.C.: Center for Strategic and Budgetary Assessments.

Weinberger, Caspar. 1984. *Report of the Secretary of Defense Caspar W. Weinberger to the Congress on the FY 1985 Budget, FY 1986 Authorization Request and FY 1985–89 Defense Programs*. Washington, D.C.: GPO.

Weintraub, Jeff Alan. 1997. "The Theory and Politics of the Public/Private Distinction." In *Public and Private in Thought and Practice: Perspectives on a Grand Dichotomy*, edited by J. A. Weintraub and K. Kumar. Chicago: University of Chicago Press.

Weiss, Linda. 1988. *Creating Capitalism.* Oxford: Basil Blackwell.

———. 1998. *The Myth of the Powerless State.* Ithaca, N.Y.: Cornell University Press.

———, ed. 2003. *States in the Global Economy: Bringing Domestic Institutions Back In.* Cambridge, UK: Cambridge University Press.

Weiss, Linda, and John M. Hobson. 1995. *States and Economic Development: A Historical and Comparative Analysis.* Cambridge, UK: Polity Press.

Welser, Jeffrey. 2011. Statement before the House Committee on Science, Space and Technology, Subcommittee on Research and Science Education, hearing on Nanotechnology: Oversight of the National Nanotechnology Initiative and Priorities for the Future, 112th Cong., 1st sess., serial 112-15, April 14. Washington, D.C.

Wessner, Charles W., ed. 2001. *The Small Business Innovation Research Program (SBIR): An Assessment of the Department of Defense Fast Track Initiative.* Washington, D.C.: National Academy Press.

———. 2004. "The Military R&D Myth about US Innovation." Presentation to Innovation, Security & Growth: Perspectives from the U.S. Innovation System, Myths, Realities and Opportunities, Six Countries Programme Workshop, Defense & Security R&D, Brussels, November 19 (online).

———. 2005 "The Myth of Military Spin-Offs." In *Local Heroes in the Global Village: Globalization and New Entrepreneurship Policies,* edited by David B. Audretsch, Heike Grimm, and Charles W. Wessner. New York: Springer.

White, Richard H. 1996. *A Survey of Dual-Use Issues.* IDA Paper P-3176. Alexandria, Va.: Institute for Defense Analyses.

Wilson, Robert W., Peter K. Ashton, and Thomas P. Egan. 1980. *Innovation, Competition, and Government Policy in the Semiconductor Industry.* Lexington, Mass.: Lexington Books.

Winarsky, Norman. 2012. "The Defense Industrial Base: The Role of Independent Nonprofit Research and Development Organizations." Testimony before the House Committee on Armed Services, Panel on Business Challenges within the Defense Industry, 112th Cong., 2d sess., serial 112-95, January 23. Washington, D.C.

Wirls, Daniel. 1992. *Buildup: The Politics of Defense in the Reagan Era.* Ithaca, N.Y.: Cornell University Press.

Wong, Joseph. 2011. *Betting on Biotech: Innovation and the Limits of Asia's Developmental State.* Ithaca, N.Y.: Cornell University Press.

Woo-Cumings, Meredith Jung-En. 1998. "National security and the rise of the developmental state in South Korea and Taiwan." In *Behind East Asian Growth,* edited by Henry S. Rowen. London: Routledge.

Yannuzzi, Rick E. 2000. "In-Q-Tel: A New Partnership Between the CIA and the Private Sector." *Defense Intelligence Journal* 9 (1): 25–38.

Yergin, Daniel. 2012. *The Quest: Energy, Security, and the Remaking of the Modern World.* London: Penguin.

Yonkers, Terry. 2011. Statement to the Senate Committee on Commerce, Science, and Transportation, Subcommittee on Aviation Operations, Safety and Security, hearing on Aviation Fuels: Needs, Challenges, and Alternatives, 112th Cong., 1st sess., serial 112-209, July 28. Washington, D.C.

Zenko, Micah. 2013. *Reforming U.S. Drone Strike Policies.* Council Special Report No. 65. New York: Council on Foreign Relations Press.

Zhu, Tianbiao. 2002. "Developmental States and Threat Perceptions in Northeast Asia." *Conflict, Security and Development* 2 (1): 5–29.

Acknowledgments

I have the great pleasure of thanking the colleagues, officials, friends, and family members who helped this project along the way. My special thanks go to Col. Bernard Chachula (USAF Ret.) who read an earlier draft of the entire manuscript, generously shared his report on government-sponsored venture funds, and put me in touch with various NSS program managers who could answer my queries. I am indebted also to Michael Yamaner at the National Science Foundation who went out of his way to locate material that had gone AWOL from the online database. Barry Watts at the Center for Strategic and Budgetary Assessments was equally generous in divulging sources for updating some of his earlier graphs. Harold Morgan and George Friberg at Sandia National Laboratories, and Robert Smith in the Office of Naval Research, helped me to understand some of the intricacies of NSS organizations and programs. The librarians at the Law Library of Congress provided invaluable assistance in locating documents.

Some of the research for this book was stimulated by invitations to participate in workshops supported by the International Studies Association (New York), the France-Berkeley Fund (Sciences Po, Paris), the Academy of Social Sciences in Australia (Sydney), and the Ford Foundation (New York, Berkeley, and Rio de Janeiro). For the opportunities to try out early versions of the argument at some of these events, I would like to thank Fred Block, Leonardo Burlamaqui and Ana Celia Castro, and especially Shelley Hurt and Ronnie Lipschutz, who organized the ISA hybridization workshop.

Since 2007, when I began working on this project in earnest, I have chalked up quite a few dress rehearsals, refining the argument in seminars and symposia that took me to Aarhus University in Denmark; the universities of Ferrara, Udine, Modena, and Ancona in Italy; Koch University in Istanbul; the Federal University of Rio de Janeiro; Hebrew University in Jerusalem; the

Beijing Forum; Seoul National University; the City University of New York; the University of Queensland; and back home to the University of Sydney. For these opportunities and for their collegiality, I wish especially to thank Stephen Bell, Fred Block, Kyung-Sup Chang, Mette Kjaer, Atul Kohli, Pietro Masina, Georg Sorensen, Patrizia Tiberi, and Marco di Tommaso. For useful comments I also thank Geoff Dow, Tim Dunne, Jason Sharman, and my very own colleagues in the Department of Government and International Relations at Sydney. With their searching questions, graduate students at many of these venues played no small part in stimulating and refining my thinking.

If I were handing out a prize for stamina and creative commentary, it would have to be shared by Elizabeth Thurbon, Sung-Young Kim, and John Mathews, who read and reread successive drafts of this book—and always found room for improvement! I cannot thank them enough. Judiciously framed comments from Peter Katzenstein and one anonymous reader helped me to sharpen my argument. For helpful comments on parts of the argument and manuscript, my thanks also go to Will Clegg, Ben Goldsmith, Bill Lazonick, David Levi-Faur, Herman Schwartz, and Naomi Sussmann. Until his doctoral program beckoned, Will was a highly motivated research assistant who helped me get my head around the early formative years of the national security state. For technical assistance with graphs I thank Petra Sandulache for her efficient, can-do approach. In the creative titles department, Ken Wallace was my first port of call.

The legendary partnership of Roger Haydon and Peter Katzenstein has made the process of turning the draft into a book a uniquely rewarding experience. I thank them both for their engaged, hands-on approach. Susan Specter oversaw the editing and Gavin Lewis brought exceptionally fine editing skills to bear on the manuscript.

For their many supportive roles that cannot be enumerated: intellectual, emotional, fun—you name it—I thank heaven for Liz Thurbon ("daughter-sister-best friend" rolled into one) and John Mathews, partner in life.

Index

Note: Page numbers followed by a "t" indicate tables.